THE
INVENTION
OF ETHIOPIA

Bonnie K. Holcomb
Sisai Ibssa

THE RED SEA PRESS
Publishers & Distributors of Third World Books
15 Industry Court
Trenton, NJ 08638

JQ
3758
.H641
1990
153069
May 1991

The Red Sea Press, Inc.
15 Industry Court
Trenton, New Jersey 08638

First Printing 1990

Cover design by Ife Nii-Owoo

Book design and electronic typesetting from author's disk
by Malcolm Litchfield
This book is composed in Janson

Library of Congress Catalog Card Number: 90-60990

ISBN: 0-932415-57-1   Cloth
         0-932415-58-X   Paper

This book is dedicated to
William H. Silverman
and
the memory of Warqee Odaa

CONTENTS

List of Maps vii

Glossary ix

Preface xiii

Acknowledgements xix

1   Introduction 1

2   The Changing World 27

3   The Birth of a Dependent Colonial State 71

4   The Dependent Colonial State Is Tested: Challenges
    from Taytu and Iyasu 145

5   State Consolidation under Haile Selassie, 1916-1944 . . . 171

6   Ethiopia Enters the Era of Finance Capital, 1945-1974 . 215

7   Resistance to the Formation and Consolidation of
    the Ethiopian State 279

8   The Opposition Movements: The Forces of Reform . . . 315

9   Continuities of Empire in Ethiopia under Soviet
    Patronage, 1974-the Present 329

10 Summary 387

    Bibliography 409

    Index 425

LIST OF MAPS

Between pages 73 and 74

Map 1   Location of the Horn of Africa

Map 2   Enlarged View of the Horn of Africa

Map 3   Abyssinian Areas, 1870

Map 4   Oromo Areas, 1870

Map 5   Somali Areas, 1870

Map 6   Afar Areas, 1870

Map 7   Sidama Areas, 1870

Map 8   Location of Major Peoples of the Horn of Africa, 1870

Map 9   Shoan Conquests, 1872

Map 10   Shoan Conquests, 1876

Map 11   Shoan Conquests, 1886

Map 12   Shoan Conquests, 1887

Map 13   Shoan Domination of Abyssinia, 1889

Map 14   Shoan-Dominated Abyssinian Conquests, 1893

Map 15   Shoan-Dominated Abyssinian Conquests, 1897

Map 16   Ethiopian Conquests and Acquisitions Following the signing of the Tripartite Treaty, 1910

Map 17   Ethiopian Boundaries, 1962

GLOSSARY

awaraja (Amharic)

an administative unit of the Ethiopian state, in size immediately below that of a province; roughly equivalent to county

atbia danya (Amharic)

the name given during the period of Haile Selassie to a judge presiding over the smallest jurisdiction recognized by the state

balabat (Amharic)

literally, owner or the one responsible for a given area; the term applied to persons from the conquered regions who cooperated with the Ethiopian state in return for benefits such as landholding rights; the one responsible to the state for roughly a kebele-sized region of conquered territory

chaffee (Oromo)

literally, a flat grassy area; term used to refer to both the site and the kind of open Oromo assembly regularly held in such a place during the Gada period

dejazmatch (Amharic)

a high position within the traditional Abyssinian social and military hierarchy; literally commander of the leading forces; immediately below a ras

finfinnee (Oromo)

the traditional name for the Oromo site on which the city of Addis Ababa was built;

Glossary

literally means site of the spring which refers to the hot springs located there; the Amharic word (filwuha) for hot springs often applied to the location has the same meaning

gabbar (Amharic)

literally, farmers brought into submission through payment; refers to people who pay tribute in produce, labor or cash to settlers who moved in with the backing of the Ethiopian state to become owners of lands previously held by the residents under traditional arrangements

gada (Oromo)

the term used to refer to the total combination of social institutions within the Oromo society prior to incorporation of the Oromo into the Ethiopian state; superstructure of a distinctly Oromo system of production

kebele (Oromo)

the smallest administrative unit of the Ethiopian state; a geographical area equivalent to a neighborhood

mehal sefari (Amharic)

traditional Abyssinian upper class arbitrators; persons considered to hold a neutral position with regard to settling disputes or advising decisionmakers; persons well acquainted with the intrigues of the elite

mekwannint (Amharic)

tradtitionally, members of the Abyssinian ruling elite, those who had attained high social, economic and political position; later came to include the upper echelon of the settler class as well; connotes arrogance and self importance

neftegna (Amharic)

literally, the owner and carrier of a gun (neft), term used to refer to the armed Abyssinian settlers who arrived in the conquered regions to claim land and play a role in the establishment of the Ethiopian state; the settler class

Glossary

ras (Amharic)

term of military origin referring to the chief commander of the military forces; the highest ranking member of the social, political and military hierarchy under the royal family

shifta (Amharic)

one who operates outside the law, a bandit or rebel who causes trouble for the regime in power

woreda (Amharic)

a geographical unit created for administrative purposes; roughly equivalent to a district; several kebeles comprise a woreda, several woredas comprise an awaraja

zemetcha (Amharic)

an expedition usually involving massive numbers of participants; term traditionally used to refer to a large military campaign; in 1974-5 applied to a large-scale program in which the government ordered students from the urban areas into the coutryside

PREFACE

This book is a work of interpretation. Its central ideas were developed for an introduction to a book we began to write on the issue of self-determination, to be titled Exploring the Bases for Self-Determination. We originally set out to examine the cultural and political content of liberation movements in the Horn of Africa. But we found that it was not possible to conduct an adequate analysis of liberation movements without a close look at what they are resisting and why. We found it necessary to characterize the nature of the Ethiopian state that is in conflict with these national movements.

Despite many claims in the literature from Ethiopia and about Ethiopia that major transformations have taken place there, neither of us has found that to be so. Each of us had independently seen the need for a systematic reexamination of the Ethiopian state and each of us had undertaken to do the work separately. Eventually we agreed to collaborate and this book is one of the results of that collaboration. We shared the opinion that no available treatment of the history of Ethiopia dealt adequately with the factors that shaped the empire, that is, factors that generated the political and economic relations still found there and which account for the conflict currently raging within the empire.

In deciding where to begin this work we noted that whenever either of us had summarized our viewpoint about the causes of intense crisis in the Horn of Africa, either verbally or in writing, people had asked for further reading material. There was nothing

Preface

satisfactory to give them. It was not possible simply to cite others who had developed this outlook. Only an article here and there was available which addressed the central issues. Even the most diligent student became discouraged by the paucity of materials on this subject. We decided to do the job ourselves. Most of what is currently available offers Ethiopianist interpretations of the Ethiopian state which recount the classic features of what we call Ethiopian colonial mythology.

We have observed a remarkable continuity over time in the form and the purposes of Ethiopian state institutions. This continuity demands an explanation. It is our opinion that such an explanation might begin to answer some of the questions coming from a sector of the public that is sincerely seeking to understand how Ethiopia developed, what are the forces in conflict there, and what impact their involvement there might have whether political, humanitarian or otherwise. So we put aside the other book on self-determination in order to present in this book our explanation for how Ethiopia came into being and persists into the present day. The book is written explicitly for those who are seeking to comprehend the complex situation in the Ethiopian empire.

When we began to cooperate in writing and in making presentations in the early 1980s on matters of concern in the Ethiopian state, each of our papers had a sizable historical section. We were not able to say what we had to say without turning to history. Like others did, we had included introductions which enabled us to better approach the current issues. Finally, at one of the conferences, a commentator asked the crucial question, "Why is it that yours and every other paper I have heard about Ethiopia has an enormous historical introduction going back to the time of Emperor Menelik and beyond? We can't ever seem to do without that!" All those attending the session concurred that, yes, all the papers had this component, and, no, none could do without it. Yet the histories of Ethiopia that were available did not prepare one for understanding current dynamics. When we began work on a book-length piece, we discovered that the historical issue was again a central one. Different features of the history of Ethiopia had to be emphasized in order to

Preface

explain the roots of conflict raging in the Horn. The commentater had fingered an important matter. The history of Ethiopia as it has been written by Ethiopianists up to the present has been written from a perspective which does not include the background to what is going on in the empire now.

There is a clear reason why people hark back to the period associated with Menelik when they are trying to cover an issue of current importance in Ethiopia. It is not a matter of fashion, preference, or obsession with history per se. It is because the Ethiopian empire was created during that period; its processes were set in motion at that time, the infrastructure was laid out, and the institutions fashioned at that juncture of history continue to function in the present day with only superficial alterations. The fundamental societal arrangement fixed at that time remains intact despite claims to "modernization" and to "socialism." The roots of the current conflicts lie in the past. But it is not satisfying simply to amass more detail about Menelik and his court, Haile Selassie and his court (then called his "cabinet"), or Mengistu and his court (now called a "politburo"), fascinating as that might be. Knowing every detail of the lives and the intrigues of the rulers and their cohorts still offers no special insight and no guarantee that issues involved in the current conflicts will be clarified. Though explanations of current dilemmas go back through periods during which Menelik, Haile Selassie, and Mengistu have ruled, they do not lie with the individuals. These men have presided during periods when processes were occurring that have engulfed all of Africa. The eras when these emperors have been in power were also periods when industrial and then finance capital expanded due to internal pressures in the system of capitalism and embraced Africa, including northeast Africa, in specific ways as part of the changing worldwide economic order. Ethiopia was invented and maintained as part of these processes.

We have titled this book The Invention of Ethiopia to draw attention to the fact that Ethiopia has been from its formation an artificial unit, not a naturally-occurring one as so many believe and it should be recognized as such. Its creation was the result of an alliance struck between imperial powers of Europe who were seeking

Preface

to manage their own conflicts in those days and Abyssinia that was attempting to resolve its internal crises. This alliance gave rise to the set of state institutions that constitute Ethiopia today. These institutions were the product of a European ruling class that had to send representatives to northeast Africa to serve as advisers to members of a local nationality willing to colonize the region with them.

European powers were attempting to do away with problems that had emerged as part of the development of capitalism on their continent, and Abyssinia was struggling to consolidate tiny kingdoms into a single polity. The connection between these interests created Ethiopia, and a full understanding of developments there cannot minimize the role of either partner. The resultant alliance accounts for the invention of Ethiopia. The connection between these two parties is the crucial sustaining component of the Ethiopian formula, whether it is the connection between Menelik and France/Britain, Haile Selassie and Britain/the United States, or Mengistu and the USA/Soviet Union. The central institutions of the state were set in motion from outside the boundaries of the empire and represent forces external to the empire in ways that need to be examined. Other writers have only touched upon the interaction between European and Abyssinian leaders, and they have not sustained an analysis that places at the center of attention this alliance itself, the marriage of interests that generated an empire in the northeast corner of Africa when the rest of the continent was in the throes of direct colonization by one European state or another.

Ethiopia is always treated as an exception to the general explanations offered for developments in the rest of colonized Africa. But it was not an exception; in fact the creation of Ethiopia was an extension of dependent colonial policy and carried in it the seeds of a plan for the future of the continent—Ethiopia became a test case for what is usually called neo-colonialism or corporate access to regions already sugjugated.

Much of the current writing available as analysis of Ethiopia reflects a confusion about the nature of this state and of the events taking place there. Though many are now willing to criticize Menelik and Haile Selassie up to a point, they seem to hold the

Preface

attitude that since revolution is violent, and since there has been a great deal of violence in Ethiopia, therefore, there must have been a revolution in Ethiopia beginning in 1974. Several writers have asserted in fact that a revolution has occurred in this empire (Harbeson 1988, Marina Ottaway 1987, Clapham 1988, Schwab 1985). Some have written of the "transformation" that has taken place in Ethiopia. Two recent authors have gone so far as to title their books, The Ethiopian Transformation and Transformation and Continuity in Revolutionary Ethiopia. It is one of our central theses that Ethiopia has not undergone a social transformation at all; its central institutions are intact.

We have chosen not to debate the numerous recent writings on the area. The differences will be clear to anyone who decides to conduct his or her own comparison.

We have also decided that it is important both for those who would agree and those who would disagree with us that we be as explicit as possible about our use of terms and about our orientation to the material. We offer this interpretation in anticipation that the issues will be taken up and debated in the future in whatever way our readers choose. It is our hope that it will generate further research by scholars interested to explore crucial areas of concern that have been neglected because of their politically controversial nature.

ACKNOWLEDGEMENTS

Looking back over the course of work that has been inherently controversial, it is those people who encouraged us to keep at it and who reminded us of the value of offering a new perspective on the Horn of Africa that stand out as the ones to whom we owe the greatest debt of gratitude. Not all of these were persons who agreed with our approach. Even those who argued strongly against us caused us to realize the importance of offering this interpretation of events to open public discussion.

At the outset, then, we would like to thank both individually and jointly those of you who have shown an interest in what we were doing, who have relentlessly bombarded us with questions, and who have encouraged us to meet the challenge of the work. It is the spirit of those who realize the implications of this work that has kept us on track. We are indebted to you.

In addition to moral support, several people have offered us opportunities to present and test several of these ideas in public conference and university forums. We particularly appreciate Edmond J. Keller in this regard; he has always been alert to create opportunities for lively and productive discussion among allies and adversaries alike.

From the moment that we began to talk about writing, Mohammed Hassen made available to us all the considerable documents he has in his possession. We are very grateful to him for his generosity of spirit as well. Of the many people who helped us to track down seemingly untracable printed and oral information, we thank Tom

Acknowledgements

Garnett of the Smithsonian Institution for going out of his way at critical junctures to help us find obscure materials of the former variety and Ammanuel Nagassa for assisting us trace obscure information of the latter type. We also want to thank Ammanuel for being the one person who never expressed dismay about whether or not the project would ever be completed.

To our publisher, Kassahun Checole, who encouraged us to transform our work from a pile of conference papers into a book, who waited for us to finish despite missed deadlines, and who appreciated the scope of the job while continuing to agitate for its completion, we extend special thanks. Bereket Habte Selassie also deserves special mention for his unflaggingly positive contributions from the coffee shop to the political and academic forum.

We also would like to express our indebtedness to our readers (in alphabetical order): Ammanuel Nagassa, Bereket Habte Selassie, Bill Silverman, Ibssa Ahmed, Lubee Birru, and Mohammed Hassen. Each of these people spent valuable time day and night to read the entire volume in a short time and to offer spirited observations, comments, criticisms and suggestions. We are grateful for this valuable contribution.

We particularly want to acknowledge Bill Silverman who helped us throughout all the difficulties we faced. He was there with technical, monetary, and moral support any time we needed his assistance. He has played a major role in bringing this project to fruition. We also want to mention young Braden Silverman, who has been surrounded by aspects of this project all of his short life and whose first sentence was, "Mommy's upstairs working." He has taught us more about patience than we have been able to teach him and both of us are grateful to him.

Last but not least, we would like to express our indebtedness to Ralph and Velma Holcomb, who, having come the long distance from the West Coast to Washington, D.C. took over our physical and emotional burden for the last two months while we completed the final draft. Without them, our work would still not be finished.

It would not have been possible to complete the work without the participation of all of these people, and our thanks go out to you

Acknowledgements

all. When all is said and done, however, there were suggestions made that we chose not to accept, there were omissions noted that we did not fill. So none of these people is responsible for the presentation, format, or interpretation found here. We bear the sole responsibility for it.

Bonnie K. Holcomb
Sisai Ibssa

December 27, 1989
Washington, D.C.

1   INTRODUCTION

Historical Overview

"Ethiopia" is the name that was eventually given to the geographic unit created when Abyssinia, a cluster of small kingdoms in northeast Africa, expanded in the mid-1800s by conquering independent nations in the region using firearms provided by European powers. Throughout this book *Ethiopia* refers to that empire formed in the late 1800s by means of conquest, and *Abyssinia* refers to the historic homeland of the Semitic-speaking residents of the group of highland kingdoms. Hence, Ethiopia includes independent nations that were conquered and occupied at a time when major European imperialist powers, in the midst of an intense worldwide rivalry for territory and global dominion, were unable to resolve a stalemate over which of them would claim the area called the Horn of Africa. Having occupied the rest of Africa, they clashed over occupation of the region that was strategic due to its location near the recently opened Suez Canal and near the headwaters of the Blue Nile. The solution to this conflict was to encourage, up to certain limits, the expansionist ambitions of the leaders of various Abyssinian kingdoms, then to establish a collective agreement among themselves to recognize and assist the resultant entity as a dependent colonial empire, claiming that an ancient "neutral" sovereign state existed there. Such a defense became the basis for the mythology of "Greater Ethiopia."

The Invention of Ethiopia

The entity established in this way persists into the present. What is the nature of this state? How are we to analyze Ethiopia? It is a question which has been rarely raised, postponed even on those occasions when it was raised, and never the subject of sustained debate among those who identify themselves as either "left" or "right." Now that a military government has declared that it has led a "National Democratic Revolution" in the empire at the same time that national liberation movements of the peoples of once-conquered nations have gained unprecedented strength and virtually surround the old Abyssinian "heartland," the time is long overdue to raise this question. The question retains its relevance as long as there is eager and bitter contention among several groups who aspire to take the place of the Derg by assuming state power and holding the empire together.

It is our thesis that Ethiopia is a dependent colonial empire whose control over the colonies is being challenged by the colonial subjects; that the historically established economic and political subjugation by Abyssinia of alien nations begun at the time of conquest in the late 1800s has never been relieved, let alone eliminated and that the objectives of the national liberation movements in the empire are appropriately compared with others who have risen up against colonial domination.

Since claims for "uniqueness" as well as historical and even sociocultural unity for the empire have prevailed in Ethiopian Studies, much of what follows challenges received wisdom about the region. We believe, however, that without a new direction to thinking about the area, the issues at the heart of the conflict there will continue to mystify observers. Above all, we invite inspection, testing and discussion of the perspective and the interpretations offered here of events in Ethiopia. Rethinking and rewriting colonial history is a daunting but highly rewarding task, one that is part and parcel to finding solutions to problems grounded in colonialism.

Ethiopia encloses many nations. For our purposes in this book we have often chosen to utilize the example of the largest and first-conquered of them—that of the Oromo people now referred to as Oromia. Its lands constitute about 275,000 square miles, over half

Introduction

the present land area of the empire, and its people account for over 60 percent of the population of present-day Ethiopia. The Oromo issue is central historically, structurally, geographically, numerically and theoretically to any consideration of the nature of the Ethiopian state and of the political economy of the region. Other nations surrounding the precapitalist Abyssinian polity, such as Sidama, Ogaden, and Afar, also bore the experiences of conquest and colonization. Land seizure and the policies of this hybrid form of colonial state apply systematically to them. As a consequence of the way in which Abyssinia came to hold the colonies, the people of Tigray were subdued, and Eritrea was later attached or annexed to the dependent colonial state.

We maintain that Ethiopian colonialism is the result of an intriguing alliance formed between capitalist states and a loose assemblage of Abyssinian kingdoms that is usually erroneously designated as "feudal." Ethiopia therefore exhibits many features that do not fit classic patterns of either feudal or capitalist formations and consequently confuse observers and thwart analysis. Indeed there are aspects of the Abyssinian hierarchy that appear "feudal." Capitalist relations are also evident. In addition there are sociocultural groups with completely separate histories—all interacting within what appears to be a single system. In this book we argue that it is in fact a single system, a dependent colonial one, historically constituted and maintained in a form acceptable to settlers who were primarily of a single nationality and to a series of imperial backers through the eras of Menelik, Haile Selassie and the Derg.

Our approach is to examine the empire through analytical discussion with enough historical and structural description to indicate the direction of our thinking. This is not a work of history, though history is a significant part of it, nor is it a work of theory, though theory is a central concern. It is one of interpretation.

Our basic concerns are (1) how the fundamental economic relations which characterize the empire came to be established, (2) how they have been maintained and by what means the structure of the Ethiopian state has been supported up to the present day, and

The Invention of Ethiopia

(3) why many widely-held beliefs about this empire and the historical account do not correspond.

We will also examine the widely accepted notion that Ethiopia is unique in Africa due to the fact that the territory was not occupied by European powers. Ethiopia is declared on maps and regarded by the world body as "Independent" among the states of Africa. Was it that *only* the peoples of Abyssinia and its colonies, together referred to as Ethiopia, out of all the nations of Africa, could successfully resist and defeat the European superpowers when they arrived in the late 1800s to begin dividing the entire continent among themselves during the Scramble for Africa? This is what the supporters and defenders of the dependent colonial state assert. Had this part of northeast Africa reached a level of development that allowed them to defend themselves against the European technology and military organization where the rest of Africa failed? They had not. Did the nations of that particular region unite to form some kind of strong irresistible united front against imperial powers that made it impossible for them to be defeated by the European arsenals? They did not. What then is the reason for this unique case of "Independent Ethiopia" and how did it come to possess such a vast area in a rich, heavily populated, strategic region of Africa? How significant is its "unique" history in analyzing present-day events in the empire?

These important questions must be answered in historical perspective particularly in light of the dynamics of an expanding capitalist world order and in light of events in that area at the time of the arrival of Europeans in Africa during what is called the Scramble for Africa.

We argue that, contrary to popular belief, the Horn of Africa before the advent of imperialism was the home of several independent nations who inhabited separate geographical and topographical homelands and represented fundamentally distinct languages and modes of livelihood. The most well-known to Europe, however, was the Semitic-speaking highland kingdom of Abyssinia, which had attracted the interest of Europeans primarily because its people practiced what was recognized as an aberrant form of Christianity.

Introduction

Travellers and explorers from Europe occasionally ventured into that area to learn about the reputed "Christian island" and to report back to interested readers and supporters at home. Fascinated Europeans paid little attention to the fact that south of the Abyssinian kingdom in a different ecological zone were the Cushitic nations of the region. Each of these nations was unrelated to Abyssinia in terms of mode of social oraganization or norms, values and beliefs.

Among these, the most populous of the entire region of northeast Africa, was the Oromo nation whose homeland was well watered central zone highlands and lowlands that stretched across the center and south of the Horn of Africa. The Oromo, for example, at this time were organized under a participatory form of government that was based on five grades often called "parties" that incorporated persons of agricultural, pastoral and mixed forms of livelihood into public service. For at least five centuries of recorded history prior to the Scramble for Africa in the late 1800s, the Abyssinians and Oromos had tested each other and maintained consistent and clearcut boundaries between their homelands.

Actually, in the 1800s the arrival of the Europeans in the Horn of Africa introduced new factors into the area and changed the balance of power in the region. This intervention set processes in motion and shaped events in a fundamental way not only in Africa and the Horn, but on a global scale. A powerful new force from Europe was unleashed based on heavy industrial capital seeking raw materials for production and markets for its products. Very quickly competition that had been going on between rival capitalist powers in Europe changed to worldwide competition. Control and access to materials and new regions were essential to keep the motors of industry going and to minimize the power of the labor movement. The law of value and the contest between labor and capital had become globalized. No region of the world was exempt. Suddenly major competitors began grabbing huge sections of the African continent and her great untapped resources. This rush became the order of the day, and control of these regions became a necessary condition to remain a viable force in Africa and in Europe itself.

The Invention of Ethiopia

At about the same time, a new route to the Persian Gulf, Indian Ocean, the East and the Far East opened up, providing a means of reducing the transportation costs such as general operation and maintainence, travel time, oil use, etc. In an economy based on maximizing profit, whoever controls the route is destined to gain economic supremacy. On this basis the opening of the Suez Canal increased the value of real estate in the Horn of Africa. From this time on, British and French behavior in the Horn of Africa have to be seen in a global economic perspective. The economic conditions in Europe and the cost of transport led the French to dig the Suez Canal and the British to try to gain financial control of it. Following the opening of the Suez Canal in 1869, British companies were planning to lay a major railway line from the Cape to Cairo, with all the outlay of heavy industrial capital, political control of surrounding regions and easy access to critical abundant raw materials from south to north thus implied. The French empire was to be connected by equally extensive rail lines from West Africa to the Red Sea. For awhile there were no holds barred on the part of British and French interests intent on forcing their plans through to completion. Competition over control of these grand railway schemes in Africa was desperate and ruthless. The British takeover of the Suez Canal by purchasing its majority shares led France to Obok in order to position France to move by way of Abyssinia to control the source of the Nile, threatening livelihood in British territory.

Thus British activities were orchestrated around a grand design to run a railroad from the Cape in South Africa to Cairo while French investment focused on connecting all her tentative contacts by means of an east-west railway to the Red Sea. When these efforts clashed, accommodation had to be reached in several places in order to avoid war. These two major powers employed a model of conflict management in which each tried indirectly to block the other from attaining supremacy. It was during this period and for purpose of avoiding debilitating war between temselves that both powers turned to focusing on the Abyssinian kingdoms in the contested region. By supplying or officially recognizing individual entrepreneurs whose

Introduction

task it was to establish contacts and intelligence about the area, both Britain and France made entrees into Abyssinia.

Finally the British made the decision to back Yohannes IV, an Abyssinian Tigrayan emperor who had assisted them during a major foray into the region known as the Napier Expedition, while the French took the liberty of supplying huge amounts of weaponry primarily to Menelik, the Abyssinian king of Shoa. Menelik's territory was strategically located at the gateway to the sources of gold, coffee, ivory, etc. The Italians tried to become involved on their own and shipped large numbers of arms to Menelik too, but the French were successful in hijacking that supply to their cause. When Yohannes died and Menelik became full emperor, the British were left without their local ally. They could not act on their own behalf in the region because of their relation with Egypt. Their strategy shifted to providing indirect encouragement to Italy to block France in the region. Even the famous 1896 battle of Adwa between Italian and Menelik's forces, known as the occasion when "black Africans defeated the European colonizers and chased them away from their territory," was actually another indirect battle between the British and French over control of the region.

After the British and Italians failed at Adwa, the French began to proceed to build a railway from Djibouti to the White Nile. The British used every means to block this move.

These incidents demonstrate that the imperialist powers had their own agendas and interests in the entire continent, including the Horn of Africa. Neither Britain nor France could find a way to stop the other in the Horn. So they reached a stalemate, an impasse, a period of backdown from direct competition over monopoly control of this region. They were unwilling to bring on a world-scale war between themselves yet. Such a clash was postponed until World War I in 1914. They reached a political accommodation, resolving the issue by making the region a part of a general detente. What did not happen here was as important to them as what did happen. Each worked to prevent the other from developing the means to gain an economic or political advantage.

The Invention of Ethiopia

Their primary interests were guaranteeing that no one European power controlled the area completely, avoiding war, assuring stability in the region, protecting access to the Red Sea, confirming a constant flow of raw materials from the rich lands. Especially after Adwa, the railway company battles and the illness of the Emperor, they agreed that it was in their best collective interests as imperialists to prevent fragmentation and disintegration in the Horn. They proposed and then implemented an agreement which essentially internationalized the empire of Ethiopia.

This is how the Tripartite Treaty of 1906 among Britain, France, and Italy was born. This agreement stated, "We the Great Powers of Europe, France, Great Britain, and Italy, shall cooperate in maintaining the political and territorial status quo in Ethiopia as determined by the state of affairs at present existing and the previous [boundary] agreements" (Hertslett 1909: Article 1, #102). With this treaty, Ethiopia became an example of what would later prove to be a useful model of conflict management in the continent and elsewhere. This agreement introduced the colonial mythology—the idea of an "independent, neutral" Ethiopia—that protected or safeguarded the interests of all the imperialist powers in the region. It created geographical, political and economic space for what has subsequently been referred to as Ethiopian sovereignty.

It is in that space, that kind of political safety zone, that Ethiopia survives until this day. To create a dependent empire was a collective imperialist decision and it has remained in the collective interest to maintain a "stable" regime, i.e., a regime that perpetuates this arrangement by protecting the dependent colonial formula in that part of the world. The nature of the Ethiopian state cannot be appreciated without attention to the collusion of imperialist interests there. Their mutual agreement to allow this state to exist gave Menelik and, more substantially, his successors a type of "independence" conditional upon controlling the area in the prescribed way.

The Ethiopian rulers upon whom this mantle fell were primarily Shoan Amharas of Abyssinia who became settlers in the conquered regions and ran the newly formed state apparatus. Their rule took the form of an idiosyncratic type of colonial domination which

Introduction

contained a large component of Abyssinian patrimonialism enforced by the imported firearms with which they bludgeoned huge nations, some their equals and one several times larger than themselves (the Oromo), into submission. To retain control they literally eliminated some peoples, ruthlessly attacked others and settled an armed occupation force throughout those conquered territories to maintain control. How the colonial system was established is one of the themes of this book. The creation of the Ethiopian empire was carried out with the full participation of both these Abyssinian and superpower forces. Understanding the relationship of the imperial powers and Abyssinia is primary to understanding the nature of Abyssinia's assisted conquest and of the Ethiopian colonialism that followed.

Due to the place that has been carved out for Ethiopia as a junior partner of imperialist nations and a colonizer within the international sphere, and also in order to maintain its prescribed position in the world economic order, each successive Ethiopian regime has had to face and successfully meet three basic requirements to retain power. Each must (1) maintain an alliance with an imperial superpower, (2) provide an adequate basis for the growth and protection of the Abyssinian settler class, and (3) maintain control over a colonized majority within the empire. Confronting the same basic challenges has led to the use of such remarkably similar devices to retain power that these devices can be identified as basic components of the Ethiopian dependent colonial formula. Throughout the book the consistent use of these devices to keep that peculiar type of colonial system intact will be demonstrated.

First, from the time of the invention of Ethiopia itself to the present day, dependence on a strong imperial power has been an essential component of Ethiopian colonialism, leading to (1) extensive use of foreign technology and (2) the critical role of foreign advisers. The dependent relation has given rise to (3) a systematic policy of "showcasing" on the part of the Ethiopian state—presenting to the imperial powers carefully designed programs and policies which conform to all the formal characteristics necessary to win acceptance, favors, and a partnership with imperial powers but which are facades

9

The Invention of Ethiopia

without base or foundation within the empire. One counterpart of this policy is (4) to deny access, inspection or sustained observation from representatives of foreign states. This goes hand in hand with (5) the aggressive use of a colonial mythology. The claims to grandeur, uniqueness, sovereignty, internal unity, shared history of peoples, and independence have played a critical and decisive role in Ethiopia's ability to maintain her position in the international sphere. She has pushed herself forward and has been pushed forward by her patrons as the representative for African independence and has ridden the wave of international tensions over racial conflict for at least three decades.

Second, the creation and maintenance of a settler class derived primarily from the Abyssinian heartland has also been a basic requirement for the Ethiopian state to stay together. This need has led to consistent policies followed by each regime. The primary one has been (1) the use of conquered and colonized land as a compensation for loyalty and service to the state. Related to this is the single most significant feature of all three regimes: (2) settlement of state-sponsored Abyssinians into the conquered regions to lay claim to land. Other policies important to relations within the colonizer nation are (3) concentration of state control in the hands of the settlers themselves who originate in large part from the Shoan Amhara segment of Abyssinia, (4) shaping the state according to terms acceptable to that segment, including elevating to official status the language of the Shoan Amhara, their orthodox Christian religion, customs, and history, that is, establishing and maintaining Amhara hegemony, and also (5) continuing to assure that the state acts as a provider for the members of this colonial ruling elite with jobs, scholarships, privileges and rank.

Third, the continued existence of the Ethiopian state requires maintaining firm control over the colonies. The devices used for achieving this control in Ethiopia are quite similar to those that were used in other colonial systems across Africa: (1) confiscation of the means of production, (2) demanding high payments in rent and tax to support the state, (3) heavy militarization in the colonies to "maintain order," (4) requiring assimilation to a colonial identity for

Introduction

participating in or obtaining benefits from the state, (5) suppression of local cultural or organizational life, and (6) a virtual blackout on information or access to the colonies.

In summary, Ethiopia is an imperialist invention consisting of Abyssinia with its colonies held together by institutions that were fashioned by superpowers in competition with each other for control of the area.

Colonialism Identified

The task taken up in this book is to demonstrate that Ethiopia is indeed a colonial empire. Since the histories of Ethiopia that are currently available have been written from the point of view that Ethiopia constitutes a unique case of an ancient nation that valiantly staved off European colonial aggression to survive into the present day intact, the position offered here runs counter to "received wisdom." There are several reasons why this kind of image of Ethiopia has prevailed in the literature. One is that scholarly thinking on colonialism as a social process has been very narrowly defined and has progressed very little if at all since the voluminous writings on the matter in the 1950s and 1960s when enormous monopolistic empires, particularly of the British and French, were undergoing dramatic changes. Another reason is that both the mystique and mythology surrounding Ethiopia as the only country able to hold out against worldwide colonial expansion have been advocated and actively circulated by those very powers who benefitted from the variation of colonialism implanted in northeast Africa via the Ethiopian empire.

In order to broaden the perspective on the subject of colonialism itself it is necessary to look at the phenomenon at its most basic. Colonialism is best viewed as one of several modes of interaction among nations of people. It does not occur between individuals or groups. Rather it involves a change in the entire social and productive life of a people. Each nation of people, through the process of living together, develops a distinctive pattern of production and a distinctive set of rules or what could be called a code of conduct for safeguarding that particular pattern and for managing its affairs within given boundaries. Colonialism occurs when those boundaries are penetrated by outsiders who are products and carriers of a different system intent upon forcefully changing the pattern of production and imposing a different set of rules. Put another way, colonialism takes place when invaders use force to take possession of elements vital to the economy of the invaded society of people and to reorganize those components according to a new and forcefully imposed system of production. What occurs is that a colonizing society violently seizes the economic substructure of colonized society and rearranges it by replacing its organizing superstructure.

Colonialism is a complicated and violent process involving massive use of manpower, technology, and strategy to overcome the inevitable resistance of victims who fight to preserve their livelihood, the values embedded in their patterns of life and their very means of existence. It can only be accomplished when the colonizing force is vastly superior to the conquered in terms of technology, strategy, or manpower. Colonialism has not been limited to the era of capitalism alone, however, as is usually assumed; it is a process which has gone on throughout every era of history. In fact history is full of accounts of colonized nations being violently sacked and occupied by colonizing powers from before the feudal period. V. I. Lenin has documented and argued convincingly that colonial policy existed before capitalism (see also Salmon 1970). The Ottoman empire is a case in point, but Rome was perhaps the best known case. Lenin pointed out that:

> Colonial policy and imperialism existed before the latest stage of capitalism, and even before capitalism. Rome, founded on slavery, pursued a colonial policy and practiced imperialism. But general disquisitions on imperialism, which ignore, or put into the background, the fundamental difference between socio-economic formations, inevitably turn into the most vapid banality or bragging, like the comparison: "Greater Rome and Greater Britain" [footnote in

Introduction

Lenin's original to C. P. Lucas, Oxford. 1912] Even the capitalist colonial policy of *previous* stages of capitalism is essentially different from the colonial policy of finance capital (1917: 260).

The different ways that colonialism has been carried out over time has depended upon the level of the development of the productive forces of the colonizing country and the means used by these colonizers to suppress the various forms of resistance put up by the victims.

But ever since "colonialism" became a political watchword among Western and third world intellectuals in the 1950s and 1960s, literature produced on the subject has addressed exclusively the type of colonialism implemented by monopoly capitalists in the preceding century. The assumption is fairly widespread that monopoly capitalism even created colonialism. This view implies that unless a country is itself a capitalist country, it could not possibly be involved in the practice of colonialism at all. This assumption simply is not supported by history. It is much more accurate to argue that colonialism itself generated monopoly capitalism in the process of creating institutions to control from a distance peoples and resources that previously had been organized under distinctive forms of social organization.

It is true, however, that once capitalism burst out of the boundaries of Europe and extended its reach globally, initially by extending and controlling massive apparatus of transportation and communication, it eventually pulled all other modes of production existing at that time into its orbit. There is no quibbling among historians over the global import of the rapid expansion of capitalism; the only debate exists over whether the effects were positive (the argument of the right) or negative (the argument of the left). The worldwide dominance of capitalism established in the latter half of the 1880s meant that all other forms of socioeconomic organization were forced to function directly or indirectly as its subsystems. No part of the globe remained isolated. Since each region has come to function as a subsystem in one way or another it is not possible to

13

The Invention of Ethiopia

portray an accurate picture of the dynamics of any specific area of the world without using a global perspective.

Most historical writing about the period since the explosion of capitalism consists of documentation of how specific social systems came to be dominated. The case of Ethiopia, however, has almost always been declared to be an exception to the general process of capitalist domination through colonial control. As a result, the emergence of Ethiopia has escaped the careful scrutiny applied to other regions of Africa. But Ethiopia was by no means an exception. The way in which it was made to be and remains a subsystem within the process of colonialism is the focus of this book. The place that it held and continues to hold in the global order has to be understood in order for the processes going on inside its imposed boundaries to be properly interpreted.

Most writers who have dealt with the subject of colonialism have described a particular colonial experience within the era of monopoly capitalism and have crystallized certain observable features of that experience into some formula intended for universal applicability. It is usually implied, if not asserted outright, that anything that falls outside of those parameters fails to qualify as colonialism. This approach does not proceed from a general theoretical outlook to the particular case at hand. As a result several variations of colonialism are simply defined away. Since the bulk of writing on the matter of direct colonialism in Africa was done during the rush for "decolonization" in the early 1960s, it is confined to issues that were germaine to countries aspiring to independence in that period. Later, in the 1970s, writers assessing the cases of Portuguese colonies exposed a variation that had not been regarded as fitting the pattern. Until then Portuguese claims had been taken at face value—claims that her Lusitanian empire constituted an exception to the rule in colonial Africa because of the complete unity that had been attained between the motherland and the "overseas territories." Analysts writing during the period of resistance against Portuguese rule challenged the boundaries of received wisdom regarding colonialism by calling the Portuguese variation "ultracolonialism" (Anderson 1962 and Cabral 1973).

14

Introduction

Since that time, despite assertions made by representatives of peoples from the Horn of Africa and elsewhere that they continue to live under colonial rule, analysts of both the left and the right have failed to recognize what they consider to be the identifying characteristics of colonialism in Africa. The issue has often been reduced to a simplistic association of colonialism with the racial features of the direct carriers of colonialism from Europe rather than a tough look at the system of rule. If representatives born in Europe were not sitting at the desks in the offices of a colonial bureacracy, scholars showed no interest in further investigation of the circumstances. Had careful investigation been conducted in Ethiopia, a variation on this pattern would have been revealed quite close to the surface. For example, in Ethiopia a European or foreign-born adviser would have indeed been found in the next room or behind the door in every office of the bureaucracy. But no one chose to question the bold assertions of complete independence made by the Ethiopians and their allies and fellow beneficiaries. The assumption that every form of colonialism looks the same both historically and in the present day has contributed to confusion about the past and also has hampered analysis of newly emerging forms of the phenomenon. The approach to colonialism per se has prejudged each case and severely limited understanding of social process.

Tools of Analysis

It is argued here that recognizing colonialism is a matter of identifying the basic features of the social organization of specific societies in question and determining whether or not a fundamental repatterning of either the economic base or the superstructure (or both) has been imposed by force. In this work the terms *economic base* or *substructure* are used to refer to the relationship in a particular society among material components that determine how its productive life is organized; the term *superstructure* is used to refer to any and all dimensions of the society that safeguard that basic economic relation and guarantee its continuity and centrality. The

15

mode of production refers to the configuration of the total societal entity, the combination of the base and the superstructure in which one social formation dominates by bringing all forces in the society into alignment with its values so that all social forces are ultimately made to contribute to its objectives. The term *social formation* is not as all-encompassing as mode of production; it refers to a specific distinctive set of social and economic institutions arranged according to the norms and values of a discrete group within a society. When a particular social formation does not dominate others, its constituent features are made to conform to the strictures of the social formation that does prevail. However, the dynamic and growing strength of subordinated social formations within any distinctive mode of production provides a constant source of pressure upon the one that predominates. There is a constant tension created when groups within society act to dismantle the controlling social formation in order to replace it with a new one which would introduce a new mode of production. This tension provides a strong impetus upon the social formation that does control the others to reform in order to remain in authority over them and to continue implementing its own values at their expense.

These conceptual issues are best seen within the larger question of *social transformation*. It can be said that a social system has undergone a transformation only if either the economic base or superstructure has been fundamentally rearranged. This rearrangement can occur two ways, either through the imposition of the production system from another society, which is what happens in the case of colonialism, or it can occur through the emergence of a fundamentally new form of social organization from within the parameters of an existing economic system such as with the emergence of a new social formation. This latter represents *revolutionary transformation*, an historic departure from previously known types of social order, capable of introducing and enforcing new relations of production from within the prevailing order. Transformation is often confused with *reform*, its polar opposite, which refers precisely to those adjustments in the superstructure made for the purpose of protecting

Introduction

the relations of production which lie at the heart of the prevalent economic base.

In most of the political economic literature these terms are used exclusively to apply to so-called modern societies with complex institutional forms. But this usage limits analysis. All societies may be analyzed in terms of the economic base and the superstructure that maintains it. In fact, a fundamental requirement for people to live together in communities at all is that a clear code of conduct govern their lives both day-to-day and over generations. This code regulates their production, consumption, distribution, and patterns of exchange. The codes of conduct that have been enforced through institutions designed to direct and protect the life, safety, and interests of each society are what comprise the superstructures of those societies. It is not only complex societies that can be said to have a mode of production, but all societies, since they have all operated under sets of guiding principles that affect all aspects of production.

The code of conduct may be written as law or not, depending on how the society transmits information to its members, but it is also embodied in the culture, values, and beliefs of its members and serves as the guiding force in shaping their judgments and behavior. Colonialism as a process bypasses or attempts to undermine and destroy the basis, or the code, by which the colonized society has organized its life; this is done in order to divert the material resources under the control of that society to a different end determined by the colonizer.

The involvement of invasion and force to impose a new code of conduct constitutes *conquest*. But conquest cannot guarantee control. The desire to control the conquered region leads to occupation, which is a separate and necessary step in colonialism. Settlers sent to occupy a conquered area begin the process of altering the economic relations of the conquered nation. At this point the two forms of socioeconomic organization, those of the conquering and of the conquered societies, come into full confrontation. *Occupation* is the sustained and intimate involvement of settlers in attempting to install institutions that will guarantee a permanent alteration of the

The Invention of Ethiopia

production relations, including channelling the application of force necessary to accomplish the task. In order to create a new production relation in the conquered regions, the members of the occupier community bring with them the code of conduct that guides their society of origin. The settlers impose upon the conquered peoples the superstructure of their own, the colonizing, society, something that is unknown to the natives of the area. This process of imposition is colonization. Once the new arrangement prevails, the conquered nation becomes a colonized nation.

It was Karl Marx who first argued in *The Critique of Political Economy* (1970) that colonialism is characterized by a change in the mode of production of the affected societies. For the conquered nation or community of people, day-to-day activities are altered, the relations that determined the organization of their society are realigned so that they are no longer patterned according to the institutions that were produced by that society. Instead an intruder has entered and brought the means to impose a new set of relations upon them. In imposing and enforcing new relations, the intruder has effectively seized the economic base of the society. This seizure and forcible reorganization constitutes the impostion of a new mode of production.

The above process is generally applicable regardless of the era or complexity of the colonizing society. With the advent of the kind of class society that emerged with capitalism, however, came the *state*. The *state* is a particular set of institutions that a specific ruling class has fashioned to organize the rest of its own society in ways that promote the interests and objectives of that class in opposition to the interests of the others. The emergence of the state occurred when classes holding different positions in a given economic system developed distinct interests and objectives for the organization of the total society. These differences gave rise to the expression of a distinct form of ideology, politics and economics by each class.

Simply put, *ideology* is the summation of the historical experience of a particular group or class; it is the blueprint according to which that class aspires to organize the entire social formation. *Politics* constitutes policy formulation, the implementation of the ideological

Introduction

blueprint that represents the interest of the group or class; and *economics* is the fundamental relation that is effectively established between the members of a society and the material forces required for the survival of that society. The basis of state formation is the making of institutions that embody the ideology, politics and economic objectives of the dominant class. Once fashioned, these institutions are capable of orienting central features of the entire society toward the objectives of that class. The advent of the colonial state meant that subsequent colonization was directed to serve the interest of a particular dominant ruling class.

Specific characteristics of colonialism that transcend the particular era in which the colonization takes place are:

1) settlement of aliens on territory originally in the possession of a distinct nation or nationality,

2) the reliance on externally derived resources, personnel, and ideas to administer the occupied area and to control its inhabitants,

3) the use or redirection of indigenous labor and the extraction of surplus from the conquered to serve ends determined by the conquering nation,

4) the suppression of the organizational and cultural life of the indigenous people,

5) assimilation programs conducted to enable selected indigenous personnel to blunt opposition to imported rule and eventually to function in the apparatus of administration,

6) heavy militarism of the settler group for the enforcement of newly introduced mechanisms for administration of the region,

7) harsh suppression of the resistance encountered from the local inhabitants,

8) development and reliance upon an elaborate ideological justification of the occupation for use both internally and externally.

These features of colonialism have been implemented differently in every historical era. For example, conquest and occupation by the feudal class during the era of feudalism manifested the institutional features of feudalism, the use of slaves, and reliance on the types of weaponry, communication, and transport facilities that had been developed in that period. After conquest, the societal configurations of these conquered peoples were rearranged and feudal institutions were forced upon them, reorganizing their communities according to the code of conduct demanded by the feudal mode of production. Once mercantile capitalism emerged from the era of feudalism, it had developed the capacity to decolonize the feudal and impose its own mode of production and institutions upon the colonies. Likewise monopoly capitalism had the capacity to reorganize the arrangements of the mercantile period; finance capitalism in due course was able to replace the configuration imposed by the monopolists. In each era colonialism has implemented the features of that era and organized the mechanisms of extension within whatever technological, political, social and logistical limitations that the world economic order of that day would allow.

Colonialism has been an enduring feature of social relations because it provides immediate benefits to the colonizing system. By extending the superstructure of the colonizing society, colonialism offers to the society a powerful means of mitigating or attenuating its internal contradictions. Exporting internal sources of tension to the domains of other nations to be worked out in a new context at a distance, prolongs the life of a colonizing system by affording it the opportunity to apply its resources to resolving or controlling one crisis at a time at home. This mitigation of tension can be accomplished in many ways, the most notable being 1) to remove to a distant land surplus or problematic populations, 2) to export surplus products generated through overproduction due to imbalance in the colonizing society, 3) to develop further the available technology and resources by means of extending them and thus increasing the capacity of the economic system beyond what was possible within home boundaries, and 4) to obtain for use in production raw materials from outside the finite supply of the home country. These kinds of measures have provided means for deflecting unrest temporarily correcting imbalances in economic systems that were expanding rapidly and could not satisfy simultaneously the growing demands of participating groups.

Introduction

Colonialism during the Eras of Monopoly and Finance Capital

From the time that monopoly capitalism developed the capacity to operate as a global system it was able to determine the direction of the world economic order. After that, all the economic processes that had been previously set in motion during the feudal and mercantile periods were subordinated to it. Colonialism in this era began to function as an extension of the state system established by the monopoly capitalist class. The new capitalist class had the ability to turn all other economic processes either to serve or to accommodate its own ends through the management of the state. No region or social system was exempt.

Any type of expansion carried out by a noncapitalist society after the rise of the monopoly capitalist class was subject to the influence and direction of class representatives resident in several major countries of Europe. Control by the monopoly capitalist class of the state in these countries is what made them monopoly powers; the institutions in each of these countries were made to serve the purposes of capital. Once control of any one country had become concentrated in the hands of a group of nationalistic capitalists, that group extended its reach worldwide trying to bring other regions and peoples under the control of its own European flag. Though the state institutitions of European countries that were controlled by capitalists were roughly parallel and shared the same kinds of economic objectives, members of the capitalist class in one country competed with those of another for control of the market and global supremacy for their particular nation. This competition went on until members of the class eventually acknowledged their common objectives, merged their resources and began to share multinational institutions. This class merger launched the era of finance capital.

While the terms monopoly capital and finance capital are sometimes, though not always, used interchangeably as they are in Baran and Sweezy's book *Monopoly Capital* (1966), we have adopted and consistently applied a very specific usage. *Monopoly capitalism* and *monopoly capital* are utilized quite literally here to refer to the

The Invention of Ethiopia

capitalist system in Europe which operated when the capitalist class was segmented, its members overtly nationalistic and striving to bring new acquisitions of territory, resources and peoples under the sole control of the institutions of their particular nation-state. In other words, nationalistic capitalists sought to "monopolize" and consolidate into rival empires all the regions of the world that they were able to conquer or colonize by some means.

Ultimately, however, tensions and competition among these European nation-states erupted into two worldwide conflagrations, a new model, that of *finance capital*, was adopted which called upon the common features of the state institutions in each capitalist country and effectively guaranteed collective access to the colonies of all the empires. The new model was the model of multinational institutions which embodied the common values of the merged capitalist class—the finance capitalist class. The shift to international reliance on the institutions of finance capital was completed by the mid-twentieth century and constituted an adjustment in the world order.

Each variation of capitalism has introduced different strategies for maintaining the advance of capital, including different forms of colonialism. During the period of monopoly capitalism, rivalry among the European colonizers was characteristic. This condition of competition gave rise to a specific form of colonialism relevant to the subject of this book. Smaller countries were supported by larger ones to occupy contested regions with the result that the occupied region would be accessible to the big power. During this era, if any small society occupied another, it did so not on its own, but it did so only in the interest of monopoly capital and with the assistance of a particular guardian from among the monopoly powers, who at that time openly called themselves "the Big Powers of Europe." Smaller societies who were assisted in occupation of other regions became dependent colonizers. In this book the system of assisted occupation which extended the objectives of monopoly colonial control through weaker countries who then became partners in the process is termed *dependent colonialism*.

Introduction

In the dependent colonial model, an agent country was made to carry out the work of colonizing a designated region in alliance with a specific national capitalist class. There came an intervening force between the capitalists and the colonized nations. This force was the dependent colonizer who gained benefits from the domination and exploitation of other nations by controlling them in ways it would not have been capable of without the intervention of capital. Dependent colonizers were empowered by larger powerful nations. The expansion of the dependents, made possible by holding, subjugating and exploiting other nations as colonies, served to extend the superstructure of a capitalist state into new territories.

During the conquest of Africa, several countries became dependent colonizers—Abyssinia, Portugal, Belgium, and South Africa. The Abyssinian, Belgian, and Portuguese cases offer good examples of conditions in which a weaker power, by allying with imperialists, was able to accomplish the expansion that each had aspired to but that none had been able to achieve alone. Expansion offered certain benefits to the weaker countries as well as to the monopolists by creating avenues for exporting some of the elements that contributed to pressures and contradictions that created internal social and economic crises. In several places in Africa where European capitalist powers faced an impasse over the direct incorporation of specific regions into one monopolistic empire or another, weaker countries were empowered to establish the amount of control necessary to ensure access to the region by the concerned superpower. A dependent colonial system that has been ignored by analysts of Africa and of colonialism resulted from major powers managing potential conflict among themselves by accommodating each other in several regions of Africa. This system minimized competition and extended the viability of monopoly capitalism as a world system a while longer.

The collaboration between some superpowers of the day and smaller countries who became dependent colonizers worked to the mutual benefit of the metropolitan capitalists and the countries who became their agents in Africa. The agents, as junior partners, benefitted by furthering their own internal ambitions and relieving their own internal problems. Therefore, because the world economic order was operating to their advantage, the dependent colonizers did not (and still do not, in the Ethiopian case) want to challenge or question that order or the position they have taken in it.

It was stated above that the specific form of colonialism found at any one historical period manifests the features of that epoch and the world economic order which characterizes it. The model of dependent colonialism fits this pattern. It emerged as a means of managing or containing conflict between monopoly capitalist powers. It is interesting to note that the kind of solution reached in forming dependent colonial states provide evidence of the birth of finance capitalist forms of organization in the womb of monopoly. The solution to the problem of providing access to the Ethiopian empire for several European monopoly powers, for example, presaged the eventual model of corporate access to all the colonial countries which was proposed and accepted forty years later, after finance capitalist institutions were strong enough to move in to replace the old forms of monopoly worldwide.

It is reasonable to ask what the difference is between dependent colonialism and what is widely termed neocolonialism in the rest of Africa and the world. Neocolonialism, which is referred to in this book as *corporate colonialism*, developed later after finance capital had become dominant. It was instituted in areas where the advanced industrial capitalist countries of Europe had already carried out their own colonizing. These regions had originally been colonized directly by representatives of their own capitalist class, born and trained in the European mother country, who travelled out and settled in the colony. Once there, the settlers had been in control and directly responsible for establishing the institutions necessary for transforming the subject area into a peripheral supply zone for and an extension of the metropolitan centers. When the separations between the monopolists were eliminated, and the institutions of finance capitalism were brought in, a new form of colonialism was introduced; this is what is called neocolonialism or, better, corporate colonialism.

The decolonization of the empires that has been constructed directly by national representatives of the monopoly capitalist class amounted to a change of personnel. By that time the institutions built to accommodate the interests of capital were operational. The move to neocolonialism constituted a withdrawal of European-born representatives and their replacement by locally born persons who were put in charge of the intact institutional structures. These African-born representatives had been equipped to serve as faithful guardians of the interests of the capitalist class, equipped through training either by a metropolitan-style educational system set up in their country or often through training and socialization abroad in the metropoitan center itself. Advanced modern education enabled these individuals to acquire the skills and to develop the interests necessary to defend enthusiastically and preserve effectively the smooth operation of capitalist institutions which had been firmly established in their countries during the colonial period. Through this process of so-called decolonization, countries that had been forced into the capitalist economic system in the position of subject remained in the same subject position. A change in birthplace of the personnel administering the state had no effect on the basic production relations. The adjustment in the world order that was made when finance capital became dominant ensured that capitalist production relations were able to continue unmolested.

The basic difference between dependent colonialism and what eventually emerged as corporate colonialism is that the two were implemented in different eras and therefore in a slightly different manner. Dependent colonialism was established in the period when monopoly capitalism was expanding. It was fashioned out of the desperate need of monopoly powers who were very nationalistic to secure access and some form of control over disputed regions without destroying each other. Monopoly powers of Europe turned individually and collectively to weaker countries that they could influence to exert indirect control over these regions. Dependent colonizers were selected because they were already situated near the contested area and were equipped, by means of technology and the strategy provided through foreign advisers, to move further inland and take on the job of changing indigenous institutions. In the process of establishing dependent colonialism, competing members of the monopoly capitalist classes in Europe reached across the national boundaries separating them and acknowledged their common interests enough to make arrangements to manage their conflicts successfully. These accommodations, made in order to achieve objectives that they all shared, contributed to the emergence of new forms of institutions and a single finance capitalist class worldwide.

At the time that corporate colonialism was established, the institutions that characterized finance capital had developed to the point that they had become capable of dominating the world order. In fact, ensuring collective access to all the formerly monopolized areas by implementing corporate colonialism signalled at last the global dominance of finance capital. The objective of corporate colonialism is similar to that of dependent colonialism—to retain secure access and to achieve the indirect colonial control by the dominant capitalist class over specific regions. In corporate colonialism the agent is different. This system has been implemented in areas where a direct colonizer had already entered the region and imposed a capitalist superstructure, which included new norms and values, upon the colonized. The agents of corporate colonialism are themselves products of that very colonial institutional superstructure. The the specific group that forced the original institutional changes upon the colonized nations is no longer present. It has formally and very publicly withdrawn. Consequently, there can be no face-to-face confrontation between the finance capitalist class and the indigenous people who have been colonized. The conflict between the class who designed and benefits from the system of corporate colonialism and the indigenous people who remain colonized is one in which actual representatives of the colonizing class are absent from the scene. In the case of dependent colonialism, however, the colonized directly confront one of the groups responsible for instituting their oppression; they can and do confront the settlers directly.

Let us turn to examine the developments in Europe and elsewhere in the world that gave rise to the conditions that created and continue to fashion Ethiopia and other dependencies.

2 THE CHANGING WORLD

The key to why the Ethiopian empire was created and sustained as an internationally recognized state lies in understanding the dynamic of the world order at that period. The purpose of this chapter is to present relevant information about the global context in which Ethiopia came into being and survives. It concerns the shift that occurred on the world scale from the dominance of competitive industrial capitalism in which single countries of Europe vied to monopolize specific portions of the market (monopoly capitalism) to the dominance of the institutions of finance capitalism.

Ethiopia occupied a specific position within the shift from single-country monopoly to the control of financial institutions. It is not possible to appreciate or interpret the specific juncture of either history or geography that Ethiopia occupied without standing back and surveying the forces at work on the world scale at the time of Ethiopia's formation. The background information here is presented without continual reference to the Ethiopian case, however, since understanding the problems of any given socioeconomic area requires an understanding of the world economic order of which it is a part. The relevance to the case at hand will emerge as the argument unfolds.

The Invention of Ethiopia

The Transition from Regional to Global Economy

Historically, the demise of feudalism in Europe together with the advent of a merchant capitalist class advocating "free trade" saw the pioneer take on great importance. Pioneers had a strategic role to play in making possible the expansion of capitalism into a worldwide system. They were explicitly rewarded for extending a burgeoning capitalist system from Europe into new territories and for "discoveries" in those territories of resources to be used in the development of industry on the mainland of Europe. The "discovery" of America as far back as 1492 was part of this process, as were the major expeditions which took European pioneers to Asia and to the continent of Africa. The pioneers and those who supported them eventually became the masters of the new discoveries.

By the late 1700s, however, this kind of initial pioneering effort had resulted in the establishment of groups of settlers who wanted to disengage from the motherland, such as the American colony, who declared their independence from the European countries that had sent them out. Disengagement of the colonies of the mercantile period, coupled with the internal conditions in Europe, set the stage for a new condition of intense rivalry in the continent of Europe. Powerful Britain lost one of its largest and most significant colonies (later to become the United States), largely due to the strategic assistance of the French which enabled it to break free. France, on the other hand, by the opening of the nineteenth century, had been able to conquer and colonize several European countries themselves, bringing the major countries on the continent of Europe under Napoleonic rule. For a while most of continental Europe became either a colony of France or fell under French domination. This situation changed when this French empire lost a crucial war over control of Spain in 1808 and Spain, with British help, was eventually able to declare itself independent. Soon the interior colonies of France in the heart of Europe stepped up their struggles for independence. France's support for America's independence that was followed by English support of Spain confirmed these two states as enemies and rivals on the continent, contributing to heightened tensions and competition.

By 1815 Napoleonic rule, the rule of what is often referred to as a bourgeois monarchy, in Europe had ended. Such a monarchy had enabled the bourgeois class to develop across Europe. The Congress of Vienna was held to address the new conditions (sometimes called "the new reality") that had emerged on the continent during this period. This congress marked a milestone in a series of formal agreements to maintain peace by acknowledging a "balance of power" in Europe. The bases for the agreement indicated that strategies important to the growing class of capitalists were beginning their ascendancy. The bourgeoisie had begun to monopolize resources and control conditions within specific national boundaries in Europe and nationalism had begun to flower. Monopolistic capitalism began to emerge as an economic system. The major concern in Europe had become peace, and people had begun to express in various forms their rejection of war. Mass movements such as demonstrations and large-scale protests developed whose main objectives were the renovation of the economic and political systems. According to David Thomson, one of many who have chronicled this period from the point of view of diplomatic history, during the next twenty to twenty-five years in Europe "human energies were devoted more to seeking an overhaul of internal political and social systems than to pursuing the nationalist causes of war against foreign states" (Thomson 1957: 91).

During the period when the Europeans were able to stop the general wars, the war economies that had been built up experienced serious reorganization. The continent of Europe as a whole experienced several economic crises. The story of the acute and widespread economic crisis of 1818-1819 was repeated in 1825 and in much greater intensity in 1838-1839, and again in 1846-1847. In the midst of these conditions a movement had begun to develop among the working class, and a new class was emerging capable of affecting government, what several writers have called a "middle" class.

The Invention of Ethiopia

> The chief way in which industrialism affected government and politics was in its conferring new wealth and power upon the growing middle class of enterprising traders, manufacturers and financiers, and in its creation of a new industrial proletariat. (Thomson 1957: 162)

Through this period antagonistic classes spawned by industrialism began to consolidate and to face off against each other—the industrial bourgeoisie and a new wage-earning class of factory and mine workers, the proletariat class.

At the initial stage, the demands of these classes had appeared similar—they both wanted to improve the supply of food and to change the nature of political participation. By the second half of the century, e.g., the revolution of 1848, monarchical rule was crushed at the hands of these new classes, in France especially (see Marx's *Class Struggles in France* and *The 18th Brumaire of Louis Bonaparte* for an account of these events). A new order was to be organized by the new capitalist class, one with a new ideology and new politics. This period marked the birth of their power. The rise to power of this class came at a time when the European population was increasing dramatically. That population in 1800 was 180 million, whereas by 1850 it was 266 million (ibid.). It was also a period which witnessed both the emergence of advanced technology and technical know-how and the problems of industrial development which accompanied them.

Soon once-peaceful Europe began to face a new series of external conflicts. The Crimean War of 1854-56 which involved Britain, France, Russia and Turkey, was generated from outside the signers of the Treaty of Vienna and marked the breakdown of the formal balance of power. New wars of a different kind broke out, most of which had their origins in the internal conditions that existed within European nations. Such were the war between France and Austria in 1856, the war in 1864 which pitted Prussia and Austria against Denmark, the Austro-Prussian War of 1866, the Franco-Prussian War of 1877 as well as the Russo-Turkish War of 1877, which came close to becoming a general European conflict.

The Changing World

While the ascendancy of the new capitalist class represented a consolidation of capitalism as an economic system, this incoming class did inherit from the previous class rule two problems from the recent economic crises, however. One of the consequences was an extreme shortage in the food supply. Food was being imported from "America and Soviet [sic] Russia, and payment for it drained away gold .... There were large scale mercantile failures, bankruptcies and closures of banks" (ibid.: 163). Famine conditions resulted in uncontrolled exploitation and a growing mass discontent.

The other heritage from the past was the peace treaties that earlier had been agreed upon. The new class in power moved to reinstate and to respect the principles of the treaty of Vienna (1815) that had articulated the concept of the "Concert of Europe," the idea that had left Europe without a major regional war for almost half a century. They also accepted the principles of the later treaty, that of the Congress of Verona (1822) that made explicit the form of conflict management that relied on maintaining a "balance of power." They agreed upon a formal set of principles that disavowed "annexation without ratification." It was this principle that called for an alliance of forces in Europe to fight together any party which tried to take any more territory from any other European state. The principle had clearly stated, "No state should gain additions of territory in *Europe* without the agreement of the other state" [emphasis added] (ibid.: 221).

Since these agreements only constituted a restriction in taking away territory *in Europe* but not in any other place, and since taking from Europe brought the danger of direct retaliation, the new industrial bourgeois class was confronted with a dilemma. The only thing that remained to be done was to go elsewhere—outside the boundaries of Europe—to find a solution to the critical problems associated with population explosion, unemployment, and a growing working-class movement. As it turned out, acceptance of the principles of the Treaty of Verona provided the impetus for seeking solutions to growing problems outside of Europe.

These new problems provided intense pressures for expanding and extending the institutions of the new bourgeoisie. This led to

The Invention of Ethiopia

changes in the nature of the type of colonialism that had been practiced up to that time. Earlier colonialism had been an extension of the mercantile system based on exploration and establishing trade. This new class had developed institutions whose objectives were to monopolize, that is, to completely control the resources and populations within their domain. By extending their reach abroad, the new bourgeoisie, the monopoly capitalists, sought a means to expand, not alter, these objectives, thereby relieving the internal contradictions that they faced in Europe.

At this time, the period when the industrial class took over from the merchant class, in the mid-1800s, the majority of the globe was already occupied by industrial powers. The problem was, where to go. South America was protected by the "Monroe Doctrine." Australia and the major part of Asia and New Zealand were already occupied by European powers, namely Britain, France, Portugal and the Dutch. By the second half of the nineteenth century the only "open" areas, meaning the only areas of the globe not already occupied by a power in Europe, were Africa and Polynesia (see Hobson 1902, Lenin 1917, Hobsbawm 1975).

It was in this kind of political climate that the new pioneers, the entrepreneurs, were sent into Africa explicitly representing the interests of these monopolists. Several of this group arrived on the scene in Abyssinia.

By the opening of the era of industrial capital, then, the stage was set for a rush into the remaining territories. Every indicator showed that a "scramble" into Africa and Polynesia could be anticipated. In actual fact, however, the grabbing was delayed until power relations in Europe itself had been sorted out. When Britain came out of the Crimean War of 1854-56, she proceeded to extend her influence elsewhere. Meanwhile, France and Germany were engaged in regional wars until 1870, so they did not extend themselves as early, nor did they begin the process with full swing (Thomson 1957: 91). But after the end of the Franco-German War in 1870, it appeared that all of Europe turned around to see nothing but the need to feed and supply its enlarged population and its growing industry. They saw boundless new supplies abroad and raced to

The Changing World

obtain them. Colonialism in this period was seen clearly as a "bread and butter" issue for Europe by the last quarter of the nineteenth century.

This is when the process began that has often been described by both its advocates and its detractors as a Scramble for Africa. It became a ruthless campaign to take all that was possible to take wherever a European power had not already staked a claim. The scramble was particularly intense over the last bits to be claimed. By the end of it, Britain and France came out with the most gains among the participants, primarily because of the positions they had already held as world powers before the conquest. Each of them had significant previous acquisitions. And their experience in other places poised them to move quickly. The number of their colonies alone proves the level of their technological capacity.

Before 1876, Britain had either occupied or had been present in one form or another in the North Atlantic, in Canada, the Caribbean, India, Ceylon, Burma, Australia, South Pacific ports, in West Africa, Cape Colony, and a chain of intermediate islands between the Atlantic region and the Indian and Pacific Oceans, and had a treaty with the United States. France, on the other hand, held Algiers, Tahiti, Ivory Coast, Peking, Syria, Dahomey, Guinea, New Caledonia, Indochina, Cochin-China, Cambodia, as well as having more say in the regional economy of Europe. The Netherlands had the holding of the Dutch East Indies. Spain held the Canaries, Cuba, Puerto Rico and Caribbean. Portugal claimed the Atlantic islands of the Azores, Medeira, Cape Verde, Angola, Mozambique and Goa (Thomson 1957: 231-237).

This scramble among the European powers who divided Africa was nothing less than a full-scale land grab. When it began, the only countries that had a footing in the continent by way of trading posts from the mercantile era were Britain, France and Portugal. The rest were equally new to the region. In fact, the events that unfolded reveal that the major contention remained to be one between two superpowers who were only beginning to be cognizant of the potential power of others.

The Invention of Ethiopia

The building of the Suez Canal was a crucial part of the laying down of the physical and material infrastructure which made possible the extension of European institutions and the control of remote regions.

With all this taken into account, the entire occupation of the African continent can be viewed as a contest between Britain and France on the one hand and Britain and Germany on the other, with others brought in only to play a secondary role (see Anderson 1962 for a concise summary statement of this argument). The key to why Belgium, Spain, Portugal, Abyssinia and Italy came to hold colonies in Africa at all lay solely in this contest. They were there not by their own power alone but by the position they held in relation to the balance of power that existed in Europe, particularly between the two major powers, Britain and France. Among all of these "smaller" powers, the weakest were Abyssinia of Africa, and King Leopold of Belgium in Europe.

At first there was a very rough division of the territory, made with sweeping strokes; in fact, there were times when one major power would suggest to another power to move into a particular region. Thomson says, "occasionally one power made gains with the encouragement or assent of others. Bismarck encouraged France to expand into Tunisia" (1957: 465).

When, by the beginning of 1884, however, Britain and Portugal set up a joint commission to control navigation of the whole Congo River, the intention was to block Belgium. What was at stake here was how to avoid recourse to war when national strategies abutted each other in Africa outside the mainland. While treaties had established principles of operation on the continent, there had been no rule provided for behavior in the newest region. The Congo matter provided the occasion for the Congress at Berlin. Bismarck of Germany and Jules Ferry of France, cooperated in 1884 to summon an international conference at Berlin to settle amicably the future of the Congo in central tropical Africa and the future of Belgium in European society. The purpose was to lay down general rules by which monopoly control could be established in Africa. The objective was that arrangements for control of this area based on ideas of monopoly could be made according to the same pattern that Europeans had used to solve their problems in Europe.

The conference was attended by most of the states of Europe. The superpowers of the day, Britain and France, arrived at the conference with their own subordinate governments in tow. Britain opened by asserting that she recognized as belonging to Portugal all areas that Portugal had claimed on the continent dating back to the mercantile period of free trade. The reason for this move was clear and has been clearly summarized by Amilcar Cabral as follows:

> Since 1775 Portugal has been a semi-colony of Britain. This is the only reason that Portugal was able to preserve the colonies during the partition of Africa. How could this poor miserable country preserve the colonies in the face of the ambitions and jealousies of Germany, France, Belgium, and the emerging American imperialism? It was because Britain adopted a tactic. It said—Portugal is my colony, if it preserves colonies, they are also my colonies—and England defended the interests of Portugal with force (Cabral 1973: 82-83).

France had her own interest in the Congo area; Germany had an interest in the Cameroons. At the same time both Germany and France would rather deal with a weaker force, i.e. Belgium, than with Britain; King Leopold of Belgium was aware of the situation and looked to France and Germany for help.

Lenin summed up the situation in 1917 saying:

> Alongside the colonial possessions of the Great Powers, we have placed the small colonies of the small states, which are, so to speak, the next objects of a possible and probable new colonial "shakeout." Most of these little states are able to retain their colonies only because of the conflicting interests, frictions, etc., among the big powers which prevent them from coming to an agreement in regard to the division of the spoils (Lenin 1917: 259).

The Invention of Ethiopia

Though the conference was called upon the issue of Belgium, ostensibly to determine the future of Belgium, the real issue or the primary concern of all present was the issue of extending European "spheres of influence" to Africa. The conclusion reached by the participants was indeed a series of resolutions to extend the principles embodied in the European treaties of Vienna (1815) and Verona (1822) regarding European holdings on the mainland. The frequently confused issue of Abyssinia's place in this process cannot be understood apart from this context.

The decisions and agreements of the Berlin Congress were no different from the kinds of rules that capitalists had utilized in Europe to preserve their interests, that is, rules for maintaining a balance of power. It was said that "... in the future any power that effectively occupied *African territory* and duly notified the other powers could thereby establish possession of it" [emphasis added] (Thomson 1957: 466). They left open-ended the matter of who specifically could participate and how "effective occupation" was to be determined. Eventually the scramble became an intense competition for territory within these guidelines. The participants resorted to acquiring land and resources by both direct and indirect means. The battle for the control of northeast Africa fit this pattern perfectly. The envoys and entrepreneurs who struggled to bring the land and peoples of the Horn region under the control of one European power or another used the same tactics that were used across the continent. The Horn was no exception, as it is usually considered to be.

Abyssinian leaders were carefully advised and encouraged by entrepreneurs representing the larger powers to enter into the marathon in much the same way as Belgium and Portugal did, as a placeholder for the major powers who planned to apportion the areas in the larger chess game they were engaged in.

When the occupation of Africa was completed, the biggest beneficiary appeared to be Great Britain. British views on the importance of occupation were clear; Harrison Wright has characterized them as follows:

The Changing World

However costly, however perilous, this process of imperial expansion may be, it is necessary to the continued existence and progress of our nation; if we abandoned it we must be content to leave the development of the world to other nations, who will everywhere cut into our trade, and even impair our means of securing the food and raw materials we require to support our population (Wright 1976: 31).

By the end of the 1800s, according to Hobson's estimation:

Great Britain during these years (1884-1900) acquired 3,700,000 square miles of territory, with 57,000,000 inhabitants; France, 3,600,000 square miles with 36,500,000; Germany, 1,000,000 square miles with 14,700,000; Belgium 900,000 square miles with 30,000,000 inhabitants; Portugal, 800,000 square miles with 9,000,000 inhabitants (cited in Lenin 1971: 224-225, refer to Hobson 1938: passim).

To fill out the record, we must note that Italy obtained 185,000 square miles and 750,000 people (Thomson 1957: 464), and Abyssinia acquired 800,000 square miles with a population of 12-13 million (Perham 1969: 293-295).

It was Germany who was extremely dissatisfied with the outcome of the scramble. Her response was to try to establish a relation with Britain in order somehow to acquire the colonies of Portugal. Germany was especially intent on taking Angola from Portugal so that Germany could connect the two colonies of German Southwest Africa and German East Africa. In 1898 when Britain and Germany met, Britain informed Germany that her support of Portugal was still firm, thus confirming the role of that smaller nation in the British strategy. Germany's interest in this area provided an additional British rationale for supporting dependent colonialism—protection of property from the direct control of Germany. Germany at this time began to express her dissatisfaction with the arrangement.*

By this time Germany's industrial development and its naval power were not only catching up technologically and creating a threat to Britain but also posed a threat to the colonial holdings of all the colonialists of Europe. In naval, military, and commercial abilities, Germany was approaching the strength of the old power brokers who represented the chief rivalry in Africa. The German threat was felt on the continent of Europe and elsewhere, not just in Africa.

At the turn of the century several participants, directly or indirectly (as in the case of Abyssinia), were all engaged in wars which represented challenges to the conquerors. Each wanted to take some territory from the conquered, but none of these had consolidated positions.

By the end of the nineteenth century Britain and France were in conflict over Egypt, Sudan and control of the upper Nile region of northeast Africa; Britain and Germany over southern Africa; Britain and Russia over Persia; Germany and Russia over the Balkans; Japan and Russia over China; Germany and France over Morocco; and Abyssinia and Italy over the Abyssinian colonies of Oromia, Sidama, etc. These conflicts were part of specific drives to connect empires, consolidate positions, and fine-tune the spheres of influence that had been established by treaty. Diplomatic arrangements prevailed in several instances, e.g., the Tripartite Treaty of 1906, but ultimately the rules were burst asunder in the First World War, which began in 1914. These conflicts are usually blamed on Germany, but Britain and France were as much responsible by demanding, for economic and political motives, that their colonies be connected. Connecting the colonies would satisfy the colonial

---

* Kaiser Wilhelm II of Germany had sent a congratulatory note on the activities and sayings of Kruger, who when toasted for the birthday of the Kaiser, said of Germany that it was "a grown-up power that would stop England from kicking the child republic" (Thomson 1957: 479).

economic desire by increasing monopoly and reducing costs of protection and transportation.

Eventually they had to sacrifice these schemes because their interests were overlapping. As Thomson summed it up:

> By 1900 and mainly since 1870, the great powers of Europe had divided up most of the African continent.... Their separate holdings were so distributed that Britain, France and Germany each aimed at linking up their holdings: the British by a Cape-to-Cairo line running South-North; the French by linking their large western territories with French Somaliland on the east; the Germans by a triangular thrust across the Congo and Angola.... These thrusts led to colonial collisions at Fashoda and to the Boer War and to international agreements to preserve Belgian power in the Congo and Portuguese in Angola. (ibid.: 462),

The international agreement that was reached in 1906, the Tripartite Treaty, represented a significant and innovative mechanism for diffusing the tension and competition among the powers intent of preserving their interests in Africa. As we shall see, they arranged to invent and recognize an "independent" African-run state in an area where they were at loggerheads over control. Their accommodation was to preserve Abyssinian rule in the regions of Oromia, Sidama, Ogaden, etc. Their solutions contained the seeds of the model that was later to be used to maintain indirect control over the rest of Africa.

By 1907 after the signing of treaties for the protection of all these powers, most African colonial disputes had been provisionally settled. However, Europeans entered the twentieth century without achieving what they had been dreaming about ever since the end of Bonapartism in Europe; they were still without a true balance of power. Each was watching the other endlessly.

By the opening of the twentieth century, new and powerful monopoly states emerged that had been developed on capital and institutional bases unencumbered by the concerns and obligations of

The Invention of Ethiopia

Europeans obsessed with finely honed balance-of-power issues. These were the United States, Russia and Japan. The United States, by the close of the century, had flexed its muscle by taking over the Philippines and stepping in to protect the former Spanish colonies by means of the "Monroe Doctrine." Japan asserted itself by taking Formosa and competing with Russia for the control of Manchuria and Korea. These acts were known as Sino-Japanese War of 1895 and Russo-Japanese war of 1904-05.

Such acts ushered in the twentieth century amid tensions on a worldwide scale, throwing off the carefully constructed balance of power that had prevailed among Europeans and had been extended to the rest of the globe. Besides the newcomers—the new colonial forces—which had come into the picture, Germany had begun to prove that she was a power to be reckoned with, replacing France as the leading force in Europe. Britain remained as the leading power worldwide, but Germany had begun to imply that had she so desired, she could have easily overtaken Britain. Germany had even begun to assert that she did not need that island because she could build a ship as large as the British island itself (ibid.: 493-498).

By 1907 one can see that the division between the European powers fell into two blocks; one was the alliance between Germany, Austria-Hungary, Italy and Rumania, and the other was an alliance between France, Britain and Russia. The build-up of war materials in both Germany and England continued. An English journalist, J. A. Spender, explained the nature of the European situation:

> The stage which Europe had reached was that of a semi-internationalism which organized the nations into two groups but provided no bridge between them. There could scarcely have been worse conditions for either peace or war. The equilibrium was so delicate that a puff of wind might destroy it . . . . (quoted by Thomson 1957: 500)

Under these conditions each block considered that if one was touched they were all touched. These alliances and colonialist agreements now would not only involve them, it would involve the whole world, because the colonies were considered to be a part of each camp. Activities reveal that they all participated in these wars. Any action by one group would trigger a world war.

Redirecting the World Order

The year 1907 marked a point in the history of Europe by which most of the older European powers had come to realize that they had to protect their own interests at home as well as their colonies abroad. Recent developments had shown that if they did not have a power base at home, they could easily lose not only the colonies they held but they could themselves become a colony of a stronger power. This marked a period when the older powers, Britain and France, the powers that stood to lose the most if the existing arrangements were tampered with, began to show real concern about the growing force of Germany. Germany represented new capitalist power and had effectively demonstrated that she could no longer be discounted or pushed around.

Even prior to the final unification of Germany, German states had participated in, even hosted, some of the European peace treaties—including those of Vienna in 1815 and Verona in 1822; then a unified Germany hosted conferences at Berlin in 1878 on the eastern European question, and again at Berlin in 1884-85 on partition of Africa, and participated in Algeria in 1906 on the Morocco dispute, and in London in 1912 concerning the Balkans. Nevertheless, she was considered a young capitalist state. It fell upon Germany to raise a serious challenge to the status quo in European power relations. She began to assert that she had always been discriminated against by Britain and France due to the type of formula utilized to construct the agreements. As far as Germany was concerned, the treaties were based on outmoded European-style tactics designed to buy time until one of the old powers was in a position to annex territory that had been lost.

The alliance of forces and the treaties that existed between "the Powers" (as they called themselves) amounted to little more than a

The Invention of Ethiopia

series of promissory notes that could be redeemed at any time that the holder could claim maximum face value. A British prime minister once summed up this sort of situation by asserting that there was no such thing as a permanent agreement, only a permanent national interest.

By the first quarter of the twentieth century, all countries had realized that there was in essence an open market for any one "small nation" to sell its alliance or its loyalty to the highest bidder in this power game. The small states and dependent colonies, however, were kept locked into a subordinate position by the great powers and were used as pawns in the political gambits of the big powers. Several writers have used chess game analogies in referring to this period (for example see Work 1935, Louis 1978). By 1907 one could see the alignment of capitalist forces—the old monopolists led by Britain, France and Russia on one side, and the young monopolist powers led by Germany, Austria-Hungary and Rumania on the other, with Italy representing the real condition of the political market, selling or offering her alliance to the highest bidder. Playing this kind of position to her advantage was what enabled Italy to silence Britain and France when she moved in and take over Ethiopia in the 1930s. Italy signed treaties with both the Allied (Triple Alliance) and the Central (Triple Entente), as the old and young powers began to call themselves. At this time the development of war materials on both sides had reached an unprecedented scale. The growth of Germany's naval power and economy created a general tendency for distrust and fear. Thomson summed up this development as follows: "The system of rival alliances marked the liquidation of nineteenth-century relationships, the abandonment of traditional foreign policies, the adoption by others of the new, mobile, dynamic diplomacy . . . " (Thomson 1957: 493).

Now this meant that the old order was being challenged by a new force demanding a new order. The new order demanded of the small and powerless nations of Europe that they become a part of it through alliance with a larger power. If any one of the small nations tried to break away, one of the big powers was able to regain it by annexation. This created the condition that led to World War I—

The Changing World

that if any one were to attack another who was a member state of one of these alliances, such an attack was instantly recognized as an attack on the entire membership. As these armed camps faced each other, both parties were ready to start the first contest at home. The situation at this juncture has been characterized as follows:

> ... the European nations were passing through a strange twilight era of mixed systems: not a stabilized balance of power, but a newly recreated and precarious balance of power; not a concert of Europe, but a residual and imperfect concert, with which was blended a system of divisive alliances; not an international community but only an embryonic international society in which all political and military decisions remained the jealously guarded preserve of separate sovereign states. ... (ibid.: 503)

After some time, the national bourgeoisie in each country of Europe could accept in principle the advantages of making the world one arena, governed by one ruling class. But they could not agree, however, on which national bourgeoisie would direct the job. They had not yet developed the political-economic or the ideological base for implementing such a shift, which would involve transferring the leadership of the world order to values and institutions dominated by finance capital. European countries were in the position of asserting that one national bourgeoisie was better than the other and that one refused to trust leadership to another. International contacts had increased and so had domestic friction. That condition existed when the Archduke of Austria was shot by a Serb and the Viennese government declared war on Serbia on July 28, 1914. All of Europe took the position that it was time to go to war. This declaration instantaneously lined up all alliances referred to above to test the power of their war machines. The clash between European alliances quickly spread to a worldwide arena, thus acquiring the name "World War," for the next four years.

The Invention of Ethiopia

> From that decisive act everything else followed. Russia ordered a general mobilization on July 30, Germany on July 31, and Germany declared war against Russia on August 1, against France on August 3. Germany's ultimatum to Belgium on August 3, and its rejection as being a violation of Belgian neutrality, ensured Britain's entry into war the following day. The bonds of the alliances held firm, and the two armed camps clashed in open battle at last. (Thomson 1957: 507)

The fact that such an incident could immediately trigger worldwide conflict demonstrates how precarious the balance was.

The First World War marked the beginning of the end of the old formula for balance of power. The major outbreak of clashes among the European powers affected the world order by disclosing the erosion that had taken place within the old order and by creating the conditions for a new model of capitalism to emerge, one that showed the capacity to establish mechanisms that could dominate production on a global scale. The nature of the crisis revealed the inherent need to overcome the several diverse and competing systems and to begin to function as a single world system, within a single set of values, that is to say, within a shared superstructure. The realization of that ideal took some time to develop.

The war had to be fought on a global level so that European nations could establish who was to become the dominant decision-making force over the European institutions that had been established worldwide. Simply to control them in Europe was not sufficient. The war was not over quickly, however, and when the situation was at a standstill, the October revolution in Russia broke out. Germany was soon ready to make good on her threat to try to take over Europe by dominating Great Britain. Britain's base was not in Europe but in the colonies. France's base was grounded in the continent. Germany felt that if she took both, she could have the last word.

The United States had stayed out of what it considered to be a "European conflict" until she was able to see clearly where her

The Changing World

interest lay. She finally entered the war on April 2, 1917, declaring herself to be defending peace in the following terms, which reveal the U.S. agenda:

> ... We shall fight for the things which we have always carried nearest to our hearts—for democracy, for the right of those who submit to authority to have a voice in their own Government, for the rights and liberties of small nations, for a universal dominion of right by such a concert of free peoples as shall bring peace and safety to all nations and make the world itself at last free (quoted in Thomson 1957: 530).

With this, the United States brought her fresh forces—naval power, the military prowess and strategic power—to the side of the Allied powers, at a time when they needed it most. Had the United States not entered the war, the outcome would have been far different. The heavy reliance of the Allied powers on U.S. loans during the early part of the conflict, was one factor in the United States' decision to intervene in the war on their side (Kennedy 1987: 268-9). By 1918 the forces of the Entente powers, beginning with Bulgaria, began to surrender one by one. Hostilities finally came to an end at the eleventh hour of the eleventh day of the eleventh month in the year 1918 that brought an end to the power of the Entente alliance.

When the Central powers surrendered, however, influenced greatly by the U.S.-led finance capitalist class, the Allied forces did not take over Entente countries; instead, they immediately called an old-style peace conference where they began to make plans for the future. This setting is where the U.S. interests received formal recognition. The significance of this to the matter of colonialism is that the United States' entry into the war was said to be in "defense of smaller nations." Though not ostensibly related to the primary issues of the war, Thomson has noted that there was some justification for the U.S. position from a European point of view: "From the outset, the attacks on Serbia and Belgium had made the indepen-

The Invention of Ethiopia

dence of small states an inherent issue of the war. Restoration of their independence was an original war aim" (ibid.: 534). In fact, this "small nations" issue had been on the U.S. agenda for as long as the U.S. finance capitalists had been frustrated by their lack of access to the colonies monopolized by the capitalist powers of Europe. The war conditions provided the U.S. opening to offer the rationale for a transition to a new system for access to the colonies—trusteeship. And indeed the United States did use the opportunity to introduce a new formula for eliminating wars over the colonies, i.e., what they called a formula for maintaining "peace." United States President Woodrow Wilson, in January 1918, put forth a fourteen-point program (see Benns 1954: 90ff., Scott 1973 and Thomson 1957) which embodied the new formula. These points eventually became the basis for the charter of the League of Nations. In essence the United States' President was putting forth the elements for a new superstructural model to operate on the world scale to replace the increasingly troublesome balance of power model that prevailed.

The old-style peace conference called by the Allied nations soon after they became victorious was held in Paris in January 1919 for the purpose drawing up a peace treaty. This Paris Peace Conference, held at the Palace of Versailles, was attended by the leaders of the Allied forces, the United States, Britain and the Commonwealth, France, Belgium, Serbia, Italy and Japan. The resultant treaty, though signed by the nations that attended the first plenary session, was not signed with Germany until June 28, 1919.

The new ideas and purpose of world peace were addressed in the Versailles treaty. The main objective was said to be establishing a "collective security." At this conference, a "world" organization was proposed in the opening statement by the United States President. He told the conference of the necessity for defending the rights of small nations and the rights of nations for self-determination. He further suggested that the nations of the world should work to defend each other and to provide a covenant for each other based on this principle. It introduced a new global formula in response to what was a clear demand for a shift in the situation of the capitalist world.

The Changing World

In recognition of this need, the League of Nations was established. But just as it was to start to function fully, the U.S. Congress failed to approve United States participation in it. The debate over the matter in the U.S. Senate indicated that the class base required to fully implement the program was not yet fully consolidated in that country. Consequently, the United States was not a member. Russia did not join, and Germany was not in it, either. That meant that the league started from a very weak vantage point, a membership made up of those who had not generated the guiding ideas of the organization. The absence of the United States, whose President made the proposal, but whose Congress was not able to rally support for it in the U.S. Senate, was the fatal blow. In the final analysis, the weakness of the organization and the equivocation of its participants reveals that the conditions required for the institutions of finance capital to emerge dominant had not yet matured. This was to come.

This weak, unorganized, and powerless "world" organization thus proceeded with trepidation, and it was not long before member nations were consumed again by old monopolistic national interests. The league became an assembly of overseers of empires and of dependent colonial nations, and soon its principles were put to the test. Japan, a founding member, was first to challenge the league's strength, then Germany, followed by Italy, and Russia. All these nations who were testing the new organization had signed the Paris Peace Treaty and had entered as members of the League of Nations. The failure of the league to respond when the Japanese took away the right of Manchuria, violating both the Paris Peace treaty agreements and the principles of the league, was when the League of Nations died. The "Ethiopia" incident only proved that this was already the case.

Germany soon wanted again to test her power to extend monopoly control by trying to swallow the Balkans. By doing this she could regain some of the kinds of benefits from holding colonies that she lost as a result of the outcome the 1914-18 war. And Italy, who had been disappointed by what she had gained as a great power, wanted to take over the territory of a member country of the

The Invention of Ethiopia

League, the Ethiopian empire (see Scott 1973: 320-360). Then Japan extended to take over China. There was nothing to stand in her way. By the end of the 1930s, "[t]he smaller powers, which had joined the League for the security against aggression they could not provide for themselves, were conscious that what had happened to Ethiopia could happen just as easily to them" (Scott 1973: 359).

The United States, who had declared herself to be the defender of "small nations," was not present. The big states that responded to the attack on Serbia at the outbreak of the First World War were not responding now in the same manner, rather, they were all trying to secure their own national interests. Yet all dependent nations who were members of the league were expecting the big powers, under whose umbrella they were present, to protect them. As Haile Selassie's telegram of February 20, 1936, "to his Britannic Majesty" expressed it,

> Because England has been the main defender of the case we were hoping England / would have aided us in a way which would not have touched her honor, integrity or armed forces by giving us arms ammunition and loans to carry on our defensive fight. But though it has been judged against Italy that she was the aggressor she has not found a way to help the aggressed state neither to stop the war or to strengthen us (Scott 1973: 351-2).

While the telegram contains the expression of the specific victim in this case, the reaction of the other dependent states was also overwhelming. They instantly recognized their vulnerability and expressed their feeling of insecurity. Statements issued by two of them reveal this quite clearly. One such statement was made by the representative from Haiti, Alfred Nemours, after he had observed the "Ethiopian case": "Great or small, strong or weak, near or far, white or coloured, let us never forget that one day we may be somebody's Ethiopia" (cited in Scott 1973: 340-341). The role of the dependent colonies and the powerlessness of the "small nations" had been clearly revealed.

The Changing World

Ethiopia's empire became the most infamous test of the new notion of "collective security," probably because the countries involved were both members of the league. Mussolini, by taking over Haile Selassie's empire by force, violated not only the Versailles treaty (Paris Peace Treaty), but was also the principles of the league itself, yet Italy remained, without effective challenge, as a member of the league in good standing (see Sbacchi 1986 for a full discussion). The British decision to support Italy in the 1930s was a political ploy to prevent Mussolini from joining the Entente powers at the outset of World War II, but, this act only signalled to the dependent states in the league exactly where they stood. Soon all small nations were exposed to the unbridled power of Germany, Italy and Japan. By the end of the 1930s, the new imperial forces began to realize their strength. The old forces were justifiably fearful, not only of their colonial possessions, but also again of their own home territories.

The demise of the old powers seemed to be just a matter of time. Japanese, German and Italian forces were ready to take over directly Russia, France, and even Britain herself. For Germany it was a matter not only of regaining a lost colonial empire but also of breaking the backbone of the former Allied forces of the previous World War.

Germany's objectives were primarily to assert herself within a framework which recognized single-country monopoly power rather than to impose a new framework altogether. In this she differed fundamentally from the objectives of the United States. Germany aimed to replace the old powers at the top of the existing order of things. As Germany began to flex her muscle, the once-big powers began to taste the bitter medicine that they had previously inflicted on weaker and "small" countries. Germany, assisted by Italy, came into direct confrontation with the once-great powers. As Germany had predicted, they all fell into her hands. First came Belgium and the Netherlands; then Germany occupied Norway, Denmark, and later France, and much of the Russian empire. For her part, Italy took over Albania, Serbia, Greece, Finland, some of the Balkan states, and East and North Africa. The only unoccupied states on the European continent by the beginning of the 1940s were Sweden, Ireland, Switzerland, Portugal, Spain and Turkey.

After the defeat of France, Hitler felt it would be impossible for anyone to stop German power, and Germany could move into the position that she coveted—she could operate as the new leader of the world powers. She had waged an effective challenge to the leaders of old order for that position. Germany became confident that she could be the one to set the specific terms of a new peace treaty in her favor, as a message sent by Hitler to Britain to force the issue, indicates, "[o]nce more to reason and common sense in Great Britain as much as elsewhere—I can see no reason why this war must go on" (Thomson 1957: 731).

When Britain did not accept what amounted to an ultimatum from Hitler, Germany launched an invasion of Britain herself in July in a maneuver known as Operation Sea Lion. This act was to put Britain under pressure to consider a compromise peace; when British response was to resist, Germany bombed London and other industrial cities. The Second World War began as a battle of the old powers of Europe against the new powers aspiring to dominate on the old balance of power model. All the defenders of the Allied powers rallied behind Britain. The defense became an act of revenge or a united front of all the countries Hitler had tried to destroy in Europe.

But there was a lot more going on in this war than just those battles in the European theatre. Elsewhere, significant forces were involved. True, the Germans and the Italians were newly united and overtly nationalistic, but Russia was busy both in the Balkans and fighting against Germany and Japan on the Asian front.

The other young power operating far from Europe but very much a part of the second imperial war was Japan. Japan had been isolated from the rest of the world for centuries after she deported all foreigners from the country as far back as the mid-1500s. As she came out of isolation, she had concluded that her defeats were not because Europeans were strong, but rather because Japan herself had become weak.

The Changing World

Japan silently built what she was lacking. She reformed her system, and before too long she found herself competing with the Europeans: "Her merchants and her ships became the rivals of the Europeans in the neighboring seas, where her commerce has increased far more rapidly than that of the Western nations" (Robinson and Beard 1908: 343). Japan by 1900 had become a power to reckon with. She took over Korea, then Manchuria, and soon after that, even defeated Russia. After the 1904 war, she began to control her surroundings; she became master of the sea in her area. By the second quarter of the twentieth century, she had become a young contending imperial power, and by the 1940s she initiated a clash with the United States by attacking Pearl Harbor, the United States naval base on Hawaii. This attack, on December 7, 1941, marked the official entry of the United States into World War II.

The Shift to the Global Dominance of Finance Capital

By the outbreak of World War II there were too many forces operating on a world scale for a return to the old "balance of power" formula for keeping peace. The world was changing. The old forces of monopoly could no longer contain even the demands of the rising monopolists, represented by Germany, let alone the new the new forces of finance capitalism, represented by the United States. The old order was knocked asunder. The Second World War accomplished what the first had failed to do—create the conditions for the introduction and the enforcement of a new superstructural model grounded in the values of finance capital. What was lacking was a specific new design for containing these forces that could be implemented to ensure peace.

The United States entry into the world conflict again changed the course of events in Europe. The United States had already pledged that she would work toward world peace. At a conference between Britain and the United States in August 1941, even before the incident at Pearl Harbor, plans were in the process of being laid

The Invention of Ethiopia

for a new model of world order. Prime Minister Winston Churchill and President Franklin D. Roosevelt:

> ... met on a battleship off the coast of America and together shaped the Atlantic Charter. It was a public pledge to the world of their faith in ultimate freedom. Two months earlier Germany had invaded Russia, and four months later Japan attacked the United States naval base at Pearl Harbor. So, through universal disaster, the Grand Alliance between Britain, Russia and the United States was born (Savage 1962: 16).

Once again, as it had been the case in the first World War, the United States lined up on the side of the Allied powers, who had become debtors to the United States over the course of the war (see Kennedy 1987) and with whom the United States had historical links, to save the old imperial powers of Western Europe from being crushed by the mighty forces of the new rising powers. The old imperial powers (Western Europe) were only able to prevail because they were supported by the fresh powerful forces of the United States, much superior to theirs on all counts and by all standards— on the sea, on land, or in the air. With this support brought to their side, Allied forces were able to drive away the challengers from all areas that had previously been Allied-occupied.

Before the war ended, the United States began to move swiftly to implement more "security" for the "world" than it had done after the First World War—the security of the institutions of financial capital. This was possible because the design of its new formula for world order was already prepared. The United States called a meeting, held at Dumbarton Oaks in Washington, D.C., which was attended by representatives of the United States, Britain, Russia and China. The purpose was to present the new design for avoiding the old style of war, that is, direct conflict between monopoly powers. This conference was a meeting of representatives of finance capital and marked for the first time the real emergence of the global dominance of the class of finance capitalists. It was billed as a "prelimi-

The Changing World

nary peace talk," and it is here that the basic infrastructure of the San Francisco conference was laid down. At this time the war with Japan, Germany and Italy was still going on, but the United States was confident of the final result and took the initiative early. The issues at stake were those of how the United States would assume a leading role in the determination of the changing world order. A key part of this was what is of interest here—determining what would happen to the colonies.

With the United States involved, the Allied forces made a series of strategic decisions that included all-out attack on German holdings through air, sea and ground attacks. Italy was forced into unconditional surrender on September 2, 1943, and on May 7, 1945, the Nazi force laid down its arms. The Nazi regime also agreed to the Allied terms of unconditional surrender. This assured an end to the Second World War in Europe, bringing not only the end of the German empire and German power in Europe but also marking the end of the dominance of monopoly power on a world scale. The war continued in the Far East until Japan was defeated in all of the areas it occupied and surrendered in August 1945, marking the end of World War II.

Meanwhile, the Allied forces turned full attention to what should be done about ensuring peace and managing conflict among countries capable of imperialism in the future. As mentioned, the United States had already focused considerable attention on this matter by providing at Dumbarton Oaks the infrastructure for a world body that would improve upon the old League of Nations model. The task of deciding the future of Germany also presented itself. To do this, Britain, Russia and the United States met in February 1945 at what was known as the Yalta Conference.

The representatives of these three countries—Roosevelt, Churchill and Stalin—all agreed to hold an international conference in April at San Francisco to form an organization capable of governing international affairs. What their work amounted to was protecting the interests and imposing the conditions under which the institutions of finance capital could flourish. At this conference, the United Nations was conceived as a "permanent international organization."

53

The Invention of Ethiopia

This marked the first gathering of the Big Five (the Dumbarton Oaks group—United States, Soviet Union, Great Britain, China—plus France, who was not present at Dumbarton Oaks). The former members of the League of Nations were formally invited to the founding conference of the United Nations. Among the world powers, Germany, who had lost her African colonies in the First World War and lost her own independence in the Second World War, Japan and Italy, who had surrendered completely to the Allied powers, were not invited to be present at this victors' conference. It was the United States and Soviet Union who stepped in to replace "the powers" of Europe as the new authoritative world powers based on their performances in World War II.

This change brought in new masters for the colonies and new policies for the management of world economic order. How the control of finance capital would be implemented in the colonies is the part of this arrangement that is of interest.

Though the United States had stayed out of the direct European conflict for much of the war, as soon as she stepped in she quickly assumed the leading role among the world imperial powers. The United States was quick to point out that past conflicts had not well served the ambitions even of the old European monopoly capitalist class. It was not only in the United States' interest to fashion a different set of strategies to deal with the interests of the monopolists at home, but it turned out to be in the interest of the monopolists themselves to accept it.

Trusteeship: The Transition to Corporate Colonial Control

The ideology and political agenda of the emerging class of finance capitalists was embodied in the model of the United Nations. This organizational blueprint provided the key—an avenue for making a break with the direct single-country control of colonial regions which had led to the insecurities brought on by wars over ownership, in favor of a model of "collective security." The plan's corporate model offered members maximum return on international

The Changing World

investment. It allowed all imperial forces proportional access to the world market.

The U.S. model realized the power of finance capital by legitimizing institutions shaped by it. This model provided for colonies of the defeated powers to be temporarily held collectively by a world body. The proposal evolved into an arrangement providing international access to the regions on a shareholder system. The world was presented as composed of three elements: (1) the old and new monopoly powers, home to the representatives of the finance capitalist class, (2) middle-class technocrats whose role was to serve the interests of finance capital, and (3) the colonies. This proposal essentially brought into the institution the plan of a corporate company of capitalist countries which enabled all participants to share world resources according to their capital investment in a giant common market. It would not be necessary to go to war to readjust or reorganize power. The colonies' role would be to function like wage-earning employees of a company.

The administrators and agents who had functioned under the old colonial system were to be invited to serve in the same sort of middle-man roles they had filled, this time as managers in the new institution without the old competitive loyalties. It was provided that eventually individuals from the colonies were to be trained to move into the spots vacated by these colonial administrators—whose job was to ensure the smooth operation of the institutions that were fashioned according to the ruling ideas of finance capitalism.

This set of ideas was put together, and drafted into the United Nations charter. The charter mapped out the future of the colonies. The proposed organization addressed, above all, the matter of rearranging the conditions for access to the colonial market. The matter of trusteeship embodied the means for opening up the market, in effect, the means for internationalizing the colonial market.

Initially, both Britain and France objected to the proposal, but it was beyond their power to stop the United States when the United States was supported by the Soviet Union, representing a regional finance class, on the grounds of eliminating monopoly control, and also supported by the dependent states responding to the U.S. role in championing "independence." These old powers clearly preferred tinkering with the old "balance of power" once again, but the United States would have none of it.

The former colonial countries did not give in easily. Each of them put forth proposals for maintaining their former colonies in Africa within a merely enlarged colonial empire—to be administered by the educated elite of one "tribe" from each colonial region. Each country would be divided into provinces so that each tribal group could be brought into the administration by means of a "council." In this way, the colonies could have a symbolic part politically and economically in the British empire. France also attempted to maintain her colonies in a dependent relationship by proposing to make them "overseas provinces" of France. They required that the native administrations behave like French. These were both dubbed by their authors as programs for "decolonization" (see R. D. Pearce's *The Turning Point in Africa* (1982) and the volume entitled *Decolonization and After: the British and French Experience* (1980), edited by Morris-Jones and Fischer).

William Roger Louis' book, *Imperialism at Bay: the United States and the Decolonization of the British Empire* (1978), directly addresses the response of the old powers to the transition from the old model of single-country colonial control to the corporate model introduced through "trusteeship"—the one promoted by the United States and Soviet Union—which allowed equal access to former colonial market areas. As Louis puts it, the old colonial powers represented by Britain:

> ... believed that the very existence of the British Empire would depend on the British being able to protect the trade and commerce of the colonies and Dominions from an economic takeover by the United States. On the American side, Cordell Hull and Sumner Welles regarded the question of Imperial Preferences as one of the vital issues of the war and, if their own words are to be believed, a threat to the future peace of the world. They wanted "Free Trade"

The Changing World

and the "Open Door", cliches meaning, in practice, equality of economic opportunity and access to colonial raw materials. Amery [the British secretary of state for India and Burma] wanted to keep this door closed and if possible to lock it even tighter. He once commented that he would prefer the "New Order of Hitler" to the "Free Trade" of Cordell Hull. Such were the flights of rhetoric (Louis 1978: 24).

It should be noted, however, that France was not as hostile as Britain, though "... to deGaulle, who, like Churchill, viewed the scheme for trusteeship as a disguise for American expansion" (Louis 1978: 28). Although these were the sentiments of both great monopolists and colonial holders about America's plan for the former colonies, when the actual implementation of the program came, they abandoned their opposition in exchange for significant roles in the future after their recovery from the war. In effect, they accepted a franchise in the new system.

The Americans were unswerving in their conviction that the current economic order demanded the implementation of the kind of program they had put forth.

The role of the United States in shaping the future of the capitalist world consisted primarily in taking the lead to plan the direction and to legitimize the activities of a new economic class, the class of finance capitalists. During this period the rationale behind the United States plan for the world system began to come to light. She had already opened discussions with potential rivals such as Britain, China and the Soviet Union regarding the economic and political future of colonies.

The United States' proposal for dealing with the former colonies of monopoly powers finally provided a remedy to the difficulties the United States had experienced throughout the world where American trade had been virtually locked out of areas within the domain of primarily British and French colonial empires. The writing of R. J. Skinner, an American envoy sent by Theodore Roosevelt's government, reveals the United States had experienced

The Invention of Ethiopia

difficulty competing with both Britain and France in areas where each had established bases for operation. Skinner had written that the United States went to Ethiopia in 1906, "for the avowed purpose of protecting and extending commerce, and without a political issue of any character to discuss." He observed that,

> It will be said, perhaps, that the ultimate aim of all the European Powers is to promote commerce, and that it is only for the purpose of promoting commerce that colonies are established and official relations maintained. This may be perfectly true in principle, but in practice, at least, that matter of frontiers, balance of power, and kindred questions, are so far in the foreground that the ultimate commercial ambition is entirely overshadowed (Skinner 1906:91).

He explained the American situation as follows,

> [w]e [the United States] had enjoyed for years a trade in certain of our goods, notably cottons, more valuable than any other import trade in the empire. To reach these customers of ours, our merchandise had to cross either British, French, or Italian soil. The frequently abused missionary had gone into Africa many years before present political conditions prevailed, and had introduced some of our honest American cotton goods with the success above stated. This was a trade in which no American houses were directly engaged, but the benefits thereof were no less directly enjoyed by the American farmers and working men.

Skinner then describes the European partition of Africa from an American's point of view:

> Then came the partition of Africa by the European Powers into spheres of influence, the creation of Custom-houses, and all those administrative measures whereby trade is made

to follow the flag. The French took hold of Madagascar, and as abruptly as Napoleon announced that the House of Braganza no longer reigned in Europe, our long-enjoyed cotton trade ceased to be. In the Congo Free State, where cotton sheetings are still known as "Americani," the merchandise was now coming in fact from Belgium. Then our British friends, whose shibboleth is Free Trade, had in fact extended special privileges to their own manufactures in many of the colonies, creating conditions which made American transactions difficult of accomplishment. The methods by which this had been done were no doubt perfectly legitimate, but none the less effectual for all that. There remained to our credit, however, in spite of the unfavorable conditions that had been gradually created elsewhere, the coveted export business in cottons, known as the "Red Sea Trade." The greater part of this was in Abyssinia, where it amounted to a monopoly.

Our business in Abyssinia had grown up under shadowy political arrangements, when the Abyssinians had claimed an outlet to the sea, and which the Egyptians had contested with them by force of arms. In our time, the Abyssinians had been forced back, land-locked like Switzerland, with Italy, France and England standing guard on the Red Sea (1906:92-3).

After providing details concerning the politics and the logistics of the then newly constructed railway, Skinner offered the following understatement, "No spirit of prophecy seemed necessary to perceive that the forces at work for the development of Ethiopia were, at least, not being created for the furtherance of American commercial ambition" (ibid.).

Skinner's observations, voiced in 1906 just before the issuance of the Tripartite Treaty, provide a telling example of how U.S. business in general perceived the old colonialist position, i.e., as a threat to its own expanding interests. The United States' formula for trusteeship, the collective holding of the former colonies, provided

The Invention of Ethiopia

a transition to collective administration of the colonies and dissolved the privileged entree to the colonial regions that the monopoly powers had enjoyed.

Joint approval of the new program was required, a design that kept the imperial powers from entering into direct conflict. Along these lines, Lord Keynes had even suggested the necessity of a central world bank to eliminate capitalist conflict. This notion was seriously considered by all the conference participants.

The United Nations Model for World Order

The massive superstructural framework of the United Nations included bureaucratic components found in all forms of Western political administrative, executive and legislative bodies. The many agencies were equivalent to departments or ministries of energy, industry, education, health, finance, labor, food and agriculture, justice, etc. (of several volumes available regarding the structure of the United Nations, see Bailey 1963 and 1964, Savage 1962). Since the proposed organizational form, consisting of various departments and subdivisions resembling the bureaucratic models of the United States and Western Europe, was familiar to the former colonial countries, the proposal was approved without dissent. By the year 1945 the structure became functional.

The leading organs of the United Nations were established as follows: the General Assembly (a forum for discussion of issues presented to the body and for recommendations, but without power to enforce its recommendations), the Security Council the body that limits armaments and "prevents war by settling disputes between nations"), the Economic and Social Council, ECOSOC (the body that deals with problems of the once-colonial third world supervises the activities of agencies, decides budgets for commission and advises agencies which have their own budgets), the International Court of Justice (which considers legal disputes between members of the United Nations), the Secretariat (the administrative body of the United Nations).

The Changing World

What replaced colonial administration was the body created as the Trusteeship Council. This is the body that was established specifically to look after territories of the former European colonies. As Savage has described it:

> The Trusteeship Council acts as a temporary guardian until the people are trained to form a national government. It appoints a member nation to administer each territory and makes progress reports twice a year to the General Assembly (Savage 1962: 24).

When this enormous international apparatus began to operate, its leading bureaucrats were former colonial officers considered to be qualified due to their "international" experience, but out of a job as a result of the decline in direct colonial rule. They brought all the experience and "expertise" in handling the "colonial world," with them. The headquarters, significantly, was placed in the United States. So, from its first days, the United Nations resembled the apparatus of the state in developed capitalist countries writ large. Although the United States and the Allied forces who supported the initiative of the United States stated that the purpose of the United Nations was "preventing war," they found it necessary to establish a plethora of agencies whose actual standard of operation often fell below that of the developed countries themselves. It is quite clear that the agencies were designed to serve primarily the countries that were then colonies, but that were slated for "independence" from the single colonial power to which they had been linked.

The General Assembly was empowered to recommend or deny what is termed the "independence" of areas that were under the monopoly control of one power or another. Between 1950-1960 several colonial areas were "decolonized" according to the procedures spelled out by the United Nations system. What this amounted to was time allowed to establish institutions responsive to finance capital in these countries. Once a management class was trained and willing to operate the instruments for this control, the official presence of the overseer country could be withdrawn. Here is the key. In 1959 alone ten "trust territories" were recommended for "independence," and by 1961 they were allowed to declare their independence. Though the process of obtaining "independence" has been termed "decolonizing" the colonized countries, it could more accurately be called "de-monopolizing" the colonies since the "independence" was only from the monopoly control of one power.

As suggested by Lord Keynes and promoted by Roosevelt, an International Bank for the Reconstruction of Europe, guided by the U.S. was proposed and planned at the initial stage, was to become the central bank for this body over a period of time; it is now known as the World Bank. The World Bank and its sister institution, the International Monetary Fund (IMF), provided a mechanism to ensure equal access to the colonial market by the capitalist world. Ultimately, however, the World Bank and the IMF did not become permanent and integral parts of the United Nations due to differences in the relative capital wealth of the leading members of the United Nations, chiefly, differences between the United States and the Soviet Union. The operating principle was that the one who invested more had greater say in the decisions and actions taken. Since the Soviet Union was not in a financial position to play a role commensurate with that of the United States, the Soviet Union utilized its veto to reject these financial instruments, calling them "imperialist institutions." The irony of this pronouncement was that the Soviet Union was a United Nations member in good standing which had a direct relationship with and benefited by all these processes.

As for herself, the United States was of the opinion that independence of the Bank was necessary to maintain her own power with regard to the world body and consequently did not force the issue.

Ultimately, the agencies of the United Nations were patterned to fill the voids that existed after the withdrawal of the direct colonizers. Each of the agencies was structured to serve a specific purpose in strengthening the structure of dependency. For example, the main function of the United Nations Educational, Scientific and Cultural Organization (UNESCO) was to ensure that the training of the required bureaucrats proceeded along the same lines as had

The Changing World

been followed by colonial standards and that the cultural and scientific standards of once-colonial powers prevailed in the new era.

Other agencies such as the Technical Assistance Board (TAB), the International Labor Organization (ILO), and the Food and Agriculture Organization (FAO), were brought in and organized in such a way as to continue dependency of the former colonies on the expertise of the former colonizer countries. These agencies were set up to be the models and the workshops to consistently reinforce what the "modernized" African has learned in the colonial schools.

Looking at the conditions that existed in the world at that time and at the process by which the United Nations was formed as part of a division of war booty, one can say that this new arrangement offered a marriage of convenience for both the capitalist and socialist countries, as well as the colonies. For the Soviet Union at that time weak, both economically and militarily, and unable to put forth a viable alternative, agreement and participation in this program were a way to avoid war, establish herself, and to buy time for reconstruction. The needs of the capitalist countries were met since the new apparatus was able to encompass and absorb the functions and the personnel from the colonial administrations. In fact it was a more efficient arrangement for them. The advantages for the young intellectuals from the colonies have already been mentioned. For its part, the United States obtained full access to the world market. As far as the working peoples in the former colonies, under this system they were not destined to achieve independence. The form of their dependency was changed. What really changed was that, "The fathers began working for the sons" (taken as the title for Sara Berry's 1985 book which graphically depicts this process in Nigeria). The sons merely became functionary elements, acting as intermediaries between the owners of the capital and the working population of the colonized countries.

Since a major function of the United Nations was to avoid wars between major powers over sole control of particular regions and to "contain" what was seen as inevitable conflict between the colonized and colonizing countries, powerful countries chose to support the idea of the United Nations. They seemed aware that it would be difficult to sustain a war of the colonies. Eventually the colonized world came to be politely referred to collectively as the third world. It was countries recognized as former colonies who were to draw on the United Nations agencies for development assistance and advice in times when they otherwise would have relied on the former monopoly power. The strategy was quite successful in extending dependency under the facade of independence and in forestalling war among the imperial powers. Because all imperial powers shared in the responsibility and in the spoils that accrued from administering the former colonies, what had been the major cause of war prior to that time was eliminated.

In the case of Africa, the children of UNESCO came into power after the agency had functioned for about fifteen years. By that time the countries that had collectively represented and defended the interests of finance capital had successfully, through "modern education," imparted to a young generation of bureaucrats from the colonies the key concepts for how the capitalist system operated from the inside. In the process of education these young people were treated far better than others of their age group in the colonies. They were told, and eventually they came to believe, that the capitalist system provided the only conceivable and practical avenue for change and improvement in the conditions of their people. Befriended by the international system, they were told that they represented the future and provided the only hope for their nations' independence.

This group continued to believe, even as they grew to be middle-aged civil servants, that it was they who would lead their countries into true "independence." To these trainees, who were often collectively referred to as "intellectuals," independence meant that they would move into the positions held by the colonial bureaucrats who had previously advised them. They had been essentially moved through an educational assembly line which prepared them to confirm only one way to independence. It should surprise no one that revolutionary change was not to come from this group. They were anxious to take over the symbols of power, i.e., to occupy the offices of their former colonial masters, fly their own flags, and enjoy the kind of life that accompanied these positions. They had little interest in changing the structure of the state and, in retrospect, they have ultimately introduced no fundamental changes.

This phenomenon of continued structural dependency, recognized in many of its features and usually termed "neo-colonialism" in Africa, is usually not considered applicable to the Ethiopian case because that empire was not monopolized and directly occupied by any one particular European country. The formation and the administration of the Ethiopian state, however, constituted the first and possibly the test case in Africa for this kind of arrangement— one in which representatives of the dominant class in Europe established institutions for managing the state, then worked primarily as advisers until Ethiopians could be trained to fill the positions that had been created. The entire structure had been designed to protect the interests of international capital in that region and beyond it. The Ethiopian case was a model of collective access constructed by major powers and applied to a specific state, one first administered directly or indirectly through European experts and advisers and later by European-trained personnel.

Superpower Rivalry Updated

Soon after the formation of the United Nations, two political-economic camps emerged, one led by the United States and the other by the Soviet Union.

It should be noted that people from colonized countries who had participated in the previous world wars—wars that had been fought largely over the issue of possession of or shares in the colonial territories—had been witness to the fact that colonizing countries could be defeated in battle. As early as the 1940s, amid several sources of dissatisfaction, several of the colonized countries (e.g., Singapore, Malaysia, India) determined that they could fight for themselves for their own independence from the colonizer, and they did fight. Once victorious, they were admitted to the United Nations to assume a structural position equivalent to that of the other members who had been formerly held as the monopoly possession of a single country but who had accepted the recognition of their independence on the basis of the shift from European to African administrators.

The militant expressions of dissatisfaction provided the opening for a renewed sort of superpower competition over the market of formerly monopolized regions. This competition took the form of battles for loyalty and the establishment of special relationships between specific colonized countries and either of the two new superpowers, the Soviet Union and the United States. The socialist-oriented revolution in Europe and the position of the Soviet Union in relation to it provided a basis for overt and covert agitation from the Soviet Union for "self-determination" of these disaffected dependencies in particular. The Soviet Union offered itself as a force that could stand behind countries taking on the struggle for liberation, which was to be distinguished from the independence that was championed by the United States. "Liberation" developed its own meaning and became a mechanism by which the Soviet Union sought to gain an advantage over the United States by obtaining privileged access to some of these countries.

The issue of liberation versus independence was raised when the matter of Singapore and Malaysia came up. At that time there was great concern that a third world war might erupt as a devastating conflict, a worldwide war not in name only, but one also between the colonist countries and the colonies. The solution supported by most United Nations members was to dismantle existing empires systematically and bring the colonies into the "world community," i.e., the orbit dominated by finance capital. This did not prove to be difficult. Since the United States had set herself up as officially opposing "colonialism," she was initially able to rally most of both the colonizers and the colonies in support of this sort of "independence" and thus retain leadership in the world arena.

The contest that developed between the United States and the Soviet Union, however, proved to become a reenactment of the kind of superpower rivalry that the world had witnessed among the European monopolists through the first half of the twentieth

The Changing World

century. This rivalry, accompanied by the same sort of nationalistic feeling and political rhetoric that characterized the one that preceded it, has proven to be another conflict over the market shares held by the competitors. The rivalry has ultimately proved to be one contained and played out within the boundaries of the United Nations with both sides not only accepting but upholding the superstructural principles that the United Nations represents. In fact the behavior of the Soviet Union within the confines of the United Nations provides an interesting insight into the position of that country in the world economic order. Despite the formal Soviet position opposing what they call neocolonialism and imperialism, the Soviet Union has acted equally with the United States to uphold the formula for world order represented by the United Nations, one of continued dependency of the former colonies of the monopolists within a market-oriented economic system. Their competition has been over dominance within that system. A great deal of confusion has resulted from taking at face value the rhetorical position of the Soviet Union, which denies this reality, when assessing the nature of the conflict.

By the same token, the Soviet Union equally with the United States has tolerated, recognized, and conducted business with the group of petit-bourgeoisie (intellectuals) that was created by the institutions of international finance capital, serving to legitimate them in their positions and play into their illusions of independence from the system that created their class. In fact, a good part of the bargaining power of the leaders of the Soviet Union in its rivalry with the United States lies in their willingness to perpetuate the self-deception of members of the petit-bourgeoisie that they constitute the hope of their countries' future.

Though the Europeans initially allied with the United States, they were also in the process of building their own economic and military blocs. Louis (1978) maps the relations among the imperial forces of Europe (the former colony holders) and some of the European countries which had not been considered by the United States as a viable imperial force. Meanwhile, the Europeans who earlier had perceived the ambitions of the United States as a threat had come together to form a bloc in Europe for their own security. These countries saw the United States as an imperial force capable of and interested in taking away their colonial holdings. There was a palpable threat that they would be pushed completely out of the market. This fear was not groundless. This bloc had observed how the United States-dominated World Bank and International Monetary Fund had been specifically designed to draw the former European colonies into that orbit. Having observed this, European strategists began to plan a European defense, both economically and militarily, for a future which guaranteed that Europe would not be pushed out of the world market. Consequently a group of six European countries formed communities of states for the purposes of economic stability and military defense. These are known today as the European Economic Community (EEC) and the North Atlantic Treaty Organization (NATO).

With similar concerns, the Soviet bloc or, more precisely, the "socialist" bloc, also moved to defend its economic and security interests within the new global economic order by organizing its allies into essentially the same kind of groupings. Economically they are known as COMECON and militarily as the Warsaw Pact.

Though Britain initially declined to join the EEC, by 1973 she decided that it was to her advantage to do so. The United States joined NATO defense forces. What has resulted from this kind of alignment is that the countries of the world have fallen roughly into two major categories for the purposes of marketing. One broad category is those countries controlling finance capital who are in search of markets, the second is the category of suppliers, the newly "independent" countries created out of former European colonies. The financier countries include the United States, acting through the World Bank and the International Monetary Fund, the European countries of the EEC, and the Soviet Union together with her allies through COMECON. In keeping with the idea that military institutions basically provide protection for the economic interests of a coherent class, the EEC members and the U.S.-dominated World Bank and International Monetary Fund come together to form a single military pact.

The Changing World

The existence of these economic and military blocs reveals that they have no basis upon which to go to war or to annex each other. Each arranged to protect its own interest.

3 THE BIRTH OF A DEPENDENT COLONIAL STATE

European Initiative in Northeast Africa

The scenario of the transition of capitalism from primarily a regionally focused economic and political system to a global one in which the conflicts that erupted across Europe were resolved through expansion outward is now a familiar one. The new jobs, new resources, and new markets that were sought required exploration and establishment of control over what was found. The motive force behind these new types of overseas empires was the attempt to solve problems at home. Cecil Rhodes captured the spirit of the era in which monopoly capitalism began to flourish when he said, "Empire, as I have always said, is a bread and butter question. If you want to avoid civil war, you must become imperialists."

To avoid civil war, Europeans began campaigns to extend their institutions specifically into Africa during this period by expanding into the hinterlands the small trading posts that had been established up to that time merely as toeholds on the coasts of Africa. These locations provided starting points for the new genre of colony generated under monopoly capitalism. The sites enabled entrepreneurs from each of the major powers of Europe to explore the

The Invention of Ethiopia

possibilities of locating or creating markets wherever the technology and expertise derived from their economic system would take them.

By the first half of the 1800s the dominance of monopoly capitalism had been so firmly established in Europe that all institutions extended from the European mainland into Africa after that period bore its definitive imprint and served to introduce and protect the values of the new capitalist class in power. Consequently all the groups and individuals who went abroad at this time, regardless of differences they may have had among themselves at home, were propelled or enabled in their ventures by the strength of this new economic system. Those who went out from Europe served, by their very presence and by the resources and ideas they used to do their work, to project the institutions of the mainland into the new region and to act as carriers of the ideology of the system that sent them.

In most parts of Africa these sometimes unwitting emissaries—missionaries, traders, adventurers, and entrepreneurs—had penetrated the inland areas by the first quarter of the nineteenth century and played a crucial role in extending the infrastructure of the capitalist system. Due to the intense national competition that existed on the European continent, each European country conducted its own program of colonization. This was just as much the case in the Horn of Africa as it was throughout the rest of Africa at the beginning stages. By the middle of the century, however, the northeast African region suddenly became critically important for strategic purposes to both of the most powerful bases of monopoly capital in Europe, France and Britain.

It was during this period that the digging of the Suez Canal through Egypt was completed. This was an event of great significance because it dramatically affected the rate of profit that accrued to the country that controlled it by reducing the time and expense required to transport goods to and from what was called the Middle and Far East to Europe. The Suez Canal was an important component in the laying out of the new global infrastructure that enabled the class dominant in Europe, the monopoly capitalist, to dominate worldwide. The intense rivalry that had developed between the

The Birth of a Dependent Colonial State

representatives of this class in each of the major countries of Europe over which of them would exercise the controlling influence within the new global structure was exemplified by the struggle that was carried on over control of the Suez Canal. Although French engineers and capital were responsible for the actual physical construction of the canal, the greater part of the shipping that passed through it was British. The British were able to obtain financial control of the canal by purchasing shares that had been held by the Egyptian partner in the project during a time when he was in need of cash. This financial ploy enabled the British to overtake the achievement of capital and technical skill accomplished by the French and foreshadowed a new era of moves and countermoves between Britain and France in this part of Africa. The creation of Ethiopia as a ground that could not be monopolized by either power played a significant role in the management of the conflict between them. It provided a means by which a balance of power between the two countries could be maintained.

From 1869 onward into the twentieth century, the history of northeast Africa became to a great extent a story of the efforts of each of these powers to maintain an upper hand at best, and, at least, to prevent the rival from monopolizing control of the lands and peoples surrounding this critical waterway. Most of the moves each European power made in this region were with an eye on the global situation and were designed to sabotage the position of the rival. The activities of these powers in the Horn of Africa must be assessed in this regard—as a extension of European politics and economics—rather than studied exclusively for some kind of internal logic.

Each of these powers required access to the Horn of Africa in order to implement both continentwide and worldwide schemes to secure control over vast new territories essential to maintaining their economic positions globally. The advent of the Suez Canal ushered in concern over the security of Egypt and of the source of Egypt's lifeline waterway, the Nile. In addition to its location on the continent and its being the source of the Blue Nile, the Horn had the potential for markets and the availability of gold, ivory, and other

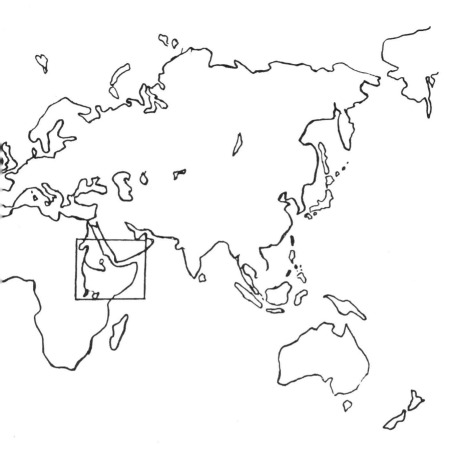

MAP 1   Location of the Horn of Africa—strategically situated at the commercial crossroads opened between Europe and the Far East after the Suez Canal was opened in 1869

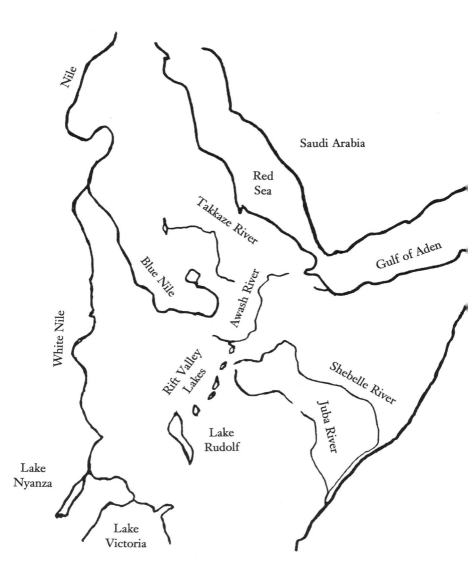

MAP 2   Enlarged view of the Horn of Africa, indicating selected natural landmarks

Tigray

Gondar

Gojjam

Manz (Shoa)

MAP 3   Abyssinian areas, 1870, indicating the kingdoms of
          Tigray (Axum), Gondar (Begemder), Gojjam, and Manz
          (Shoa)

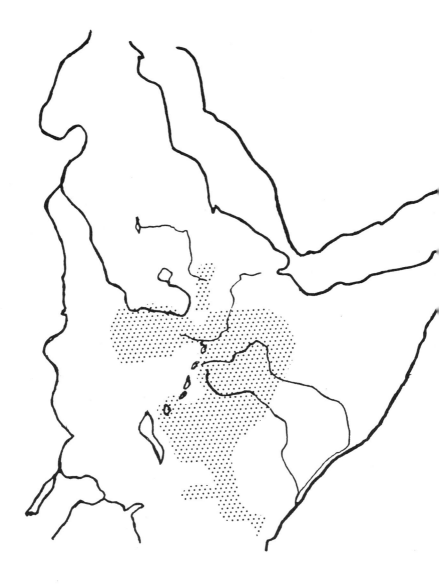

MAP 4   Oromo areas, 1870

MAP 5   Somali areas, 1870

MAP 6   Afar areas, 1870

MAP 7   Sidama areas, 1870

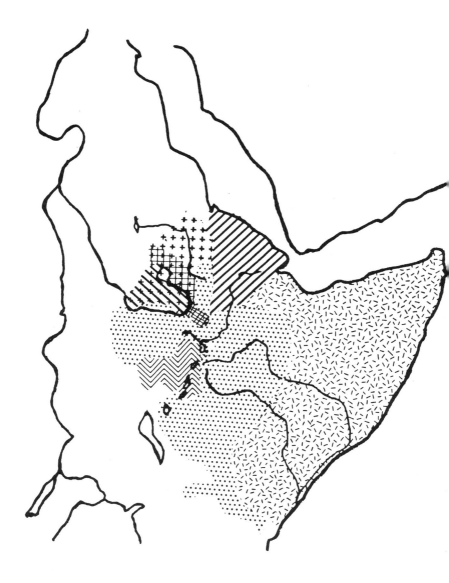

MAP 8   Location of major peoples of the Horn of Africa, 1870,
indicating the dominance of Tigray in Abyssinia

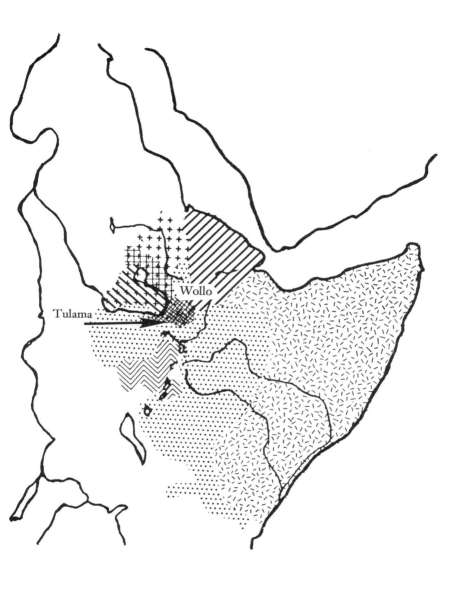

Tulama

Wollo

MAP 9   Shoan conquests, 1872, incorporating part of Wollo and
        part of Tulama Oromo

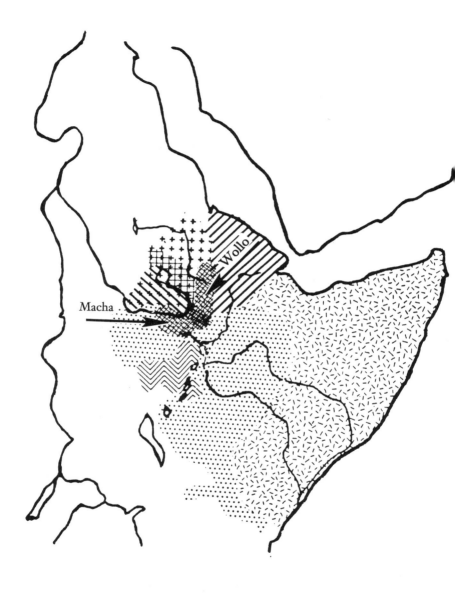

MAP 10 Shoan conquests, 1876, incorporating the remainder of
the Wollo and part of Macha Oromo

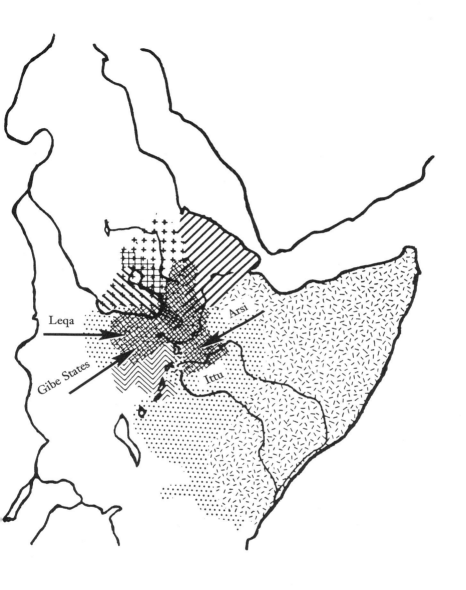

MAP 11   Shoan conquests, 1886, indicating parts of the Lega, Arsi
and Ittu Oromo and the Gibe states

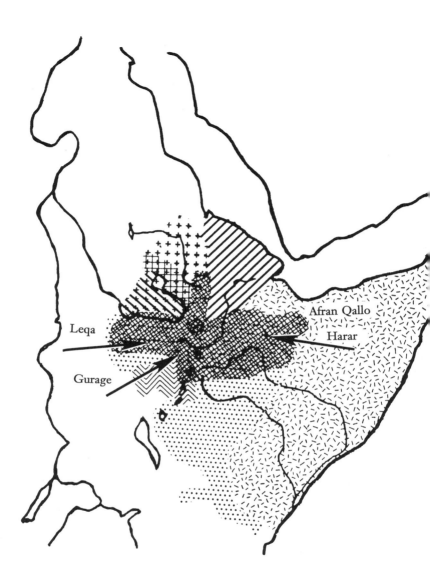

MAP 12   Shoan conquests, 1887, indicating the incorporation of
Harar, Afran Qallo, Leqa Oromo and Gurage, victories
facilitated by French-supplied weaponry while Tigray
dominated in the north with British arms

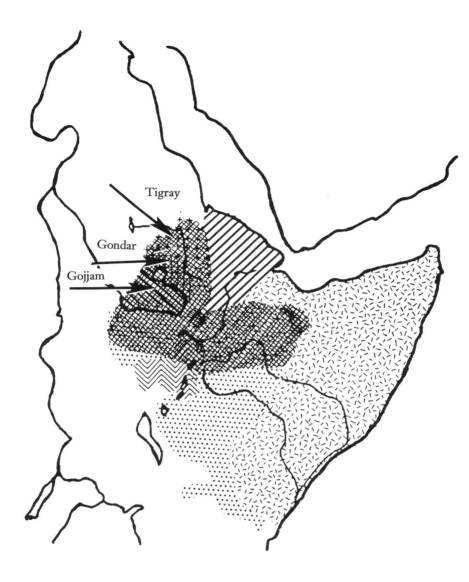

MAP 13   Shoan domination of Abyssinia, 1889, indicating the
         domination of Tigray, Gondar and Gojjam, which took
         place when menelik became Emperor of Abyssinia (King
         of Kings)

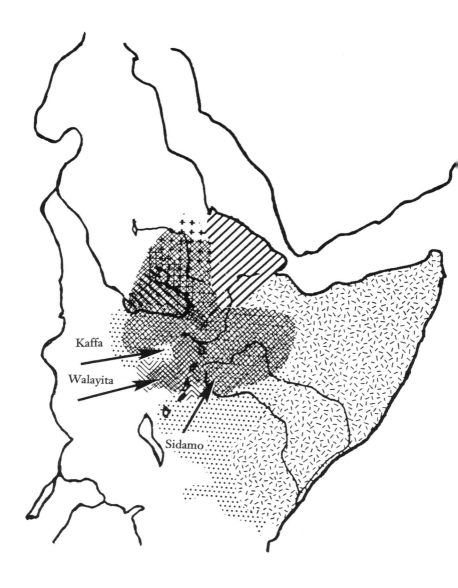

MAP 14   Shoan-dominated Abyssinian conquests, 1893, incorporating kaffa, Walayita and Sidamo

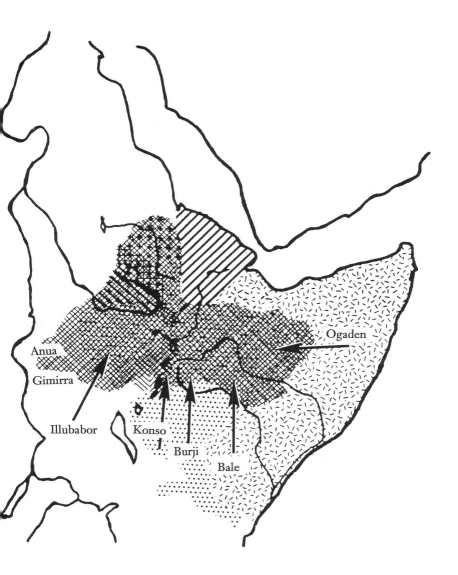

MAP 15   Shoan-dominated Abyssinian conquests, 1897, indicating
the defeat of Anuak, Girmirra, Ogaden Somali, Konso,
Burji and Illubabor and Bale Oromo

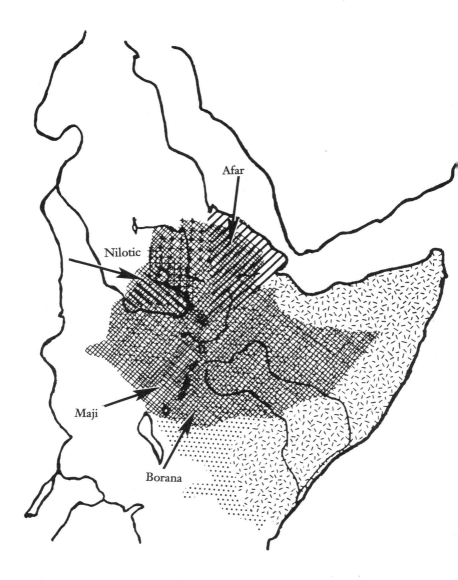

MAP 16 Ethiopian conquests and acquisitions following the signing of the Tripartite Treaty, 1910, indicating the recognition of Boundary agreements between Abyssinia and European colonial powers and the incorporation of Maji, Borana Oromo and Afar Sultanate

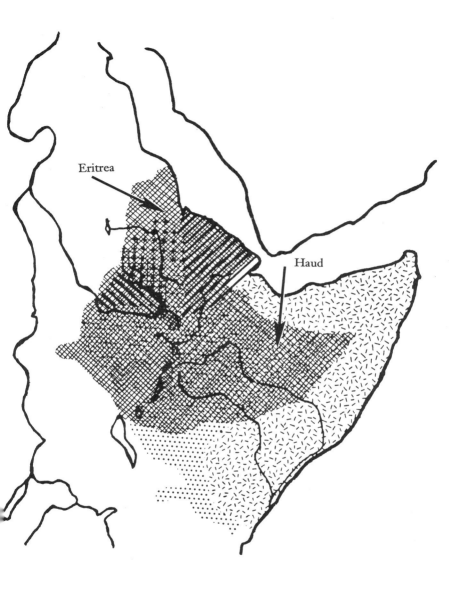

MAP 17   Ethiopian boundaries, 1962, indicating the annexation of
Eritrea and the Somali Haud

The Invention of Ethiopia

goods that were highly valued in Europe, making the area attractive to Europeans eager to extend territorial control and to secure staging grounds for more markets and greater profit.

It is in light of these developments that the first and subsequent contacts between Europeans and Abyssinians in northeast Africa are best seen. Contacts in the 1800s were initiated by Europeans who had acquired a global perspective and who represented institutions straining to become global. European entrepreneurs who served as carriers of this new outlook and forerunners of this new system arrived on the scene in Abyssinia at a time when power was extremely decentralized there. In fact the arrival and activities of the first scouts for monopoly capital had determinative impact on the direction of events in Abyssinia and beyond.

The First Acts of Abyssinian Confederation

Throughout the early 1800s Abyssinia, an overtly hierarchical society, had been divided territorially in conflicts among rases and dejazmaches—nobles who held positions of power in relation to the amount of loyalty they could rally locally. At this juncture the symbolic center at Gondar had come to be ruled by an outsider, a non-Abyssinian, Ali II, the great-grandson of a Yejju Oromo from Wollo, who was known as Ali I, or Ali the Great. In the midst of political and military chaos within Abyssinia before the turn of the century, the great-grandfather of Ali II had been invited by the emperor of Abyssinia to lead a peacekeeping force of Oromos from the neighboring country to help him to maintain some sort of law and order there in Abyssinia. The Oromo force, which displayed superior military might, was employed in effect as an instrument to be used by one of the contending Abyssinian figures to try to subdue and control the others. The grandson of the leader of this initial peacekeeping force eventually took the Crown of Gondar himself and became a powerful, though alien, ruler in Abyssinia. He had brought all rebellious dejazmatches under control by imposing law and order. This man was known as Ras Gugsa.

The Birth of a Dependent Colonial State

Abir relates that, "[u]ntil the death of Ras Gugsa in 1825, northern Ethiopia was relatively quiet. The death of Gugsa was, however, the signal for a renewed struggle for power among all the important lords of the country" (Abir 1968: 33). Soon after the death of Gugsa, the same type of pattern began to emerge that had existed prior to the importation of the Oromo force as a peacekeeping force—Abyssinian rases and dejazmatches each set out to assert authority over the others. Each wanted to rule, and they again went to war with each other. A series of wars broke out. After Gugsa, Ali II took the responsibility for keeping peace among the rases.

Eventually, after a sequence of coalitions and alliances were formed and defeated, conditions were created that provided a basis for the reunion of the Axumites (or Tigrays) under Dejazmatch Wube. This man, who was one of the first Abyssinians to deal with the reunion of Abyssinia, was also one of the first to deal with the Europeans.

Wube was not the only visible leader, however. In this period there were several other leaders in Abyssinia, for example, Dejazmatch Kinfu of Gojjam, Faris Aligaz of Damot, Negus Sahle Selassie of Manz (later Shoa), and Ras Ali II, who was reduced to only Gondar.

The institution of the church in Abyssinia had always served as the ideological basis for rule and, during this period, it came to play an active role in the effort to realize some kind of central control.

By 1840 another factor began to affect the region: Egyptians, who had earlier contact with Europeans and prior opportunities to obtain European armaments, started to attack Abyssinian territory. Egyptian involvement in the region provided a limited source of modern weaponry. The development of extensive encounters between Egyptian and Abyssinian forces produced a particular line of powerful *shifta* (rebel or outlaw) leaders in Abyssinia who had found avenues for appropriating Egyptian artillery. "These Shifta leaders, the most important of whom was Kassa-Teodros, were defying authority" (Abir 1968: 110). It appeared as though every able body had risen up to assert his right to authority. It was at this time and into the midst of this kind of situation that a greater number of

The Invention of Ethiopia

European entrepreneurs interested in expansion began to arrive in northeast Africa.

The Gun Meets the Guncarrier: European and Abyssinian Contacts

The first encounters that the warring dejazmatches and rases of Abyssinia had with European representatives were with missionaries and explorers, who reported back to Europe about their findings. Abyssinia was first visited by European missionaries and other travelers in the same way that most other parts of Africa were visited. Though the missionaries' formal goal was the teaching of the word of God, the service that they performed for the ruling classes in Europe was that of reconnaissance. Whether they intended it or not, they served as agents of the institutions of the new dominant class, the monopoly capitalists. This made the missionaries not only the agents of a form of Christianity that had absorbed much of the ideology that prevailed in Europe, but also explorers, forging the way into new regions, and salesmen, promoters of the products and, more importantly, of the ideology of European capital-intensive industrial society. Their use of several kinds of European items in the areas they visited introduced both a new demand for several kinds of merchandise—guns, medicine, and luxury goods—and a rationale for their utilization. They sent home to their European supporters crucial information about the nature of the country, accessibility, the type of raw materials available, the type and number of people present, the nature of political dynamics and the geopolitical makeup of the new areas. This was the role of missions in general throughout the continent, with little difference in the case of Abyssinia (Norberg 1977, Aren 1977).

As in other parts of Africa, missionaries came to Abyssinia with a Bible in one hand and a notebook in the other to record what natural resources were available. They traveled widely throughout the region and everywhere they visited they were reporting back to

The Birth of a Dependent Colonial State

interested Europeans at home. The missionaries were employed as teachers, doctors, trainers, political advisers, diplomats, etc.

Following the reports of the missionaries, the entrepreneurs, commercial agents, and adventurers began to swamp the area, agitating different dejazmatches, rases and any potential contenders to make some sort of visible commitment and sign treaties which were later interpreted in any way that the entrepreneurs chose. Occasionally the so-called treaties were held in case they might become useful at some time in the future.

The initiative for treaties usually lay with the European traveler who often sought to make any kind of contact whatsoever with any person who might be represented as someone of authority and who then presented the rationale for a signed agreement with the person. In such an event he immediately presented an often ready-made treaty to suit his purposes and to implement his own ambition. This was typical of entrepreneurs of the period, who usually departed for Africa with all-purpose draft treaties in their bags (Winks 1969: 95-96).

The ideas which guided the objectives and shaped these endeavors were ideas that emanated from capitalists and that were proffered to advance capitalist institutions. All types of documents were taken back to the home countries by these travelers as tools of enticement, threat, or coercion in attempts to involve their governments somehow in the regions they had scouted. The process here in northeast Africa was no different from that in other parts of Africa which were subjected to the voracious appetites of entrepreneurs.

Reviewing the provisions of the treaties and other documents produced by these early entrepreneurs, one can see that they are fraudulent agreements (Rubenson 1976: 159-163). Although the signed agreements were not between governments, the contending European states eventually utilized them and proclaimed them legal whenever they needed to justify their specific moves.

In the Horn of Africa, the requests by the Abyssinian rases who were contacted were presented to sponsoring business interests as identical—demands for weapons systems, teachers, technicians, commodities—regardless of the specific interests and demands that

The Invention of Ethiopia

the rases had originally revealed. Some reports claimed that one particular Abyssinian leader or another needed weapons systems in order to bring all rases under one central government. Some stated that Abyssinia needed technicians either to teach the armed forces how to use the guns or to produce gun powder or both. The teachers were to bring in European expertise.

The demands of the European entrepreneurs, on the other hand, were always the same and underlay the presentation of any particular ras's interest—to bring a given area under the protection of some European power, preferably (but not always) the entrepreneur's own home government. The notions that they introduced to justify and assure this end became central components of the construction of a new guiding ideology for the region. The entrepreneurs were generating a rationale on which cooperation and involvement were based.

The independent rases and the independent entrepreneurs had difficulty reaching agreements and concluding their discussions due to several factors. In the first place, the entrepreneurs were from widely varying locations, and so was their interest and their advice. While some represented Great Britain, France, Italy, Germany, Portugal, Switzerland, Russia, and Belgium, others travelled forth with the notion that they would peddle their contacts to the European state most interested at the time of their return.

For its part, Abyssinia was divided into four autonomous kingdoms, the Tigray or Axumite, the Gondari, the Gojjami, and the Manz. Each of these kingdoms contained districts ruled by a ras who could attempt to establish his own foreign relations and, in his own mind at least, was independent. It was common for rases to proceed as if they were destined to be king, which was the primary reason that wars were waged among them continuously. This period has been labelled the Era of the Princes, despite the fact that the word "prince" in English conveys a more fixed line of authority than actually existed in Abyssinia at the time. To call this period the "Era of the Rases" would more accurately represent the nature of wanton ambition that characterized the era.

The Birth of a Dependent Colonial State

Products of the neighboring Oromo country could be viewed in the markets of Abyssinia. The initial European interest in Abyssinia gave way to an interest by the businessman in the source of products available at the markets (Oromo products).

None of these kingdoms with their volatile districts was seeking expansion of markets on its own, yet the cluster of them held a key position in relation to the productive areas, south of these Abyssinian kingdoms, that were of interest to the entrepreneurs. Consequently, the entrepreneurs from various countries of Europe had to deal with Abyssinians as middle men and had to proceed through Abyssinian territory as a series of staging posts for the interior regions which held the resources of interest.

Another complicating factor was that the European entrepreneurs who entered and operated in this region had great difficulty gaining the full support of their respective governments to proceed with establishing direct control in this region. The general pattern of exploration followed by more-or-less automatic endorsement that was witnessed in other parts of Africa was not evident here. The European countries that the entrepreneurs represented in the area were many. All had a keen interest and stake in the area, but none of them was willing to become involved at the cost of direct, full-scale confrontation with the others at this stage.

The first major attempt made by Europeans interested in controlling the region was to administer it as a part of Egypt; when that did not work because an economic crisis in France enabled Britain to seize financial control of the Suez Canal, France, as the offended party, rushed to adopt a new strategy. The new strategy allowed the agents of both Britain and France to attempt to play the rases against each other until Abyssinians became consolidated under one leader. To bring about this consolidation, Europeans began supplying arms to whoever wanted them to hasten the emergence of a single victorious contender. At the beginning stages of this strategy, the Europeans were giving arms upon request to virtually anyone with a title.

The one geographic area that exempted itself from this process of fighting among fellow rases will be discussed separately below. In this region acquired weapons were utilized against external non-Abyssinian forces under the leadership of Sahle Selassie, the king of Manz (followed by Menelik II), who chose instead to expand his kingdom south against the Oromo nation.

Thus most of the firearms that the European entrepreneurs were willing and even eager to make available for their own purposes were initially of interest to the Abyssinian rases to strengthen their hands against their internal enemies in these skirmishes. Firearms were sent to Dejazmach Wube of Tigray as "a present from the French king" (Abir 1968: 111) to express friendship. Wube's objective was to protect Axum. Since he had received military materials and had the Abuna as an ideological leader, Wube openly announced that he intended first to attack Ras Ali II, the alien, on the way to consolidating power. He also proclaimed that he would "install the lawful descendant of the line of Solomon, King of Kings Tekle Giorgis, who was at the same time in his camp, on the imperial throne in Gonder" (ibid.).

Wube not only turned the guns that he had received against his enemies, he also used the Abuna to try to unite all the Christians under himself. A careful reading of Sven Rubenson's book will reveal that at the time of first contacts with Europeans, Wube was among those who at first thought that it was more important for him to establish his ideological position than it was to address military and economic matters with the willing European hustlers (Rubenson 1976: 66-129).

In trying to liberate Abyssinia from non-Abyssinian hands, Wube received the assistance of the Abuna in using the power of the church against Ali II. Abir tells us that "The Abuna was convinced by Wube of the Islamic tendencies of Ras Ali. He therefore excommunicated the ras and proclaimed the Ichege a heretic" (ibid.). Having completed this purge, Wube used all means at his disposal to establish Axum as predominant. In addition to the military weaponry, Wube used the political weapon of installing a lawful descendant of the line of Solomon on the throne and the ideological weapon of keeping Abuna Solomon at his side. At this point the firearms from Europe played a significant if not definitive role. By

The Birth of a Dependent Colonial State

the end of the year 1841 Wube was able to advance to capture Gondar. He was supported by a Birru Goshu. These two leaders advanced to Ali's residence to chase him out of the Abyssinian kingdom. The confrontation reveals the way that European firearms were utilized at an early stage in attempts to shape events in the region, as Abir's account reveals:

> The united army of Wube and Birru Goshu then proceeded to attack Ali's army and on February 6, 1842, the two armies met near Debra Tabor. Ras Ali's army, numbering nearly 80,000 soldiers, was composed mainly of Galla contingents and was supported by Dejazmach Merson and strangely enough by Birru Aligaz, who according to one source joined Ras Ali at the last minute. The battle of Debra Tabor was clearly a battle between the Christian Amhara and Tigrayan elements and the Galla, fighting desperately to preserve their predominant position in northern Ethiopia. The contesting armies were nearly equal in size but overwhelming superiority in firearms of Wube's army tipped the scale in favour of the Amhara and Tigrays. The battle was won by Wube and Birru Goshu, but during their subsequent celebrations, the victors were surprised by a small Galla army led by Birru Aligaz. Wube and his son were taken prisoner, but Birru Goshu ... escaped ... into Gojjam (Abir 1968: 111-112).

This battle of Debra Tabor, which marked the first significant united Abyssinian military effort, was waged for the purpose of doing away with Oromo elements. The ultimate failure of Wube's plan meant that the hoped-for solution among the Abyssinians was not immediately brought about. The scramble for power between brothers, and between fathers and sons, continued.

The second attempt to function in a united fashion was when Ali II ordered Dejach Kassa, who had been known as an outlaw for some time by then (later to be known as Tewodoros), to move against Gojjam. Abir reports that "Kassa ignored his master's command." By this time (1852), Ras Ali, who:

> . . . succeeded through tireless campaigning in bringing to submission most of the rebellious nobles of northern Ethiopia, was not slow to react. A strong army was dispatched to Agowmedes to chase the rebels, but for a number of months Kassa managed to avoid battle and spent the rainy season of 1852 among his kinsmen of Qwara (Abir 1968: 138).

Kassa's time in hiding was spent organizing a force that could realize the dream that Wube had recently attempted, i.e., organizing what could be called an Abyssinian national army, one that could stand against Ali's forces. This army was organized mainly from his kinsmen and, significantly, from help brought in from outside, consisting of both personnel and equipment. "Kassa was able to recruit into his service a number of deserters from the Egyptian army with whose help he was probably able to discipline his followers and strengthen the firepower of his army" (ibid.).

Kassa openly declared his aim to defeat Ali II and to reunite Abyssinia under his rule. He organized troops from all over Abyssinia. Ultimately, Kassa was victorious over Ali by bringing Abyssinian forces together on a strong anti-Oromo stance. He proceeded to fulfill his promise by marching to Debra Tabor, meeting Ali II's forces as Abir tells it, "on the plain of Ayshal, defeating Ali's forces and closing the chapter of the 'Yejju [Oromo] dynasty' of Begemeder" (Abir 1968: 140). Temporarily Kassa became the unifier and symbol of a united Abyssinia. His rule was felt over Gojjam, Begemeder (Gondar), Axum, and Manz from 1856 to 1865.

The glory of an Abyssinian united front that had chased alien elements from their territory soon again faced the same problems that had invited foreigners into their country in the first place. Harold Marcus reports that: "By 1865 the emperor controlled only a small portion of the territory he had ruled by 1856" (Marcus 1975: 21). Piece by piece, the kingdoms splintered away. By 1865 Manz

The Birth of a Dependent Colonial State

was gone; Bezzabbeh declared its independence. By 1865 in Tigray, Yohannes rebelled, seeking independence. In Gojjam, Tadla Gwalu successfully rebelled in 1865. The last was in Gondar, where Tiso Gobaze pulled away from his emperor. Soon wars were again raging among the rulers of these principalities, each seeking to become the King of Kings of Abyssinia.

External force was necessary to hold together in a single unit the Abyssinia that incorporated the four kingdoms that had been organized under the dynasty of Ali I (Ali the Great). In the mid-1800s the events in Europe that are reported in Chapter Two resulted in the arrival of an external force capable of decisively changing the course of events in this region. This was the force of European imperial power which made it possible to organize and keep Abyssinia under one emperor. Manz had not participated in these internal Abyssinian squabbles during the time that it was attempting to expand to the south; she emerged with a fairly neutral stance, something which attracted European attention and gained her several European friends. Ultimately Manz became the unifier of Abyssinia and a major driving force in the creation of Ethiopia.

Manz Becomes Shoa

The most important period in the organization of Manz' power vis-à-vis the northern rivals was that of Sahle Selassie of Manz, ruler of the Abyssinian kingdom located furthest south. Though northern authority figures had been in contact with Europeans, Sahle Selassie was the first from Manz to open a direct communication with the imperial powers of Europe, specifically with the United Kingdom, for acquiring weaponry. Sahle Selassie realized that he did not have the means to pay for the amount of weaponry he needed or wanted. He was the first to see the necessity of generating foreign exchange and translated his need into a quest for the resources that were within his grasp—merchandise that was in great demand by Europeans at that stage—ivory, gold, and coffee. These items were acceptable in payment for the quantities of armaments he required.

83

The Invention of Ethiopia

Since none of the products demanded by the European market were to be found within the boundaries of the kingdom of Manz nor even available within Abyssinia itself, Sahle Selassie utilized the classic process of moving inland from trade centers supplied by regions south of Manz to the country where the valued items were available. This quest to control the sources of these products took him inland into Oromia. King Sahle, however, was met with rejection and resistance from the Oromians themselves (see Chapter Seven).

Sahle's objectives were thus compounded. He realized that to get more arms he had to control the very lands that produced the desired capital to acquire the armament. Thus he also aimed to control Oromo territory. Sahle's choice was to go to war to seize Oromo lands. He began pushing the Oromos south of Manz, annexing part of the northern Oromo territory. During this annexation he was able to utilize effectively the weapon system provided to him during his initial negotiations with the Europeans (Rubenson 1976). Manzians were eventually able to translate this advantage into power over other Abyssinian kingdoms. Sahle Selassie, whose main campaign was to occupy his neighbor for the purpose of acquiring the raw materials that were needed in the European market, proclaimed in the name of God his intention "... to resume the lost possessions of his ancestors ... three hundred miles south of his present limits and to reunite the scattered remnants of the Christian population ..." (Harris 1844: 170).

Accompanied by British guests in one of his earlier campaigns, Sahle Selassie, whose army was "blessed" with the presence of European visitors, began its march to the Oromo country to demonstrate to them what he could accomplish with their gifts. From those who accompanied the king on this war of conquest we have the following account of how the battle was waged:

> Preceded by the holy act of St. Michael veiled under its scarlet, attended by the father confessor, and by a band of priests, with whom having briefly conferred, he turned toward the expectant army, and pronounced the ominous

The Birth of a Dependent Colonial State

words which were the well-known signal for carrying fire
and sword through the land "May the God who is the God
of my forefathers, strengthen and absolve!" Rolling on like
the wave of the mighty ocean, down poured the Amhara
host among the rich glades and rural hamlets at the heels of
the flying inhabitants ... (Harris 1844: 178).

While these forces, who were in effect demonstrating their use of
the guns given by Europeans to Sahle Selassie, began to destroy the
Oromo life and resources, the guests of Sahle, the Britons who
accompanied the mission with the king, were observing with field
glasses what was happening. They reported that when

> ... the luckless inhabitants, taken quite by surprise, had
> barely time to abandon their property and fly for their lives
> to the fastness of Entotoo which reared its protecting form
> at the distance of a few miles. The spear of the warrior
> searched every bush for the hunted foe. Women and girls
> were torn from their building to be hurried into hopeless
> captivity. Old men and young were indiscriminately slain
> and mutilated among the fields and groves; flocks and herds
> were driven off in triumph and house after house was
> sacked and consigned to the flame (ibid.).

This marked the beginning of systematic destruction of the Oromo
property and people through conquest and occupation of the Oromo
territory. A succession of further conquests inland in Oromia took
place with Abyssinian armies armed, accompanied and advised by
Europeans who were keenly interested in the spoils of battle and in
seeing the specific Abyssinian with whom they had allied become
victorious.

Sahle Selassie began to formalize his relationship with some of
these Europeans by signing treaties. He was eventually advised by
not only British but French and other powers vying for access to the
resource-rich regions to be conquered. One Frenchman, Rochet,
reportedly told Sahle that in order to become ruler of all Abyssinia,

The Invention of Ethiopia

"the King should organize his army in the way the French army operated. The necessary arms for this he offered to go and bring from France" (Rubenson 1976: 151).

Eventually the double objectives of Sahle Selassie were met, even though Rochet's objectives were not. Manz became Shoa with the expansion into Oromo country, and Sahle demonstrated that he was a potential business ally. His subsequently became the most important kingdom for the Europeans to deal with. In fact there was signed "an elaborate treaty of friendship and commerce between Great Britain and Shewa [Shoa], and a shorter, but from a political angle, more important treaty between France and Shewa" (Rubenson 1976: 144) between 1839 and 1843. Rubenson, commenting on these treaties has remarked that

> it has been suggested [by Kofi Darkwah] that Sahle Selassie, motivated by the desire to modernize his kingdom and acquire firearms, took important initiatives himself to bring about the mission. But if Sahle Selassie had a genuine, "largely strategic" interest in foreign contacts, [it was] something which exactly suited British and French plans for the exploitation of Shewan trade . . . .
>
> From several points of view, Sahle Selassie was a more promising ally, or at least trade partner, than any of the other Ethiopian rulers with whom the Europeans were involved in the 1830's and 1840's. His position was questioned by no one in Shewa; his word was the law of the land . . . (ibid.: 145).

Sahle Selassie's position vis-à-vis the Oromo regions conquered with the assistance of European firearms was what attracted European entrepreneurs to the area. During his reign a strategy was formulated and articulated by the French entrepreneur Rochet for controlling the entire region through Shoa.

> . . . Rochet had told Krapf that he intended to use the first 1,000 troops he had trained to turn against Sahle Selassie

The Birth of a Dependent Colonial State

and make himself the ruler of Ethiopia: "as there is a British India so a French Abyssinia . . . . " To gain his aims, Rochet was even prepared to unite and use the Galla tribes. With an army of 200,000 Galla, he would unite his French Abyssinia with the French possession on the Senegal river and make Africa "the continent in which France may have free hands" (Rubenson 1976: 151).

This strategy was to prove prophetic.

By the 1840s, after its expansion and conquests had proven its position in the European market, the newly created Shoa of Sahle Selassie offered to France according to Rochet, "a market of at least 1,000,000 consumers exploited by no one, a royal treasury holding at least 30 million francs which the king did not know how to use, and the opportunity of dominating Shewa [Shoa], through Shewa all Ethiopia, and through Ethiopia Egypt." (Rubenson 1976: 149).

Sahle Selassie, though aging, had played a role that effectively created Shoa as an entity that could serve as a promising center for European business and proved that Europeans could have influence in the most productive regions by acting through Abyssinian rulers. This came about only because of what Sahle Selassie could provide through controlling Oromo resources. In this pivotal role lies key to the rise of Shoa. Europeans had helped Sahle Selassie effectively and responded to him and his interests until his death in 1847.

The man who replaced him, his son Beshah Wired, later known as King Haile Melekot, ruled only eight years until his sudden death due to illness. King Haile Melekot did little to use successfully the European resources available to him references to oppose the efforts of northern Abyssinians to take over Shoa (Rubenson 1976: 164-65; Marcus 1975: 12-13). Haile Melekot died in the midst of efforts to prevent Shoa from being absorbed into the Abyssinian federation being built by Tewodoros.

In Shoa, then, following Sahle Selassie there was a lapse in Shoa-European relations. European attention was turned northward to the Abyssinian kingdoms that aspired to control Shoa and the Oromo areas that Shoa had conquered. Consequently, Shoa did not have much communication with Europe, and the activities of conquest were temporarily ceased. The much-touted Shoan commerce also seemed to die out.

It was at this time that Tewodoros of Qwara was in the process of regaining power in Abyssinia and had taken it upon himself to bring the powerful Shoan kingdom under his own control. The quantity of European firearms accumulated in the north exceeded the amount in Shoa, so eventually Tewodoros was able to incorporate at least the Abyssinian part of Shoa, i.e., Manz, into his domain.

Manz' glory waned until Menelik, Sahle Selassie's grandson, came to power and replaced the role of his grandfather, building upon the formula of enlisting European cooperation in conquering neighboring nations in order to control the territories and the sources of trade items valued in Europe.

The young Menelik had been imprisoned in the court of Tewodoros to prevent his ascension. While he was still in detention, his father, Haile Melekot, died. Meanwhile, Tewodoros had been able to subdue the Manz portion of Shoa, and it was brought under Tewodoros' rule temporarily. The Manzians, however, did not relish their position and rejected Tewodoros' overlordship. Briefly, one Shoan leader, Ato Bezzabeh, organized an army and declared Shoa to be independent of the Abyssinian kingdoms.

Menelik finally escaped from prison and returned in July 1865, planning to organize a small army. By August of the same year Menelik proclaimed himself King of Shoa. To regain the real position that he had merely proclaimed for himself remained to be done. Harold Marcus writes that

As long as Tewodros controlled Ethiopia, Menelik made no attempt to regain his hereditary kingdom. By 1864, however, the emperor's domain was shrinking, Ato Bezzabboh had proclaimed himself the independent ruler of Shoa, and Tewodros' punitive expedition to chasten him had failed (Marcus 1975: 23).

The Birth of a Dependent Colonial State

When Menelik wanted to regain his father's domain, he went to war with and defeated the independent Ato Bezzabeh and took control of Shoa. When the two men confronted each other, Menelik succeeded in acquiring Sahle Selassie's legacy in weaponry from Bezzabbeh.

> Bezzabbeh's army confronted Menelik's much smaller forces, [Menelik became victorious and] this victory gave Menelik 1,000 muskets and one cannon from the battlefield, and at Kebrat Amba he found another 1,000 guns and three cannon. He had by now become very powerful (Marcus 1975: 26).

This victory put him securely into the leadership position he had asserted for himself; he became the practical authority figure and successfully reorganized the administration as he saw fit. Quite a significant fact in considering Menelik's orientation from the outset of his rule following captivity was that he was imprisoned with Wube, the Tigray ruler who had experienced contacts with some of the first Europeans who arrived in Abyssinia. (Wube had been taken captive at Debra Tabor by Ras Ali II; when Tewodoros took over, he did not release Wube because he was a contender for power.) Kofi Darkwah mentions that Wube was Menelik's tutor while they both were imprisoned at Maqdala. Given the extensive contacts Wube had with Europeans, quite fully documented by Rubenson (1976), this is significant.

> Here we cannot do more than to point out that the policy which Menilik was later to follow as king of Shewa, especially the use which he made of Europeans, appears to have had its roots in this period. While he was at Maqdala Menilik was well treated and had for a playmate the Emperor's son, lijj Mashasha. Both boys appear to have been directly under the care of Dejaz Wube, the former ruler of Tigre, at this time also a prisoner at Maqdala (Darkwah 1975: 51).

The Invention of Ethiopia

It is safe to assume that Menelik emerged from captivity knowledgeable about the potential value of European alliance.

Early in his career as leader of Shoa, Menelik had additional opportunities to learn about the Europeans when the British expedition came to Abyssinia under General Napier. Tewodoros, having achieved the status of emperor by taking over Gondar and then subduing the kingdoms of Gojjam, Manz, and Tigray, had begun to lose control of his empire. After he had made enemies of the rulers of each of these kingdoms, he had contacted the government of Great Britain through a letter written to Queen Victoria, requesting the aid needed to assert control again. When his letter was ignored, he took several British citizens hostage in an attempt to evoke a response from Britain. The response was not what he had planned.

The British response indicated that Tewodoros II was not a valuable ally to them. There are several possible explanations. Tewodoros' location was such that one had to cross Tigray in the north, Manz in the east, Gojjam in the south, and Egypt to the west to reach him. He was involved in full-scale war with Kassa of Tigray and Wagshum Gobaze of Amhara, and the once-subdued Manz was in the process of rebelling by declaring its independence. The British response to Tewodoros was to send a massive punitive expedition, the much-publicized Napier Expedition, to free the hostages. In preparation for this expedition, the British asked Menelik for assistance. His response was typical of his pattern for dealing with Europeans; he contacted a European adviser, Massaja, to plan a strategy in response. Eventually he made a show of travelling with the requested assistance to Maqdala, the British destination, only to pull away at the last minute, offering a weak excuse for doing so, that he decided to attend a religious ceremony. There is speculation about his failure to complete this mission, including the thought that he had formed a strong personal emotional attachment to Tewodoros himself and that he already had a plan laid with France. Whatever the reason, Menelik did not materially assist the British in their effort and, consequently, neither did he reap the material benefits available to the one who did.

The Birth of a Dependent Colonial State

Tewodoros' enemy in Tigray, Kassa (later to become Yohannes IV), assisted the British at every turn, and after the completion of their massive expedition, they left him an enormous legacy of firearms, ammunition, and supplies. The war materiel was sufficient to assure Kassa victory in his bid to bring each of the Abyssinian kingdoms under his control, one by one. It is quite safe to say that Kassa was left with all the war materiel needed to achieve his goals. The British contribution was a condition for his success in uniting the Abyssinian kingdoms and ruling over a united Abyssinian empire. Kassa took the throne name Yohannes.

The significance of these events was not lost on Menelik, who reportedly said to Massaja with hindsight,

> If I had fallen in with the British army, not only would I have been consigned to the fortress of Magdala after the victory, and been presented with rifles and cannon, but I probably would have been elected and acclaimed Emperor by the Victors and by the people. Now all is lost, and perhaps another will sit upon the throne that belongs to me by right.... Don't I have reason, dear Father, to be sad and melancholy? (Marcus 1975: 30)

Menelik resolved to establish alternative arrangements to acquire what the Europeans could offer to assist him in obtaining his objectives. Before any other move, after regaining the throne of his fathers, Menelik had established a systematic set of objectives and a policy to match. His first acts in ruling Manz had been largely those of self-assertion, even boasting—necessary to announce to all that he meant business. He first had to formulate a strategy for regaining the territory that Manz had once taken from Oromia during the reign of Sahle Selassie, the territory that had so enriched Manz and transformed it into Shoa. Second, he had to create some kind of relationship with the Europeans, preferably building upon that excellent rapport that his grandfather had established (see Rubenson 1976 and Darkwah (1975:22-30). Third, he had to resolve a trouble-some ideological matter, that is, to make a law concerning a divisive

The Invention of Ethiopia

religious argument (which was in effect the problem of shaping and enforcing a unified ideological position within his region of Manz). Finally, he had to escape the restrictions of membership in the Abyssinian confederation—either by controlling the whole as emperor or by forming an independent kingdom.

In line with these challenges, he proclaimed religious freedom and prohibited anyone to fight over religion: "All religious discussion is forbidden in Shoa, where all cults are free; every Ethiopian priest convicted of having produced a religious controversy will be put to death" (Marcus 1975: 27). One year after obtaining power in the Shoan region, he had written to Queen Victoria of his victory and his wishes to reinstitute the kind of contact that Sahle Selassie had established. He decided to move slowly on the issue of regaining the colonies, initially to protect what remained until more people could be organized and armed. He asserted Shoa's independence from the confederation of Abyssinia, maintaining that he therefore did not have to indulge in the struggle for power with Kassa of Tigray or Gobaze of Lasta for the crown of Abyssinia. He apparently had decided early that he could go around the northerners and gain direct access to the Europeans by establishing his own route to the sea. This plan was a precise match with the European desires. Both were plotting to reach Oromo and other southern territories more directly. He therefore turned all his forces first toward the conquest of the Wollo Oromo in order to open a safe access route for the Europeans whom he had invited, and then turned against the Macha Oromo to prevent them from totally regaining the territory lost to Menelik's grandfather Sahle Selassie. These plans were developing while the others in Abyssinia were scheming over the crown.

Although not the type and quantity of armaments that Menelik desired, his weaponry far outmatched that of the Wollo Oromos, whom he defeated. The French assisted in this endeavor. His victories in Wollo placed him much closer to opening a direct route to the coast that would bypass Tigray, and ". . . renew . . . his efforts to obtain the technical services of Europeans" (Marcus 1975: 43). The advantage of the route he had selected was that he could avail

The Birth of a Dependent Colonial State

himself of protection offered by France against the Egyptian government that was attempting to keep all European military assistance away from Menelik. The other routes through Massawa and Assab were long, expensive to travel and occupied by Yohannes. The Italian presence was felt there, too. Since the new route offered the advantages of speed and security, Menelik devoted all his efforts in the direction of Obok.

Having seen the possibility of reaching Shoa, missionaries, technicians, businessmen, geographers—Europeans of many nationalities and of all professions—began entering the area. "[B]y 1870 there were already signs of European interest in the Ethiopian coast along the Red Sea and Gulf of Aden" (Marcus 1975: 45). Menelik wrote a letter to Theophilus Waldmeier dated 15 June, 1872: "...that he was prepared to accept missionaries and that the best route to Shoa was through Aden and Tajura.... [Menelik wrote] 'Be so kind as to send me a doctor, an engineer, a mechanic, and good men specializing in woodwork and ironwork. I will respect them and treat them well and reward them properly.'" (1975: 43). It is interesting to note that he was willing to allow proselytization among the Oromo in exchange.

The most interesting response was that of Arnoux, a French businessman from Alexandria, as quoted by Harold Marcus,

> Nothing less than to open a European route toward Central Africa via Obok and Shoa ... to furnish in the markets of Marseilles an entrepot for Ethiopian products *without any Egyptian interference* [emphasis added], to found on the high plateau a French colony, to introduce to Shoa our industry and our civilization, to assist King Menelik by all moral and material means to rejuvenate Ethiopia, to facilitate to explorers and scholars entrance into the heart of the African continent [and] finally to thwart the slave trade by our presence and our efforts (Marcus 1975: 43).

Furthermore Arnoux "... stressed, [that he] would act as the catalyst in this national rejuvenation" (Marcus 1975: 44). This was

The Invention of Ethiopia

the main program of Menelik. As he later expressed it, Arnoux's letter had definitely touched the bottom of Menelik's heart. Menelik had responded, "You have fathered my most secret desires. It is God, without doubt, who has sent you to me. I am happy to listen to your counsels. . . . The French are my friends; it is upon them that I shall base the hope of my reign" (1975: 44). He saw that he could pin the hope of his future on France. The interests of the ambitious Abyssinian king and the equally ambitious French businessman had found each other. European objectives in this region began to find a secure toehold.

As promised, Arnoux became catalyst and helped in training and equipping Menelik's army with modern weapons. "When Arnoux equipped one hundred of the royal guard with rifled carbines, the king exclaimed, 'Ah! If only I had ten thousand men like that'" (ibid.)

He meant that if he had ten thousand men armed with modern weapons he would start his conquest of the surrounding nations immediately and could also become the emperor himself. He meant that his program and Arnoux's ambition could have been satisfied. It was not too long until Menelik's ambition was fully executed, if not his friend Arnoux's. Arnoux did eventually bring a man named Chefneux, an entrepreneur who became a foreign affairs adviser to Menelik and played a key role in advancing capitalism in Ethiopia.

Menelik marched south as far as three-quarters of the way to Addis Ababa, almost the length of the Shoan region before the time of Haile Selassie. By the end of the third quarter of the nineteenth century, when the Tigray king and the Shoan king were much better armed, major skirmishes between the rivals for future power began. Emperor Yohannes, who had not yet defeated the other rases, claimed to be ruler over all of Abyssinia, a formulation that included Shoa, although the independent Menelik had done little to acknowledge that rule. Kassa of Tigray crowned himself king of kings over his rivals and became Yohannes IV. The man whom he was most concerned about was Menelik. He appears to have devised various means of removing Menelik.

The Birth of a Dependent Colonial State

There followed a series of planned attempts to overthrow Menelik, apparently with the backing of Yohannes. Among these plots one of the most interesting was the backing by Yohannes of an unlikely candidate, ironically Menelik's mate, a woman named Baffana.

He knew that Baffana was a much beloved female companion who had several children by other men before she met Menelik, but was unsuccessful in having a child by the king. Though full of ambition herself, she was primarily concerned about the future of her sons and basically wanted to secure a position for a son in power. Yohannes also knew that this woman had become an important mentor for Menelik in his early years, and her influence over him as a strategist reveals how dependent he was on crucial strategic advice. (This trait is important to note, as Menelik surrounded himself with European advisers throughout his lifetime.) When she was unable to bear Menelik a child, Baffana finally began to plot a coup d'etat against him. She planned and conspired with the Emperor Yohannes and with several Shoan noblemen. She was able to plan and get Menelik to implement specific military moves. For example, she persuaded Menelik to march against Ras Adel of Gojjam. She was able to isolate Menelik's cousin, made a deal with the religious personnel, and act as Yohannes' secret agent. She suggested and then virtually forced Menelik to go against his will to Gojjam:

> To provide legitimacy for her revolt, Baffana fostered the royal ambitions of the ageing Mardazmatch Haile; according to her plan, he would begin the rebellion and proclaim himself king during the rainy season, when it would be difficult for Menelik to effect a hasty return from Gojjam. Yohannes and Ras Adal would attack Menelik, and after defeating him the emperor would force Mardazmatch Haile to cede his position to one of Baffana's sons, who would formally submit to the jurisdiction of the imperial crown. Baffana would act as regent until her son reached his majority and would also make an act of fealty to Yohannes (Marcus 1975: 50).

The Invention of Ethiopia

Surprisingly, Baffana came very close to achieving her seemingly far-fetched goals. It is quite likely that Menelik was eventually convinced of the treachery of Baffana by his trusted European adviser and confidante, Massaja. This interpretation is supported by the fact that later when Yohannes finally was able to exact concessions from Menelik, he revealed details of Baffana's plot to Menelik (Darkwah 1975: 94). He also demanded that Massaja be deported immediately (Marcus 1975: 58).

Following Yohannes' attempt to take over Shoa with the duplicitous aid of Baffana, Menelik attempted to move from expansion to consolidation of his position, but he had a problem. Yohannes demanded his submission. His much-needed mentor was not with him. What could he do? Should he fight to the last man or should he submit to Yohannes? Interestingly, when Menelik reached his final decision, Baffana was brought back from exile to be at his side. Menelik suggested a negotiated settlement. Instead of fighting head-to-head to the end, Menelik strategically committed an act of submission. His primary interest was to consolidate his power, and to do that he needed to retain an independent route to the sea, something that he could not accomplish without controlling Wollo. Yohannes, who himself did not know which way a war between them would end, accepted the terms of negotiation. Their treaty was known as the Treaty of Wadara. The agreement of March 20, 1878,

> ... gave most of Wollo to the king, provided he built churches there and Christianized the Galla population, a task to be accomplished with the emperor's co-operation. The other conditions of the Treaty of Wadara included renunciation of the title of King of Kings; periodic tribute to Yohannes; supplies for Yohannes's army whenever it passed through Shoa; free passage for Yohannes and his army through Shoa to Debra Libanos; mutual assistance in times of need; definition of the boundaries of Menelik's domain at the Bashillo River on the north, the Abbay to the west, and the Awash to the east and south; adoption of Qarra Haymanot [doctrine of three births of Christ] by the

The Birth of a Dependent Colonial State

Shoan church, although implementation was postponed approximately a year to prepare the Shoan population for the change; and removal of the capital of Shoa from Licha to Debra Berhan (Marcus 1975: 54-55).

Both having agreed to these conditions before the occasion of the actual ceremony of submission, Menelik arrived before Yohannes on foot followed by his troops, "carrying a rock on his neck face down in the traditional form of submission. The moment he set foot on the rugs in the imperial tent, Yohannes' cannons 'thundered twelve times,' announcing the downfall of Shoan independence" (ibid). Six days later, however, in the presence of all his potential rivals and after having conversed with Menelik, Yohannes "... ordered salutes to announce the celebration of Menelik's coronation as king of Shoa." Activities and ceremonies for Menelik's inauguration and gifts of all kinds were offered him, including "four cannon, several hundred Remingtons and corresponding ammunition." On the morning of the 26th after the dignitaries had been seated

> ... the *echage* rose, bowed to Yohannes and placed a cross before Menelik; he kissed it, and on it took his oath of submission and fealty to Yohannes. The emperor delivered another short speech: "You are accordingly king and master of a land conquered and possessed by your forebears; I shall respect your sovereignty if you will be faithful to the agreements decided between us. Whoever strikes your kingdom, strikes me, and whoever makes war on you, makes it on me. You are accordingly my eldest son" (Marcus 1975: 56).

This was the formula by which Menelik's kingdom became part of the Abyssinian empire. Under Yohannes, Menelik was ordered to pay heavy tribute, which was designed to impoverish him economically, and to send to Yohannes his European mentor Massaja, which was designed to impoverish him strategically.

When Massaja, who had been in the country and mentor to Menelik for many years, with two other priests, was sent to

The Invention of Ethiopia

Yohannes as ordered, Yohannes had him deported to Europe immediately.

Significantly, Menelik did not go long without having a European strategist at his ear. By as soon as April 1879 he had found a new adviser, one who would stay with him for twenty-seven years. This man, Alfred Ilg, arrived with two other technicians, armed with an education from the Swiss Polytechnic Institute. Although he was only one adviser among several, he represented the quintessential foreign adviser to Menelik on everything from European technology to European cultural style to European diplomacy. He made himself indispensible by initiating a wide scope of activities for himself and was eventually formally employed in various capacities; he installed the plumbing in the palace, built the first bridge over the Awash River, served as translator for virtually all major negotiations between Menelik and European political and economic agents who visited the country, personally orderd Taytu's silver table service and jewelry in Europe, suggested to Menelik the idea of a railway connecting Addis Ababa to the coast through the French port, single-handedly obtained the much-desired concession to build the empire's first railroad and served officially as counselor of state for foreign affairs. He was clearly devoted to obtaining the Emperor's confidence and equally devoted to effecting fundamental changes in this corner of Africa. Ilg was one of many advisers who represented of the interests of monopoly capital and played an enormous role in constructing the technical and political infrastructure for a dependent colonial state.

The European-Shoan connection, once broken, was again functional. Soon regular commercial relations commenced between France and Shoa. In the wake of the alliance between Britain and Yohannes formed at the time of the Napier expedition, the French chose to back his opponent, Menelik, as the person most likely to dominate in the region. Ilg was widely reputed, particularly among British sympathizers, to have been on the payroll of the French government in light of his overt French preferences, but no hard evidence has confirmed this suspicion. Soon new friends appeared again from France and from Italy, making it possible for Menelik to

The Birth of a Dependent Colonial State

acquire all the war materiel needed to take the necessary steps toward fulfilling the program of conquest of Oromia, Sidama and others.

Menelik, having already begun the conquest of northeast Oromia in 1870 (a conquest that was not completed until 1879), proceeded to invade the central area and near west in 1880, the far west in 1880. (The east was later invaded in 1887.) The direct expansion of Shoa under Menelik by means of the annexation of Oromia was a logical and actual extension of the strategy devised by his predecessor.

Shoa's geographic position lay strategically between the rich southern zone and the northern principalities of Abyssinia, which gave her the priceless advantage of access and a brokerage position for the occupation and conquest of remaining parts of Oromia; it also led to the rich Sidama lands and products.

Shoa had other advantages over the northern Abyssinian kingdoms. Her early contact with the Europeans made her aware of their particular interest in specific market items important to weapons purchase, and the trade route established to what is now Djibouti ran through Shoa's territory. These advantages assured the flow of armaments. The acquisition of advanced weapons systems placed Shoa at an immediate advantage over other Abyssinians in any threat of confrontation.

Also the successive conquests and occupation of additional land further secured his friendship with the Europeans, and improved the likelihood that Menelik would become the successor to Yohannes. Menelik did face one serious challenge to Shoa's dominance and particularly to her control of the Oromo lands and people from his and Oromia's neighbor to the north. A stiff competition developed between the Shoan king Menelik and the king Tekle Haymanot of the other Abyssinian principality bordering Oromia, Gojjam. Finally, in 1882 at Embabo, an armed confrontation took place which pitted these Abyssinians against each other over control of access to Oromia and pitted the Oromos against both of them in resistance to their efforts to occupy Oromo land. Shoa emerged victorious over Gojjam and over the resistance form the indigenous people. The victory gave Shoa dominance within Abyssinia, security due to the vast economic wealth and population which she prevented the other northern principalities from tapping.

During the same period that Shoa was rising, the importance of the other kingdoms was dying. Europeans virtually took the affairs of Shoa into their hands—commerce, military, foreign relations, etc. Besides the key role of Europeans planning its affairs, another of the reasons for the rise of Shoa was the rise of trade. Darkwah has pointed out

> The trade of Showa, both domestic and foreign, like the frontiers of the kingdom, expanded with the years and there was a direct relationship between the trade and her territorial expansion ... foreign trade brought ... into the kingdom firearms. Armed with improved weapons, the Showan soldiers met with greater successes in their campaigns of conquest and the resulting [activity] opened up new markets and fresh sources of raw material.... Showa as such, indeed Christian Ethiopia [*sic*] as a whole, had very few commodities of her own to offer the coast; her trade was therefore a transit trade of which the coast and the southwest constituted the opposite ends (Darwah 1975: 152 & 156).

Shoa's access to Oromo resources shielded her from the twin disasters of drought and continuous war which plagued the north. When Shoa was recognized as the ruling power, a convenient arrangement was found—Abyssinians who needed food obtained it by joining Menelik's campaigns to conquer Oromia and her neighbors. Menelik, who needed additional manpower to carry out conquest and colonization, was able to obtain supplementary troops for his armies and more settlers to swell the occupying force with personnel form northern Abyssinia.

The Birth of a Dependent Colonial State

Abyssinians Share the Spoils: Conquest and Occupation of Conquered Regions

By the end of Yohannes' era, 1889, Menelik of Shoa became emperor of Abyssinia with little resistance from contending kings of the other Abyssinian kingdoms. There were several reasons for this. Primary among these was that Menelik with his southern conquests and promises of more booty could supply what the others needed. He was successful in dealing with the other Abyssinians because he had rarely turned his guns against them, but rather had aggrandized his kingdom by turning against the southern neighbors gaining secure access to resource-rich lands there. Ultimately this was welcomed by other Abyssinians. Famine brought on by wars between Abyssinian kingdoms and drought had severely affected them all, introducing particularly serious crises into the Gondar and Axum regions. They needed food desperately and Menelik had captured a secure supply. He was able to offer them many assurances if they submitted to him: that they would benefit from his successes in the regions south of him, that all Abyssinians who needed a better life could work to attain it by helping in the further conquest of these areas, and that if they put their guns behind their desire to improve their situation, that they would get what they wanted.

Europeans observed the dynamic of this relationship among the Abyssinians. Since Menelik had consolidated his power in Shoa, and drawn on that to become the undisputed authority in Abyssinia as well, he became the only figure that the Europeans chose to deal with. This was a crucial feature, especially in light of the Europeans' prior decisions not to become directly involved in the region for reasons of wanting to avoid outright confrontation with each other there and elsewhere. No potential Abyssinian challenger received assistance sufficient to oppose Menelik.

From the position of emperor, Menelik kept his promises to the Abyssinians. He brought together troops from throughout Abyssinia to accomplish the conquest of the expansive regions south and east of Shoa (Oromia, Sidama, etc.) whose peoples' resistance threatened to reverse Menelik's earlier incursions. Once he had completed the

The Invention of Ethiopia

course of conquest, Menelik brought areas that had remained free of European control under his own control.

Europeans had been interested in the products and the markets of these territories all along, and through supporting Menelik, they finally were able to deal with those areas, though indirectly, thereafter. This was a great advantage since the area could now be accounted for on their global map, and they had access at little expense to themselves.

After Menelik's ascendency as king of Shoa positioned him to assume power upon the death of the Tigrayan Emperor Yohannes, Menelik was left without an effective rival for the emperor's crown. By 1889 Menelik had become the king of kings of Abyssinia. He had a green light from the superpowers of the day to complete the annexation of territories that were inaccessible to the European powers because of their stalemate, so long as he continued to be responsive to their needs by maintaining strategic access to the region and to the economic resources of the most productive area.

In order to wage the kind of full-scale campaign required against Shoa's neighboring nations and nationalities, Menelik had earlier requested assistance from the powers of Europe. As letters Menelik sent to Britain, Italy and France demonstrate, he made direct requests for cannons, guns, and military, technical and political advisers. Besides requesting actual firearms, Menelik revealed in his letters his willingness to employ any European willing to work for him. He was eager to bring European expertise into the country. Not only the letters demonstrate Menelik's ambition; so does the eventual presence in the region of more firearms than the Abyssinians could use demonstrate the European willingness to cooperate. A close observer of Abyssinian affairs once remarked that "[i]t is impossible to travel between Harar and Addis Ababa without repeatedly meeting caravans of rifles and cartridges." He later observed, "I should think that at present there are more rifles, Gras and Remington, in the country than there are men to carry them" (Pankhurst 1968: 603).

The employment of several French, Russian and other European military experts and other regular mercenaries in the Abyssinian

The Birth of a Dependent Colonial State

military clearly shows the agreement of the European capitalists to participate directly in the war against Oromia and against other nations and nationalities in this empire.

Each battle was fought against full-scale resistance by the Oromos and others who had maintained the boundaries between theirs and Abyssinian/Amhara territory for at least four centuries of recorded history (Getahun 1975). The discrepancy in armaments created by the Euro-Abyssinian alliance not only accounts for the ultimate outcome, but for the decimation of the population in many Oromo regions during the campaigns.

European backing enabled Menelik not only to carry out the military aggression but equipped him to begin to consolidate his control over the areas thus conquered by employing policies of settlement in Oromia and other regions by the end of the nineteenth century. This kind of presence was encouraged and then acknowledged by Europeans. Once he was able to conquer most of Oromia, Menelik was advised by an Italian resident consul to make an application to be recognized as a legitimate colonial power. This was done based upon the terms of the agreements made at the Berlin conference of 1884-1885, specifically requiring "effective occupation."

The way in which the conquests were actually carried out differed from region to region. Occasionally European observers took the time to record what they witnessed. Harold Marcus has made available in English much of the account of a Frenchman in the country for commercial purposes who was one of the many Europeans visitors who became fascinated by the process of incorporation of new areas into the empire. In this case the attack was against the Walayita people, erroneously called "Gallas" in this passage:

> Of the actual mechanism of Shoan conquest we are fortunate to have an excellent description by J.G. Vanderheym, a French commercial agent, who accompanied the Emperor Menilek on a large-scale military expedition against the Wollamo Galla [*sic*] in December 1894. The Wollamo Galla

had been raiding into the Empire, and these raids threatened to become more serious. Several small expeditions against these Galla had failed, and the Emperor wished to reverse these defeats while keeping his troops in trim; he went along himself, claiming that he wanted to see if the country was as beautiful and fertile as he had heard. On a Saturday in early August 1894, the royal drums announced the organization of the expedition into Wollamo, and a royal edict was read ordering each soldier to prepare his provisions and equipment to be ready to go to war under the leadership of Ras Wolde Giorgis and Ras Mikail. For three months thereafter, Addis Ababa had an air of "unaccustomed activity," and, on November 1, Ras Mikail with ten thousand troops joined the waiting armies of the Emperor and Ras Wolde Giorgis in the capital. The next day, long files of women took the road for the first camp, each one carrying something or driving cattle and sheep. The soldiers started their march the next day, and Menilek left on November 15. By this time, the roads had been repaired, and Menilek quickly caught up with his armies. On December 1 they arrived in Wollamo where, the army of the advance guard of Ras Mikail had already burnt the houses abandoned by the Wollamos, fleeing before the invasion.

From the evening of December 1, when the Shoans fought some preliminary skirmishes with the Wollamos, the soldiers chanted war songs and songs of self-praise, "every day and every hour. These cries never ceased to resound and became a veritable obsession." As the object of the campaign was to reduce the country into submission, there was, from the very beginning, "looting of houses and crops, slaughtering of animals, sacking of the country, [and] burning." Every day the conquerors came back to camp with slaves and booty. With their superior weapons the Shoans slaughtered large numbers of Wollamos. "It was a terrible butchery, a debauchery of living or dead flesh ... by the soldiers drunk from blood." As the Galla warriors

The Birth of a Dependent Colonial State

left cover to throw their spears, they would be shot dead by the Shoan troops, armed with Remington or Gras rifles. By December 11, the resistance of the Wollamos had been broken, and on the march that day, "our mules turned aside continuously from recently killed corpses which encumbered the country. The wounded, horribly mutilated, were trampled by the cavalry men." On that same day the seriously wounded King Tona of the Wollamos was captured. He was brought to Menilek the next day and severely reproached for not yielding until forced to do so in the face Menilek's superior strength. Tona told Menilek, "It is the wickedness of my heart which made me resist such an enemy. The death of my compatriots falls upon me ... guilty of having heard only my pride. I should have submitted myself to you before allowing the devastation of my country and the massacre of my subjects."

On December 18 and 19 Menilek divided up the rich booty, keeping eighteen thousand head of cattle and eighteen hundred slaves for himself. He then returned triumphantly to Addis Ababa, taking along King Tona (Marcus 1969: 273-274).

By 1887 there were hundreds of thousands of rifles and artillery pieces complete with ammunition available to Menelik's army. Some of the clearest accounts we have of these battles and the destruction come from Europeans who went along to observe the use made of the weapons supplied by their governments. Several observers mention the Oromos' pleas for assistance in providing arms so that they could fight back and one British observer who accompanied Menelik noted that if the Arsi Oromo had been armed with rifles, Menelik would probably not have been able to defeat them.

The plunder taken out of these conquered regions has been described in various sources, especially by people who watched the victorious army marching into Addis Ababa with hundreds of thousands of head of livestock, slaves, tools, clothing, etc. Eventually this flow of goods and animals was maintained by the establishment of

105

The Invention of Ethiopia

a systematic Abyssinian colonialism which institutionalized the extraction of resources through the establishment of a new economic base and a set of institutions to keep it in place.

Settlement

By the turn of the century active military aggression had ceased, the outcome of the Battle of Adwa had forced the European powers interested in the region to devise a new formula for access to the region, and the boundaries of the empire were recognized by the neighboring colonizers in treaties reached between Menelik and the European powers who controlled the territories surrounding Menelik's claims (Hertslet 1909). This was the time that colonizing processes began in earnest to establish control over conquered regions.

Crucial to the process of installing a permanent occupying force is a permanent administrative center. As Abyssinian incursions continued southward from Shoa, an Ethiopian city was built in the midst of Oromia for the purpose of organizing colonial control. The site was the location of a natural hot springs called "finfinee" by the Oromo indigenous to the area. Finfinne literally means spring waters in the Oromo language. The Amharic word felwuha which has the same meaning is often applied to the region.

Menelik and Taytu, each afflicted with health problems, were initially attracted to the site because it was known to have curative powers. Following military conquest of the region, the first Abyssinia settlement was erected near the springs. Once the settlement was established, the site was renamed Addis Ababa, "new flower."

> ... at the end of the rainy season of 1886 Menelik and Taytu, accommpanied by their retinue, went down for the second time to Felwaha where a large number of tents were erected. Taytu, admiring the beauty of the scenery from the door of her tent, and remarking on the softness of the climate, asked Menelik to give her land on which to build

a house. He replied, "Begin by building a house, after that I will give you a country."

"Where shall I build my house?" she inquired.

"Here is the place" he answered, "which my ancestor, King Sahla Sellase ... like the prophet Mikias, made the following prophecy: One day as he sat under that great tree not far from May Heywat (or water of life), mead was brought to him while he was playing chess, when suddenly he said, 'O Land, today you are full of Gallas, but one day my grandson will build here a house and make of you a city.'" "It was," the chronicle declares, "the will of God." That very week Taytu decided to construct the house; her steward received orders to start at once. The work began and not long afterwards, a beautiful edifice was erected (Pankhurst 1968: 699-700).

Finfinne was made Addis Ababa by 1887.

Oromia and other nations of the south were occupied by the forces of Abyssinia aided by technical and strategic help from the European capitalist class interested in seeing this part of Africa play a role in their master plans for the development of the continent. During the conquests referred to above, military operations had eliminated or driven the people from their land. Their territory and even villages were occupied and declared to be "owned" by the colonizers who shared the land and people among themselves according to their rank and status. This was land that the indigenous peoples had cultivated and grazed with their herds for generations.

Not only conquered land but conquered laborers living on the land were granted as compensation to the victorious soldiers in amounts and numbers according the soldiers' ranks and backgrounds. When the northern soldiers moved out to claim their farms and the human work force to support them, most of the settlers themselves discontinued farming as an activity and were assigned to perform administrative functions in Menelik's state apparatus.

The Invention of Ethiopia

Oromo and other conquered peoples were turned into serfs and were forced to cultivate their own lands for these Abyssinian foreigners, who became their masters. The Abyssinians were able to accomplish this rearrangement of productive relations through the indiscriminate use of force, i.e., massive slaughter and plunder which devastated the fertile zones were designed to render the remaining population submissive. One foreign traveler had "an Ethiopian leader" explain to him that "if an invasion did not completely ruin a country, the inhabitants would sooner or later rebel 'and it would be necessary to send a great *zemetia* [expedition] and start all over again'" (Marcus 1969: 274). Many Oromo and other indigenous peoples, who had been displaced through the expeditions and were now prisoners of war, were sent to work without pay in cash or in kind for the interests of the Abyssinians and Europeans, and many were sold as commodities into slavery (Pankhurst 1968: 73-134).

The beginning of this settlement process marked the birth of the settler class in Ethiopia. The initial manpower for the aggressive imposition of this system of control came from members of the peasant armies who had chosen to fight and plunder
with Menelik rather than remain at home in the midst of what has been called the Great Ethiopian Famine of 1889-96. This is the route that brought most of the soldiers to become guncarrying overseers of the conquered Oromos and others. The incoming Abyssinian peasants, now transformed into soldier-settler landlords maintained an explicit interest in preserving and strengthening the system that kept their own privileges in place. Although many of them had themselves cultivated land in their home regions, once they were settled onto state-confiscated land, their work, their status and their interests changed. Their position was maintained by the newly forming Ethiopian state alone; their only legitimacy in the new territory was one created for them by the new laws imposed to enforce the arrangement. Their relation to Oromos and others who worked the land for them had become a vertical one. The term used to describe the relation between the settlers and the indigenous people is "neftegna-gabbar" (*neftegna*, the Amharic word for these settlers, literally means "gunowner"; *neft* means gun). In this new

The Birth of a Dependent Colonial State

economic arrangement, the conquered people became tenants, their previous rights in the land abolished at conquest.

The opportunity for Abyssinians to gain access to conquered regions, labor and resources through settlement was a key mechanism established for sharing the spoils of conquest. It has remained a centerpiece of Ethiopian dependent colonialism.

By the opening of the twentieth century Menelik II had settled his soldiers in every territory of Oromia and of other nations that he had conquered. They were transformed into colonists. Everywhere the colonists went the church followed, attempting to establish control beginning with proselytization. This process was described by witnesses in 1897 as follows:

> An interesting feature of the process of conquest, but apparently found only in pagan areas, and in territories directly administered by the northerners, was the almost immediate attempt by Ethiopian Christian clergy to proselytise. A Roman Catholic cleric traveling through Ethiopia in 1896 reported that Menelik was always eager to Christianize the Pagans, but that he did "not always employ to that end the method of persuasion." Some Ethiopians had informed the Monsignor that, on Menelik's orders, groups of five hundred Galla were assembled and ordered to go to some nearby watercourse.
>
> Then the Amhara Priest necessary for the occasion divides the group into two, gives to those who are on the right the name of Wolde Mikail and to those who are on the left the name of Wolde Giorgis; then ... he distributes meat slain by Christian hands to them. The Galla and the Abyssinians who have witnessed this ceremony are profoundly convinced that it is a perfect baptism and that it imprints on the unhappy [Galla] the indelible mark of the Christian (Marcus 1969: 274).

In return for the role that the ideologues played in the occupation of the conquered regions, huge portions of land were allotted to the church just as it was to the army. The law of this newly

The Invention of Ethiopia

forming state provided that the villagers had to provide manpower and supplies to the alien landlords. The law was imposed by force of European-supplied armaments that had been transferred to the rural areas following the wars of conquest.

The rule of settlers was introduced systematically. Military garrisons were built throughout the conquered regions for the purpose of bringing indigenous people under control and to protect the settlers from the resistance of the conquered indigenous people. These outposts became the towns (ketema) and administrative centers for the colonial state from which colonial rule was introduced. With the extension of these settlements into conquered regions and with their connection to each other and to the newly constructed center that maintained contact with Europe, the infrastructure for the Ethiopian empire was established.

Again Marcus has summarized in English the observations of a foreign eyewitness to this process:

> Once the Ethiopian government had effectively occupied an area or conquered a country, it governed and policed the subject peoples by establishing *Ketemas*, or fortified garrison towns, in strategic high places. 'Many of the villages ... are really permanent corps of armed men. These are always perched high upon the summit of the loftiest hills, and are quite a feature here. A Frenchman described the *Ketema* of Dendi, near the Awash:
>
>> It is built upon a hill and surrounded by a tall hedge and by a ditch; entrance is controlled by two gates above which is found a little square house in the form of a pigeon house with an opening on each side; it is there that stands the night-watchman. These Amhara towns are often ... the subject of attacks on the part of the Galla.
>
> Such "skillfully planted Abyssinian posts" were meant to achieve strategic control over the adjacent countryside. For

example, Arero in Borana was "a stockaded village, the only Abyssinian post south of Sidamo. From this centre the Abyssinians control the whole of Dirri, Tertale, and the inhabited part of Liban." Not only were centers like these used to govern the Empire, but they also "form ... a line of defense around Shoa." There was a system of communication between the posts which made it possible for thousands of rifles to be rapidly concentrated at any point. Thus, these *Ketemas* effectively controlled subject peoples, as well as representing to the adjacent European powers the visible evidence of effective "occupation" (Marcus 1969: 277-278).

These outposts were inhabited primarily by the Abyssinian soldiers with their families or those people specifically attached to some branch of the state.

It is these settlers who are of special concern in this analysis because it is this group of actual settlers and those concentrated around that state formed to protect the settlers' interests who form the only viable "Ethiopian" class.

The settlers and their descendants as well as those who managed the state did not have the socioeconomic basis for generating the institutions that comprise the Ethiopian state. Those institutions were the product of the expanding European capitalist class characterized at the outset. The capitalists influenced and made possible the state development at every stage. The Abyssinians willingly became the guncarriers, though, and moved onto land that they could not hold in previous centuries, manned the state, and brought with them cultural practices with which they felt comfortable.

Settlers rushed to take advantage of the new opportunities that miraculously opened up for them in the conquered regions. Not aware of combination of forces that enabled them to move into rich, long-coveted regions and to become established there in positions of authority over the indigenous peoples, these Abyssinian settlers assumed that their own innate superiority over the local residents accounted for this accomplishment. This assumption and the

The Invention of Ethiopia

associated attitude have become central components of a distinctly neftegna outlook. Many persons who did not enjoy land security in their northern home regions travelled south to take part in the settlement of the colonies. Soon the garrison posts became towns bustling with the activities of the new beneficiaries.

The transition between the kind of aggressive, brutal subjugation of the surrounding nations carried out during the military campaigns, and the kind of sustained occupation of the country that was required for colonization was a gradual one. In his campaigns Menelik utilized advanced firearms obtained from Europeans to equip these huge armies of northern peasants seeking opportunity outside the declining economy of rural Abyssinia. Upon occupation, the weapons were stationed with the settlers in conquered regions. Together they comprised the material and human instruments for maintaining and regularizing the relations between conquered and conqueror, and together they provided the means for enforcing the new pattern of relations that constituted the economic base of the dependent colonial state.

When the military campaigns were stopped, the same large-scale use of arms apparently continued, directed against the conquered nations as the settlers met opposition from the indigenous people to their presence. Aside from the oral histories of many of the conquered people, one piece of evidence comes from the whereabouts of the firearms used by Menelik to conduct war against the south. The total number of rifles in the central army of Ethiopia in 1896 was 112,000. In 1903 there were 600,000 rifles in Menelik's possession at the seventh anniversary of the Adwa battle. But by 1935 when Haile Selassie's army met the Italians, the central army had only 60,000 rifles, most of them newly purchased. The remainder of over 500,000 rifles were not in the capital, but in the conquered areas for the purpose of maintaining control, establishing a "stable" system of administration for the empire against the violent resistance of the resident populations (see Getahun 1974: 62).

As the colonial system developed and the structure of this new state emerged, every dimension and every branch of the apparatus was shaped on terms acceptable to these incoming Abyssinian

The Birth of a Dependent Colonial State

settlers in order to communicate with them, to utilize their services more efficiently, and to equip them to perform the tasks expected of them—defining and keeping "order" and transferring wealth to the central capital.

To assist and legitimize the settlers' control over the colonies, the language of the Amharic-speaking settlers was made the "national" language. The languages of the conquered peoples were outlawed, including the Oromo language, the first language of over 60 percent of the population in the empire. The religion of the settlers, Orthodox Christianity, was made the state religion, and their ancient law code, the Fetha Nagast, was made the basis for the Ethiopian Civil and Criminal Codes at this time (Perham 1969). For the settlers' children, schools were built where they were taught that their cultural behavior was civilized and legitimate, and further, that their rights were guaranteed. What they considered to be their national history was taught in the schools and presented to the external world as the history of the entire people in the empire. Authority was concentrated into the hands of the neftegna. These gunowning settlers became the landlords, the tax collectors, the administrators of justice (as they defined it), the priests, and the enforcers of the church and civil law.

The landlords who held larger tracts in the conquered regions, who presided over their own personal forced labor reserves, were often members of the northern aristocracy who had little to do with the Abyssinian peasant in their home country. But in the colonies, the former Amhara peasant who went south as a soldier with his family to share the spoils of victory held the same interest as did the nobles in keeping Ethiopia intact as an empire. Their interests (those of peasants and nobles) may have clashed in their homelands, but they converged in the colonies. Even the lowliest soldier in Menelik's army was awarded three farmers from the colonies, who together with their own families, lands, tools, and livestock, had to support the neftegna and his entire household for the rest of both their lives and those of their sons as well. The Abyssinian settlers *as a group* related to the conquered indigenous peoples *as a group*. Internal differentiation of the groups was (and is) of secondary

113

importance to that relation. The colonizer and the colonized saw it (and still see it) that way. This convergence of interest of the settlers marked the birth of the neftegna class. Specific measures have been taken by subsequent regimes to expand the base of this class. But its core group remains to be those who benefit directly from the colonial arrangement generated by Abyssinian and European collusion.

Conquered Regions Become Colonies

As previously mentioned, one of the regions conquered by the Abyssinian-European alliance was the homeland of the most populous nation in northeast Africa, the Oromo, whose territories contained well-watered central zone highlands and lowlands stretching across the center and south of northeastern Africa. Prior to conquest, Oromos had developed a republican form of government which enforced the principles of its own independent superstructure generally referred to as Gada. Gada embodied the particular code of conduct historically developed by the Oromos. Gada organized the population into five parties incorporating persons of agricultural, pastoral and mixed forms of livelihood. Institutions for education, defense, adjudication, religion, and welfare gave shape to an Oromo redistributive mode of production.

After the conquests, a new colonial superstructure was imposed on the Oromos, one that exhibited components of the Abyssinian precapitalist system and features derived from the European capitalist system. The synthesis of these elements formed the new Ethiopian dependent colonial superstructure. This combined product was brought to the conquered nations by the arriving settlers. This process reduced fully functioning modes of production and social organization in the conquered regions to the status of partial social formations within a colonial empire. In other words, what had been autonomous production units became subsystems within the new empire.

114

The Birth of a Dependent Colonial State

In the Oromo case, for example, Gada was dismantled and replaced. Nationwide features of the Oromo polity became merely local expressions and what had had powerful political and economic implications was often reduced to ritual. The Oromo people themselves were subjugated and reduced to serving the new neftegna as gabbars (tenants) on their own land. Those of the conquering group who became settlers acquired rights in the Oromo lands by virtue of their relation to the new state and were installed by that colonial state into the positions of landlord and administrator.

The essential economic relation between these two groups was a transfer of products and labor services from the conquered peoples to the conquering system in the form of either land rent, tax, tithe or days worked per month or week. The basic means of production, the land of the conquered people, along with the agricultural and pastoral people themselves was declared to be in the possession of either the conquerors from the north or those who had agreed to recognize the crown.

This colonial method was totalistic. It stripped the conquered nations of their ability to develop their own productive forces by first requiring the farmers to transfer to the setters three-quarters of the crops produced there, then by destroying the former mechanisms for organizing production and distributing the product, and finally by investing nothing for reproduction. Since the colonial lands were completely monopolized and divided, there was no opportunity for any development which could challenge the new Ethiopian power base.

Especially in the aftermath of wars of subjugation in which two-fifths of the population of some areas was eliminated, labor was the critical shortage for production. The residents of the conquered regions were assigned by the head to work for the neftegna. All the reproduction costs were carried by the Oromo serfs themselves—tools, seeds, fertilizer, new laborers—based on their now-impoverished and distorted pre-conquest system of production.

In the Oromo case, the superstructure of the society, the traditional overarching organizing and integrating mechanism, Gada, was overthrown together with the language, the religion, and the

The Invention of Ethiopia

legal and administrative systems. The territory-wide conventions and long-range exchanges among agricultural and pastoral producers were forcefully eliminated. These were replaced by the superstructure of the colonial state which implemented a new economic base embodied in the new production relation.

This arrangement spawned the fundamental contradiction between the neftegna colonial settlers and the institutions which were established to hold them in a dominant position, on the one hand, and the Oromo and other colonized tenants together with the remnants of their previous superstructure, on the other. This contradiction was manifested in conflict from the first days of the conquest and was continued through the period of colonization into the current era. This is the most basic contradiction, the deepest faultline that runs through all other sectors of the society—a contradiction between conquered and conqueror. This is the essence of the colonial relationship. At the heart of the conflict, each contending force strives to establish and maintain control of the means of production.

The task of carving out the Ethiopian empire geographically was essentially completed by 1906 when the Tripartite Treaty was signed. The latter part of Menelik's life was occupied with the work of consolidating his rule. He had to establish a firm control over the basic means of production extant within the boundaries, which is to say that he had to lay the foundation for an Ethiopian state apparatus. All the successors of Menelik have retained the basic objectives and consequently have retained the same basic infrastructure of the state designed during his era. The structural continuity into the present day is remarkable despite attempts at "modernization" and establishing "socialism." For this reason above all others it is important to look at how the control was established and how the state was formed.

The Birth of a Dependent Colonial State

Organization of an Economic Base for Ethiopian Dependent Colonialism

The declaration after conquest that conquered lands belonged to the crown and the conquered people were to be subjects of the crown signalled the shift to a new economic relation among peoples in the region. The Ethiopian state imposed and safeguarded that new relation, the new economic base. The neftegna soldier-settlers arrived in the conquered regions to play a role in implementing this new arrangement and remained there solely by virtue of their connection to the Ethiopian state.

When the conquest of non-Abyssinian nations that surrounded Abyssinia was complete, or, rather, at the time that full-scale military aggression ceased, vast numbers of Abyssinian peasants needed to be fed. They had been hit by a famine which was brought on by incessant internal skirmishes exacerbated by drought, and then they were recruited into a professional army. Michael Stahl described the situation of Menelik's forces in these wars as follows: .

> The troops were hungry. Menelik's resources in hard currency were limited and the Abyssinian legions were more exhausted than probably ever before in the aftermath of the famine. The situation had deteriorated further through the deployment of the armies throughout Abyssinia. Thus the problem of rewarding the troops could only be solved by granting land and labourers to the victorious soldiers in the newly-conquered South (Stahl 1974: 44-45).

It was these troops who became landlords and administrators in the newly conquered regions. As they took on increasing functions of administration, adjudication, and police work, the state expanded. This basic arrangement laid the foundation for the relationship between the sectors of society. The social and cultural consequences which the conquered have found so distasteful and deleterious flowed from this configuration that was patterned following conquest. As Margery Perham has pointed out,

117

The Invention of Ethiopia

The land was regarded in most part as confiscated to the crown, a varying proportion being allotted to the conquered chiefs and people, and the rest used to reward or maintain Amhara, and especially Shoan, soldiers, officials, and notables.... By the end of these wars Menelik had collected a very numerous army and, to provide for these men and to hold down the conquered territories, large garrisons were distributed. The conquered people were allotted as *gabars* to the soldiers in numbers according to the latter's rank, as follows: Governors—varying numbers often running into three figures; district commanders—from 30 to 80 each; officers—from 7 to 10 each; and soldiers—from 2 to 5 each.

It will be imagined that Amhara soldiers in charge of the conquered tribes [*sic*], which were mostly pagan or negro, or both and far from such supervision and restraints as existed nearer the centre, were not likely to treat their *gabars* with much forbearance (Perham 1969: 295-296).

Distribution of land and people to an army of occupation was one thing, but for Menelik to control systematically even his own soldiers was quite another. Realizing this, Menelik set out to find methods of control that could be effective and could also be understood by his fellow soldiers in order to ensure compliance and comprehension. He ultimately introduced a type of land tenure with which the soldier-settlers felt familiar. He transferred some elements of the land system, specifically, the terminology, from their own homeland. Though it sounded familiar to the settlers, the system did not function in the same way in the conquered regions as it did in Abyssinia. In fact it bore no resemblance to that in the settlers' homeland except for the terminology. The land tenure system in the south, decorated with the same language that the Abyssinians used to talk about their land tenure in the north, created among them the false sense that the tenants on the conquered lands shared the same experiences that the settlers had had before moving south. This confusion has carried over to analyses of land tenure in the conquered regions to this day. The conquered peoples who worked the

The Birth of a Dependent Colonial State

land in the newly colonized regions cannot accurately be described as peasants because their relationship to the land has been one of laborer within an alien production system.

Michael Stahl has described the arrangement which was implemented:

> The privileges which the officials received in relation to the peasantry in the southern provinces [the areas referred to here as conquered regions] and which constituted their salary, were institutionalized in new forms of land tenure. The new tenures were modifications of the old gult privileges of the Abyssinian kingdom. The three most important tenures were maderia, rist-gult and siso (Stahl 1975: 47).

The subtleties of the Abyssinians' land tenure as it functioned in the northern kingdoms were dropped when the major categories were applied to the conquered regions. Hoben (1973) has described the finer workings of land tenures in the Abyssinian homelands, and Ellis (1976) has discussed the differences in application of land tenure in the north and south. The types that were transferred in name only were rist land, communal or maderia and gult land.

In Abyssinia, rist land is land that can be inherited for use but cannot be sold; it is land in which the holder has usufruct rights. The maderia (communal) land in Abyssinia was land owned by a household and its use right vested in membership in a parish or kin-linked neighborhood (or both) that oversees land utilization. Gult land is part of an estate from which the government has lifted its tax. It cannot be inherited—it has a use value free from tax for the person to whom it is granted. Whoever receives the rights to gult land can receive and consume any revenue that it generates. These arrangements were applicable for the most part for individuals and religious establishments in Abyssinia.

When Menelik tried to convert these forms of tenure in order to utilize modified versions, he came up with rist-gult, maderia and siso tenures. Maderia land came to mean a type of government land that was given to the lower-ranking members of the army from which to make a living. Since all land that was conquered technically belonged to the crown and the crown did not have the capacity to develop payment in cash, it gave land limited in use to the life of the particular person in question as payment. After he died, the land rights reverted to the crown. Just as the meaning of maderia in the Amharic language is "living expenses," it covered the lifetime of that individual, and in fact closely resembles a salary for the individual. The beneficiaries, or those who profited from these arrangements, changed over time.

Rist-gult was a type of land allotment of a higher order. It was granted to the leaders of the conquest and was permanent, that is, it was inheritable. It had both use value and exchange value. The other type, siso, was the land awarded to members of the indigenous populations of the region known as balabat. These were people who had assisted in the conquest of their own nations. Siso could be best designated as payment [in kind] to those who had sided with the Abyssinians in one way or another.

Whether rist holder, maderia holder or siso holder, holders of land formed a privileged category. The design created the material basis for an economic unit that could act together as a class. The actions that gave them land laid down the infrastructure of the Ethiopian empire by creating simultaneously a conquering class and a conquered one. For every person who was rewarded, there were entire categories of previously independent people who lost everything they had. They were forced to change their way of relating and making decisions about their own land and its produce in order to feed the gun-toting strangers. This new arrangement constituted a transformation of the management and the organization of production, a fundamental alteration of the previously existing norms for production and distribution. This arrangement introduced new production relations. It created two opposing forces in an antagonistic contradiction.

Though there were fine differences among the soldiers in terms of rank, and there were the differently named forms of tenure mentioned above, those differences did not alter or blunt the new reality that this group of professional soldiers became the owners

The Birth of a Dependent Colonial State

and controllers of land and labor in societies and cultures that had been operating according to independent methods of organizing production. The finer points of whether the soldier had only usufruct rights, whether he had been given his land and labor for only his lifetime or whether his new privileges were inheritable were of little consequence to the conquered people. Regardless of prior internally significant differentiation in the conquered societies, the members were reduced to laborers for the soldier-settlers. This gave rise to two distinctive groups which it is accurate and convenient to call classes; one was the class of soldiers who became the settler overseers, and the other was the class of formerly autonomous agropastoral people who were reduced to tenant laborers. This arrangement was held in place by means of the Ethiopian state that was created for that purpose. The new production relation which was established was, without any question, a colonial relationship.

This new infrastructure created a set of arrangements which have persisted through subsequent shifts in regime. In fact adjustments have been made precisely in order for these basic production relations to continue.

To establish enough control to secure the extraction of resources, the conquering coalition divided the conquered lands and people territorially into a series of geographical units. The boundaries of these units dismembered the meaningful units of the previously existing societies. Peoples of alien societies and cultures were drawn together into awarajas, the awarajas into woredas, and the woredas into miktel-woredas in which the only thing they had in common was their relation to the conqueror. It was a system familiar to colonial administration, but not one derived from units recognizable to the conquered people. The administrative units themselves were a product of the blend of European and Abyssinian notions that comprised the Ethiopian state. The designations were set up in a ranked order. To impose law and order as they were defined by the new Ethiopian state, a system was introduced among the settlers whose job it was to control the colonies. They were reinforced from the center when need arose.

The Invention of Ethiopia

The church also played a colonial role by effectively conducting what amounted to a propaganda war in the conquered regions. Building churches at all points where garrisons were established, the church served as the ideological arm of the new settler-run state, and was compensated with huge land grants which were called semon land.

This entire process of social reorganization was started in motion by the representatives of two classes which acquired a solidity of interest over time. There were the European entrepreneurs who had worked so diligently to establish Ethiopia as a European outpost and the Abyssinian rases who benefitted from the alliance as agents. These sets of actors were able to assist each other from the beginning.

Not only did the early European entrepreneurs advise the rases of Abyssinia to acquire guns, they also advised them to obtain people who could show them how to use the weapons. As a result, the Abyssinians found and employed European trainers. The European entrepreneurs, themselves products of a capitalist system in Europe, pushed to establish the basic requirements for commercial success, i.e., they introduced the need to build and expand a solid infrastructure for communication.

The importance of communication was not a problem faced only by Europeans. Limitation on communication was a problem faced by Abyssinian kings who had tried to attract commerce, to provide raw materials to the market and to get European products, especially guns and ammunition, to their destination. This was true of those Abyssinians who bordered the Oromos' territory, Oromia, for example. Kings Tekle Haimanot of Gojjam and Menelik of Shoa had faced as fundamental a problem as crossing the rivers that separated them from Oromia and lands further inland to extract efficiently the goods highly valued by the European entrepreneur.

A Greek resident in Gojjam, Giyorgis Iotis, advised the building of a bridge over the Abbay (the Blue Nile) to do away with the "river problem," he began the process of utilizing European technical expertise to solve a long-standing Abyssinian problem. In agreement, Negus Tekle Haymanot wrote an invitation to an Italian

The Birth of a Dependent Colonial State

company to build a bridge for him. He said, "In the Galla countries, ivory, gold, civet and coffee are to be found, and thus the bridge will be a good thing for your Assab" (Pankhurst 1968: 298). A more convenient marriage of interest would be difficult to imagine. This bridge construction began in 1884 and by 1885 the first of two bridges that could take Tekle Haymanot to "the Galla countries" was built. Richard Pankhurst offers extensive detail on the process of the bridge construction, a process which provides insight into the more general challenge of implementing European ideas and designs by force in an environment and among people who had no familiarity with the undertaking.

[The Italian Count] Samlimbeni was accordingly sent to undertake the work at the king's [Takla Haymanot's] direction.... The foundation stone was laid by Takla Haymanot on December 15, 1884. Explaining that the sovereign was motivated in the selection of the site by fear of attack from Shoa, Salimbeni relates that preliminary investigation revealed good supplies of limestone, rocks, pebbles, clay and sand in the area, but that timber was unobtainable as the only nearby trees were in the vicinity of churches and could not therefore be touched. Large quantities of supplies were used: 34,000 porter loads of sandstone, 12,00 loads of sand, 8,000 loads of limestone, which had to be carried a distance of three days, and 60,000 locally-made bricks. the work was based on improvisation: trowels were made of the engineers' frying pans, hammers out of local ploughs and rope out of twisted cowgut, while bamboos were set in straw-strengthened mud to serve as scaffolding. Women, many accompanied by their children, were given the task of baking the bricks, while two Italian assistants, Bianchi and Andreone, trained eight workers to use the lime kiln and twelve others to lay bricks (Pankhurst 1968: 298).

The other bridge crucially important to further the interests of both the entrepreneurs and the rases and, thus, to the economic base

123

of the new empire was the one over the Awash River. This bridge also represented the forcible implantation of a European strategy and design into a hostile political and physical terrain. Alfred Ilg, himself the consummate agent of French capitalist ideology, had built three models for a bridge over the Awash before he could convince Menelik to grant approval for the project. In a letter written upon completion of his first attempt, Ilg revealed that he himself was striving to elevate Shoa towards some higher external standard. He wrote,

> Shoa has advanced a step forward. A few weeks ago I completed the first brdge in the country; it spans the river Awash. The beams had to be carried 15 kilometres on human shoulders. For the bridge heads I had to square up the stones on the spot. I even had to burn coal in order to forge the nails rivets, screws and bolts required. Add to this the tropical sun with all its dangers, heavy rains with resultant dysentery, intermittent fever, cyclones which almost pulled out my beard and carried the tent in all directions. At night the hyenas almost stole our leather pillows from under our heads; jackals and other rabble plundered the kitchen and obliged me to obtain respect with strychnine. I had with me an army of 1,200 men, 1,000 Gallas and 200 Abyssinians. In order to carry a beam 10 metres long and 25 to 35 centimetres in diameter, not less than 300 men were necessary and they required 3 full days to carry it 15 kilometers (cited in Pankhurst 1968: 299).

Once completed, "[t]he Awash Bridge was of great strategic and economic importance, as it enabled the river to be crossed without difficulty during the rains. It was soon destroyed in fighting with the Gallas; but Ilg in the following year built a second bridge" (ibid.). It is important to note that since the Oromos destroyed it immediately, it is clear that they did not share in the benefits of the bridge in any way. They saw the bridge as an element of invasion—and indeed it played a significant role in the construction of a foreign superstruc-

The Birth of a Dependent Colonial State

ture. It was used as a tool of aggression against the indigenous peoples.

The feature of physical infrastructure that most picqued European interests was the prospect of introducing a railway into the region. Railway construction across the full length and breadth of Africa absorbed heavy industrial investment of both British and French monopoly capitalists intent upon securing at reduced costs supplies of raw materials for home industry, and expanding markets for home products. Equally important was the need to establish enough political control over strategically sensitive and potentially productive regions to effectively remove those regions from the grasp of capitalist competitors. This latter motive appears to have been primary for both Britain and France due to the location of the headwaters of the Blue Nile river in this part of northeast Africa and its proximity to the Suez Canal, the major global crossroads between Europe and the East before the advent of the airplane. It is not surprising that the prospect of a railway line to be built in this region became a focal point for political strategy of several European representatives at Menelik's court.

Quite significantly it was Ilg who first proposed to Menelik that a railway be built to link the new capital city with the coast where it would connect with shipping lines. Pankhurst reports that the initiative lay with Ilg, that the very idea of a railroad in this area was "conceived by Menelik's Swiss adviser Ilg who arrived in the country in 1877" (Pankhurst 1968:304). Ilg apparently took up the task of educating Menelik thoroughly on the matter, constructing model railroads for him and discussing endlessly the advantages. Ilg's biographer wrote, "[t]he conception of the railway preoccupied him all the time" (quoted in ibid). Having seen how a small railroad had been used to British advantage during the Napier expedition, Menelik expressed reluctance to become associated with a scheme so unlikely to win Yohannes' approval. It is interesting to note, however, that on December 6, 1889, within days of Menelik's own ascension to the emperor's throne, he wrote to the president of France indicating his decision to have a railway constructed (Pankhurst 1968: 305).

The Invention of Ethiopia

By 1893 Menelik authorized Ilg in writing to set up a company for construction of a railroad and Ilg immediately turned to Leon Chefneux, a French businessman who had also served in official diplomatic capacity for Menelik. Once enough interest was aroused in France to secure the necessary capital, a legal concession for the undertaking was required and eventually granted directly to Ilg personally, authorizing him to establish an Imperial Ethiopian Railway Company.

British-French colonial rivalry in the Horn was highlighted over the issue of the railway, which was the only heavy capital investment made in the region. It was in January 1896 that the Paris firm of Duparchy and Vigoroux signed a contract to build the railway. This move was in keeping with the usual pattern for establishing spheres of influence in Africa—commercial ventures would take an initiative for investment in a given area and the role of the European government was to acknowledge successful ventures, legitimizing and politically protecting them. At the initial stage, the French government was hesitant to authorize the construction of the line through French Somaliland because of the international diplomatic crisis that it would have caused with the Italians and indirectly with the British.

Significantly, the Battle of Adwa occurred at this point, the famous military encounter between Italian and Ethiopian forces in which the Italians were routed and Menelik won the day. The crucial point is that Menelik prevailed while armed with primarily French weaponry. The battle was an indirect confrontation between the major superpowers of the era, Britain and France, who were unwilling to go to blows with each other over the region.

After the Battle of Adwa on March 12, 1897, the French government gave official permission for the formation of the Imperial Railway Company. French capital that was initially secured for the venture was inadequate. British investors were called in and the International Ethiopian Railway Trust and Construction Company Ltd. was formed. This trust established authority over the Ethiopian Railway Company. The company was French in name but controlled by British capital. The interests of these powers were clear; the French financiers were eager to secure the intervention of

The Birth of a Dependent Colonial State

the Paris government in the construction of the line and the British were equally concerned that "the French should not occupy the predominant position in Abyssinia which the construction of the railway will probably give them" (Cromer to British Foreign Office cited in Marcus 1975: 202). Extensive public debates were held in France, making the matter of the invasion of British capital into a French enterprise a threat against French national interests and revealing perceptions about the political as well as economic advantages of controlling the railway. The content of these debates, held prior to a general election, reveal French ambitions: ". . . the line must remain French, for through it Ethiopia could become 'a kind of colony' with all of the advantages of a colony and none of its responsibilities" (Pankhurst 1968: 316). Finally the French government did intervene to legitimize the company but without Menelik's knowledge or consent.

The British representative in Ethiopia, John Harrington, reported these developments to Menelik and encouraged him in sabotaging the venture's financial success in various ways, chief among which was refusing to allow the construction of the second section of the line to Addis Ababa. Harrington was able quite successfully to influence Menelik against France, to sign a treaty with the emperor in 1902 that was advantageous to Britain, and eventually even to supplant Ilg's influence at the royal court. But until France, Britain and Italy had defined their positions, interests and responsibilities in the region capital could not or would not proceed.

When the railway came to need additional funds between 1902 and 1904, Lord Chesterfield, the President of the British company, proposed that the Ethiopian railway be internationalized over its entire length and that Djibouti be made a free port (Work 1935: 312). After some extensive debate, Menelik appeared to favor the proposal and so did the British, but it was not acceptable to the French (Gilmour 1906). The Tripartite Treaty represented an innovative political accommodation to further the business interests of all parties—they internationalized the region itself instead of the railroad.

127

The Invention of Ethiopia

The communication media then began to operate explicitly as tools of control over the colonial areas by a newly-empowered local ruling class. One example of the tight control that Menelik established over the internationally supplied resources and the way he shaped those resources into tools of repression is found in the way the other communications systems developed within Ethiopia's empire. The telephone and telegraph system immediately became a powerful tool in Menelik's hands for centralizing power in his own palace compound. It strengthened his authority over the colonies and the settlers stationed there. He called those administrators almost daily to supervise their activities. Telephone stations were established at Kela (customs ports) and followed caravan lines which allowed the emperor or his representative to check on the movements of traders and caravans. The Bank of Abyssinia opened in the rich trading areas of the southwest only after the telephone had been installed (Garreston 1980: 64ff).

Media were placed exclusively in the hands of Shoan Amhara elites and were accessible to a few traders. Thus their use was totally controlled. Menelik's minister of Post, Telephone and Telegraph was one of his closest confidantes. Telegrams were sent only in Amharic and for the telephone Amharic had to be used at least to obtain initial contact. Foreigners were allowed to use it at a fairly steep price which brought a tidy profit to the emperor. The costs of the telephone and telegraph were carried by the peasants in a direct levy to maintain telephonists and costs of installation and upkeep. This is an example of precisely how the introduction of "modernization" brought increased burdens on the peasant for changes in the society that not only failed to benefit him but actively worked against him by strengthening the very state machinery historically designed to exclude and exploit him.

The telephone network was introduced by 1889. In 1890 Italian engineers installed in the emperor's palace the first telephone. It was one that had been given to Ras Makonnen by the Italian government during his visit to Italy in 1889. Having tested it, Menelik had approved the project over the strong objections of the major hierarchy of Ethiopian orthodox priests who rejected it as the devil's work.

The Birth of a Dependent Colonial State

Menelik was often depicted as an "advanced" and "innovative" thinker by Europeans amused to observe him tinkering with the new device and overruling the priests in this matter. In fact he was a man who had a European adviser constantly at his ear suggesting ways that specific tools available from Europe could enable him to conquer and control new regions and could bring him closer to his (and their) goals.

By 1894 a European-style postal system was imported, i.e., established by decree, significantly on the same day that the concession for the railway was signed (Pankhurst 1968: 337). The idea of producing postage stamps came from Chefneux. The stamps were designed and issued in Paris, bearing the emperor's head and Amharic script. Efforts to have Ethiopia admitted to the International Postal Union were handled by Ilg personally in Europe.

European entrepreneurs systematically advised and introduced those dimensions of communication infrastructure that could assure their commercial development in the region. Since the rases were not familiar with the technology and could not manage the operation of these innovations, they had to leave the implementation entirely to Europeans. The Abyssinian rases did see clearly that they had benefitted in the past from European technology, primarily guns and other weapons, and they could see also that they would benefit from these new phenomena as well. They readily entered into alliance with their new partners, but for reasons of their own. On the matter so critical to the European interests, the railway, for example, an Abyssinian "nobleman" commented to the British envoy, Rennell Rodd, "We don't want rapid communication with the coast; the railway will be useful to us in the interior; we shall wait till it is finished and then destroy its connection with the sea" (Pankhurst 1968: 308).

Both the entrepreneurs who had direct contact with Abyssinians and the European governments that eventually stepped in, could see that the new Abyssinian position and privileges were totally dependent on the Europeans. They were aware that without European advice and technology the Abyssinian group that they had assisted into prominence was doomed.

The Invention of Ethiopia

With a critical mass of strategically placed personnel and technical inputs introduced into the area, Abyssinia was recognized by Britain, France and Italy as an empire and a legitimate force. This formal recognition opened the door for cooperation of all three major powers of Europe to assist in fashioning the Ethiopian administration. This development is usually credited to Menelik as in the following quotation: "The Emperor Menelik, keenly interested in the new world suddenly impinging upon his country and determined to modernize his administration upon European lines, began the creation of ministries. These were set up in 1907-8 for justice, war, interior, commerce and foreign affairs, finance and agriculture, and public works" (Perham 1969: 89).

In the current work the state is regarded as a mechanism for implementing a specific value system and the institutions which comprise any particular state are seen to emerge from the historical and economic experience of the society whose values are being enforced. In the case of the Ethiopian state the institutional design was imported; it was not a product of Abyssinian values. Consequently, the workings of an administrative system based on a European model were alien to individuals from Abyssinia proper. Far from organizing such a system, without European "counterparts," Abyssinians were not prepared to utilize it efficiently to fulfill the values for which it was designed. Since Abyssinians were not privy to how the Europeans ruled their own colonies, it is not possible to say that Abyssinians devised the ministry system. It was devised by, and in large part for, the Europeans who took an interest in Ethiopia's functioning as an "independent" state on European terms.

In contrast is the case of settlers from industrial countries; transplanted groups who carried with them the outlook and the capacities of the capitalist system that produced them were able to secede from the sending power to form their own independently operating state. The dependent colonies were not able to do this, not because they would not like to, but because they did not have the know-how born of intimate familiarity with the values embodied

The Birth of a Dependent Colonial State

in the institutions—familiarity that would enable them to function independently.

Europeans who lived and worked in Ethiopia were intent on "stabilizing" the region and attracting business to the area for themselves. The corollary of this arrangement was that this type of administrative structure created a strong central government capable of reinforcing its own power by subduing any rebellion, whether by settlers attempting to secede from the agreement or national discontent in the colonies.

By the end of Menelik's era, two systems had begun to integrate for the purpose of ruling the empire. The settler (neftegna) system found its fullest expression in the colonies, being safeguarded by the imperial powers. The European system found its fullest expression in the forms of administration visible in the urban areas. In its very conception, however, it was a single hybrid system, and interpenetration was the hallmark.

As a result of the interaction of these systems a new form of social organization was introduced by the end of Menelik's era, one whose tenacity has been proven. It is a dependent colonial system. Within it a distinctive capitalist socioeconomic formation combined with an Abyssinian feudal socioeconomic formation to form a hybrid. All other types of autonomous polities that had functioned as modes of production in their own right were subordinated at conquest to form colonies, i.e., they were reduced to subjugated social formations elements of which were functional only in closely prescribed, largely local circumstances.*

All development of the infrastructure of the state was built starting from the period when the two forces met. Intensification began in earnest only after the British-supported Italians lost the Battle of Adwa to the French-supported Abyssinians. Only then did all governments of Europe begin to devise a different formula for

---

* The impact and form of this subjugation is the subject matter of a work in progress in which we argue that that elements of the subjugated social formations are generating new institutional forms capable of autonomy (Holcomb and Sisai forthcoming).

obtaining access and ensuring "security" in the region. Abyssinia's application to be considered as a different case was approved.

Organization of the Political Basis of the Dependent Colonial State

While the European economy and the monopoly capitalist class were expanding, Abyssinian rases and dejazmatches of different kingdoms were squabbling and struggling among themselves over relative positions in the Abyssinian tributary system. Most of the battles concerned who should be tribute payers and who tribute receivers.

European entrepreneurs, independent of and oblivious to these conflicts, arrived in the area carrying both samples of European products and prewritten treaties to be signed, bent on their own expansionist agenda. The Abyssinian rases and dejazmatches saw the arrival of Europeans both as an opportunity and as a solution to their immediate problems. They all sought advice and weaponry to further their own internal objectives. Since initially the entrepreneurs did not know who was who among the Abyssinians, most received what they asked for at the early stages of contact. By the same token, since the Abyssinians were not aware of the differences among the entrepreneurs, some signed the treaties or otherwise agreed to the conditions set by the Europeans for the acquisition of the weaponry and other equipment. The Abyssinians regarded particularly the guns as the critical ingredient in enabling them to seize power.

Eventually, however, the entrepreneurs, as products of societies that had used occupation and colonization of other countries as a means for solving their own internal conflicts, began to focus on the regions that produced the items most desirable in Europe. They turned special attention and advice toward the rases and dejazmatches of Manz and Tigray because of their location in relation to the sources of supply and the major trade routes. These Europeans were aware of the advantages of entering the productive regions not

132

The Birth of a Dependent Colonial State

only to raid and plunder for the desired resources, as was the pattern of the Abyssinians, but to occupy and colonize the supply regions in order to control them. The technology and advice of the Europeans gave rise to policies of conquest and occupation that were applied in regions to the south and east of Abyssinia. These initial acts of collusion and alignment of interest and technological capacity marked the genesis of Ethiopian settlement and dependent colonialism and set in motion the process of creating the conditions for the development of a new political entity in northeast Africa.

The interest of the European entrepreneurs from the time of their arrival was to create an enterprise and, acting as direct agents of the growing European capitalist class, to introduce ideas and activities that would further the interests of monopoly capitalists of their respective nations. These germinating ideas, as the seeds of capitalist formation, were brought into Abyssinia from outside during this time. This marked the introduction of the germs of capitalist institutions into the region and gave birth to the very idea of Ethiopia. The entrepreneurs introduced their own priorities, aligned them with those of the Abyssinians and provided the means to achieve both. The empire of Ethiopia never existed without the European component.

Take for example the introduction of the commodity that represented the interests of both—the introduction of guns. The training of people to acquire systematically, utilize and maintain the guns was necessitated by their import. The training of people meant, in turn, the introduction of specific characteristics of capitalist socioeconomic organization. For example, the weaponry itself introduced a particular mode of military organization on the model of a European military structure. This eventually required the introduction of European personnel. It was in the same manner that the transfer of several central features of the external system necessitated the introduction of other features. Eventually, even the dimensions of Abyssinian social organization that were expanded to extend to the newly acquired regions were changed fundamentally. Some features of Abyssinian society were retained in the colonies, but these were the trappings. The fundamental shape of the political structure was new, something that accommodated the capitalist needs as much as the Abyssinian. Ethiopia was as much a European creation as it was Abyssinian.

It is possible to trace the direct and indirect meshing of these interests and policies throughout the development of this new empire once this basic point is grasped. For example, when the Abyssinians were advised to do away with their slave-raiding, it was not without an alternative, the very system that was constructed in its place accomplished both the Abyssinian and European objectives, that is the policy of occupation. Occupation of the lands from which slaves had previously been taken allowed for a long-term control of both people and resources, a feat that the Abyssinians did not have as an objective nor the capacity to accomplish prior to the advent of European advice and direct participation.

The political collusion gave rise to the policies described above, policies which led to the building of the types of garrisons and to the creation of distinctions between towns and the rural countryside, and between settler colonists on the one hand and the conquered people of occupied territories on the other. The colonial relationship was introduced to accommodate the objectives of both equally. Europeans were quick to provide advice and equipment to introduce all the necessary infrastructure for communication and control, such as the building of roads, bridges, and trains, as well as the installation of telephone, telegraph and telegram only because these devices opened up the area to achieve the access and control necessary to advance the long-term strategies of European capitalists. They were intent upon linking this region with the global infrastructure of communication and transportation. All of these guaranteed the consolidation of the regions occupied and literally laid the groundwork for the incorporation of more colonial areas.

As the European advice was put into practice and as the infrastructure was in the process of being built and implemented, the real foundation of a new colonial empire was being laid down idea by idea, brick by brick, and piece by piece. Slowly the necessary elements or ingredients of (a) capitalist social formation and of (b) a settler colonial relation were formed.

134

The Birth of a Dependent Colonial State

Only with the introduction of an externally imposed social formation was the basis laid down for the uniform subordination of the conquered regions whose resources and people were the primary incentive for the Euro-Abyssinian alliance. The gun (from Europe) and the guncarrier (from Abyssinia) arrived in the colonies as one unit and this unit basically expresses political alliance that created the neftegna-gabbar relationship, the relation that lay at the heart of the emerging Ethiopian colonialism.

On that basis, a state apparatus was constructed by European ideology, utilizing a European model to hold the assemblage together by design. The essential and formative features were the products of a capitalist social formation. The Abyssinian features were organized around this formation's gridwork.

In actuality, then, it was in the name of first Abyssinia, then of Ethiopia, that Europeans built all the necessary dimensions of the administrative apparatus including defense, communication, security, etc. These central aspects were organized in a recognizable European model befitting the capitalist classes of Europe. Due to the specific conditions of conflict between major capitalist powers an arrangement was made for Abyssinians to fill the positions created by the formation of the state apparatus.

At the initial stages of development of the ministry system, though, Abyssinians were barely able to find their way around in the apparatus, let alone organize or be put in charge of affairs in any branch. They became at best functionaries assisting foreign bureaucrats who were the real state employees and masterminds behind each department. This arrangement served the interests of both Menelik and of the Europeans quite well. Furthermore, this formal structure marked the beginning of a systematic administrative center that successfully divided the city and rural communities and provided a mechanism for the cities to impose a form of control over the conquered indigenous people who resided in remote rural regions. The way the administration was established, it invited the participation and support of the contending factions of the aristocracy and of other peoples of the northern Abyssinian kingdoms. It also

The Invention of Ethiopia

provided an effective vehicle for dealing with the imperial powers whose support the new empire needed desperately.

In constructing a bureaucratic apparatus that could be operated in a manner familiar to and acceptable to European friends of Abyssinia and that was capable of housing or accommodating Abyssinian interests, the European capitalists and Abyssinian expansionists formed an intriguing alliance. Once the essential features of the administrative infrastructure was laid down according to the design of the advisers, foreign experts were called upon to supply the conceptual and technical know-how required to make the system function.

The Role of Foreign Advisers

Abyssinian social organization did not prepare its members to initiate or produce the framework this state apparatus, Abyssinians could not operate the new colonial system independent of the Europeans. This had nothing to do with innate ability of individuals, it had to do with the configuration of the society. It was not an extension of their social organization. At the beginning stages, the Europeans could not provide enough training to enable Abyssinians to assume management of the growing empire on their own. This bottleneck explains why the Abyssinians imported the expertise and skilled workers, personnel which could be called mental laborers, to do the job for them. In fact, within a relatively short time, Abyssinia came to rely on not only Europeans, but also on people who had been imbued with the ruling ideas in other colonial settings, Arabs, Indians and others. These latter were trained from experience in previous colonial settings.

The immigration of small and big businessmen began immediately after the Battle of Adwa and their role in developing new avenues for petty capitalism began to flourish. Each group within each foreign community began to carve out a specific role for itself. The Armenians became small-scale traders and artisans, Indians became merchants largely in textiles, manufactured goods and

The Birth of a Dependent Colonial State

several kinds of food stuffs, Arabs became merchants with broad-based commercial contracts, Greeks took on small business and artisans, such as goldsmiths, restaurateurs, cafe and shop owners, etc., and clerical employees in the Abyssinian banks. Members of the conquered nationalities of the empire were brought in to supply the labor force for these new endeavors; Abyssinians were rarely among them.

Nationals of the imperial powers, the architects of the state apparatus, had a particular division of labor. Pankhurst describes the breakdown as follows:

> The French, who were the most important of the smaller communities, were both wealthy and influential, and included several large traders, entrepreneurs and concession - holders. The Italians comprised some employees of the Ministry of Posts and Telegraphs, several architects and entrepreneurs, and two or three traders and hotel keepers. The Germans included a handful of concession holders, as well a small number of professional people, among them one or two doctors and a pharmacist, Hakim Zahn. The British community comprised the governor of the Bank of Abyssinia and several members of his staff, as well as a handful of merchants and missionaries, and was sufficently wealthy to collect donations for the purchase of two warplanes in World War I. The Swiss included several wealthy traders and concession holders, as well as an army instructor, C.R. Miller. The Egyptians consisted of the Abuna, or head of the church, several members of his entourage, and the teachers of the Menelik II School. The Syrians and Lebanese were mainly traders engaged in import-export business, the Afghans being also largely merchants. The Russians, as we have seen, consisted of several military officers, as well as some hospital doctors and an artist called Senigov (Parkhurst 1968: 63).

The Invention of Ethiopia

Britain encouraged the sending of personnel trained in her colonies because they would be capable of implementing a specifically British organizational design. The same would hold true for the other colonial powers. This explains why the increased numbers of non-Abyssinian employees arrived in Ethiopia immediately after the Battle of Adwa. The figures are available in Table 1.

The total number of foreign or expatriate employees increased from 205 individuals in 1906 to 1,096 in 1910. This represents an increment of 535 percent. Then from 1,096 in 1910 to 14,320 by 1935 represents a further increment of 1322 percent. Almost all the new positions were being filled by foreigners. This was an increment of 6450 percent from the base value derived in 1906. What does this mean? What does it say about the emerging political economic structures? It provides a graphic depiction of the dependent colonial state. As the table shows, the immigration was not at the higher job levels. Those types of jobs were reserved for personnel from the advanced imperial powers French, British, Italian, or the like. But the role of the work of lower clerks for whom positions expanded rapidly should not be underestimated. These positions were being occupied by the growing immigrant community.

Abyssinians did not and could not yet fill those positions or do those jobs for two major reasons. First, because they had not been trained and could not comprehend well enough what the Europeans were doing to be able to operate as efficiently in those positions as the expatriates. Second, large numbers of Abyssinians were playing a very different role. They took on the specific task of administering the conquered lands to consolidate control and to take advantage of the particular form of compensation offered there, land and laborers. As they moved into areas conquered to the east and south of Abyssinia, they were provided with land and tenants to work the land. They were engaged in a different dimension of establishing the dependent colonial state. They were armed and settled in the colonies and became responsible for overseeing the work of the indigenous people who had been made into tenants. Simply put, the Abyssinians who filled this kind of position developed a specific role of monitoring the day-to-day activities of the conquered peoples and

The Birth of a Dependent Colonial State

Table 1 Foreign Employees in Ethiopia

Nationality	1906	1910	1935
Greeks	65	334	3140
Arabs	?	227	4000
Indians	?	149	3000
Armenians	44	146	2800
French	35	63	350
Italians	21	42	350
Germans	12	20	
Hungarians	9	13	
Turks		15	20
Swiss	7	13	
Britain	6	14	75
Egyptians		11	60
Syrian/Lebanese		10	40
Afghans/Ba'uchis		8	
Portuguese, Goans		6	
Russian/Bulgarians		6	31
Caucasians		5	
American		3	103
Austrians		2	50
Belgians	5	1	28
Swedes		1	50
Georgians		1	
Danes	1		
Jews			125
Czechs			50
Japanese			4
Poles			2
Dutch			2
Chinese			2
Estonians			2
Lithuanians			1

Source: Pankhurst 1968: 62-65

The Invention of Ethiopia

establishing ways and means of bringing their labor and resources to the service of the new state. Their activities in this regard contributed to their developing a set of common interests and practices that set them on their way to becoming a distinct class.

Meanwhile the crown and the displaced Abyssinian aristocracy—the dislocated rases and dejazmatches—took on the special role of providing a facade in the capital and urban areas, setting in offices and meeting the public while expatriates ran the affairs of their departments.

By the end of the century the organization of the administrative apparatus had been completed. It was divided into five main bureaus which were called ministries. These were Justice, War, the Interior and Commerce; Finance and Agriculture; Public Works; Post and Telegraph; and Foreign Affairs.

By officially recognizing the initial infrastructures of the Abyssinian/Ethiopian state, the imperial powers of Europe were able to legitimize it as a dependent colonial state, a test case for the kind of model for the control by finance capital (usually referred to as neocolonialism) that was to flourish later throughout Africa.

The Ideological Basis for the Dependent Colonial State

The specific circumstances in which the set of ideas that constitute the ideology of Greater Ethiopia was generated have been described earlier in the chapter. These are the ideas that were formed in the process of creation of the empire itself, ideas were brought in by the participants who had an interest in the perpetuation of this new entity.

For example, the very notion that Ethiopia was an ancient kingdom that had merely been recognized *as is* by the Christian states of Europe did not originate with any Abyssinian. It was suggested in 1891 by Crispi, an Italian official to the Italian resident-agent in Addis Ababa, as part of a plan to have Menelik send a letter outlining the extent of his boundaries. Harold Marcus, who has provided this information from the Italian, has written,

140

The Birth of a Dependent Colonial State

Count Augustuo Salimbeni, the Italian Resident-Agent in Addis Ababa, received instructions from Francisco Crispi to inform Menelik that the European powers were establishing their boundaries in Africa and that the emperor should, with Italian assistance, circulate a letter defining his borders in order to guarantee the integrity of his empire. Crispi suggested that in the letter, Menelik ought to point out that Ethiopia was an ancient Kingdom which had been recognized as independent by the Christian states of Europe. Crispi thought that such a letter would help Menelik sustain his title in areas where Ethiopia had claims, but over which it did not exercise sovereignty. Menelik thought this idea a good one and asked Salimbeni to prepare the proposed letter. Salimbeni's draft circular than became the basis for Menelik's letter to the Powers, which was, however, distributed without the assistance of Italy (1969: fn271).

So even the key notion of claiming antiquity for the recently expanded Ethiopian boundaries was authored by an Italian whose country claimed a protectorate over Ethiopia and planned to extend her own territories by means of this ploy! The ploy was successful since the Italian's letter served as the basis for Menelik's famous circular letter to the powers, claiming the territories she aspired to control with European assistance. The rerouting of the letter itself was very likely planned with the collusion of Menelik's ever-present foreign adviser, Alfred Ilg.

As in the case cited, the Abyssinians did not originate most of the basic framework of Ethiopian ideology. Since its primary purpose at the initial stages was to ward off interference from specific European powers who aspired to control northeast Africa, many of the concepts were framed by one set of Europeans seeking greater influence against other Europeans. Each part of the ideology itself provides justification for the arrangements and the relationship between this part of Africa and Europe that the authors were trying to implement. For this reason a great portion of the colonial mythology of Ethiopia was generated for external consumption. The

The Invention of Ethiopia

Abyssinians have embellished it and updated it in each new era, but the essential components have remained constant.

Abyssinian society, though divided into numerous segments and kingdoms each led by a ras or a dejazmatch who considered himself independent, shared the same pattern of social organization, hence, ideology, whose base is to be found in the church. The values and behaviors understood to be appropriate were dictated according to the code of conduct produced by the Abyssinian traditions and protected by indigenous Abyssinian institutions. These institutions have been described in detail elsewhere (Hoben 1973, Levine 1965, Crummey 1972). What is of interest is that the institutions that formed the basis for the Ethiopian state were not structured according to Abyssinian norms nor enforced by means available to Abyssinian society prior to the arrival of Europeans.

It is undeniably a deeply held belief in Abyssinian society that Abyssinians entered the colonies and claimed the conquered territories by virtue of their superior mode of production. This idea forms the basis of the notion of Abyssinian feudal expansion. It is a central idea of Abyssinian rule in Ethiopia that Abyssinians were not only present in the colonies by their own right, but that they took with them their own institutions to conquer and to rule the colonies. Part of the ideological defense is the notion that Ethiopia was the only country that defended its independence against European colonialism. There has been in effect a challenge go up from Ethiopians backed by some international scholars that Ethiopia's so-called defeat of Europeans must be honored as a symbol of black competence. Those who would fail to accept this notion are subjected to a kind of ideological terrorism—accused of dishonoring black people in general. This has effectively silenced scholars who espouse liberal values. Such a threat, however, has ultimately accomplished the sequestering of many times over as many black nations who were victimized by Ethiopian mythology that denies their history.

The ideological arm of the new state largely consisted of institutions of education and propaganda which trained Abyssinians to acquire the knowledge necessary to operate the state, and pre-

The Birth of a Dependent Colonial State

pared some intellectuals to refine and publicize some kind of ideological defense of the new empire.

The creation of a dependent colonial state required a series of components to satisfy each group that harbored an interest there. This resulted in the building of an elaborate myth which each party that benefitted was willing to defend and elaborate.

The components of that myth at the outset were (1) a dependent state has to be all things to all people; (2) it is at the mercy of the monopolists, who demand that it fulfill all the requirements they have asserted for it yet say that their client did it; and (3) it is also the tool of the settlers who actually adopt a sense of superiority over the people of the colonies because they themselves do not understand how they came to be thrust into the superordinate position—they actually come to believe that they deserve to be where they are.

The Abyssinian settlers' contribution to Ethiopian mythology consists in part of the erroneous notions that their society had reached a superior evolutionary stage at the time of conquest, making them able to move in and take over Oromia and others conquered peoples. The illusion plays a critically important role in holding the entire complex together, the ideology of Greater Ethiopia.

The essential features of the ideology of Greater Ethiopia are

1) that Ethiopia is, above all, unique in Africa and the world
2) that her boundaries, though recently drawn, are sacred
3) that an ancient polity has survived intact into the present day only to be recognized in its pristine condition by members of the international community of nations
4) that the current state is the embodiment of that ancestoral unit
5) that the peoples within the current state have shared 3000 years of common history
6) that the peoples of the empire have intermarried and shared so many features of social and cultural life that they form one people, invisible
7) that during the nineteenth century, Abyssinian society represented an advanced level of social and economic organization in

143

comparison with the other peoples in northeast Africa, which gave it the capacity to expand under Menelik and share the benefits of a superior way of life with the neighboring, more primitive peoples

8) that Abyssinian influence and the extension of Abyssinian institutions to surrounding peoples constitute a beneficial civilizing force

9) that peoples resistant to this civilizing influence are backward, pagan, warlike, and hostile by nature; therefore, extreme measures in dealing with them are justified

10) that the conversion of resistant peoples to the ideological beliefs of the Abyssinian governors has a beneficial effect on the people themselves

11) that Eghiopia more than any other part of Africa symbolizes the power of black African people, because they resisted the tide of European conquest and preserved their ancient political institutions while others were collapsing.

The Ethiopian myth has been embellished as the state itself has grown, but its essential components have remained intact.

While this new kind of social organization was being fashioned and concretely materialized, the Shoan Amhara architect Menelik became ill. The new landlord group, the neftegna, and all rases and dejazmatches as well as the European powers who had an interest in the area, began wondering who would be the man who could guide them in the direction they had charted for the alliance. The actions taken and the battles that ensued reveal the clear alignment of forces that took an interest in the preservation of the formula that had been devised for control of this new empire.

4 THE DEPENDENT COLONIAL STATE IS TESTED: CHALLENGES FROM TAYTU AND IYASU

By 1904 a specific set of arrangements had been carefully worked out under Menelik's auspices that 1) ensured access to the region by Britain, France and Italy, 2) subjugated and established a firm military control over the lands and peoples of the productive regions surrounding the old Abyssinian heartland, 3) created a socioeconomic category of settlers to administer and to benefit from control of the colonies, and 4) fashioned a set of institutions whose purpose was to maintain that colonial relation. At the heart of the economic base of the new polity was the neftegna-gabbar relation, the critical distinction introduced between conquered and conqueror. As long as Menelik presided over the administration of this entity, it seemed secure.

Just at the time that all of the vital components for the experimental Ethiopian state had been put into place and a new form of social organization was being fashioned and implemented to assure its operation, however, the Shoan Amhara architect Menelik, became ill. This man had established a highly workable pattern of responsiveness to both European suggestion and input on how to shape the empire and to the influence of his wife Taytu who represented in the palace the interests and concerns of the northern Abyssinian aristocracy. At the same time he had safeguarded the basis for Shoan settler dominance, and had come to seem indispensable to each interest group. Subject to a series of debilitating strokes, each of which left him weaker than the previous one, Menelik could no longer serve as the indispensable focal point for success of the new system. Each group of beneficiaries of the Ethiopian system moved to secure its position in the case of Menelik's ultimate demise. In the ensuing conflict, the dependent colonial formula was put to a series of severe tests.

It had become known in the foreign community by 1904, when Menelik was examined by a French-trained doctor, Vitalien, that he was suffering the long-term effects of having contracted syphilis at an early age (Rosenfeld 1978 and Prouty 1986: 284). This knowledge caused considerable concern in the foreign diplomatic community, and forced the powers who had specific objectives in the region to take some action to guarantee their interests beyond the life span of this particular man. The timing of the Tripartite Treaty of 1906 among the great powers of Europe, as Britain, France and Italy called themselves, should be seen in this light also. Of course there were other pressing matters which instigated the framing of the Tripartite agreement, as discussed above. Primary among them was the issue of control over the railway which tested to its very foundation the matter of diplomatically resolving competing interests of monopoly powers at the turn of the century. The tension had mounted to such a crisis point that E. Work has written about the period of 1905, "The tension became so great that it was feared Addis Ababa might become the spot upon which some event would occur to disturb the peace of the world" (Work 1935: 314, citing E. rouard de Card). Also, in a major effort to forestall armed conflict, France and England had reached a general accord termed the entente cordiale, which focused a great deal of attention on the need to reach accommodation in regions such as Ethiopia where their interests clashed directly. The mounting threat posed by German willingness to move into Ethiopia and assist in the matter of completing the railway line caused great concern in Britain and France, highlighted by the arrival of a German diplomatic mission

146

The Dependent Colonial State Is Tested

in Addis Ababa in 1905. The additional factor of Menelik's ill health coming to light contributed to making this place at this time a critical pressure point for finding a solution to the European impasse. The prospect of losing the cooperation of an undisputed ruler was enough to transform this issue into a crucible for creative conflict management among the Europeans. Most of the year 1905, the Europeans were involved in negotiations over the issue of what they would do in the absence of Menelik (Work 1935: 317).

All who had an interest in the survival of the Ethiopian formula, the new landlord group, members of the northern aristocracy, as well as the European powers, began wondering who would be the person who could protect the direction they had charted, who could keep their alliance and the empire together long enough for it to prove a viable and secure foothold both locally and internationally.

At the first signs of weakness in the emperor, speculation became rampant. There were two issues that came to the fore. One was that Menelik needed some form of assistance to aid him personally in governing as his strength failed. The other was that a successor had to be named. Various conflicting steps were taken. A European-style cabinet composed of nine ministers who "had only the vaguest ideas about their responsibilities" (Marcus 1975: 228) was arranged with the objective of assisting him and later his heir. As he got weaker, Menelik assigned the role of prime minister over the other ministers of this cabinet to one of his highest ranking, shrewdest, and most trusted associates, Fitwrari (Fit.) Habte Giorgis.

Then by 1907 all attention focused on the traditional Abyssinian requirement that an heir, preferably male, succeed the monarch. Amidst a series of stroke-like incidents, Menelik remained lucid enough to name his own heir to the throne. Since he did not have a male child, in 1909 he finally designated the healthy son of one of his two daughters as his heir and ultimate successor "and presented him to the notables with an impassioned plea for their loyalty" (Perham 1969: 61). This was Lij Iyasu, the son of his daughter Shawa Ragga by Ras Mikael of Wollo. Lij Iyasu, however, was very young, only ten years old at the time of the decision. Consequently, a series of steps were taken to ensure that decisions could be made

The Invention of Ethiopia

on his behalf until he reached majority. A regent was named to govern in his place until that time and also a regency council was set up that drew on dignitaries from throughout the empire, mixing those who represented the northern and the Shoan settler interests.

Taytu's Challenge to Shoan-European Dominance

All of the contingent provisions for rule began to create conflict as Menelik became incapable of governing, but had not abdicated the throne in favor of the named heir. In 1909 governmental affairs were handled by a crown council that included the named so-called prime minister, the regent and guardian of the heir and the Empress Taytu who acted on her husband's behalf as the council's chair. Since this body drew on persons from all of the factions, the situation was ripe for a power struggle among the different internal groups eager to advance their interests and to take over the government in the developing power vacuum.

Empress Taytu, throughout her marriage to Menelik, had actively represented the interests of the northern aristocracy. She was a descendant of Ras Wube, a nobleman from Semien, probably of mixed Tigrayan and Amhara parentage. Her influence had been a contributing factor in making Menelik's rule successful. When placed in a position of what Marcus calls "de facto head of government" (1975:236) she immediately moved to establish northern dominance over the entire government, undermining Shoan advantage and, in effect, abandoning the balanced combination that had characterized Menelik's reign. She assembled a group of supporters who were willing to challenge Shoan privilege and she demonstrated open disdain for the European delegations who had held her husband's ear. She went so far as to attempt to block the public pronouncement of Iyasu as heir to Menelik (Marcus 1975: 236-7 and Prouty 1986: 322-331). This provided the occasion for both the Europeans and the Shoans to turn against her openly. She began to use various strategies to concentrate control of the empire into the hands of northern aristocracy and away from Shoan, such as remov-

The Dependent Colonial State Is Tested

ing Menelik's appointees and replacing them with her own men, arranging marriages that would tie powerful key people to her through traditional obligations. One of her attempts to block Iyasu's ascension to power was to play upon a deep-seated rivalry between Iyasu and Ras Makonnen's son Tefari by elevating the young Tefari to the governorship of Harar along with the title of dejazmatch. This put a highly ambitious peer in a better position to challenge Iyasu.

Ironically, however, Taytu's attempt to challenge the formula for dependent colonialism by shifting the internal power base to the north had the effect of consolidating Shoan strength and revealing how inflexible the combination really was. Her tactics provided a rallying point for pro-Shoan forces against her and focused Shoan political energies. Their basis for privilege had been constructed by Menelik and, in the face of the threat that Taytu posed, they began to realize where their interests lay. They were now prepared to move against any attempt to shift the balance of power from Shoa elsewhere.

Interestingly, through the period of internal struggle between Taytu and the Shoans who were led by the appointed guardian of the heir, Ras Tasamma, each side always punctuated its acts by informing the foreign legations, something that suggests that legation approval was recognized to be a necessary component for ultimate success. Indeed, when Taytu "tried to force the diplomats to bring all questions to her rather than to Habta Giorgis and Tasamma [the regent], which would have been 'a tacit acknowledgement by the Powers of her right to the supreme voice in Ethiopian affairs'" (Colli, the Italian representative, cited in Marcus 1975: 243), the Europeans met and agreed to refuse to accept her as head of state. Their official position was that they "could not intervene in the internal affairs of Ethiopia and that the empress should bow to the will of the people" (Love cited in Marcus 1975: 245). Information available in Prouty's detailed writing, however, indicates that this was only a public stance, since the primary legation chiefs "engaged in unabashed meddling in Ethiopian affairs" (Prouty 1986: 332). Taytu's final act in the face of a Shoan coup against her was to appeal to the European diplomats for support. They remained intransigent.

At the heart of the matter was whether or not the carefully-constructed Ethiopian empire was going to survive. The European refusal to accept Taytu as head of state gave the Shoans an opening to assert themselves and to establish self-conscious unity. From the point of view of European interest, it was Shoa that was located as the gateway to the productive colonies; no other Abyssinian region could offer that. It was Shoan Amhara who constituted the vast majority of the settler group in control of the colonial lands and peoples, their language and culture that had already been officially recognized by the state. It was they who could be counted on to maintain and protect the state in its present form, since they owed all of their benefits and privilege to its creation. Taytu's attempt to challenge that part of the formula only proved how strong that part of it was.

Taytu was officially ousted from power on the grounds that she had interfered with the work of the council headed by Ras Tasamma. The account of this event offered by Ras Tefari in his self-serving autobiography sheds some light on the way this was carried out.

A few days after my appointment to the governorship of Harar, all the nobles assembled in the house of the Archbishop, Abuna Mattewos, made very seditious charges against Empress Taitu and proffered advice, expressing their thoughts as follows: 'We do not want you to enter upon the affairs of government, but henceforth remain in the Palace looking after the sick [emperor].' But Empress Taitu had many partisans and consequently things remained in abeyance, because it caused difficulty to determine the matter. Empress Taitu was strong-willed and an expert in the art of ruling. At the time, I was an admirer of Empress Taitu's regal qualities. Since it was with her help that I had been appointed to the governorship of Harar, the nobles did not dare talk to me about it and reveal the matter.

The Dependent Colonial State Is Tested

After things had remained in abeyance, without a decision having been reached, for about 15 days, a meeting was called in the house of Fiawrari Habta Giorgis, and all of us were summoned on 11th Magabit (= 20th March 1910) and went there. Ras Bitwaddad Tasamma also came, summoned like the (other) noblemen, in order to let it appear that he had not entered upon the matter. Afterwards Fitawrari Habta Giorgis, being the spokesman of the meeting, declared: "We are not pleased about all the work which Empress Taitu is carrying out, and particularly about the appointments and dismissals. Only Dejazmatch Tefari's appointment to his father's governorship in Harar is fine and his alone may stand, but the remaining appointments and dismissals are to be cancelled. In future she is not to interfere with us in the business of government" (Haile Selassie 1976: 33-34).

This was agreed by all in attendance and the decision was conveyed to Taytu. Despite her objections and accusations that Tasamma had undermined her by inviting her to participate and then accused her of working without his knowledge, Tefari goes on to say, "Nevertheless the business of government—in accordance with the decision taken in the house of Fitawrari Habta Giorgis—was transferred in full into the hands of Ras Bitwaddad Tasamma and began to be carried out by him" (ibid.).

Taytu was thus placed under house arrest by the Shoan group who still met in secret and forced to be at the side of her husband, acting only to care for his physical needs in his last years. The Shoans together with those who had taken up the cause of pushing Taytu out of power (a group which included a key Tigrayan nobleman, Dejazmatch Gebre Selassie) systematically replaced all of her appointments, and established primarily loyal Shoans back into the administrative structure (for specifics see Marcus 1975: 247). Prouty refers to the "dismantling of the 'Taytu network,'" including even the dissolution of the marriages that she had forced upon people to extend her influence (Prouty 1986: 333).

The Invention of Ethiopia

Characteristically, the younger Shoan elite who had led the coup against Taytu had one overriding interest—they wanted to be named to the government positions vacated by the deposed northern sympathizers. This premier aspiration of settlers who have acquired their benefits from the state itself, made its first appearance at the time of transition from the Menelik government to the subsequent regime. It is a feature that has remained an enduring one in the transfer of power from one group of state beneficiaries to another in this empire.

Iyasu's Attempts to Alter the Dependent Colonial Prescription

Though Taytu had been effectively removed from power, Menelik lingered on, alive but without the mental or physical capacities even to formally abdicate power. For a year, Iyasu's regent, Ras Tesemma, governed in both of their places. As it turned out, the Shoan elite, both young and old, who had successfully risen up against Taytu's efforts to challenge their coveted position of privilege did so in the name of defending Menelik's legacy and Menelik's chosen heir. Fit. Habta Giorgis, Menelik's loyal minister of war, an assimilated man himself, summarized in a clear statement the position of the upper echelon Shoan settler elite (mekwannint) and their supporters,

> Lij Iyasu is the designated and recognized inheritor of the Ethiopian throne. The Wellos and the Amhara have agreed to conform to the desire of the king, to accept and support Iyasu. The pact between the mekwannint [proud members of the ruling elite] is sufficient to maintain the present dynasty on the throne; as for the people, there is no need to worry about them; they will follow. The Gojjamis, men of Kafa, Tigreans, inhabitants of Jimma, the Arussi, the people of Sidamo, Borena, Harar, and Gondar, in a word, those [in the] conquered regions are not to be feared, If

The Dependent Colonial State Is Tested

they arouse themselves, which is likely, we, the true Ethiopians ... will be strong enough to reduce them to silence and restore them to our domination ... if it takes ten years for that, we will take ten years; but at the moment we are assured that the real Abyssinians would never recognize any master other than the one designated by the Emperor; we do not doubt final success (cited in Marcus 1975: 237) [emphasis added]

This statement is a clear revelation of who considered themselves to be the "true Ethiopians"—those who were capable of reducing the conquered regions to silence and restoring them to "Ethiopian" dominion.

This position struck an effective posture as long as one of the loyal members of this elite corps ruled as regent, i. e., Ras Tasamma, who himself had been chosen by Menelik. But anything that threatened this arrangement was directly dealt with. Ras Tasamma himself realized that during her short period of influence, Taytu had planted the seeds for the undoing of Iyasu by elevating Iyasu's boyhood rival, Tefari, to the governorship of Harar. Ras Tasamma took the step of bringing the two boys and their counsellors together to safeguard Iyasu's, and by extension, his own, position from foul play. Tefari reported that

... it was Ras Bitwaddad Tasamma's plan to cause Ledj Iyasu and me to enter into a covenant and thus prevent anything from happening that might be an obstacle in his work. Thus he took me and my father's senior officers to the house of the Archbishop, Abuna Mattewos, and all of us entered upon the following covenant with oaths and invocations:

(1) That I would not seek, by trickery or rivalry, Ledj Iyasu's throne.

(2) That my officers would not give me bad advice to seize Ledj Iyasu's throne.

The Invention of Ethiopia

(3) That Ledj Iyasu, looking upon me with eyes of rivalry, would not depose me from my father's governorate of Harar.

(4) That Ras Tasamma, by giving bad and deceitful advice to Ledj Iyasu, would not dismiss me from the governorship of Harar and would not bring about my destruction on account of my (alleged) rivalry (Haile Selassie 1976: 35).

In light of subsequent events, it is quite significant that Ras Tasamma found such a covenant to be necessary. Tasamma's opportunities to secure rule for his group in the name of Iyasu ended shortly thereafter with his death in 1911.

Ras Tasamma's death immediately raised the issues of who might become the next regent and guardian, who would be entitled to make the appointment, whether Lij Iyasu would accept a guardian at all, and whether the neftegna would allow Iyasu to rule. It was soon disclosed that the Shoan elite, despite avowed loyalty to Menelik, strongly disapproved of his choice as successor. It had not been long since the Oromo great-grandfather of this youth had seriously threatened to dismember the Abyssinian socioeconomic system. Opposition to him had formed the basis for the first Abyssinian confederacy, the one which European-provided arms had made possible. These events had not been forgotten in the least. Menelik's plea for loyalty to Iyasu at the time of the boy's selection was matched with the curse that "anyone who turns against my grandson shall give birth to a black dog." Such measures reflect his awareness that his choice would not be a popular one. And indeed it was not.

The leaderless council faced the practical dilemma of how to handle or avoid the transfer of power to Iyasu. Their solution took the form of a ploy to prevent Iyasu from assuming full, legitimate power until the physical death of the emperor who remained alive but completely incapacitated. Rumors were spread and public opinion influenced to the effect that it would be disloyal and insulting to Menelik for the coronation of his successor to take place prior to his funeral. This tactic of Iyasu's opponents was effective in

The Dependent Colonial State Is Tested

preventing him from assuming power. Public opinion shifted to their side on the matter and plans for the inauguration of Lij Iyasu were officially postponed until the death of his grandfather. The appointed heir was granted no legitimate right for decisionmaking.

In the Annual Report of 1912 of Wilfred Thesiger, British Consulate officer in Ethiopia, Thesiger had the following observations to make to the British Foreign Office concerning the situation of Lij Iyasu,

> Lij Yasu's [sic] position was thus one of responsibility without power, and it soon became obvious that the council of Ministers, while determined to keep as much of the real power as possible in their own hands, while endeavoring to place on his shoulders in odium of deciding all those questions which they themselves had not the courage to face (Thesiger to Grey 1912: 2).

In the same report, Thesiger went on to point out that

> Lij Yasu, however, was evidently not disposed to accept any longer the unenviable position of a puppet in the hands of his ministers, and early in the year he suddenly announced his intention of visiting his father, Ras Mikail, at Dessie (ibid).

Not surprisingly, his decision to leave town elicited protests from the council members, who demanded that he stay at his job. Iyasu, who had just witnessed the success of the Shoan intrigue to confine Taytu to house arrest, was determined to demonstrate his autonomy, his freedom, his abilities and his manhood. He ignored their demands and proceeded as planned, arguing that they were the ones who had retained the decision-making position, so they should be the ones to stay in town. He went on to visit his father, went hunting, travelled widely (to the west side of the empire) and went to war, leading a battle between Abyssinia and the government of Sudan at Odonga in which two British officers lost their lives. These

The Invention of Ethiopia

activities were ones which appealed to Oromo standards for earning public respect and for proving a man's maturity and capability for leadership. Having accomplished these feats identified with manhood, Iyasu returned to Addis Ababa full of confidence. The inhabitants of the regions through which he travelled were not the only ones who were impressed. In the conclusion of his report Thesiger stated that "... the boy has returned a man. He has, I think, clearly shown that he will not be content to be a possive in the hands of his advisers, and for good or ill to take a line of his own" (ibid). Iyasu emerged to be recognized as his own person.

Iyasu returned to a government in complete disarray. In Addis Ababa, the council that had never been set up for administration had failed badly. In Thesiger's view,

> ... everything has fallen into arrears, and corruption of the officials has reached a point which has been hitherto undreamt of. The finances of the country are in disorder and the country is in a general state of discontent.... To remedy this condition of affairs Lij Iyasu will need strong officials and a definite system of reform, and it is difficult to see where either are to be obtained (Thesiger to Grey, 1913 January 7, Addis Ababa).

This period was significant because it revealed how completely dependent the central government was on the revenues from the colonies. Salaries were not paid, corruption became commonplace and foreign affairs suffered (Marcus 1975: 250). It became clear what happened when the Shoan neftegna were not held in tight control under a government to their liking—simply the taxes were not paid. Without the revenues extracted from the southern colonies of Oromia, Sidama, Kaffa, etc., the state ceased to function.

Having just returned from the outlying areas of the empire, Iyasu's perspective on the needed reforms that Thesiger refers to was bound to be different from the perspective of those who had remained in the capital, even had all else been equal.

The Dependent Colonial State Is Tested

All else was not equal, however, and through the process of achieving what he had been taught by his father was necessary to rule, Iyasu had accumulated a relatively diverse experience within the empire. Away from the capital he had witnessed the battles of warlords and the oppression of peoples based upon national and religious differences. He returned to Addis Ababa with notions of what kind of changes were necessary—notions that were very different from those of the council who were trying to keep state power in the hands of the Shoan elite.

Changes of the kind that Iyasu began to pursue, such as reconciliation of national and religious distinctions which led to oppression, required not only reform, but the assistance of an external power. In that year, 1913, there were two camps emerging in Europe, as discussed in Chapter II. The Allied powers, who together with the Shoan settler group had shaped the Ethiopian state as Iyasu had found it, and the Entente powers. The two world forces were aligning for a major global confrontation. Ethiopia was not exempt as an arena in which the tensions were acted out. Unlike the Shoan group that was already committed to the Allied powers, Iyasu took a neutral position on the global conflict. He viewed the position of the powers in terms of how their support might affect his efforts to redress some of the imbalances he had encountered in the empire. His failure to declare loyalty openly to the Allies was another of several issues that separated him from the Shoan elite.

Eager to implement the changes he envisioned, Iyasu finally took power with the backing of Menelik's loyalists when the death of his grandfather was made known. Ultimately, however, Menelik's heir himself did not honor or commit himself to protect the interests of those loyalists who considered themselves "true Ethiopians" in the sense Fit. Habta Giorgis used the phrase in his speech of support. And in the final analysis, Iyasu's short period of rule became a test of whether or not the Ethiopian dependent colonial prescription could be tinkered with by anybody, even the designated heir of the renowned architect of that empire.

The entire system was tested again when Lij Iyasu came into power. From the outset, he became clear that his concerns were

The Invention of Ethiopia

quite different from those of the Shoan establishment. He carried out the job with a great deal of independent decision-making, independent of the forces involved in the designing of the empire, and consequently played a significant historical role.

If there was any radical attempt to change the direction of that empire it came from Lij Iyasu. His actions, whether economic, political or ideological, were contrary to the European-Abyssinian establishment.

Initially, Iyasu was intent upon reform. He desired to do away with the religious and national distinctions that prevailed in the empire, he continued to leave the capital for long periods and began to build a foundation for some kind of national unity on a different model from that which was already in place and to establish a base of support different from that of the Shoan establishment. Chris Prouty reports that Iyasu "held many informal talks with people of all faiths showing compassion and interest in all his people, whether Christian, Muslim, pagan, northerners or southerners. [H]e won their liking and forgiveness for his personal foibles, which they attributed to his youth" (1986: 339, citing Brice and de Coppet). Marcus cites one Italian observer who wrote, "Lij Eyyasu [sic] had met with more sympathy from the population than from the chiefs, many of whom have been punished for their hostility and taken in chains to Addis Ababa" (1975: 258), and one "well-placed Ethiopian partisan" who commented that the prince would "astonish everyone by his intelligence and by his system of government, which would be carried out according to some European criteria with justice, especially for the Galla [Oromo] population" (ibid.).

As Iyasu built churches for the Christians, so did he build mosques for the Muslims. He began to take away land that had been confiscated from the indigenous people and gave it back to the them. He expressed the sentiment that Ethiopia be made for all Ethiopians; if Ethiopia were composed of Moslems as well as Christian, and if the Ethiopian flag represented the symbol of the people, then he saw no reason for the Ethiopian flag to have a cross but not a crescent. So he approved of a flag with a crescent as well as a flag with a cross, and with Arabic as well as Ge'ez. He saw no

The Dependent Colonial State Is Tested

reason why the Oromos, the Somalis, the Afars, etc., could not carry guns if the Abyssinians were allowed to carry them; so he gave them guns. He saw no reason why the Abyssinians and the Allied legations enjoyed freedom of expression while other foreigners and the indigenous were not granted the freedom of speech. So he announced his willingness to work with any foreign power who would support his program. Consequently, the Allied began to consider him dangerous, while the Entente powers regarded him as a democrat.

Since the imperial powers had cordoned off a specified territory, that is, the land mass of the empire protected by the agreement of France, Britain and Italy, they reacted strongly when Lij Iyasu immediately challenged their role and the sacredness of their boundaries. Harold Marcus reports that ". . . Iyasu saw an opportunity to unite Somalis and Ethiopians to eject the hated colonizers" (Marcus 1987: 14), an indication that he did not recognize the essentially "untouchable" nature of the boundaries drawn by the Europeans. Furthermore, the wishes of the foreign diplomats to have matters taken care of quickly were ignored by Iyasu who spent more time in the rural areas than in the capital.

Iyasu spent a great deal of time trying to prove that he had respect for Islam, and he showed sympathy to the Central Powers' promises to unite Muslims in the region if victorious in the World War that was building up. His public show of support for Islam, together with his openness to discuss the German-Turkish plans for Moslems in the region, further alienated those Europeans who had powerful interests in maintaining Ethiopia according to the formula reiterated above. He introduced a ". . . policy of equality between Muslim and Christian . . . " (ibid.). This political act greatly alarmed Allied Europeans and Abyssinians because it struck at the heart of their alliance. By this act he was treading on sacred distinctions between Abyssinian Christians as rulers and others as subjects that had already become part of the new Ethiopian mythology. In Abyssinian politics this was akin to thrusting a dagger into the heart of the neftegnas. They had established religion as an ideological

The Invention of Ethiopia

weapon to retain control. To challenge this was to trample on a key element in the ideological basis for dominance in Ethiopia.

Economically also Iyasu had created much opposition among those who benefitted from the existing Euro-Abyssinian alliance. His changes threatened the relation which stood at the very heart of the economic base, the neftegna-gabbar relation. He turned upside down the decree of his grandfather that "all conquered land belongs to the crown and all conquered people are subjects of the crown." He openly opposed the neftegna-gabbar system that had generated the new and dominant relations of production in the empire. Since the introduction of this new system had generated a process of labor exploitation that made the empire rich, it was feared by those who benefitted directly from this arrangement that Iyasu's plan might liberate the laborers. They had cause for concern. Iyasu felt that people should be made to be equal and that somehow that change should be guaranteed. Iyasu had introduced the regular taxation of neftegna not only in the conquered regions of the empire, but also established tax rates for land and property in the capital, Addis Ababa, where most of the big landholders resided (Marcus 1975: 269). By recognizing and sympathizing with Oromos and Muslims as groups that deserved to have rights protected by the state, by raising the taxes of the neftegnas, and by sending Shoan administrators to Addis Ababa in chains, he threatened to eliminate the basis for their privilege. He was tinkering with the critical distinction between conquered and conqueror, and between neftegna and gabbar.

In the final analysis, as he demonstrated while in Harar (see Marcus 1987: 13-16), and in fact in all his activities (ibid pp.13-58) during his period in power, Iyasu was in his own way exhibiting anti-imperialist behavior and indicating that he was against empire-building. Iyasu explained to an Italian in the country during his reign

> that he sought to reduce the tyranny under which Muslims lived and to lessen the exploitation they suffered. He wanted to transform himself into a more national and neutral

The Dependent Colonial State Is Tested

figure, not inflexibly identified with the Christian ruling caste. He wanted to reconcile Ethiopia's Muslims to their Christian compatriots, thereby reducing the country's chronic unrest, benefiting the economy, and permitting a program of modernization. He sought to release the energies of his empire's Muslim population which [he said] "up to now has been abandoned and persecuted." He offered them brotherhood: "though we differ in religion and tribe, I would wish all of us to be united through a nationalist sentiment ... cooperation with the rest of your Ethiopian brothers and sisters will keep your country united and her frontiers secure" (cited in Marcus 1987 :15).

When Iyasu had taken charge, he began replacing several people in positions that could enable him to implement his new programs without heeding the advice of those both Abyssinian and European who had worked so successfully behind the scenes in his grandfather's government.

This period, as stated earlier, was the period during which the European countries were organizing allies for the First World War. It was when Iyasu ultimately threatened to reach beyond the cozy alliance that Abyssinia had formed with Britain, France and Italy to create a relationship with the enemies of the Allied forces that he provided the opportunity for his enemies to force him out. In short, Ethiopia's secure niche under the wing of the Tripartite Treaty powers was threatened by Iyasu because he believed that Austria-Hungary, Germany and Turkey could be his allies in carrying out his new programs. This was a major blow to the foundation of the politics of this empire. In fact this was the last straw and the basis on which the Abyssinians were able to rally Britain and France to oust him. His sympathy with Germany, Austria, and Turkey alarmed the Allied countries, and prompted their representatives to issue a warning and a promise to strengthen the hands of those who opposed Iyasu.

All the while Iyasu was engaged in attempting quite dramatic reforms, the settler-neftegna group led by Dejazmatch Tefari was

161

The Invention of Ethiopia

compiling a case against him to take to the Allies. Tefari seized the opportunity to treat the breach with the Allies as Iyasu's critical lapse and even decades later, recounting the event of Iyasu's disposition from power, he recalled the Allies complaint against Iyasu as the deciding blow in the eyes of "the leaders of Ethiopia." To use Tefari's own words,

> At the time of the Great World War, when some foreigners presented to him (ledj Iyasu) their view: "even though you cannot help the English, the French, and the Italians, who are Ethiopia's neighbours at the frontiers, with armed force, it would be good if you would at least assist with provisions, i.e. with food," yet he did not listen. Instead, he had begun on an exchange of secret correspondence with the peoples surrounding Ethiopia, the Adalites and the Somalis, with a view to resisting the Allies. But as the representatives of the three governments resident at Addis Ababa had discovered the exchange of secret letters, they made an official approach and, it is reported, presented [the correspondence] to Bitawaddad Hayla Giorgis.
>
> When the leaders of Ethiopia found out about this whole affair, they became convinced of the need to depose Ledj Iyasu (1976: 46).

Here it is clear that while the political, religious and economic activities that Iyasu became engaged in had already antagonized the Abyssinian ruling class, it was when the Europeans rose up against him intent on maintaining the status quo in the new empire that the Shoans made their move. Both the Europeans and Abyssinian settlers could see and feared that Iyasu was in effect leading an attack against dependent colonialism. Iyasu did not last long, due for the most part to a European advised and Shoan-led conspiracy against him. In agreement they waged a coup.

It was in bringing down Iyasu that young Ras Tefari (later to become Haile Selassie) saw his opportunity. In the midst of the political confusion, Tefari began to execute a long-term ambition.

The Dependent Colonial State Is Tested

His advisers lined up behind him to carry it forth. Tefari, who had seen the direction of Iyasu and who knew that Iyasu's policies were heading toward a fatal reversal of key components in the Ethiopian formula, kept up with him by reporting and distorting his every move, by spreading rumors and by sending information about Iyasu to key persons. The face that Tefari presented to the officials, however, was that of most intelligent, humble man, who submitted to the appropriate powers and who was qualified in every detail, even married according to the requirements to step in to fill Iyasu's position should it be vacated.

The "leaders of Ethiopia" that Tefari wrote about were the self-appointed Shoan neftegna group conspiring to defend and to save their own particular formula for government, the one that Iyasu was bent on tampering with. Tefari describes their manner of conspiracy,

> But as it appeared to them likely that their secret would be betrayed if they were assembled together for consultation, they chose servants as trusted messengers and began to correspond through them as go-betweens. But some met by night at a hidden place and after talking to each other face-to-face, separated again ... the party which approved of Ledj Iyasu's deposition began to grow steadily (ibid).

It was a classic Abyssinian coup, conducted for the most part by rumor, circulation of unverified—and unverifiable—stories which played upon the fears of the participants, psychological warfare, and intimidation. Tefari not only leaked what damaging information could be had about Iyasu, but he was the source of many falsehoods that were disseminated. Interestingly, the accounts that exist of this period contain very little eyewitness testimony of events that were alleged to have taken place. Documentation, such as it is, consists of letters written by Europeans present in the empire, primarily in the capital city during that time who got most of their information selectively from Abyssinians interested in a particular outcome. Ras Tefari turns out to have been the source in several cases where stories are traceable.

The Invention of Ethiopia

Dejazmatch Tefari proceeded primarily by agitating and distributing rumors to two key groups. Stories that Iyasu was organizing the indigenous peoples against the interests of the "Ethiopians" were exaggerated and embellished for neftegna listeners. These were not enough to be successful by themselves, however.

But when finally additional rumors that Iyasu had staged some kind of "demonstration" in support of the Entente and that the Austro-Hungarian, German and Turkish alliance supported Iyasu's actions were passed to Abyssinia's European friends, that was when Iyasu's fate was sealed.

The actual charges against Iyasu were read out at a meeting in the palace. Tefari has provided a full listing of Iyasu's "crimes,"

On the 17th day of Maskaram 1909 (= 27th Sept. 1916), on the day of the great feast of Masqal, it was arranged that the nobles with the army, and the Archbishop Abuna Mattewos, and the Etchage Walda Giyorgis with the priests, should assemble at a prepared place with in the precincts of the Palace and when they had all arrived and taken their seat according to their rank, the following indictment against Ledj Iyasu, which had been secretly prepared, was read out:

The Christian faith, which our fathers had hitherto carefully retained by fighting for their faith with the Muslims and by shedding their blood, Ledj Iyasu exchanged for the Muslim religion and aroused commotion in our midst; in order to exterminate us by mutual fighting he has converted to Islam and, therefore, we shall henceforth not submit to him; we shall not place a Muslim king on the throne of a Christian king; we have ample proof of his conversion to Islam:

(1) He married four wives claiming: "the Qur'an permits it to me." Of these wives one is the daughter of Abba Jiffar of the Jimma nobility; the second is the daughter of Hajj Abdullahi of the Harar nobility; the third is the daugh-

ter of Abu Bakr of the Adal nobility; the father of the fourth, Dejatch Djote, became a Christian and baptized his daughter; while she lived under her baptismal name Askala Maryam, it was to Dejatch Djote's daughter that he (Ledj Iyasu) later on, after his conversion to Islam, gave the Muslim woman's name of Momina.

(2) He built a mosque at Jijjiga with government funds and gave it to the Muslims.

(3) At that time he sent to Mahazar Bey, the foreign [Turkish] consul resident at Addis Ababa—as he was celebrating the Ramadan Feast—our Ethiopian flag (on which there was written "The Lion of Judah has prevailed" and adorned with the sign of the Cross) on which he had caused to be written the following words (in Arabic): "There is no god but Allah and Muhammad is the messenger of Allah."

(4) He wore Somali Muslim clothes and the Muslim turban, held the Islamic rosary, and was seen to prostrate himself in the mosque.

(5) He was seen praying and reading the Qur'an, having had it transcribed in Amharic characters.

(6) On the headgear of had special guards he had embroidered the legend "there is no god but Allah."

(7) H. H. Ras Makonnen had built a church at Harar and had made the area adjoining the church into a dwelling for the clergy, giving the Muslims a place in exchange; then, 32 years later, he (Ledj Iyasu) expelled the clergy and restored it to the Muslims.

(8) When a girl was born to him he saw to it that she would grow up learning the Muslim religion, and he gave her to the Muslim Madame Hanafi and said: "Bring her up on my behalf."

(9) He despised the descent of Menelik II, which comes direct from Menelik I, and claimed to be descended from the Prophet Muhammad; assembling the great Muslim sheikhs he spent the day convincing them of his genealogical calculations.

The Invention of Ethiopia

(10) The day on which our great king, Emperor Menelik, who had bequeathed him the throne, died, instead of mourning and of arranging lamentations he went out horse riding to Jan-Meda and spent the day playing combat games. He forbade Menelik's body to be buried with dignity and thus it has remained up to now. We possess a great deal of similar proof (against Ledj Iyasu) (Haile Selassie 1976:48-49).

Iyasu saw this all too late and did not move against it soon enough. The coup took place before he implemented an adequate retaliation.

Attention turned to finding a replacement for Iyasu. Since Menelik himself had selected Iyasu as his successor, replacing him was a major challenge and responsibility on the shoulders of the king's council. When they had finally acknowledged that Iyasu could no longer be sustained in power, Fit. Habta Giorgis, then the minister of war and appointed by Menelik earlier to serve as "chief" among ministers, came forward as the most powerful decisionmaker. Fit. Habta Giorgis asked Iyasu to come to Addis to explain himself. When Iyasu refused to do so it has been said that Habta Giorgis has called upon the traditional mahal sefari to assist him. The mahal sefari were a group of respected "elders," experienced members of the interest group, who were basically empowered to give impartial decisions on important matters, but whose opinions had no legal impact. This is the group that was called upon to make suggestions for a successor to the throne out of Sahale Selassie's line.

In response to this call, the counsellors put forward thirty-two names of ostensibly qualified individuals. During the search, a French consultant and tutor for Tefari suggested that his name be entered into the campaign. All thirty-two, including Tefari's, were rejected by Habta Giorgis in the first round of consideration on one basis or another. Thinking that Habta Giorgis might have rejected the others because he preferred to have the position for himself, the council requested that Habta Giorgis himself takeover. Habta Giorgis rejected this suggestion as well on the ground that he had

The Dependent Colonial State Is Tested

been prisoner of war and that he was the son of a family that had been made slaves. He said "the crown won't be becoming on us."

When Tefari heard about this decision and learned that influential opinionmakers were reopening their search for a successor to Iyasu, Tefari came up with a new plan. He acted upon a suggestion from his French counselor and tutor that he needed to secure the attention of Habta Giorgis through private channels. According to K. Teferi (1987), an eyewitness who was present in the palace, the intrigue went like this: Tefari's new scheme was to approach the (Elifingi Askalkaye) the private secretary of Menelik, who had been a good friend of Tefari's father, Makonnen. This man knew someone who could take a message to Habta Giorgis.

He located a Dejazmatch Beyene, a friend of Habta Giorgis' son-in-law Dejazmatch Seyoum who had a longstanding grudge against Iyasu dating back to a time when Iyasu had had an affair with Beyene's wife. Drawing on this perfect contradiction, Tefari approached Dejazmatch Beyene and convinced him to tell Dejazmatch Seyoum the following rumor: that Menelik had actually planned to pass the crown to Ras Makonnen, Tefari's father. This would set up a route of legitimacy for Tefari to receive serious consideration during the second round of discussion. Beyene agreed to cooperate, not because he was convinced that there was any truth to the story, but because of his personal antipathy for Iyasu. He wanted to see Iyasu destroyed and replaced. Beyene's cooperation in planting the seed of suggestion with Dejazmatch Seyoum was convincing enough that it brought Fit. Habta Giorgis to reason that had Makonnen lived he could logically have taken the crown. Had he died after taking the crown, Tefari could conceivably be eligible. Since both Makonnen and Makonnen's only other son Dejazmatch Yilma had died, Tefari was perceived to be a legitimate successor. Using this logic as a basis to justify response to pressure from both the Allies and the Shoan group to select a candidate acceptable to them, Habta Giorgis reached his decision and presented the counselors with its merits. Tefari's plan was successful. They agreed to accept Tefari as regent and successor to the throne, with Zewditu on the throne, a mere figurehead.

The Invention of Ethiopia

The final words of the indictment and deposition of Iyasu were made to read

> Therefore, having deposed him (Ledj Iyasu), we have placed on the throne Wayzaro Zawditu, Emperor Menelik's daughter. We have appointed Dejazmatch Tafari, the son of H. H. Ras Makonnen, Crown Prince, with the rank of Ras, and Regent of the Empire (Haile Selassie 1976:48-49).

Zewditu was also asked to divorce her husband who was the governor of Begemeder, Ras Gugsa. Apparently the Shoan mekwannint were afraid that he might find an angle to become king and they did not want the crown to get out of Shoan hands. Zewditu agreed to divorce her Gondari husband and thus became the empress. Tefari moved into position as her heir.

Tefari described their division of work as follows,

> But God in his goodness had caused Ledj Iyasu to be deposed and us to be chosen, Queen Zawditu to Ethiopia's crown and throne and me as Ethiopia's crown Prince and Regent Plenipotentiary, we marvelled at this and lived in amity and concord.
>
> Previous to that, on 17th Maskaram 1909 (= 27th September 1916), the officers with the troops, the Archbishop and the Etchage with the priests, being assembled together and proffering advice, while choosing the Queen for crown and throne and me for the succession to the throne and the regency plenipotentiary, had defined for us the following allocation of duties for our establishment and our work:
>
> (1) That the Queen should take the honor of Crown and Throne and be Called Queen of Queens;
>
> (2) That I, being called Crown Prince of Ethiopia, should take the regency plenipotentiary and carry out in full all the work of the government;

The Dependent Colonial State Is Tested

(3) That I, selecting the officers of the army, should appoint and dismiss them;

(4) That I, sitting in Court, should judge all the civil and criminal appeals which the judges had handed down in the first instance;

(5) That I should conclude by negotiations any matters whatsoever concerning relations with foreign governments (Haile Selassie 1976: 63).

The selection of Zewditu as successor to Iyasu is probably best understood in light of her unimpeachable bloodline, the fact that there was antipathy between her and Iyasu which would prevent any attempt on his part to reclaim the throne through her cooperation, and the fact that she was a malleable figurehead who posed no threat to the council. To place Tefari directly on the throne would have aroused problems, particularly among the northern faction who still held key positions. Tefari's position gave him full powers to clear the way for his own ascension, which he used to full effect.

This coup and the compromise political arrangements made in secret were not immediately accepted throughout the empire by any means. An attempt to arrest Lij Iyasu himself in Harar failed, but troops from Addis Ababa were able to enter and take over the city of Harar, causing Iyasu to flee as a fugitive. Iyasu's father, Negus Mikail, gathered forces largely from Wollo and marched to Addis Ababa to challenge this group who had resorted to this coup d'etat against his son. Expecting Iyasu to challenge the move from Harar, Mikail was slow enough in arriving that Tefari had the time to gather a Shoan force to meet him at Sagale, north of Addis Ababa. The new government was baptized with the blood of 20,000 soldiers from Wollo, 12,000 Shoans and incalculable numbers of maimed and wounded (Marcus 1975: 280). The Shoans were victorious and Iyasu's father Negus Mikail was captured at Sagale to be marched through the streets of Addis Ababa in chains, forced to show submission to the new government.

The Invention of Ethiopia

The first order of business after Zewditu's coronation ceremony was the dismissal of all of Iyasu's ministers who had not collaborated in the coup and the appointment of new loyalists in their places.

Iyasu's brief reign was ended. Both his attempts and those of Taytu to tamper with the dependent colonial model upon which Ethiopia had been built turned out to be the exceptions that proved how rigid these rules really were.

Having moved into the coveted central position, the man later known as Haile Selassie began to plan to secure political power in his own hands. He had already proven that he knew where the power lay that kept the empire together and that his most outstanding characteristic was deliberate and painstaking planning. Nowhere was it more evident than in the way he next planned to seize the emperor's throne.

5 STATE CONSOLIDATION DURING THE PERIOD OF HAILE SELASSIE, 1916-1944

Ras Tefari Comes to Power

After Ras Tefari had planned and executed a successful coup d'état against Lij Iyasu and a series of moves that placed him into the position of crown prince, Tefari's preoccupation turned to working toward reaching the next higher level, becoming emperor. He was keenly aware that to assume that position he faced several internal and external challenges. He must first remove from his path several men of established social power in Abyssinia. He chose to attempt to trap or capture them in some kind of wrongdoing. Others who stood in his way were many of the ministers, then the mahal sefari (high ranking counsellors to the throne) and finally the queen herself.

But these were not the only obstacles he saw. The European component was at least as significant as the Abyssinian, and Tefari's actions prove that he was well aware of this. He placed great importance on having European powers recognize him as the modernizer of the empire. To accomplish this he had to find a way to prove himself by performing as a statesman.

As soon as he became the crown prince he took charge and began systematically to pursue these objectives. To eliminate

171

The Invention of Ethiopia

ministers en masse proved a great challenge. He was unwilling to wait until he could entrap each of them individually in some kind of mistake. People who were part of the court during that time such as K. Teferi (1987) report that Tefari secretly agitated and was known to have bribed several counsellors to air their opinions regarding the corruption of ministers. This process of rumor-mongering and grumbling took some time but was quite effective. After a long period of sustained agitation, he finally succeeded. The rumors of corruption among the ministers surfaced, and a highly publicized gathering in which the ministers were openly condemned gave the opportunity for Tefari to call for a meeting of the mahal sefari. When brought together, the members of the group were asked for their advice about what to do about the situation of corrupt ministers. As Tefari had calculated they suggested that all the ministers resign en masse. Tefari (following this impartial counsel) asked for the resignation of the entire group of ministers with the exception of Habta Giorgis, a man of the colonized regions who was widely known to oppose corruption and who posed little threat to Tefari because he could make no traditional claim to the throne.

This ploy was successful. The ministers resigned (though the usual interpretation is that they were fired [Marcus 1987:32-35]). Thus, Tefari was rid of the major hurdle to his acquisition of full power. These ministers represented the highest echelons of the traditional Abyssinian aristocracy. They had achieved their positions as part of the pattern used during Menelik's era—a pattern of securing the cooperation, or at least deflecting the opposition, of the powerful figures of the northern kingdoms by compensating them with rank and privilege. Tefari's battle against them was part of the larger struggle for consolidation of neftegna settler rule over the entire empire. As long as the aristocrats remained at the top of the state, Tefari and the group of settlers that he represented would be insecure. This internal coup meant that the avenue was open for Tefari to bring in men from his own settler group, loyal to a very specific interest and aspiring to protect and expand their newfound power.

State Consolidation

The second most significant source of real political power in the country was the group that served as counsellors to the throne, the mahal sefari. These men were also members of the most prestigious families in traditional Abyssinia. Their membership among the mahal sefari was based on respect and honor deriving from the values embodied in the old Abyssinian system. The position of the counsellors had been recognized in the early period of the new Ethiopian state as a customary remnant of old Abyssinian forms of rule, but it had not been embodied as part of the new set of institutions; therefore, their power had no formal legitimacy in the new state. The counsellors had to be recognized and called upon by the current formal or legal leaders in order to have influence. Consequently, their influence could easily be deemphasized to the point of elimination by a ruler threatened by them and wishing to move the state in new directions. The leader at this time was Tefari himself and Tefari exercised the option of never calling upon them again. The ministers who might have turned to them were gone. Over time they were forgotten and simply lost their power. Their last act was to assist Tefari to get rid of the ministers. By that act (known subsequently as the Great Demonstration Against Corruption), they effectively eliminated their own socio-political viability. They thus swept away the traditional basis for their own political and social function. No one of the northern power group was in a position to rally support against Tefari.

Reorganization of the Bureaucracy

Tefari had systematically eliminated the major political elements who would have been capable of challenging his power, including the pressure groups. Having accomplished all this, Tefari was in a position to become officially the chief minister over all existing ministries. From then on, he was able to appoint his own hand-picked people to the positions of commissioners (called Shum) and to all the ministries that were now under his direct control. These were the especially trusted (or best understood) neftegna elements, many from his home station of Harar.

The only remaining potential internal political threat to Tefari, besides the ousted but still living Iyasu, was the governors of awarajas, the geographic administrative units established following a European design during Menelik's era. Tefari knew firsthand what people assigned to fill this position were capable of doing since he himself had served as a settler officer. He then took it upon himself to weaken their power. Tefari approached this task with the efficiency of a man who had the experience of having been a former awaraja governor himself.

Knowing from the outset that the real basis for the social and political power on which the awaraja governor depended was the balabat, Tefari's next moves were deliberate attempts to undermine that particular relationship. He reorganized the structure that had been set up under Menelik for local administration; the structure still remained intact at the time Tefari reached power. At that point the empire had been divided into twenty-seven relatively independent administrative awarajas. In fact these had become so independent that they were in effect small fiefdoms. Each awaraja was divided into three or more smaller geographical districts called woredas, and each woreda was carved up into three or more regions that were usually under the administrative control of the balabat, a local resident recognized to have authority under the Ethiopian state. The physical domain of the balabatship was several gashas of land, usually between 15 and 40 gashas. (A gasha is 40 hectares.) A chain of command had been established such that an order passed from the king went to the Ministry of the Interior, or any other concerned ministry, to the awaraja, then to the woreda and finally to the balabat.

The balabat was the member of the bureaucracy in direct contact with the people residing in his designated area. Especially in the case of public mobilization, such as in time of war or for tax collection, the balabat's position was a strategically important one.

Tefari saw that if an awaraja governor was to rebel against the central power, he would necessarily depend upon the institution of

174

State Consolidation

the balabat and the balabats' ability to raise funds and forces for him. Tefari's move was to introduce a centralized municipal government made up of police and local magistrate (danya) courts responsible solely to the central government, a move that neutralized the critical function of the balabats. The tight central institutional control over the awaraja governors that resulted from this move is usually cited as evidence of Tefari's "modernization" of the bureaucracy, but the outcome that had the greatest immediate effect for the crown prince was that of securing him in power.

In the meantime, there were only a few powerful individuals at the center who could effectively challenge him or stand in his way to complete power. They were Fit. Habta Giorgis, the specific dejazmatches whose anti-Iyasu forces had helped thrust Tefari into power, and Queen Zewditu. These powerful people died under mysterious circumstances within a fairly short period of time. There has been much speculation about the manner of their deaths. Presumably they all died of poisoning. In the absence of hard evidence, it is fair to say that it was Tefari who was the chief beneficiary of their demise. He was able to force some of the remaining individuals to submit to him through the system of promotion and demotion, rewarding and punishing people to the effect that he finally did become undisputed king of the empire.

As stated earlier, however, Tefari's preoccupations were not only to clear the route to power by eliminating local contenders from his way, he was also working on gaining acceptance for himself among the external powers, especially France and Britain. This had to be done while retaining approval from the neftegna elements internally. He very well knew from the experiences of Taytu and Iyasu that without the approval of these forces he would not be successful at achieving what was essential to all Ethiopian rulers, to satisfy the objectives of the settlers, to implement the designs of the Europeans for the region, to contain the colonies and to keep the regions incorporated by Menelik within the control of the empire. He had to be capable of continuing in the manner that Menelik had conducted business with these forces. Tefari did just that and gained recognition both internally and externally.

The Invention of Ethiopia

A major advance in this regard came when Tefari took a trip to Europe in 1924 in connection with the effort to gain admission for Ethiopia in the League of Nations. This tour around Europe, with several European and an American adviser in tow, had a profound impact upon the ferociously ambitious king and upon the powers of Europe who remained interested in seeing that their arrangement to keep a representative of the settler class in power in the northeast African empire not crumble. He immediately became the darling of the media and received an inordinate amount of media attention. During this visit of Tefari's to Europe, there was extended public discussion of Ethiopia's place in the world community and a great elaboration of the Ethiopian mythology initiated by European writers for a European public.

Rave reviews in Europe introduced Tefari to the political power of the media in Europe and also accustomed him to media popularity there. Commentators remarked about his "extraordinarily handsome face, next door to black, with high standing curly hair, a crisp black beard, a fine hawkish nose, and large gleaming eyes" (*Manchester Guardian* July 8, 1924, cited in Marcus 1987: 67). When *The Times* applauded the ras' "devotion to modernization," he saw that the positive reaction would benefit him greatly over time. Once Ras Tefari had been widely advertised and praised by the European media, *The Times*, the *Manchester Guardian* and *Observer*, he clearly saw that his being applauded in Europe greatly strengthened his prestige and power in Ethiopia as well. His experience laid a basis for his expectation of becoming a media figure at home during this time. It was as expected "upon his arrival in Addis Abeba on 4 September." Awaiting him were leading military and civil officers, the diplomatic corps, and thousand of Addis Ababans and soldiers (Marcus 1987: 70).

Tefari acted quickly to set in motion a long-range plan to install powerful media capacity in his empire. He was sensitive to the fact that despite the critical value of these modern media to his purposes, no Ethiopians were trained to understand their operation, including himself. He immediately assigned members of the European intelligentsia and technocrats including Europeans and Americans in all

State Consolidation

the positions critical to keeping this apparatus functional. Some served as "advisers"; for example, an Englishman was hired as the supervisor of the Ministry of the Interior and a Frenchman for the Ministry of Posts, Telephone, and Telegraph (Marcus 1987: 100-102). Tefari's decisions to place Europeans rather than Abyssinians into these slots were opposed by several rases as articulated most clearly by Ras Gugsa. "The ras was equally unhappy about Tafari's use of foreign experts and advisers, because their presence revealed the inability of the old ruling classes to administer an increasingly complex Ethiopia" (Marcus 1987: 93). In this kind of opposition Gugsa was joined by the Orthodox clergy who had begun "grumbling about a foreigner [an Egyptian] holding the best ecclesiastical job in the realm" (Marcus 1987: 103).

Once his power was fairly firmly established, however, Tefari further developed the communication apparatus as part of the job of reorganizing the ministries. As mentioned earlier, the communication system was of central importance as an instrument in the construction of an international infrastructure, one that would guarantee the type of access to and control of the region that Europeans needed to have in return for their support of this experimental political entity. It was also vital to the settler government's ability to consolidate its internal position. As with the other central institutions, the development of communication basically extended the design of the state apparatus that had been constructed during Tefari's predecessor's time. Some alterations were required to facilitate the operation of the departments, and some updating was in order. But Tefari made no fundamental alterations in Menelik's civil administration, and communication was certainly no exception.

The development of mass media in this empire state was built to safeguard the control and to transmit the ideas of the classes that cooperated in rule. The settlers used them to control the colonies by minimizing internal contradiction and by projecting a particular image among contending Abyssinians. Here is where the marriage of the European image-making on Ethiopia's behalf and the settlers who were placed in charge of the state resulted in very interesting progeny—what can accurately be termed the Ethiopian colonial

The Invention of Ethiopia

mythology. Italians had suggested that Menelik should claim Ethiopia to be an ancient empire recognized by the Europeans in order to expand the lands under his and, by extension, Italian control. This idea was put forth as a straightforward political ploy by the players angling to find their best advantage. But when the idea was brought inside Ethiopia, the myth was accepted and substituted for the facts of history. Henceforth, the state's version of the history of the empire came to include the ideas listed above, including that the territories recently conquered by European-assisted Abyssinians shared 3,000 years of common history with Abyssinia itself and that the people of the empire actually constituted a single "Ethiopian" nationality.

The state-controlled media began to propagate the mythology, and the other instruments of the state were utilized to force adherence to this version by all persons who expected to benefit by it. The media operated explicitly as tools of control by the ruling class over the Oromo and other colonial areas and emitted the ideas necessary to achieve that control.

Tefari did not change the pattern of utilization of the media that had been introduced during Menelik's time. Like Menelik, Tefari learned well how to use the media to his advantage. For example, as far back as 1910 Tefari had been acutely aware of the political importance of the new "innovation" when the Minister of Telephone and Telegraph under Menelik kept him fully informed of Taytu's planned "coup," thereby helping him to thwart it and to assert himself (Garretson 1980). The telephone could be and was used to establish loyalty to him on the spot and thereby consolidate his rule and increase his dominance and the dominance of those who had access to the device.

During the rule of Tefari, communications lines built on this new technology were extended to tie more colonial regions into the center. A map of telephone and telegraph lines (Peter Garretson 1980) shows that there is not one exception to the rule that all avenues lead to Addis Ababa.

Later, when Haile Selassie turned to the wireless radio the same pattern emerged. He attempted to gain international assistance for

178

State Consolidation

introducing a technological device that would operate overwhelmingly in the favor of his own politically loyal social elite (cf. Gartley 1981). Maps showing the locations of these communication lines, telephone, telegraphs, even roads and radios are maps of where power and influence flowed out to the periphery and goods or services used to maintain the system flowed in. There was a collusion of European foreign suppliers and Abyssinian utilizers against conquered people who had no access to the very system they were making possible by paying the bill.

Construction of these means of communication, such as telephone and telegraph, which had begun during the period of Menelik under the direction of "an Italian envoy," was extended under Tefari. By the time Tefari was in the position to move into complete power "100 or so telegraph offices were operative" (Pankhurst 1968: 340) and a considerable portion of the telephone lines which had been planned were operative in almost all the provinces of the empire. He had weakened persons and institutions that might be inclined to oppose him and strengthened those that were positioned to support him. The strategic use of the modern technology represented by rapid and ubiquitous communication media played no little part in his reaching that point. Given the European concern over development in the areas of communication and transport, demonstration that he was capable of completing these systems may have had more to do with his ability eventually to assume power with European backing than has usually been recognized.

En route to full power, Tefari oversaw the development of commerce. This should not be seen as an incidental or personal whim. This was another critical area of interest to the Europeans who had a stake in the maintenance of this curious empire. Tefari had to be able to demonstrate his ability to develop this crucial area in order to earn the full diplomatic and strategic assistance of the Europeans to attain power. It was not because of the European excitement over his good looks alone that he became their choice to replace Iyasu. His ability to implement commercial infrastructure had to be proved prior to coronation. Like Menelik had done before him, he dealt seriously with the European obsession about the

179

The Invention of Ethiopia

railroad and other forms of ground transportation, even warding off internal opposition to its development. The critical importance of the modern medium of transportation in holding together and controlling the huge empire was becoming increasingly apparent to the settler class aspiring to rule. They supported Tefari in his efforts to satisfy the European concerns over the infrastructure. Prior to assuming the position of Emperor, Tefari turned a good deal of his attention to improving and introducing new dimensions of the transportation infrastructure.

Menelik's second concern had been securing a commission to lay the railway line from Djibouti to his capital, Addis Ababa. But Menelik died before that was accomplished, much to the horror and concern of the European capitalists. The Tripartite Treaty itself reflects their interest in this regard. When they could not manage to find a way to internationalize the railway line itself, they had essentially agreed to internationalize the empire over which the railroad was to travel. Now, made to distrust Menelik's appointed heir, they were above all intent upon finding someone who could see that their premier interest was protected and developed. Tefari provided the proof they needed that he was the man who could complete what Menelik was unable to do in this regard. As soon as Tefari became crown prince, he began to work diligently on updating and extending the means of transport. Most significantly, he oversaw the completion of the railway project which had lain dormant until his ascent to the regency. By 1917 railway service to Addis Ababa—and that meant all 487 miles—was operational. The Djibouti to Addis Ababa service began. This single achievement accomplished in a relatively short time probably did more than all others in assuring him the favor of the European capitalists who were to assist him into place and hold him there for half a century.

The thought in Menelik's day was that bridge building was to become the most important means of reaching the colonized areas inhabited by non-Abyssinian subjects; but by the time Tefari reached power, the technology had changed considerably with the advent of motor cars and air travel. Also, to reach the colonies was one thing, but to efficiently exploit the natural resources that would penetrate

State Consolidation

the European market was quite another. Tefari demonstrated his openness to developing new lines of access to the outlying regions, lines that would benefit both capitalists and settlers.

Even during the era of the railway, people usually walked by foot or drove pack animals along dirt roads. When Tefari had observed the function of two cars in Addis Ababa owned by the British and Germans, he desired such vehicles and wanted to oversee the construction of the kind of roads required to utilize them in his home country. He saw that cars could serve him personally as a symbol of status in the eyes of both Abyssinians and Europeans. So during his visit to European countries in 1924, he had brought back a number of cars for his own use even before there was a place to drive them. Following that visit it became widely accepted that going in a car rather than on the back of an animal was more prestigious. This provided an incentive for the laying out of urban roads, which in this empire preceded the advent of extensive rural roads.

Tefari did see, however, the importance of satisfying the interests of the settlers internally. During his tenure as crown prince, he began to oversee the connection of all major garrison towns and awaraja capitals by road, especially those to the colonies, and he made it his task to intensify road building in general. By 1922 he had established a special department responsible for the building of roads. It has been said that the regent would often not only lay the first stones, but he himself would survey the work every morning with a large retinue until it was completed (Pankhurst 1968: 291, Marcus 1987: 133).

As regent, Tefari simultaneously initiated a number of road projects to different parts of the empire. The first contract was awarded on July 9, 1927, to two Greek nationals (T. Zewos and A. Donalis) to link Metu and Gore with the inland port of Gambela, a distance of 112 miles. The objective was to ". . . transport goods between Gambela and Gore, Bure, Matto, Suppe, Noppe and Sayo" (Pankhurst 1968: 290-291).

The Invention of Ethiopia

Plans for further projects for road construction were made in this same year, indicating the importance which Tefari wished to convey to potential beneficiaries. For example, in cooperation with Italians one road was planned or considered to run between Assab and Dessie, then by 1930 Tefari made another arrangement for Italians to take the contract of building a road from Addis Ababa to Lake Tana, and the J. G. White Engineering Corporation of New York began to consider building a bridge on Lake Tana. The successful projects, however, were primarily those around Addis Ababa which drew heavily on foreign expertise and equipment to drive them to completion. These undertakings were highly visible and created a great deal of speculation and goodwill among the European residents of the capital.

Significantly, each of these roads branched out in the direction of the colonies and promised to facilitate the exploitation of those regions for the benefit of both settler and capitalist. Bartleet, a British engineer who was in the country to work on a gold industry, also began to undertake the business of road construction. He took the road work around the city from Addis Ababa to Jimma and also to Shoa. Between 1928-1932 "... the old Diredowa—Harar road was substantially improved with the aid of foreign engineers and American levelling machines to allow of motor traffic" (Pankhurst 1968: 292). Another project given to a Swiss company was to "... extend the old Addis Alam road through Lakamti and the gold producing province of Beni Shangul to the Sudan" (ibid).

Generally speaking, by the time Tefari became emperor, several forms of ground transport were being developed, and their promise if not their full effect had begun to be felt. This latter can be measured quantitatively in terms of export and import. Using 1910 as a base year imports were up in 1920 by about 350 percent, by 1930 by 536 percent whereas exports were up by 1920 by about 151 percent and by 1930 by 702 percent. These dramatic increments are properly credited to the newly developed infrastructure for transport and communication, also indicating an increased capacity for expropriation of the items in which the settlers and the capitalists shared an interest.

State Consolidation

Having reorganized the bureaucracy and expanded the above-mentioned infrastructure, Tefari had demonstrated to his primary support groups that he was capable of serving their interests in the consolidation of this empire state. These tasks completed, Tefari began preparation to take the emperor's crown. He invited Europeans, Asians, Americans, Russians, etc., to his coronation. He based his claim on his record as crown prince from 1916-1928, and as negus (king) from 1928-1930.

The ultimate victory for him at this juncture was a new arms treaty signed on August 21, 1930. This document recognized Ethiopia's right to exist as an empire.

> Its preamble described the agreement as completing and supplementing the 1925 Geneva Convention, which treated Ethiopia as a sovereign state freely exercising its powers to ensure security within its territory. Toward this end, the tripartite powers undertook to assist Ethiopia "to obtain the arms and munitions necessary for the defense of its territory against all outside aggression and for the maintenance of internal public order" (Marcus 1987: 103).

This treaty represents another crucial area in which a project that was begun by Menelik was carried through to its logical conclusion by Tefari without fundamental alteration in purpose and design. The tripartite powers had finally given him the go-ahead to take and manage the empire with their blessing.

He had followed Menelik's example in maintaining good relations with Europeans and he proudly invited them all to come share in the culmination of what they had facilitated both diplomatically and technologically. The fact that Europeans approved his ascension and his leadership gave him additional legitimacy at home, sending an internal message to his friends and foes alike that to support or to oppose his coronation would be to support or oppose the forces lined up behind him.

The crown name that he took upon his coronation as emperor, Haile Selassie ("the power of God") takes on special significance in

The Invention of Ethiopia

light of the way the support of external absent forces made possible his ascension. Tefari finally became Haile Selassie, the undisputed emperor of the Ethiopian Empire, Elect of God, King of Kings, Conquering Lion of the Tribe of Judah. Evelyn Waugh's description of the coronation leaves little doubt that it was a huge organized fraud and empty facade staged largely for visiting Europeans.

> The empress died suddenly next day, and Tafari, with the assent of the rases, proclaimed himself emperor, fixing for his coronation the earliest date at which preparations could adequately be made. The coronation festivities were thus the final move in a long and well-planned strategy. Still maintaining his double ruff of trumping at home with prestige abroad, abroad with his prestige at home, Tafari had two main motives behind the display. He wished to impress on his European visitors that Ethiopia was no mere agglomeration of barbarous tribes open to foreign exploitation, but a powerful, organized, modern State. He wanted to impress upon his own countrymen that he was no paramount chief of a dozen independent communities, but an absolute monarch, recognized on equal terms by the monarchies and the governments of the great world. And if, in the minds of his simpler subjects, courtesy and homage became at all confused, if the impression was given that these braided delegates (out on holiday from their serious duties, an unusual pageant, and perhaps a few days' shooting) had come in their ruler's name to pay tribute to Ethiopian supremacy—so much the better (Waugh 1931: 25-26).

Modernizing the Empire

The first major official act that Tefari took on as Emperor Haile Selassie was to arrange to provide a "Constitution to the Ethiopian people," as he put it. In 1931 Haile Selassie issued the first constitution. Because of the timing of its issuance and the significance often attached to such a document, it deserves a bit of attention. Usually a constitution is regarded as a code of agreement among specifically constituted groups or associations of people in a government or a party. It is viewed as an embodiment of approved methods for undertakings by the members represented. Constitutions are seen as negotiated, framed through debate and discussion to consist of a preamble and several articles, the preamble articulating the shared objectives of the constituents, and the articles spelling out the mode of implementing the objectives. A constitution does render some methods of operation legitimate and others illegitimate.

The Ethiopian constitution of 1931 is quite a revealing document for the features that it does not contain as well as for the features that it does.

Assessing the 1931 constitution, it is clear from the recounting of the history thus far that it could not represent the democratic product of constituent groups because the political mechanisms for producing such a document had not been developed in the empire; but oddly enough neither is it the embodiment of an indigenous ruling group. Rather it contains a framework for administration and law produced directly from a Western European administrative model. Norberg mentions (1977: 127-8) that the very carefully selected Swedish adviser, Kolmodin, was asked to give his views on the Constitution of 1931, but she states that he was the only foreign adviser to be consulted. This view is at odds with Earnest Work's comment published in 1935 in his own insightful book on the empire:

> The ruling class here claims, of course, to have descended from Solomon and the Queen of Sheba.... The present emperor, Haile Selassie I, affirms the same within the constitution which he has recently granted his people and *the preparation of which I have the honor of having played some little part* (Work 1935: 6) [emphasis added].

Given the interest shown by the international community in the Ethiopian experiment in African self-government, it is quite likely that all concerned foreign representatives must have had a hand in it, possibly with each one given the same impression that he was the "only foreign adviser to be consulted." The content and the very structure of the document strongly suggest heavy European influence (some might prefer the term "inspiration"). For example, it guarantees the empire a set of ministries to run the day-to-day affairs of the land and a parliament to make law. But ironically, at the time that the constitution established the ministries, there were not enough qualified Ethiopians to manage them or to fill the slots created for ministers. Rather than respond to a locally expressed and felt need, the document embodied an imported system of principles unfamiliar to the inhabitants of the empire. The constitution did legitimize already existing ministries, all of which had been designed and administered by Europeans from their formation. It formalized the foreign ideology that had already been implemented into the administration of the empire.

The legacy of cumbersome constitutionally ordained institutions has remained an enduring characteristic of Ethiopian administration. Margery Perham in the historical survey chapter of the 1969 edition of *The Government of Ethiopia* comments that the parliament, despite its potential significance, received very little attention from the public at large in Ethiopia. In fact she recalls a very telling image that was circulated on an election poster in Ethiopia conveying the way that the parliament, though constitutionally established, was viewed in its relation to the people. The poster

> suggests the contemporary view that the new institution, which other peoples have fought and died to win, was a gift from heaven through the agency of the emperor who was shown with the Crown Prince receiving the document from an angel and inviting the members to enter the chamber while on the other side a polling booth is illustrated (Perham 1969: lvi)

It would be difficult to imagine a more eloquent depiction of the role of an external agency in introducing an institution that is supposed to be a product of popular demand.

186

State Consolidation

True to the analogy in the poster, the European intervention, as if from heaven through the emperor, presented him with the authority to establish and invite members of specific sociopolitical groups to fill positions in a preordained structure. It should come as no surprise that the members of the group Haile Selassie selected—who were almost entirely neftegnas—were not familiar with the operation, let alone the underlying logic of the administrative apparatus. The concepts behind it were not born out of their cultural or political experience. The concepts embodied there were expressive of an alien ideology since they grew out of a European capitalist society. Consequently, Ethiopians did not make the imported institutions run efficiently according to European standards. This reflects the more general point that if members of a group have not produced the ideas on which an apparatus is constructed, they will not make it function as smoothly as those who share the principles upon which the institution has been built. In such a situation the administrative structure itself is foreign to the ones who have been made responsible for its operation. The purposes and the objectives of the designers and the purpose of the persons who fill the positions created come into conflict.

This is not to say that in the Ethiopian case the neftegna ruling class of the empire had no abilities or notions of rule. Indeed by the time the constitution was handed down, the neftegna had begun to develop and accept a characteristic style of rule over the colonies, but even this, which would accurately represent their development as a ruling class up to that point, is absent from the constitution. Since the document itself was not grounded in Abyssinian political, ideological or economic experience, the neftegna themselves have never developed or altered it independent of the direction of an external imperial patron.*

---

* Both occasions in which the constitution of Ethiopia has been reissued have been at the instigation of the patrons of the empire at that particular time. In each case the changes have been suggestions from "advisers" to the Ethiopians, advisers who function as representatives of international interest. In 1951, the Ethiopians were advised to alter their constitution in order to

The Invention of Ethiopia

Looking at articles 30, 31 and 32 of the Constitution of 1931 reveals that the empire is required to establish a legislative body consisting of two chambers, a Senate and a House of Deputies. According to article 31, the Senate should be appointed by the emperor from the upper strata of the neftegna class. Article 32 guaranteed that the "nobility or the local bosses (shums) elect the Chamber of the Deputies."

The very idea, let alone the organizational set-up, of the legislative body was accessible to only a tiny handful of individuals who held a minimal working knowledge of some dimensions of Western-style constitutional government. These were the few elements of the neftegna class who had visited or received some education in Europe. Since these concepts were not demanded by the neftegna class and rather were part of a design by representatives of the capitalist class, the design was sophisticated enough in its appearance to serve as an effective showcase for the benefit of those Europeans who were interested to do business in the country and defend "a democratic Ethiopia" against intervention by other forces in power.

Actually, however, within the facade of a European-style constitution, the neftegna class found several avenues to advance its own objective interests, particularly in landholding. Although there is a widespread belief that Haile Selassie used the Senate in the early days to gather together all the remaining provincial chiefs who had been appointees of Menelik and "put them out to pasture," thus rendering irrelevant those who opposed the changes that he was introducing, the consolidation of their position in relation to land was a more significant development. Since the neftegna were the

accommodate the impending federation of Eritrea with Ethiopia, and in 1987, Ethiopians were so heavily influenced by Soviet advisers on the form of the constitution of the Peoples' Republic of Democratic Ethiopia that several writers have asserted that the entire document was written in Russian before being translated to Amharic; one author has written that the final form of the constitution was available prior to any of the highly publicized meetings for discussion among the population in general (Bereket 1986: 95).

State Consolidation

settlers and holders of land in conquered and settled regions, the Senate members who were hand-picked by the emperor were given every opportunity to look after their own interests in the land and the labor available in the colonies and to defend their position against any force that might threaten it in any way. They found in the new institution several avenues to secure their position, even ultimately against the interests of finance capital. Legislation introduced in the Senate served this purpose directly.

The Chamber of Deputies, on the other hand, was designed to serve the collective interests of the settlers as a group and of the people of the Abyssinian heartland from where most of the settlers originated. The way that the legislative bodies were used enabled representative members of the group of settlers to articulate and to develop their own specific set of policies from within the framework of a constitutionally established entity. The constitutionally provided legislatures provided a hothouse in which the settlers were able to thrive and to strengthen themselves as an interest group prepared to administer the colonies. A reading of the Constitution of 1931 reveals that no single article mentions the participation or rights of the colonies.

By this constitution then the Emperor created two significant groups—the neftegna sector that developed within the legislative body and a modern manager (or comprador) sector that developed within the executive, peopled by a group which would be groomed to protect the interests of finance capital. Cognizant of potential problems that had been created, the emperor was placed above any law that the legislative body might pass and also above the decision that any executive might make. The emperor became the anchor of the entire system. The specific mechanism for how he could assume this role was spelled out in Article 47 which legitimized the power of the emperor. With the emperor thus above the laws of the legislative body, the emperor assumed the role of "modernizer" and automatically gave the upper hand to his own executive branch.

With all this apparatus fully functional, Haile Selassie began to enjoy full diplomatic support from France, Britain and Italy, the major European powers. Since their interests were nicely safeguarded they were in effect making peace with each other and running the empire together with the emperor, actually in collaboration on its internal and foreign affairs.

It was not long before events on the world scene shifted again in the ways described earlier. The Italians began to develop an interest in monopoly ownership of the Ethiopian enterprise. They soon saw an opportunity, which quickly became a demand, that the Ethiopian empire become an official part of an Italian East African Empire.

The Role of Superpowers in Ethiopia During the Period of World War II

The Italian demand to possess Ethiopia is best understood against the background of events in Europe dealt with in Chapter Two. European countries were preparing for the Second World War in the mid-1930s and taking sides. Italy represented a classic case of the position of smaller nations bargaining with the super-powers in order to find their best advantage before making a commitment to either camp. In that vein, Italy presented a demand designed to pressure both London and Paris into acceptance. Its substance was that London and Paris stay out of her way as she moved into Ethiopia to form an East African empire. In return for this, Italy agreed not to side with Germany and the Entente powers in the upcoming conflict in Europe. In return for Italy's assurances, London and Paris, the other parties to the Tripartite Treaty regarding Ethiopia, effectively stepped aside while Italy entered militarily in a bid to take over direct control of the Ethiopian Empire. The bargain struck between European powers is discussed more fully below.

We have argued that it was in the interest of specific European powers to devise a new formula to guarantee secure access to the central part of Northeast Africa. This formula was safeguarded in the Tripartite Treaty of 1906 which "internationalized" Ethiopia and ensured the protection of that empire.

State Consolidation

At this point let us look with a sharper focus at the world in which Ethiopia was constructed. The great land grab in Africa (the Scramble for Africa) took place among capitalists bent on monopolizing the last remaining parts of the globe, i.e., parts that were not already claimed by some representative of that class. The agreements of the Berlin Conference of 1884-85 reflected the type of general ground rules established by the European *monopoly* capitalist class particularly for relating to the colonized world. After that time Europe itself went from waging smaller wars on the continent to finally waging the first global war among the superpowers, the war in 1914 known as World War I.

That world-scale conflict and its outcome was still fundamentally grounded in the monopolist world view, but at that point forces of *finance* capital were on the rise. The balance of power in Europe shifted a bit as a result of that war but was not basically altered. Throughout and following the First World War, new solutions to problems posed by monopoly control were suggested by the representatives of finance capital, but at that point in history the arrangements for monopoly control prevailed. For the most part, monopoly solutions were adjusted and extended. One exception to this was the proposal for the League of Nations, suggested by a United States president who himself represented the incipient forces of finance capital, but who could not yet even rally the political forces in his own country to join the organization. The league itself embodied the new formulas being developed by finance capital for solving the dilemmas posed by competing monopoly interests. But because conditions on the world scale had not matured enough to allow finance capital and its associated world view to dominate, the league ultimately failed.

Interestingly, though, the principles drawn up for the league provided for Ethiopia to be accepted as a member on the basis that it should be regarded as an independent state. The framers and defenders of the Ethiopian experiment had chosen to call Ethiopia independent because no single one of them had monopoly control over it; the formula they had finally agreed on was one of collective control, probably the more accurate implication behind the notion

191

The Invention of Ethiopia

of "collective security." The designation "independent" quickly became part of the Ethiopian colonial mythology and remains in active use up to this day.

Mythology aside, the solution hammered out among the super-powers, whose rivalry prevented any one of them from obtaining monopoly control over the area, contained the germs of a new finance capitalist model for control of colonies. Since Ethiopia represented in principle the recipe for collective access to a dependency, she could not be regarded as a typical colony. As such, allowance was made for the admission of this new type of political entity, Ethiopia, a dependent colonial empire, into the new type of world body that was being tested, the League of Nations. In general, the League consisted of empires and their satellites. Given its particular history, Ethiopia oddly represented both and arguments could not be put together to exclude her. The League endured nearly until World War II for reasons elaborated above.

It had been the issues of who owned what and of the rules by which they could share the colonial market that had placed France and Abyssinia on one side of the battle lines and Britain and Italy together on the other side throughout the late nineteenth century, particularly at the Battle of Adwa. By the late 1930s, however, these same concerns placed Britain and France on the same side of the balance sheet.

By the time that Ras Tefari had sat in the League of Nations as a member for some six years, another member of the League of Nations, Japan, began testing the strength of the league by expanding. In violation of the League's agreement, Japan attacked China and occupied Manchuria. This act of extending monopoly control over new territory was not promptly and strictly censured by the league's members. When no challenge was made to Japan regarding this offense, the implications became clear, especially to the two greatest powers of the day, Britain and France. They saw that this created a dangerous precedent, especially for Germany and Italy, who were unhappy about past colonial arrangements and who were beginning to feel their strength. Germany, who had lost its African colonies during the First World War, had been uncooperative up to that period.

Both France and Britain saw that there was a possibility that Britain's old client state and ally, Italy, could sever the old bonds and go over to join France and England's greatest threat on the continent, Germany. Their diplomats could anticipate another war coming about over this very type of issue. Britain and France began to strategize, because the issue at hand had put the security of Europe in question again.

Only four years after the Manchurian incident that had involved Japan and Russia, what is known as "the Wal-Wal incident" took place in the Horn of Africa. This was a confrontation which predictably involved a second pair of league members, Italy and Ethiopia, in direct confrontation over territory, this time in northeast Africa.

By this time it had become clear to both Britain and France that they were implicated by way of this confrontation between their old clients at Wal-Wal, an outpost station on the eastern side of the Horn, and had to take some action. Quite simply, at Wal-Wal one of Britain's former clients, Italy, wanted to monopolize the territory of one of France's former clients, Ethiopia. It was also about the same time that Germany wanted to move in and take over the Rhineland from France. This posed a major challenge to the balance of power in Europe. Since both Britain and France had great stakes in that balance, both found it in their interest to try to preserve it. The inevitability of a second world war over this matter was clear by the early 1930s.

To forestall a potential German-Italian alliance, both Britain and France sought ways and means to appease Italy. To put it bluntly, Ethiopia was a plum that Italy greatly desired in her attempt to establish an expanded African empire. Britain and France, the cosigners with Italy of the Tripartite Treaty of 1906, were willing to give Italy a green light to occupy Ethiopia in hopes that this move would keep her from the arms of Germany.

The quickly developing situation promptly became the responsibility of France and Britain, because it threatened a rearrangement of the existing superpower alignment. There were those in Britain

The Invention of Ethiopia

and France who thought that if closely checked, Italy could play power broker between France and Britain on the one hand and between the unhappy Germany and Japan on the other. It was also clear that if Italy was forced by either Britain or France to respect the old 1906 Tripartite Treaty agreement concerning the protection of Ethiopia by all three parties, or even by one of them, Italy would simply pursue her best alternative solution and proceed to join the German camp that was challenging all the old powers of Europe and their rules. It was this situation that forced both Britain and France to stay out of Italy's way when she moved in to take Ethiopia. It turned out that this compromising conduct on the part of the two major powers did not stop Italy in the end from joining Germany, as we have pointed out above, and they eventually retaliated by taking Ethiopia away from her.

Italy proceeded to conquer Haile Selassie's empire and then joined the German camp anyway. The "Rome-Berlin Axis" was established by the end of 1936. At about the same time Germany and Japan signed an anti-Comintern pact, which was expressed to demonstrate their overall dissatisfaction with the world order and the world market-sharing arrangements.

Italian Presence: The Shift from a Dependent Colonial to a Direct Colonial System in Ethiopia

Only because the European world and the European balance of power was in a shambles in the mid-1930s was Italy able to take advantage of the situation and force others to recognize her power over Ethiopia. By 1936, Italy had in fact taken over Haile Selassie's empire.

Having faced no substantial opposition to the takeover, Italy moved quickly to change the structure of the empire by altering the administrative set-up established by the European-Abyssinian system. Ethiopia became a direct colony of Italy so that with Italian Somalia and Eritrea it was part of the African Orientale Italiana (AOI). Sbacchi explains that

State Consolidation

Italian sovereignty over Ethiopia became legal on 9 May 1936. The King of Italy became the Emperor of Ethiopia, and was represented in Ethiopia by a Viceroy or Governor-General.... Ethiopia was divided into four governorships: Amhara, Harar, Oromo-Sidamo and Shoa. The governors were given wide financial, juridical and administrative autonomy. Each governorship had its local executive council and each governor could correspond directly with the Ministry of Africa and with other ministries....

... [e]ach governorship was in essence a separate entity; each region was an independent republic and acted autonomously. Individual governors ignored the problems of the neighboring governors and had no interest in cooperating with them, fearing that their difficulties would cross governorate boundaries (Sbbacci 1985: 43)

The old dependent colonial structure that had concentrated power, control, and privilege into the hands of a single beneficiary settler group was dismantled and replaced by the direct Italian system. The arrangement called for Italian governors to deal directly with Italian decisionmakers in Europe. There was no longer a go-between class of elevated Ethiopian settlers. All colonized peoples were treated in the same fashion by the Italians, including the former settlers who decried their loss of privilege.

The educational system was a good example. From the time that Menelik had established a few schools to prepare Ethiopians to take over the new state bureaucracy until Ras Tefari came to power, there had been no expansion of institutions for education. But as Patrick Gilkes describes, during the mid-1900's, "... especially after his crowning as emperor a number of schools were established not only in Addis Abeba but also in the provinces. All of these were primary schools and the instruction was either in French or English" (Gilkes 1975: 89, and see for detail Perham 1969: 247 and Markakis 1975: 143-159).

Occasionally there were individuals who were sent to different destinations outside the empire to be trained in the schools there.

The Invention of Ethiopia

Offers had come from all Western countries to send students for study, "to equip the leaders of tomorrow."

Haile Selassie literally saw in those educated abroad the hope for the future of his empire. He watched with pride as a farmer watches his crops grow. When the Italians moved into Ethiopia, they literally mowed down his first crop of educated young men, brutally executing them. It was part of their move to replace dependent colonialism with direct control. They were prepared to fill the state positions—positions that these trained Abyssinians were destined to take over—with Italians who would serve Italian interests directly. Haile Selassie considered it the greatest atrocity they could have committed. The day the educated young people were murdered was always officially remembered. With those educated neftegnas who had acquired the outlook and skills necessary to keep the state running went his hopes for his independence from the constant presence of European personnel and for concentrating control into the hands of his own group. He never forgot it. He was determined never to be vulnerable on that point again.

What was once Haile Selassie's empire had now become the Italians' empire. The Italians then built several schools, but not in the pattern that Haile Selassie had used, limiting access to the children of settlers in a few selected areas. Instead they built schools throughout the conquered areas—areas that they had declared to be autonomous regions. In these locations they built schools for both Italian children and for the children of the subjects. They built separate schools for Amharas in Amharic, and for the Oromos in Oromoffa. For the Islamic people who wanted to pursue their education in Arabic, they built schools that taught in Arabic. Margery Perham reports that they initiated "... a training center for agriculture and crafts in Galla-Sidamo" (Perham 1969: 249). By mid-1938 the Italians reported that "... there were 10,598 native pupils in seventy-five schools ... " (ibid).

When Italy took over, she made little adjustment in the basic infrastructure of the Ethiopian empire; in fact in several ways she strengthened it. But Italy did damage the system of dependent colonialism in Ethiopia by reorganizing the institutions for education that had been set up by the imperial forces who forged the original agreement with the Ethiopians.

Herein lay one major distinction between dependent colonialism and direct metropolitan colonialism. The dependent colonizers had concentrated the flow of information and skills training to their own neftegna group in the country in order to maintain tight control. The Italians changed that for a short time, dealing with all the populations as subjects of Italy without providing privilege for any one group.

Though the Italians eliminated the Ethiopian class of state settler-managers, they did not find it necessary to change the basic nature of the state itself. It has been a mystery to some people why the colonized people seemed to prefer Italian rule over Abyssinian. Under the Italian occupation, an additional layer of overseers was removed which the colonized people no longer were forced to support. In comparison to dependent colonialism, direct colonialism seemed a relief, though many of the colonized continued to resist any kind of colonial rule at all. Oromos, for example, made an unsuccessful appeal for help from Britain for recognition by the world body as a sovereign nation after the Italian occupation. Instead they were pushed back under the British and then the Ethiopian colonial control.

Before Italy had accomplished a complete colonial reorganization, however, she broke the agreement she had made with London and Paris. She opportunistically wanted to build her empire and at the same time join the forces on the continent that were ready to destroy her European rivals there. Italy calculated that Ethiopia's old friend France was too weak to come to Ethiopia's aid now because of the German threat. She assumed also that Britain would ultimately be weakened and would have no interest in taking up the cause of Haile Selassie against the Italians. In this, the Italians miscalculated, however, as they discovered later. It had become Allied policy to attack enemy forces wherever they could be found globally. In fact, a major strategy for Allied defense was to begin hitting the enemy at a great distance and then to take that war to the mainland.

The Invention of Ethiopia

British strategic response at first was to continue to agitate Italy in order to keep her from allying too closely with Germany. It was with this strategy in mind that Britain had chosen to recognize Italy's rule over Haile Selassie's empire. It was not enough to prevent Mussolini from joining the Entente, however. As an old friend of Britain, Italy understood the British strategy and was not deterred by it.

When the Conquering Lion of the Tribe of Judah sought refuge at the prospect of the Italian conquest, Haile Selassie, who was an active member of the League of Nations, initially could not find any country to accommodate him. Although he was historically much closer to France than to Britain, he was forced to take refuge in the place that offered him the strongest support. London took Haile Selassie because they saw a strategic possibility that he could be useful to them.

The main objective of taking in the so-called enemy of an old friend, which is what Haile Selassie had become, was not concern for his safety. British admission of Haile Selassie was meant as a signal to that old friend, Italy, to discourage her from opposing Britain. Italy, who had herself been in the position of a bargaining chip in the past, knew that Britain held the emperor in that position.

By 1939 Germany had become so powerful that she had almost succeeded in subduing the major European countries. She had harassed France into a defenseless position and had attacked British interests in many parts of Europe. In the meantime Britain had also officially declared or notified the world at large and particularly members of the British Commonwealth that she was at war with Germany. By this time Britain was also expecting Italy to declare war, and as expected, Italy by 1940 declared war on both Britain and France.

Britain then reversed her compromise position of 1938, in which she had recognized the Italian move into Ethiopia, and declared Ethiopia to be a sovereign state and Haile Selassie its rightful ruler. Haile Selassie turned out to be Britain's ace in the hole to be brought back supposedly to the process of "rebuilding." The British position was to launch a crusade to return the emperor to Ethiopia.

State Consolidation

Ethiopia became part of the Allied global strategy of attacking the enemy abroad first in the area of the enemy's holding. Led by Britain, the colonial army from Africa and Asia was put to the test in 1940. On this basis, Britain immediately began to help Haile Selassie to establish a base of operation for his return through the Sudan, a British commonwealth country. Haile Selassie entered into the general picture of long-range British military strategy as had Menelik before him. The plan to keep Haile Selassie as a refugee paid off, and in the diplomatic battle to oust Italy and to champion Ethiopia, many of the elements of Ethiopian colonial mythology were called forth and were expanded in an effort to justify this move. Among many explanations the rationale for this move was that Haile Selassie was "leading his countrymen into battle." These were said to be "refugee patriots returning" for the purpose of safeguarding the "independence" of Ethiopia. John Spencer's account on the whole confirms this interpretation:

> On June 10, 1940, Italy declared war on Britain and France, and Churchill and Eden lost no time in profiting from their earlier decision to hold the Emperor in reserve in England. Recognition of the Italian conquest was declared withdrawn, and on June 24 Haile Selassie was flown to Egypt and then the Sudan where his presence could inspire the Ethiopian patriots to revolt en masse against the new enemy of Britain and France (Spencer 1984: 89-90).

Upon a closer examination, the British and French concurrence in holding the emperor in England was bound up in a general strategy for holding their empires together. The strategy was based on Britain's and France's colonial holdings in Africa and in the world. It was understood that in case a major world war took place, their position in their colonies would give the Allied nations an upper hand. When conflict did break out, Britain engaged the Italian forces in their colonies by way of British colonies. This was effective in neutralizing the belligerent.

The Invention of Ethiopia

In fact, Britain began to implement this type of battle plan as soon as Britain and Italy had reached a diplomatic impasse. In Ethiopia, in the name of "liberation," Britain without hesitation activated a colonial defense and began attacking the Italian position from every corner—from the west, from the east, from the south. Within a very short time, the Italians surrendered to the British forces one after the other. This quickly brought defeat and an end to the Italian occupation of Ethiopia. This time, instead of sitting behind the scenes, the British took direct charge of everything, began to rebuild directly with their own hands in their own way. The British army was brought in to replace the Italian as occupying power.

The British Role in the Reorganization of the Ethiopian Empire

After the defeat of the Italians in 1941 the future of Haile Selassie's empire became a major debate between two powerful offices, each representing strong internal forces in Britain, the Colonial (War) Office and the Foreign Office. This debate represented precisely the ongoing struggle over which type of colonial formula would ultimately determine how the capitalist system would organize itself to control the world at large. In a general sense, the Colonial Office represented the old strategies of monopoly capital, and the Foreign Office represented what has subsequently been shown to have been the rising forces of finance capital. The debate between these two offices within the British government epitomizes the type of battles being waged in thousands of arenas in the capitalist world as finance capital rose to dominate on a world scale.

The immediate issues at stake between the British Colonial Office and Foreign Office were that the Colonial Office wanted Ethiopia, along with the rest of the Italian colonies, to become part of British East Africa.

The position of Foreign Office was that the Ethiopian experiment be continued, the old facade of "independent Ethiopia" be

State Consolidation

retained as promised, and the empire be returned to Emperor Haile Selassie with indirect control called "special assistance" used to dominate his government.

The Colonial Office, however, was for a short time in the more advantageous position, being represented by trained military personnel on the scene, so the position of the Foreign Office was temporarily undermined. This became clear when Haile Selassie reentered his empire. He was no longer allowed the appearance of independence upon his arrival; the limits of his authority were starkly revealed. In the view of the Colonial Office Ethiopia was "occupied enemy territory." He deeply resented this, for he had enjoyed the illusions under which he had previously lived. As John Spencer has pointed out,

> [t]he degree of that control [the control of the Colonial Office] was demonstrated when less than a week after his re-entry into Addis Abeba, the emperor appointed seven cabinet ministers and the governor of the central province of Shoa, Brigadier Lush promptly told him that he had no authority to do so (Spencer 1984: 96)

The insistence of the British Colonial Office on extending its empire was out of keeping with the formula for Abyssinia that had been emerging, that of a locally managed colonialism dependent on superpower—at that time British—support. The Colonial Office approach reflected the old school and reveals an ignorance of and/or a resistance to the new dynamic of the world economic order. The Colonial Office failed to take into account in its strategies that the power of the British empire was in decline, only to be replaced by the power of a new world champion, the United States. The Colonial Office position on issues in the colonies represented the old-style settlers within a colonial empire built up on the principles of monopoly control. Those in charge could not accept the sweeping changes that were affecting Britain and refused to accommodate in policy the new world situation. The winds of change, as it turned out, were blowing in the direction of the Foreign Office position.

The Invention of Ethiopia

The British Foreign Office, aware of the rise of finance capital due to its daily interaction with problems in the British colonies and as a result of its role in the war with Germany, represented a different outlook. It had been forced to function within the limits of its current powers and had been forced to confront the reality that rigidity and refusal to accommodate change could cause Britain not only to lose its colonies to the Axis powers but could bring about the downfall of her own nation. It was the British Foreign Office that eventually engaged in secret negotiations with the United States, setting in motion a new type of colonial program that acknowledged both the power of the United States and the new power of finance capital, recognizing that these new formulas safeguarded many key British interests (see below). As early as 1938, the United States had proposed a "program of world peace" which in effect placed the United States in the position of go-between to prevent a major war in Europe. The primary question posed by America to Britain concerned what would become of the people of the British colonies.

While an agreement between the United States and Britain—the Atlantic Charter—had been signed and negotiations regarding the other regions of the world were underway, the United States was attacked by Japan at Pearl Harbor on December 7, 1941, and entered into World War II without delay.

Despite the fact that the United States had rushed to enter the war on Britain's side, she did not alter any of her demands or proposals concerning the future of the colonial world. The issues raised by the United States concerned the "self-determination" of the colonies and the United States' interest in the world market. William Roger Louis writes that

> In studying the "colonial question" during the war, Roosevelt and many other Americans increasingly believed that the principle of self-determination would work in favor of the creation of independent states out of the European colonial empires (Louis 1978: 4-5)

State Consolidation

These interests had been made clear as early as the First World War and also had been made clear in 1938 (Scott 1973: 381-88) during the time when President Roosevelt's "plan for world peace" was advanced. These concerns of the U.S., the changes in the European balance of power, and the resistance movements in the colonies all put together made it unavoidably clear that the dynamic of the world order was changing. In the face of these clear signs, however, the block of British military, settler and other forces represented in the Colonial Office rigidly rejected the prospect of worldwide alteration in British colonial policy. And while Britain remained in the midst of the war, the position and perspective on events represented by the Colonial/War Office prevailed, and that office implemented a military occupation of the Ethiopian empire.

The dominance of the Colonial Office position over that of the Foreign Office was asserted in British policy not only in Ethiopia but also with regard to other situations Britain faced at that particular point, such as the ongoing war with the Axis powers, the liberation struggles in the Pacific, the decline of British economic power, problems raised by the Commonwealth nations, and the growth of United States power and the United States demands concerning the issues of self-determination of the colonies in general.

Resolution of these other issues in the direction of the Foreign Office positions eventually also dictated that British military rule had a short life in Ethiopia. After several unhappy moments for both the emperor and the British military administrators in charge of the empire, direct British military occupation of Ethiopia gave way to what amounted to a compromise British protectorate over the empire. Churchill and Eden established British policy regarding the region. An agreement was signed on the last day of January 1942. This agreement is now known as "The Anglo-Ethiopian Agreement and Military Convention." It is cited in full as Appendix E in Margery Perham's book *The Government of Ethiopia* (1969: 464-473). John Spencer has summarized the conditions established by the agreement:

The Invention of Ethiopia

The Agreement and the Military Convention signed on that occasion made it certain that Ethiopia still remained under the firm control of Britain. The British representative was to be ex officio dean of the diplomatic corps, to be followed in rank by the general officer commander in chief of British forces in East Africa or his representative in Ethiopia. The Emperor was to appoint British advisors, a British commissioner of police and British police officers, inspectors, judges and magistrates. No additional advisors were to be appointed without consultation with the British government. Judges of the High Court, in such number as His Majesty would consider desirable, were to be British ....

The presence of the emperor and other Ethiopian representatives was virtually incidental. Spencer goes on to say,

... Further, the Military Convention provided that British forces were to have freedom of entry into, movement within, and exit from Ethiopia without authorization from the Ethiopian government, and military aircraft and personnel were to be permitted to fly freely into, over, and out of Ethiopia.... The British military authorities were to continue to use and occupy without payment any immovable property formerly belonging to the Italian state.... The high-power radio transmitting station, the telephone system, and the railway were to remain under British control. The Ethiopian army was to be trained by a British military mission to Ethiopia ... the British East African shilling was to be made the official monetary unit.... Imports and exports were controlled from London and the foreign exchange generated by exports went to British currency reserves. (Spencer 1984: 98-9)

Spencer observed that "Ethiopia was for all practical purposes a British protectorate."

State Consolidation

Upon close examination, the agreement reflects those conditions on the world scale that affected these two parties. In the first place no local material condition existed for Haile Selassie to be left to his own devices to organize political and economic institutions for an empire appropriate to the new age that was dawning. The British terms reveal that she felt that to leave the emperor on his own was to hand the Ethiopian empire right back over to the Italians. Such an eventuality would create the perfect opportunity for the Italians to expand into other British colonies at worst, or at least would mean the disintegration of the Ethiopian empire.

Neither outcome would serve British or U.S. interests. Thus, after direct military rule lasting some eight months, the above agreement, the Churchill/Eden program, was implemented in Ethiopia. Hence the Foreign Office prevailed over the Colonial Office.

One point that is quite often overlooked concerning this period is the nature of British rule in Ethiopia. The British did not change the infrastructure of the state in Ethiopia. They did not need to. The infrastructure that had been constructed through the cooperation of several European powers, including the British, during the early years of the twentieth century was quite functional. It had not been changed significantly; it had only been substantially enhanced during the Italian occupation. The British merely refurbished and utilized the infrastructure that was in place when they arrived. When the Italians surrendered, the British simply took over the functionary positions and ruled instead. Even during the eight months when the British War (Colonial) Office ruled, the British comfortably executed all aspects of administration that had been developed by the Italians. This was possible only because the Italians themselves had been able to move to utilize what was essentially a European-organized apparatus. Ethiopia functioned as a multipurpose, generic state system.

When the Italian occupation ended, the Ethiopian state emerged as the same basic Euro-Abyssinian organization altered slightly by the Italians to suit their own style of rule. Neither did the British find much reason to alter what was in place when they arrived.

The Invention of Ethiopia

Their behavior mimicked that of all ruling groups involved in the management of Ethiopia—the Italians, the British and the Ethiopians—revealing at key points of transition a familiarity with the form of institution that had been established. During the year 1941, from April to the end of the year, the Ethiopian state apparatus functioned without much interruption, just as it had during the shift to the Italian occupation.

The agreement reached between the British and Haile Selassie did arrange for the empire eventually to be returned to the settlers and administered along the lines that had existed prior to the Italian takeover of the 1930's. Basing their policies upon the Anglo-Ethiopian agreement of January 31, 1942, and operating under the guise of the Constitution of 1931, the British cadre reinstituted the type of administration that would accommodate British interests without incurring further British expense and obligation. In short, the British chose to return to reliance on the neftegna managers, thus returning to the dependent colonial state as a form of administration.

The British Return Ethiopia to the Neftegna Model of Colonial Control

The British form of reorganization of the Ethiopian empire required remapping the political geography of the empire. The British dismantled the regional model that had been used by the Italians from 1936 to 1941 because this model did not fit the political objective of a dependent colonial empire. Such a move was necessary in order to secure the neftegna in the position of state beneficiaries and state managers over the colonized peoples. To allow the Italian divisions to stand would have allowed the colonized national groups to retain their national identity and to remain in contact with each other. Any situation that fostered national consciousness or social or economic cooperation was seen as a threat to the power of the minority settler class.

In essence the British returned the empire to the old woreda organization that had been in place prior to the Italian occupation.

State Consolidation

This arrangement had carved the territories of the colonized peoples into small units, restricted travel and communication between the parts, and lumped different nationalities artificially together. However, the Italian interruption did provide some opportunity for reform of the previous neftegna pattern, and the British decided not to return to every letter of the old woreda system. They introduced refinements to the woreda model retaining the essence of the centralization the Italians had used. This shifted the units in order to put specifically the Abyssinian Amharas in control. The empire was organized into twelve provinces, and each province was divided into several awarajas. Each awaraja was again subdivided into several woredas, and each woreda into several localities. Part of this design was that it provided opportunities for the state bureaucracy to be expanded. Positions of authority were multiplied to accommodate the growing population of neftegnas. Authority was made to flow through the administrators of these new units. The administrators were all centrally appointed. Both the provinces and the awarajas were governed by individuals appointed by the emperor, and each woreda was governed by appointees chosen by these higher officials. All governors and branch office appointees were to be directly accountable to the Minister of the Interior. Control over these positions was so tight that each one was considered a salaried employee of the emperor himself and as such was also subject to be recalled at his discretion.

This refinement of the pre-Italian pattern of organization was chosen because the old pattern, despite the centralization mentioned above, had left some substantial loopholes. For example, the awaraja governors had still been capable of establishing their own independence. A governor, especially in the Abyssinian heartland of the empire, could build his own power base for his own purposes, and indeed this had happened. Some governors had paid the required taxes to the emperor only periodically. Since governors in the pre-1936 period had not been accountable to any particular ministry, they had been able to build up their own armies, which often meant that if they were dissatisfied they could, and occasionally did, declare war on the central power figure. The previous system had the

The Invention of Ethiopia

potential that the old governors could order the woredas to mobilize the general public (often through passing orders along through the balabats). Although as crown prince, Tefari had moved to weaken the position of the balabat, he had not managed to eliminate it entirely.

It is reasonable to surmise that the Italian organizational model, despite also being a centralized and logical model better suited to development than Haile Selassie's old system, was rejected at this point because the British team feared that the Italian model might facilitate the ability of the nations in the colonies to organize themselves efficiently around their cultural identities. Since they were relying on a form of reorganization that would reinstitute dependency, they sought to avoid such an outcome. Over the long term the configuration that the Italians had introduced was bound to foster national identity and provide a better platform for coordinating resistance, particularly against a settler regime. Since settler (dependent) colonialism relies to a large extent on the presence of alien settlers in the midst of the colonies, both the British and Abyssinians were intent on implementing a divide-and-rule strategy. These arrangements were essential to securing the economic base which characterizes dependent colonialism.

The second adjustment was in the political area and was designed to tighten control. A cabinet ministry was inserted to operate above the provincial governors. The provincial offices were considered branch offices of the Ministry of the Interior, with all regional governors answerable to the appropriate office of the respective ministries.

What these changes amounted to was not a reorganization of the administration of the colonies, but a return of Ethiopia's empire to the previously functioning organizational model. The difference, however, was a more refined relation between departments and a very carefully implemented chain of command.

The other form of political refinement undertaken was that of refurbishing the legislative body. The parliament provided for in the Constitution of 1931 was brought out of mothballs. The legislature was apparently regarded as useful for managing conflict among the

State Consolidation

various factions that comprised the neftegna, The members of the former aristocracy, the former governors and other people well-known to the emperor were to be nominated by the emperor to a Senate. The other house, the House of Deputies, was akin to a House of Commons. Rather than allow this body to be elected by nobles and chiefs as it had been previously, rules were set specifying that anyone was eligible to represent a given region if he lived in the area and owned property. One stipulation was that the property owned should be non-moveable, i.e., land. This policy automatically turned the campaign for the House of Deputies into a campaign solely for and between landlords over who would become the representatives in the government of an exclusively landlord class.

Elsewhere we explain the limited access to land. What this provision ensured, therefore, was a government comprised of settlers from the conquered regions and lords from the Abyssinian heartland, i.e., representatives of the landholding class that held a major stake both in the colonies and in the dependent colonial formula. Persons who previously had been holding rist, maderia, or siso land, became "titleholders," owners of land, under the new arrangements, making them eligible for Parliament. Although the rist and maderia landholders previously had independent linkage with the state and had nothing in common with each other in terms of the experience of holding land, the new land policy and the Parliament provided a common ground for all landlords and landholders collectively to protect their interests.

Within these conditions, Abyssinia and its colonies (the dependent colonial empire) faced life under a British administration that was intent on refurbishing Haile Selassie's rule and turning it into an internationally acceptable government. This process amounted to a polishing of the state.

One of the clauses in the Anglo-Ethiopian agreement was that it remain in force, that the British should continue organizing the state for two years and "[the agreement] thereafter be terminated at any time by either party giving three months' notice to the other to this effect" (cited in Perham 1969: 469). This amounted to an understanding that the agreement would stay in force until one of

The Invention of Ethiopia

the parties, either Haile Selassie or the British, felt that the state could be ruled by Haile Selassie. In fact he eventually found a way to proceed on his own path, which was essentially the settler colonial path.

In the process of perfecting the institutions of the state, the British began by endorsing the age-old Constitution of 1931, reactivating the basic structure of ministries. In addition to actions that have already been mentioned, the following was done in accordance with that constitution: (1) The security apparatus was reinstituted, (2) the judicial system was reestablished and several courts were set up—the Supreme Imperial Court, the High Court, the Provincial Courts, and the regional and communal courts, (3) as agreed, the British Government raised, trained, organized and armed the Ethiopian army at its cost, until by 1944 the infrastructure of a "modern" military institution was set up, (4) a formal education system based on the British model was established, and (5) as has been mentioned, the regional organization of the colonies and provinces was returned to the form that had been established before Italy redrew the provisional boundaries.

Although the new relationship was created, the role of the British was not ended. By 1946 Britain had achieved her minimum objective of keeping the old feudal-bureaucratic machinery together, as she had promised, and she had produced a new road map for the now Amhara-dominated Ethiopian state to follow. Thus the state institutions had been refined, and the state apparatus had begun to function in the old way. It should be remembered here that during these five years following 1941 primarily Amhara Abyssinians were trained by the British to replace the British bureaucrats.

Securing the Neftegna Class Base: Land Reform

Just as the need to update the state structure was confronted, so was the need for Haile Selassie's government to update Menelik's landholding system. The gabbar system had served several overlapping functions for Menelik: it had provided compensation for his

State Consolidation

northern Abyssinian officers and allies (such as the church), assuring their continued loyalty to the state; it had provided the labor essential to productivity in a technologically deficient system; and it had supplied a means for suppressing resistance. Under Haile Selassie the functions of the gabbar system were separated, but the essence of the system was retained. While the British architects were engaged in renovating and seeking international recognition of the model for the new state, Haile Selassie was engaged in tinkering with his own version of colonial land policy.

Haile Selassie had left Menelik's old land program intact up to the time of the occupation by Italy. Then as soon as he came back to power in 1941 he began to expand on Menelik's strategy of compensating loyalty to his regime with land. He transformed Menelik's maderia holding system (which was, in fact, a tenant system) by instituting a program of "free land grants" available to specified groups of people. For example, in a 1942 proclamation, those who had remained loyal throughout the Italian occupation were declared to be entitled to a freehold grant of forty hectares (100 acres). Just two years later, in 1944, soldiers and specified civil servants who had served the government were made eligible for these grants. (Stahl gives a complete listing of the recipients 1974:63 ff.). This policy marked a new direct and systematic policy of control of the means of production, and it was meant to last. As Haile Selassie himself made explicit on one of the occasions when he announced expansion of the policy, "The purpose in granting you land besides increment in pay is to enable you to have a lasting capital which can be inherited by your children" (Stahl 1974: 67). The significance of this was that it provided the basis on which neftegnas as a group were to develop into a class of landowners.

The land granted was from huge holdings recognized by the state as "government land." It should be recalled that all government land had been conquered and colonized land. During Menelik's time, the imperial crown had emerged as the landowner of greatest magnitude in the conquered areas, the regions usually euphemistically referred to as "southern Ethiopia." Haile Selassie moved to grant portions of this land to a carefully selected group of recipients.

The Invention of Ethiopia

Consequently, the land granted was primarily in "the south" where the bulk of once-conquered government land was situated.

Stahl writes that

> [a] case study of the social background of those who had received grants of two gashas or more showed that 80% of the grantees held titles as dedjazmatch, leul, ras, fitawrari, bejrond, kantiba, afanegus, etc., which means that they belonged to already privileged groups (Stahl 1974: 64).

Of course, the highly significant but unmentioned aspect, one that is central to our analysis, is that these grantees constitute the colonial ruling group. This essential feature of how this colonial system operated was increasingly formalized and expanded, but its essence was not changed. Land grants to these specific categories of people from the Abyssinian elite was the mechanism by which they were placed in control in the new state system.

This land grant system was the means by which the governing class in the empire organized and broadened its economic base. The system continued to function at the lowest levels as a straightforward tenant system for the conquered peoples. "Land reform" constituted nothing more than the continual conversion of state land into private property under very tightly controlled conditions aimed at creating an incentive for new landholders to defend their interest as a class. This assured an ever-widening neftegna class base. Michael Stahl had this comment about the difference that these changes had on the tenants; he said that

> [t]he judicial change from ownership of land by the imperial crown to private ownership meant little in the daily life of the peasant. They were still the subjects of military officers, civil servants, balabats, etc. who now emerged as the sole owners of the land which they cultivated as tenants (Stahl 1978: 68).

212

State Consolidation

Along with the "free land grant" program, Haile Selassie introduced a new form of payment—tax in monetary value rather than in kind (tribute). This change ushered in a period in which the colonizing group began to be openly identified as a "landlord class." Although the labels and identities of the landholder category shifted over the course of these changes, the structure of relations between those who held land and the state that protected their rights in land—the rulers—on the one hand, and those who were ruled, on the other, remained unchanged through the end of Haile Selassie's period.

When this new land grant system was first introduced, taxes were required from all the granted land. In the 1940s this resulted in substantial government revenues, but there were diminishing returns. Eventually the landlords themselves were able to utilize their own political power in endless bureaucratic devices to avoid paying taxes and to prevent increases in the tax rates. Rather than confront directly this group which was his major political power base, Haile Selassie turned to foreign investment and foreign technical assistance to speed up production, increase investment and bolster state revenues.

6 ETHIOPIA ENTERS THE ERA OF FINANCE CAPITAL, 1945-1974

The Search for a New Partner: The Pawn Changes Sides

Following the British reinstatement of Haile Selassie as ruler, it took very little time for the emperor to take the steps necessary to make the empire his own domain. Within a year of signing of the Anglo-Ethiopian agreement of 1942, he came to realize that the agreement in essence deprived him of virtually all the freedom he had had before the Italian occupation. In his dissatisfaction, he desired to turn to the United States. Such a move would put his fledgling empire under the wing of the most powerful of the world superpowers of the day, the hegemonic leader. To implement a shift, he sought and obtained proven American advisers. Then he and his American-trained advisers turned the rhetoric that had surrounded the internationalization of Ethiopia, i.e., that it was to be an "independent" entity, around on its authors. He asserted that he strongly desired to return to his former position of independence and authority. Following his lead it took very little time for Ethiopians everywhere to begin complaining about British control.

The problem was that Haile Selassie and his company had never wished to understand the British interpretation of the "liberation" of Ethiopia in 1941. As had always been the case, the invention and

The Invention of Ethiopia

reinvention, now referred to as "the liberation," of this empire was part and parcel of the general efforts of Europeans to solve their own problems. In this case it was part of the war package used by the western Europeans against contending powers. As far as Europe was concerned Ethiopia had already played out the role she was invented for—the role of the smaller nation used to achieve a larger end—just as she had during the European colonial expansion in the second half of the nineteenth century. The "help" Britain gave for the "liberation" of the Ethiopian empire was a part of Britain's war strategy to combat her own enemies, the Axis forces. Unless this is the perspective adopted, analysis goes astray.

Again one thing to be kept in mind is that Britain herself was operating under a set of constraints fairly new to her. The shift in power taking place globally at the time was one in which the old British-dominated strategy for dealing with colonial holdings by monopoly control was forced to give way to a new U.S.-dominated strategy leading to corporate control. Ethiopia maximized its own position by appealing to the United States in complaint about British policy and found a sympathetic response. The United States responded to Ethiopia positively because her case provided an excellent opportunity to test the general package of United States strategies for a new global order, not because it was much interested in Ethiopia apart from of these specific global concerns.

A major concern for President Roosevelt of the United States at that time was to introduce specific elements of his country's new formula for world order (see Chapter 2). Preparation for this project had been extensive. The United States position on global order, one that had been defined by Roosevelt, was that the primary cause of major European wars had been battles among economically powerful nations over monopoly control of the colonial market. It was also Roosevelt's position that the ongoing war of his time (the Second World War) was at its base a negation of this old method for the colonial occupation and regulating the colonial market. Roosevelt concluded that American business interests could play a major role in rearranging or readjusting the balance of power on the global scale both at the level of specific interactions and on the internation-

216

al scale. They were essentially prepared to introduce and to enforce the new game plan dictated by the power and the rules of finance capital. It was considered relevant that even the powers of Europe did not have conflicts anywhere that there was free economic access to a region.

Before putting forward the concept of trusteeship, America had begun to negotiate about the terms of a future peace (Louis 1978). It was while negotiations were underway between Britain and the United States that Japan attacked the United States, stepping up United States involvement in the global process. That situation brought the Second World War into full swing. Washington's decision to join the Allied forces changed the direction of the war and its outcome. But following the war, it became clear to the Allies that the United States was not thinking along the same lines as the powers of Europe. In fact, she even expected China to become one of the world powers, one that could be brought in either as a shareholder among the big powers or to replace France.

Without exception, the European Allied forces thought that the prospects were bright for reinstating their earlier strategy for world peace, that is, their old monopoly formula for occupying the colonies and finding a balance of power. The old European colonial empires expected that the outcome of the peace process would be the same as that following the First World War—they would tinker with the balance of power a bit. They expected that they would be restored to the same position that they had held earlier. In this, they all miscalculated. Washington saw the problem differently. Her position was that all world wars had been fought among nations seeking monopoly control over colonies. Consequently, single-country control over colonies should be eliminated.

The United States' position claimed to provide a foundation for avoiding future war among the powerful by liberalizing access to the colonies. The rhetoric of the day was that this would be avoided by "liberating" the colonies, granting them independence. It amounted to a proposal for internationalizing access to the colonies by the big powers.

The Invention of Ethiopia

To achieve this objective America committed herself to forcing the other world powers to sit and negotiate concerning not only the future of the colonies but also the future of the industrial world. These negotiations resulted in the Atlantic Treaty and the Yalta agreements. These and others of the treaties when taken together provided a blueprint for the collective security of industrial countries and introduced the conceptually new formula for peace known as "trusteeship." It was an American product which the others could not effectively counter. The notion was resisted initially and identified by Churchill and de Gaulle as ". . . a disguise for American expansion" (Louis 1978: 28). Nonetheless, it was this concept that shaped the future of global interaction after World War II. As argued in Chapter Two, this shift marked the official transition to the rule of finance capital on a global scale.

The shift did not occur overnight and reaction to this idea of trusteeship or the "disguise" of American expansion at the initial stages was slow and resistant. Both France and Britain, the largest two colony-holding countries, tried to arrange responses to the American program by presenting their own formulas (Pearce 1982).

France conducted what she called her own "trusteeship." It was a feeble attempt because her position was much too weak to enable her to oppose the U.S.-backed program.

Britain, as the largest colonial holder and also as a nation in a better condition by far, had also tried to arrange an alternative future for the colonies. Britain ". . . had put forward a far-reaching and imaginative set of proposals (the Raynton-Robinson project) by which the colonial world would develop along British lines and according to British ideals" (Louis 1978: 46).

But, though Britain may have had greater clout compared to France, like France, she could not make any difference when it came to confronting the power of the United States. The United States was economically and politically equipped to carry forth its program on a full scale. Britain as well as France abandoned its own programs at an early stage and began to put energy and attention into the United States' plans, focusing primarily on modifying it. Britain argued and tried to demonstrate that the Yalta agreement was a

Ethiopia in the Era of Finance Capital

mistake and that it ultimately worked against the interest of all colony-holding countries including the United States.

Britain argued that the United States itself held colonies, the Philippines and the islands of the South Pacific, and therefore even she herself would also find it risky and disadvantageous to be guided by the Yalta Agreement in conducting all affairs on the trusteeship model.

It was during this time that Ethiopia had approached the United States to ask for help in mediating between Ethiopia and Britain. The way that this approach occurred in the mid-1940s recalls the way that Ethiopia came to be involved in the European Scramble for Africa and was able to adhere to the provisions of the Berlin Conference of 1884-1885. Advised by foreign strategists who were keenly aware of the world situation, Ethiopian leaders were able to play for high stakes, taking advantage of the contradictions that existed among the contending world powers.

Just as Ethiopia came into an extremely advantageous position in relation to the western European power struggles in the 1880s, she did so again in 1941-45. She vied to test the positions being put forth as part of the Allied power conflict. Just as a European (Ilg), who had a clear understanding of events on the world scale, had successfully advised Menelik II as to how he could best play his country's position, so did a knowledgeable American adviser to Haile Selassie, John Spencer, act behind the scenes. He helped to maneuver Ethiopia as a smaller and weaker empire into a position to take strategic advantage of the growing United States strength vis-à-vis Britain. The British expressed irritation, for example, when Ethiopia's negotiating position in 1944 indicated that Ethiopia could call upon "our American ally" to break the British hold on the Ogaden.

> London testily attributed the ploy to John Spencer, the American foreign affairs adviser, who was well aware of Washington's anticolonialism. R. A. Butler, later to be foreign minister under Eden, was scandalized that the Ethiopian note had referred to "our American ally.... I have no doubt that the American adviser is responsible for

the impertinent suggestion of reference to the U.S.G."
Whoever was the originator of the brilliant tactic, he put
London on notice that it did not enjoy the same freedom
of negotiation it had in 1942 (Marcus 1983: 36-37).

Haile Selassie, who had a good knowledge of the making of
Ethiopia's empire, had requested directly that the United States
provide him someone of sufficient caliber to understand the needs
and position of his dependent empire and the operation of the big
powers. The Ethiopians "requested" preferably the man whom they
knew and who knew them. Haile Selassie had already complained to
the United States that the agreement of 1942 had reduced his
"independence" to the status of a colony. He had complained that
he had been paralyzed. Though Ethiopia had widely circulated her
own propaganda, she had directly conveyed her distress to the
United States' State Department and had directly requested its help
explaining ". . . the need for replacing the 1942 agreement and for
a jurist to assist in the drafting of a new treaty" (Spencer 1984: 106).

When this request was officially made, the United States had
already anticipated making a new arrangement in the world order
and had been arguing with the Allies for a program of "independence" for the colonies by way of trusteeship. Consequently the
United States responded favorably to Ethiopia. Furthermore, the
United States Treasury official who had been displeased ". . . with
the current situation in Ethiopia as it existed in 1943" (ibid.) was
more than glad to become involved in the Anglo-Ethiopian affair
(Spencer 1984: 107). It was at this time that the people at the
United States State Department located John Spencer and informed
him of the invitation. In his own words Spencer testified that ". . .
the Department of State . . . suggested that I might wish to accept
the Emperor's request that I return to Ethiopia as a legal advisor to
the Ministry of Foreign Affairs" (Spencer 1984: 107). Spencer, who
had worked as a mental laborer (i.e., as an ideologue) in Haile
Selassie's Ethiopia before the Italian occupation and who had gone
to England with the emperor as an exile to help write memoranda,
speeches, etc., was eager to accept. Furthermore, at the moment he

Ethiopia in the Era of Finance Capital

received the invitation, the man was an officer in the United States navy on active duty fighting in the Mediterranean with the Allied naval forces against Germany. As a lawyer, as a naval officer, and as a man who had observed the fall of the League of Nations, he was the top candidate for the position. He knew the ins and outs of the positions of the superpowers and of the smaller empires in general through his varied experience, and in particular that of Ethiopia. The British were not only aware of but concurred in Spencer's attachment to the Ethiopian Foreign Ministry, significant in light of general British accommodation to United States leadership.

As requested, Spencer returned to Ethiopia as "Advisor to the Foreign Office" on October 2, 1943. According to Spencer, when he arrived back in Ethiopia, Haile Selassie's group was confused and did not have a clear direction for extricating itself from British control. Spencer found a chaotic situation.

As Spencer himself later wrote, ". . . the emperor and his inner circle of ministers were actually aware of the extent and degree of domination which Britain exercised over their country and their lives. The 1942 Anglo-Ethiopian agreement and the related military convention extended control over every sector of national life and, as I was soon to perceive, every proposal and every discussion pivoted on the issue 'what would be the reaction of the British?'" (Spencer 1984: 139).

Spencer reviewed the 1942 agreement in detail and actually observed first-hand many facets of the agreement at work in the day-to-day implementation in Ethiopian circumstances. He concurred with the general Ethiopian sentiment that as long as the agreement was standing, Ethiopians were severely constrained in running the affairs of the empire. The agreement guaranteed that all the highest decisionmakers were to be British nationals and that the British were to have absolute (monopoly) power.

The Ethiopians were in no way prepared to move in to take over the state system on their own in the absence of the British. They did not have any organizational alternative to introduce. Nevertheless, the emperor and those around him were intent upon being reinstated in the position of titular rulers. The intimate

The Invention of Ethiopia

knowledge that Spencer had about the differences in the global strategies of the United States and Britain, all of which he put at Ethiopia's disposal, served the aspiring Ethiopian ruling group quite well. The emperor was finally successful in playing one superpower off against the other. It should be noted that the superpowers were willing to be played. This pattern dovetailed nicely with previous Ethiopian experience in dealing with global superpowers eager both to extend their influence and to find a way out of their dilemma.

So at the time that Ethiopia diplomatically moved to involve the United States in her affairs, both the former ruling elite of Ethiopia and the American-born adviser had concluded that without some major adjustment of this 1942 Anglo-Ethiopian agreement Ethiopia's hands were tied. John Spencer saw that his first major task in his new position was to introduce tools to sidestep or to renegotiate the 1942 agreement.

Spencer offers a full account of the strategy utilized to arrange a renegotiation of the conditions of the agreement (Spencer 1984: 102-159). He advised the Ethiopians at the outset not to fear England because Washington and London were themselves in an ongoing debate over the future of the colonies.

If England were to push the matter of control of Ethiopia too hard, chances were good that Washington would stand with Ethiopia against Britain. The implication was that there was no real danger in disappointing and alienating Britain. Spencer's role was crucial here. Without him the Ethiopians had a real fear of British reaction if the agreement of 1942 were to be seriously challenged. At the root of their fear was that they had no idea what America's reaction might be if Britain responded negatively to an Ethiopian rejection of the terms of the agreement. Though certain well-educated Ethiopians had a vague idea of America's official "anti-colonial" position, Spencer's writings indicate that he was definitely familiar with America's emerging stance on the colonial issue as well as knowing the British position.

He observed that Britain was not in any position to hold on to its colonies in the old way, let alone acquire and maintain a "new" colony in the face of United States opposition. Diplomatically

Ethiopia in the Era of Finance Capital

Washington was supporting those who came out against old style "colonialism." Opposition to Britain's colonial position from any quarter was supported by the United States. A close look at the British position revealed in the agreement of 1942 demonstrates that Britain could easily have stopped any individual from taking a position within the Ethiopian state structure at the time Spencer arrived on the scene. The interesting question then is why did Britain allow two surrogates of American interest (Blowers and Spencer) to assist in establishing "Ethiopia's situation." George Blowers was sent to become the governor of the State Bank of Ethiopia, the key position for establishing the control of finance, and Spencer arrived to become the chief engineer in the office of Foreign Affairs. Spencer has characterized most of his work as ". . . behind the scenes as both adviser and drafter of the diplomatic correspondence" (Spencer 1984: 140). By saying this he seems to minimize the role of the strategist in a dependency. Either Spencer himself was so much the technocrat that he did not understand that he was empowered by the United States and Britain to act as a significant influence behind the crown, or he intentionally downplays for the public the role of the agents of finance capital in dependencies.

Two years after the 1942 agreement the world situation had changed dramatically. It was quite clear to all parties involved in the Ethiopian case, i.e. to Spencer and his client Haile Selassie, the United States and Britain, which way the World War would end. It was well understood who would be ultimately responsible for leading the reorganization of the world economic order.

Consequently any British interest or willingness to get involved in a high stakes war over Ethiopia lost its rationale. Instead Britain was concerned that Ethiopia not fall into the hands of enemy forces. Its strategy was that it was better to have the empire allied with a force that could understand the interests of the capitalist world in general and that of Britain in particular than it was to opt for direct control and lose Ethiopia completely. Britain saw that only the United States could fill the role satisfactorily. Harold Marcus has recorded the views of the British Foreign Office on this issue:

The Invention of Ethiopia

"'Anything the Americans achieve can only be to our advantage ... while if they don't achieve anything or resign, or have rows with Ethiopians, at least Ethiopian resentment will not be directed against the British'" (Marcus 1983: 42).

With this reasoning, Britain did not oppose the return of Spencer to the palace as an in-house ideologue. The coming of Blowers to the crucial position of governor of the State Bank specifically placed him as a caretaker of the institution which shaped the economic base in a way that was accessible to the finance capitalist class. Later, American economic missions also entered and thoroughly surveyed the empire without British objection.

It can be fairly assumed that the British behavior on these matters was in essence a type of advocacy for America to take charge in Ethiopia. It simply cannot be seen as accidental, as it often is, that Americans were ushered into control of the central financial institution and of foreign affairs of the dependent state. Such control was critical to determining the course of events in this experimental situation. On the other hand, as we have pointed out above, America's interest in Ethiopia must be seen in light of the United States implementation of its global strategies of "decolonization" of empires. America advocated a new formula for division of the world market share.

So it was under pressure from the United States and in light of its own economic problems in the age of a post-war new economic order that Britain agreed to the request made by Ethiopia to renegotiate the 1942 agreement (see Marcus 1983: 42). Finally, in December of 1944, Britain and Ethiopia went head to head and produced the December 19, 1944, Anglo-Ethiopian agreement. Though Britain did not agree to give everything that was demanded by Ethiopia who was supported by the United States, it must still be considered that Haile Selassie scored a major success in the outcome. It is significant that he did it with an American adviser at his ear. Harold Marcus indicated that this "... treaty generally was a triumph for Ethiopia. It proclaimed diplomatic equality between London and Addis Abeba, it provided no special relationship between British advisers and the Ethiopian government, and the

224

head of the British military mission was placed under the authority of the Ethiopian Minister of War" (Marcus 1983: 89).

With this agreement Ethiopia had totally regained the pre-1935 position that she had coveted ever since the Italian ouster and had attained a position of recognition in the body of world politics. Upon returning, she expected to play a role at the side of the newest world power, a position which would afford Ethiopia a great deal of visibility. The old relationship with Britain was quickly pushed aside. In effect, Britain technically left the responsibility for Ethiopia to America. The United States hereafter was to take over reorganizing and overseeing the development of bureaucracy in this empire, a relationship which lasted well into the 1970s.

The Transition to United States Patronage amid Declining British Influence

As early as the first month of 1945, American and Ethiopian political technocrats arranged a meeting of Haile Selassie with President Roosevelt in Cairo, Egypt, at the Great Bitter Lake of the Suez Canal, upon the occasion of Roosevelt's return from the Yalta Conference. At this time, according to "foreign affairs advisers" who were present, Haile Selassie appeared with a long wish list. Spencer's account is one among many. He recounts that six points were emphasized.

> (1) Highest priority was given to the necessity of access to the sea and a request for U.S. support for the return of Eritrea to provide a solution to this need;
> (2) the importance of Ethiopia[n] control of the management of the railway to Djibouti, with a report on negotiations to engage an American firm for this purpose;
> (3) the problems of the Ogaden, with a report on discussions with the Sinclair Oil Corporation and the expression of a wish to promote American enterprise in Ethiopia;

The Invention of Ethiopia

(4) Ethiopia's wish to participate in drafting the United Nations Charter to replace the covenant of the League of Nations and in so doing to help others profit from her own past experience under the League;

(5) Ethiopia's wish, as the first nation to enter the war against the Axis, to play a role in the decisions taken at the Peace Conference, and

(6) a request for arranging the financing of greatly needed additional arms and transport and communications equipment (Spencer 1984: 159).

The list itself provides a nice summary of Ethiopian objectives.

This first meeting not only marked the beginning of Ethiopia's pursuit of several long-awaited goals, but Haile Selassie was also able to meet face to face with the United States' leader, which contributed to legitimizing even further Haile Selassie's rule over the still-fragile empire. It also brought to the fore Haile Selassie's wish to assume a dependent role under the United States specifically at a time when the United States was in the process of establishing international hegemony.

This position promised to give Ethiopia some leverage in establishing the nature of the new form of relationship between the superpowers and the dependencies. At the outset the United States readily accepted the dominating colonial ideology of Ethiopia. In fact American scholars soon moved in enthusiastically to embellish central features of the Ethiopian myth, such as that of three thousand years existence as a single nation.

Haile Selassie, having registered with the leader of the new world order Ethiopia's primary demands and concerns for survival as a dependent state, returned to Ethiopia with a very strong position. The emperor and his aspiring elite were now able to operate with a nearly free hand in establishing themselves in power and in initiating policies which would secure the pattern of rule that had come to characterize Ethiopian dependent colonialism. Upon closer inspection, the free rein was actually a bit of an illusion since the United States very well knew that Haile Selassie was playing within specific limits. This was assured by the presence of agents who were advising the Ethiopians on all major moves and who could be relied upon to steer them clear of potential danger zones. Only a sophisticated United States adviser could know how specific Ethiopian demands would provide the perfect pretext for American actions on a world scale. The United States in fact saw several benefits from Ethiopia's behavior because Ethiopia was able to influence other dependent states to follow her lead.

A premier example of Ethiopia's role in regard to acting as a foil for the implementation of Washington's policies was the role that Ethiopia played in establishing the Organization of African Unity, influencing the new leaders of African states to accept the rule of finance capital under the guise of independence. She was able to become a model or test case for the United States' new trusteeship formula and she willingly stepped in to advocate the formula for others. The Ethiopian case was experimental during this period not only for the colonized but for the colonizers.

The United States' relation with the dependent states was one of orchestrating the direction taken but not to assume full direct control. Ethiopia was in fact encouraged and occasionally forced by Washington to strike deals and arrangements with other powers. The United States very well knew that no other power could ultimately outdistance her in terms of support; they could only supplement. Meanwhile the trusteeship model called for shared or joint holding. It *required* that other powers invest and retain interest in a single dependency. Therefore Ethiopia was sent to strike small deals with other countries. This was not only to be tolerated but also to be demanded in the name of trusteeship and free competition.

From the time of Haile Selassie's meeting with President Roosevelt, the emperor was catapulted into the position he most loved and knew best. As titular power riding the waves of international tension among superpowers he was in his element, secure in a position he knew and from which he could operate effectively. But it must be kept in mind that Haile Selassie was effectively ordained into this position beginning from the day that the United States sent

The Invention of Ethiopia

its economic and technical mission and established Americans as engineers at the center of the financial and the political branches of the state. The policies and the individuals put in place by the Americans at that juncture played a determining role in the life of the empire for several years. Hereafter it should be understood that when we refer to Ethiopia during this period or to "Haile Selassie's government" we are in effect referring to the complex of all who were employed to act "in Ethiopia's interest."

To focus on the events that unfolded after 1945, soon after the meeting of Haile Selassie with President Roosevelt, the Ethiopian technocrats began immediately to adjust to the lead and the demands of the technical and economic mission from the United States. They took on the role of arranging financial and political conditions inside the country which rendered Ethiopia capable of satisfying both financial and political demands generated from outside Ethiopia. Indeed, the first priorities of these branches of the Ethiopian government were to accommodate external requirements.

The Ethiopian agencies knew that they had to arrange suitable conditions for foreign investors, developers and financiers:

> U.S. planners saw three major interrelated economic problems: (1) repairing and maintaining the Italian-built communications network; (2) building modern social, educational, and economic infrastructures; and (3) increasing agricultural production and industrial output (Marcus 1983: 59).

Since the whole effort required foreign capital and expatriate technicians, the revised program emphasized projects which would add to foreign exchange. Emphasis was placed on an "orderly process of expansion, development and technological modernization" (ibid.).

It must be remembered that one objective of the new United States-led policy was to agitate smaller capitalist powers to take a developmental role in the dependencies. Others were invited to share in the gain as well as in the burden. Consequently it was in the interest of the United States to encourage the smaller powers to

228

Ethiopia in the Era of Finance Capital

become involved. Others had to participate in order to legitimize the very concept of market trusteeship. The financial and foreign affairs personnel who engineered new relations between Ethiopia and the external world were aware of these requirements as each engaged in their specific line of work. For example, the financial governor of the State Bank, in planning to direct Ethiopia's finances away from dependence on Britain into the role of a dependent state accountable to a broader range of creditors among the solvent powers, began to make deals for credit elsewhere. In short he initiated the search for required foreign capital by exploring several alternative sources.

As the adviser for foreign affairs, Spencer's main job was to explore ways that Ethiopia's unique position could provide opportunities for both Ethiopia and her patrons.

All the technocrats working in the name of Ethiopia were challenged at that juncture to plow new ground and to open up arrangements in the geopolitical situation that would become tomorrow's economic benefits. In the world situation existing at that time, when the world wanted peace but the big powers did not trust each other, Spencer, as instrumental in shaping Ethiopia's foreign affairs, had a major challenge requiring the utmost creativity and diplomacy. A major task that fell on his shoulders was to advise his Ethiopian "clients" (his term) on soliciting support from all potential world powers to bring about the annexation of Eritrea and the Ogaden (see Spencer 1984: 188-281).

Although the United States played an important role globally in establishing the dominance of a finance capitalist social formation, she had not been responsible for laying down the original infrastructure of the Ethiopian state. As in other parts of the world, what the United States did was to make accessible to finance capital what structures already had been established. The United States' role led to America's refurbishing and strengthening (through development and modernization) the existing infrastructure in Ethiopia. The technical mission played a significant part in this process by first specifying requirements for stabilizing the empire's economy and then issuing recommendations for meeting these requirements.

The Invention of Ethiopia

Ethiopia had requested this technical mission. At the conclusion of its survey, it suggested the following:

> ... a loan of $130,088,870 to carry out 'projects necessary to the rehabilitation and the economic development of Ethiopia.' ... The first part of the request called for $108,500,000 for the development of infrastructures. Twenty million was to be devoted to the rehabilitation and expansion of road transport.... $55 million railway project involving the construction of 890 kilometers of new line.... Fifteen million dollars was to be invested in the development of airports and related installations ... the restoration, extension, and improvement of post, telephone and telegraph systems was calculated at $5.3 million; and various hydro-electric, irrigation, and water control projects were assigned a cost of $13,300,000 (Marcus 1983: 64).

Though Addis Ababa immediately demanded these inputs of Washington, and initially presented this shopping list to a single country, she ultimately filled the list from a variety of sources. Significantly, it was her failure to get all that she initially demanded that forced her into the role that she was expected to play. Soon she began to open her doors to all who would come to invest or otherwise assist her. She turned to Stockholm, Moscow, Prague, Paris, London, Rome and others, buying and receiving all she could from wherever she could arrange a connection.

The major task given to those responsible for Ethiopian political advances was to acquire the former colony of Eritrea and the part of Somaliland known as Ogaden. She launched a major lobbying campaign in order to put herself into a better negotiating position. The content of voluminous memos and diplomatic missions (undertaken whenever physically possible) was that both Eritrea and the Ogaden had been an integral part of Ethiopia's "3000-year" history. Such a diplomatic offensive required an elaboration of the Ethiopian colonial mythology. Ethiopia and her increasing number of advocates argued with one voice that the former colonies should not be

230

separated from the "motherland." They presented the case as if the world body was standing in the way of the homecoming of two sons who had been prisoners of war.

The United States in Ethiopia

Haile Selassie's demands in the field of foreign affairs had been met by one superpower or another ever since he returned to his dependent empire in 1941. He had demanded a formal agreement in 1942; he had it. He demanded a renegotiation for a new agreement and got that, too (the Anglo-Ethiopian agreement of 1944). In the same fashion, he demanded and was ultimately granted admission into the United Nations. He demanded a full complement of technicians and advisers, earlier referred to as mental labor, and was supplied with as many persons as his state could absorb.

A key item on his list of demands when the United Nations began its work was to obtain control over both former Italian colonies, Eritrea and "Italian Somaliland." As the United Nations opened its doors for business, Ethiopia as a charter member became privy to all issues on the agendas and their order of priority. Thanks to keen foreign advisers eager to test the tenets of the emerging new international order, it was known to Ethiopia that the first order of business was to deal with the future of the colonies of former Axis countries, including the Italian colonies. Ethiopia was ready to make her claim. The task, according to the United Nations rules, was for foreign ministers to hold a meeting and bring their recommendations. Ethiopia, eager to influence the decision in any way she could, demanded to be present at the Foreign Ministers Conference in late summer, 1945, to explain her case directly through a delegate. This initial demand was rejected, but Ethiopia was invited by the foreign ministers to "submit . . . views on the question by correspondence" (Perham 1969: 484). Though Ethiopia protested and reissued her demand, she was finally convinced that she could not attend as a participant. The emperor then issued ". . . a statement of his claims

The Invention of Ethiopia

to Eritrea and Italian Somaliland in a collection of memoranda to which several references have been made" (ibid).

As it turned out, the foreign ministers at this conference could not agree on a procedure for determining the future of the ex-colonies. Every country had its own suggestion, and most refused to compromise. Some suggested trusteeship under the United Nations, others direct international administration of all the colonies. Britain suggested awarding Ethiopia some part of Eritrea so that she could have a role to play. France rejected the idea of any new power in the area and even suggested Italy should be made trustee of her own lost colonies. Since they could not arrive at any mutually acceptable solution, they postponed the matter for further study. Although each of the big powers—the United States, the Soviet Union, Britain and France—had a specific proposal regarding the rest of the Italian colonies (Louis 1978: 555-562), when they returned they did not yet have a single mutually satisfactory proposal about Eritrea, except to send the issue back to the United Nations General Assembly. This probably occurred because there had not yet been a chance for real leadership to be demonstrated within the United Nations; even members were not yet secure in its operation.

Why, under these circumstances, did the United Nations have difficulty deciding the future of Eritrea? Perham has observed,

> Ethiopia was a vigorous claimant. But there were others. There was Italy, rather surprisingly supported for a time by Russia, presumably relying on growth of the Italian Communist party. There was also Egypt, the former ruler of the coastal regions, whose government claimed that some half of the population was Muslim (Perham 1969: xxxi).

As we can see, when issues came to a vote the most important ally to have during that juncture in world history was the United States, the power that was coming into global prominence and consequently had a significant influence within the organization. Ethiopia had made the United States an ally. Besides the interest that the United States had in obtaining a base of operations for

Ethiopia in the Era of Finance Capital

surveillance in the Middle East and Ethiopia's willingness to provide it in return for United States support for her claim on Eritrea, there were several factors that influenced the American move. Though the United States had an expressed interest in "de-monopolizing" the empires of her European allies, she was not an advocate of "creating smaller nations." Wherever possible, Washington argued to bring the colonial regions into the United Nations in large units for the purposes of administrative control. The Eritrean issue was debated and, with the United States supporting the Ethiopian position, was voted in favor of Ethiopia (see Bereket H. Selassie 1989 for details). A model of federation was devised for this particular case, out of keeping with the general types of solutions that were being found for the disposition of the former colonies. Eritrea was federated to Ethiopia in 1952.

For Haile Selassie, who did not have the word "federation" in his vocabulary and whose country had no concept nor tradition akin to federation, the term was treated as a euphemism for "possession." Ethiopia was strongly advised that a change in her constitution would be required for Ethiopia to be able to implement federation at all, since the Eritrean constitution contained provisions such as the ones for democratic elections that were absent from that of Ethiopia. By 1955 Ethiopia did issue a revised constitution, one that no longer precluded outright the formal requirements for federation. But Haile Selassie continued to interpret "federation" in his own terms, i.e., to mean that Eritrea was part of Abyssinia, and he proceeded to deal with the arrangement in precisely that way. Margery Perham, noting this, cryptically commented that ". . . the concept of federation was as unfamiliar as it was probably unpopular with the emperor and his ruling class" (1969: xxxii).

Confirming this interpretation is the account of Dawit Wolde Giorgis, who later became intimately involved with the administration of Eritrea after the federation period. Of federation he has written,

> Haile Selassie set out at once to turn federalism into complete reunification. He did nothing to ensure Eritrea's

The Invention of Ethiopia

special status. Nobody in Ethiopia understood or cared to understand what federation meant; most simply thought it meant unification with Ethiopia (Dawit 1989: 79).

Eritrea had come close enough to catch a whiff of independence, but the autonomous aspect of the Eritrean federation with Ethiopia began eroding even before the Eritreans had a chance to taste it. To some Eritreans this became clear only after several years of federation, a period during which Ethiopia gained approval and legitimacy from the big powers for virtually any activities that she cared to undertake in Eritrea. Perham, a writer with a wry sense of understatement, wrote that "[l]ittle by little the federal foundations were eroded ... in 1955 some members of the Eritrean Assembly complained of interference in their internal affairs." In response to the Eritrean members' complaint in their own assembly, the emperor's representatives made it clear that they did not make distinctions between Eritrea and Abyssinia. Their official claim was that the two had been joined long before. To use his own words, Ethiopia's representative said that, "there are no internal nor external affairs as far as the office of His Imperial Majesty's representative is concerned and there will be none in the future" (Perham 1969: xxxiii). A large part of the effort to incorporate Eritrea completely within Ethiopia was what is usually termed propaganda work. Ethiopia continually presented her case for unity with Eritrea, creating confusion, at the least, among the big powers and agreement, at the most. Gradually, by 1962 through intrigues that are described from the Ethiopian side by Spencer (1984) and from the Eritrean side by Bereket (1989), Ethiopia brought about the dissolution of the Eritrean parliament and officially annexed Eritrea, pronouncing it to be the fourteenth province of the Ethiopian empire.

Spencer informs us that in the meantime his office of foreign affairs had negotiated successfully with Britain to hand over to Haile Selassie part of the Somali area that had cost Britain £1,000,000 to administer annually. This transfer had become possible because of the condition that was developing on the world scale. In the long term, Britain had little to gain by hanging on to such a costly entity.

234

Ethiopia in the Era of Finance Capital

This remaining part was in the present Ogaden—the Haud—a region along the southern frontier of British Somaliland to which thousands of Somalis from the British side migrated annually. This land was transferred to Ethiopia and annexed in 1954. Thereafter, the Haud was regarded by Ethiopia and her backers as part of Ogaden and became another section of occupied Ethiopian territory, her newest colony. This transfer marked another step in the continuing expansion of the colonial territories made available to Ethiopia by Western powers who were guaranteed access. The new empire had now added to its domain the lands and peoples of Eritrea and the Haud, the new territories from Britain. By 1962 these acquisitions were recognized as legitimate holdings of Ethiopia by the superpowers of the day. Henceforth the colonial empire took on the characteristic shape of the current geopolitical entity that is known simply as Ethiopia.

Modernization of the Inherited Administrative Apparatus under United States Tutelage

After 1951 the U.S. effectively took over as the primary Western overseer of all major features of the empire, not only in military matters. Of the many affairs to be tackled, the primary task was to renovate the administrative superstructure. This was necessary so that technological and organizational tools were in place to enable the United States to operate efficiently according to her own modern standards. To accomplish this the United States began to deal with updating each feature of the state apparatus.

To what extent was the administrative apparatus organized and at what capacity did it operate when the United States arrived on the scene?

As previously mentioned, as Haile Selassie settled with the British officials by 1943, he issued a series of orders. The key order of 1943 was the establishment of a Council of Ministers. The following ministries were reestablished and were to be guided by specifically European principles. These were the Ministries of the Pen; Public

The Invention of Ethiopia

Works and Communication; Education and Fine Arts; Commerce and Industry and Agriculture; Interior; Foreign Affairs; Finance; War; Justice; Post, Telephones and Telegraphs; and Communication.

Most of the highest positions in all of these ministries were either occupied by foreigners, particularly British personnel, or were occupied by Haile Selassie's handpicked individuals from Abyssinia with a European adviser close at hand. Just as a pillar supports the roof, European advisers sat just behind the inner door in offices manned by Ethiopians, supporting the dependent Abyssinian bureaucrats who sat at the desks. When the United States moved in, American consultants often played the role of adviser, but not always. As described for economic matters, the United States' model called for internationalizing the personnel as well as the funds.

Of all the departments in the bureaucracy, the Ministry of the Interior is the centerpiece of Ethiopian dependent colonialism. It is the most important because its function is to safeguard the economic base of the empire.

Officially the task of the Ministry of the Interior is to oversee all the "internal" affairs of the empire. The duty of the Minister of Interior was to "supervise security throughout the Empire, and the provincial administration and police are under his orders" (Perham 1969: 91). In short, the major function of this ministry was to control the colonies. The Ministry of the Interior functioned as the Colonial Office for the empire. Critical functions of state organization, such as the security system, the provincial administration and all dimensions of municipal government, were placed under the Ministry of the Interior. One of its initial tasks was to transform what had been essentially external relations between Abyssinia and once-neighboring, now colonized, nations into internal matters of the Ethiopian state. It is therefore important to address the updated function of this section of government. Most of the other departments of the administration can be seen as supplementary.

The function of this division (Interior) was to attain complete control over the provinces. Haile Selassie had laid claim on all the portions of the empire Menelik conquered. All of these portions were again staked out to be administered by the Ethiopian govern-

Ethiopia in the Era of Finance Capital

ment when the emperor was reinstated by British forces in 1941. These regions included the conquered areas that he had claimed despite efforts of the conquered peoples to govern themselves at that time. The jurisdiction of this administration included all of the area of the current empire except Eritrea and Ogaden. When these regions were officially annexed to Ethiopia, all that was necessary to place them into colonial status was for the Ethiopian government to declare them "provinces" of Ethiopia, as lands of previously conquered peoples had been declared "provinces" in earlier days, and put them under the administrative domain of the Ministry of the Interior.

When the United States arrived, Haile Selassie had divided this land mass according to classic top-down mechanisms for centralized administration, parcelling the empire into twelve provinces with each province subdivided into several awarajas and the awarajas into several woredas. By that time the woredas had been apportioned into several segments called miktel woredas, and within each miktel woreda several municipal, kebele and finance officers were still assigned to serve as the final link between the local populace and the colonial administration. Many of these linkage persons were still called balabats. The empire was initially divided into a total of twelve provinces, sixty-four awarajas, 321 woredas, 1221 miktel woredas and an uncounted number of atbias or kebeles, often referred to as balabats after the term applied to the persons placed in charge of the smallest subdivision.

Some of the individuals who served as balabats had been selected for this new "leadership" status in the Ethiopian state through recognition of preexisting traditional criteria. Indeed there were a few individuals who were even allowed to retain the titles "king," "sultan," or "petty king" from the precolonial period despite the fact that their real position within the empire had been reduced to that of extended balabat. The much larger proportion of balabats qualified for the position through cooperating in the conquest. These, who were often termed traitors by the local people they governed, were eventually brought into the neftegna landholding system. Their landholding status has often been offered as evidence

237

that local people did share land rights. Ultimately, however, regardless of previous stature attained by the individuals who served in that position, the role of balabat remained to be that of transmitting orders from above to the local populations. The role was one of messenger service for the Ethiopian administration. This was not changed under United States' supervision.

Under the United States, the same imported bureaucratic system was utilized to govern the territory. At the top sat the emperor under whom a prime minister functioned. Under the prime minister sat the minister of the Interior. The same pattern was utilized for other ministries.

It was the emperor, rather than the Minister of the Interior, who appointed a governor-general for each of the provinces to serve as the government's representative for that province and to report directly to the Ministry of the Interior concerning all matters. These officials were also directly responsible for implementing in their provinces the policies of other ministries, such as the Ministry of Finance or the Ministry of Justice. The governor-general's office was staffed by personnel who were expected to handle all provincial business, even though the officials who served under the governor-general were appointed by, and also directly responsible to, the emperor. Under the governor-general served the office of the principal secretariat, which had the responsibility of dealing with all other offices and officers directly working with issues concerning that province. In addition there was a vice governor-general and director of the province whose main job was to look after the proper use of the funds and report to the Ministry of Finance through the Ministry of the Interior. It is fair to say that this official represented a watchdog for the Ministry of Finance.

A broad range of officials was appointed in the province. These officials were technically serving under the governor but were ultimately accountable only to the emperor who appointed them. The conflict embedded in this arrangement led to endless jockeying for power and kept the emperor firmly in command. This system of rule represented the application of a traditional Abyssinian style of management to an imported European administrative apparatus.

Ethiopia in the Era of Finance Capital

The emperor retained the power to appoint the governor of an awaraja as well. The awaraja governor's office included the governor, the principal secretary and office of the municipalities (police, courts, etc.). The office of awaraja was officially responsible to report directly to the office of the governor-general of the province. Likewise, the woreda office was to report to the awaraja level and so on. This meant that the collected reports of the lower levels of administration comprised the report of the higher level all the way up the system. Finally, the aggregated sum of the provincial reports became the report that the minister of the Interior submitted to the emperor. This system was in place by the time the United States came into contact with the administrative structure of the empire. The United States left the organizational structure intact and merely introduced updated technologies that made the communications among the segments of the bureaucracy more rapid. The United States inherited, approved, and improved upon the old colonial bureaucracy.

The Legal Apparatus with its British Imprint

The apparatus of justice at the time that the United States stepped into the role of powerful patron for Ethiopia was a curious mixture of traditional judicial practice with a British facade.

It is received wisdom among students of Ethiopian studies that the Fetha-Nagast (the Book of Laws, an ancient compilation of mainly religious law) served as the historical foundation for Ethiopia's Code of Law until the 1930s. But though there is much reference to the ancient Book of Laws, there is little substantive discussion about what it actually contains. For whatever reason, very little linkage is ever attempted between that ancient document and later Ethiopian legal codes (Perham 1969: 138-140). The claim seems to serve a symbolic or ideological purpose in linking the modern empire to the traditional Abyssinian monarchy.

According to Margery Perham, the Fetha-Nagast was first compiled in the thirteenth century by

239

The Invention of Ethiopia

a Coptic churchman in Egypt from a number of sources including the Pentateuch, Roman law, the New Testament, the Canons—some of them apocryphal—of the eastern church, and the proceedings of the early councils, such as those of Nicaea and Antioch ... he also borrowed from Mohammedan law of the Cairo school (Perham 1969: 139).

This Book of Laws was available until recently only in Ge'ez. Since Ge'ez is the language of the orthodox church scribes, it could only be understood by a few clerics and kings in Abyssinia. These difficulties led to the gradual decline of the Fetha-Nagast. Kings began the practice of ruling by decree and proclamation alone.

The process of rule by legislation was not introduced until the European alliance began. Perham has commented that

... as an instrument of government [rule by legislation] is a mark of constitutional maturity; in Ethiopia it belongs to the period since Menelik and especially to the reign of the present emperor (Perham 1969: 140).

It is really more accurate to say that a constitution did not even appear in Ethiopia until after Haile Selassie became emperor in 1931 and that one was issued primarily out of concern for Ethiopia's international stature. By act of that constitution a formal Ethiopian legal system was introduced in the empire.

The preamble of the criminal code which was issued on the heels of the 1931 Constitution offered some reasons why the Ethiopians had chosen a modern or at least European-style judicial system, namely that:

... the new code is a mere clarification and revision of damages and punishments, "according to the increase of man's knowledge and according to the improvement of the conditions of his existence." Another more daring reason given for issuing the code is that the people "by learning European practice may attain to a higher degree of knowledge, because the basis of our code of laws in many places fits in with the European code" (Perham 1969: 141).

This code issued by Haile Selassie had not had time to be tested as to its effectiveness. The entire judicial structure was swept away by the Italians upon occupation of the empire, and a new code of law was issued by the Italians on June 1, 1936. The Ethiopian system disappeared so quickly that it evidently had not taken root. Since it was alien in origin and in design, many who were assigned to implement it did not even understand it. So although the structure had been formally established, there is little evidence that the judicial system had functioned according to the blueprint prior to the arrival of the Italians.

Although the Italians were intent upon totally replacing the legal system in Ethiopia, they did not stay long enough for their substitute to take hold.

Ironically, the Italian interference in the internal affairs of the Ethiopian empire provided the perfect excuse for the British to intervene on a grand scale to reestablish several of the ministries with the heavy hand of an active manager. Without the Italian episode, this would have been more difficult, in that the British could have appeared to be tearing down an "indigenous system." Ultimately, Haile Selassie's government benefitted from the British ability to put the judicial system in place in such a manner that it would function the way that Haile Selassie had desired but had failed to accomplish.

In the final analysis it was Britain that organized the entire apparatus of the Ethiopian judicial system in accordance with the Anglo-Ethiopian Agreements of 1942 and 1944. As mentioned above in another context, four categories of courts were established. As with all other dimensions of the Ethiopian state, the judicial system was an import.

The Supreme Imperial Court is appellate in its jurisdiction. It is in theory the highest decisionmaking court. The highest judge is the president or the Afa Negus (mouth of the king). Though the Supreme Imperial Court was officially part of the Ministry of

The Invention of Ethiopia

Justice, it operated as an independent entity, the highest power in the land answerable only to the emperor on legal matters. It came under the Ministry of Justice only for administrative purposes.

The High Court was given full criminal and civil jurisdiction anywhere in the empire. However, sentences of death had to be confirmed by the emperor (see Perham 1969: 154).

The provincial courts were also filled by judges appointed by the emperor. Appeals went to the High Court. There were several restrictions, such as how many years of imprisonment, how many lashes, and how much money the provincial court could levy as fines. The days of rases sitting in independent courts were over.

> Under decree No.1 of 1942, article 10, (the important law setting up the provincial administration), the governor-general, himself appointed by the Emperor, was made president of the provincial court, but three other judges were to be appointed to sit with him. In his judicial capacity the governor-general was placed under the Minister of Justice (ibid: 154).

The various tribunals that had functioned both in the conquered regions prior to conquest and independently in Abyssinia were designated as regional and communal courts. These courts were established by fiat which provided for the incorporation of a wide variety of styles of adjudication and marked the beginning of the move toward uniformity. Perham commented on this process: "This allowed for the recognition and systematization of the large numbers of subordinate courts in the provinces" (ibid: 155).

There were other sweeping moves which were initially intended to thrust the Ethiopian judicial system instantly into the range of acceptability to Britain. These included,

> ... the Public Security proclamation (No. 4 of 1942) setting up a system of police, a large task for such a huge area; the proclamation (No. 29 of 1942) appointing a prosecutor and deputy for High Court; the Courts (Advocates)

Ethiopia in the Era of Finance Capital

Rules legal notice (No. 49 of 1944) establishing a register of advocates and a disciplinary committee for their regulation (Perham 1969: 156).

The problematic Muslim law was recognized through the establishment of the Kadis' and Naibas' councils which retained jurisdiction over questions regarding Muslim marriage, divorce, guardianship, succession and gifts. Appeal from these councils was made to a court of Shariat, "consisting of not less than three judges nominated by the Minister of Justice" (ibid.) Thus, the Muslim law was self-contained though officially incorporated into the new Ethiopian system.

This judicial system was set up and run by British personnel. Perham, writing originally in 1948, noted that

> Brigadier Willan, of the Colonial Legal Service, was the first president of the High Court, 1942-3. Brigadier Willan was followed by Mr. Charles Mathew, who has since resigned and has been succeeded by another British judge, Mr. A. Thavenot (Perham 1948: 156).

In that 1948 book Perham discusses at length the issue of, as she puts it,

> ... whether such a very advanced judicial system could be suddenly superimposed upon the medieval structure which has been described, or whether British and Ethiopian judges, so different, it must be supposed, in training and temperament, could work together harmoniously when brought into such abrupt and intimate partnership (Perham 1948: 156-57).

She observed that "... the influence of the British judicial adviser and judges is evident but it is no less evident that the Ethiopian Government has willingly used their advice" (ibid.). She comments that "... the legal synthesis and the human partnership has worked

The Invention of Ethiopia

extremely well in the High Court" (Perham 1969: 157). She stops short of saying that Ethiopia was for all intents and purposes in this period a British colony under the control of the British Colonial Office.

She does acknowledge amid the glowing commentary, however, that a "secret court" existed capable of acting on any issue outside the range of the official system. And although the entire judiciary system was organized and administered primarily by British nationals, it was very difficult to carry out the decisions reached by the courts with such apparent unanimity in this department, for there was what she called ". . . a tendency upon the part of the executive to interfere with the judiciary and it has not always been possible to carry out the decrees of the courts in the face of executive obstruction" (Perham 1969: 158). This appears to be a very politic way of saying that the courts did not continue to function properly. They, like so many other features of the state apparatus after the Abyssinian settler group took over, presented a kind of facade of modernity to satisfy the demands of the wider community of nations rather than accomplishing the administration and application of justice in the country.

After the arrival of the United States as a patron of the dependent state, a Codification Commission was charged with producing a legal code. Markakis tells us that this commission,

> composed of foreign and Ethiopian members was established in the mid-1950s to draft a Penal Code which was promulgated in 1957, as well as the Civil, Commercial, and Maritime Codes in 1960, followed by the Criminal Procedure Code in 1961 and the Civil Procedure code in 1965. The Codes, which received perfunctory approval in parliament, were cut on the most advanced models, quite removed from actual conditions in Ethiopia. . . . "The Civil Code was made for the more advanced population of Ethiopia and Eritrea," explained its principal author. "Its application in other regions is not excluded, but cannot be

244

Ethiopia in the Era of Finance Capital

envisaged in the near future except in an exceptional manner ... " (Markakis 1974: 297-298).

The main author was a Swiss jurist, Rene David, who wrote virtually all the document in Switzerland using the French language, after which it was conveyed to Ethiopia for translation and implementation. When the Americans attempted to take over training potential lawyers and judges at the Haile Selassie I University Law School to apply the "Ethiopian" law in the provinces (colonies), the difficulties involved in translation alone from the old Ge'ez, French, English, and Amharic were daunting. But the United States pressed ahead in the tradition of applying imported law to the peoples of the empire.

To understand why there was a problem of implementation, account must be taken of the fact that a large portion of Ethiopia's law did not originate there. "Law and order" in the empire has been imported along with the firearms provided to maintain it. Even the law did not reflect the historical experience of those who were being called upon to apply and interpret it. In short, the basic principles of this imported law were not understood by the neftegna class, who made up the bulk of the "potential lawyers and judges" referred to above or by the populace. Just as with much of the technology and business practice, the judicial system was not "indigenous;" it was also superimposed upon the country. It reflected in microcosm the dilemma of so many other dimensions of this young state apparatus.

The neftegnas were not in a position to reject the system, however, because they had nothing with which to replace it. They themselves were holding a place in a social structure that they had not themselves constructed. They could not simply apply law that reflected the heritage of their grandparents and use it within this system because the state was constructed from elements completely alien to that heritage. Their solution was to accept the framework—facade, as it turned out—and rule as they saw fit. They knew that ultimately they held power due to the patronage of Haile Selassie and those who supported him, so they operated with confidence within the new structure, looking beyond themselves for patrons and protectors.

The Invention of Ethiopia

Educational Apparatus Upon the Departure of the British

From the earliest days of its formation, Ethiopia had desperately needed people who were capable of performing what can be termed mental labor, the analysis, assessment, planning, strategy, organizing and implementation of the many dimensions of the European-style state apparatus. In this we are not referring to the traditional debtara or persons with church education, but rather to those who could understand and could be understood by the developers of the state institutions in which they were functioning.

When Ethiopia was in the process of formation, the ever-present European advisers who hovered around the court, trying to outwit and sabotage each other in gaining influence, did the organizational thinking and planning. These advisers, who represented the interests of the European capitalist class, implanted the political, economic and ideological instruments necessary to protect the interests of that class. Both the Europeans and the Abyssinians, however, wanted Ethiopians to be trained to be able to do this kind of mental labor and to replace the European representatives. Preparing such people, who came to be referred to as "indigenous leaders," required a full-fledged institution for that purpose as part of the state apparatus. It required an educational system based on a European ideology or what is usually called "modern education," the aim of which was to instill in Ethiopians the outlook of the class that assembled the state.

Menelik, who has usually been credited as the founder of this empire, shared the opinion of his European advisers that European education was the key to modernization. He oversaw the establishment of the empire's first European-based educational institutions. At the outset, he placed one school in Addis Ababa and the other in Harar in 1908. He also arranged for mission schools to be established with a small number of students. At the outset, of course, these had to be staffed by Europeans or persons who had somehow had the opportunity to acquire a capitalist world view, such as

246

people who had been trained in other European colonies (Indians, for example).

Ras Tefari had worked to create a coterie of foreign-educated intellectuals who were later slaughtered during the Italian invasion. The Italians' different design for direct colonial rule was reflected in the way that they handled the education of their subjects. They did not provide any special privileges to the settler group that Haile Selassie had so carefully groomed.

As soon as Haile Selassie came to power for the second time, taking over from the Italians with a vengeance, he began to reorganize the institutional framework the Italians had established. The Ethiopians dismantled the Italian institution completely because it had destroyed Amhara hegemony and neftegna advantage. Ethiopia had been constructed in such a way that education was to serve a selected few and act as a process of Amharization as well. To uproot and counteract the Italian-built institutions and to secure control firmly in his own hand on this matter—one that was critical to his form of colonialism—Haile Selassie put an American-trained Ethiopian, Makonnen Desta, at the head of the educational institution. Some time later, Haile Selassie stepped in to serve as his own Minister of Education. From the outset, a British expert, Mr. E.R.J. Hussey (who was an expert in organization in the British colonies), was placed as the first adviser to the institution of education from 1942-1944. Together they had drawn up by 1944 a completely new plan for the future (Perham 1969: 255) The only aspect of Italian education that they used for the new program was that a number of valuable buildings were taken for schools. This move provided a physical base for the expansion of modern education in Ethiopia; by 1945-46 32,000 school children were in attendance at 241 new school buildings (1969: 252-3).

This was the condition of Ethiopia's development with regard to education when America accepted the guardianship of Ethiopia in the late 1940s.

The Invention of Ethiopia

The Defense Apparatus as the United States Found It

The other institution that had a profound impact on the shaping of the society was the military which trained selected members of the society specifically to defend the state. Abyssinia, of course, had a traditional military organization, but that military was fashioned to defend the old Abyssinian society, not the new dependent colonial state. Something very different was required to defend the modern Ethiopian state that had been recently constructed against the violent resistance of the majority of the population within its new borders. That task required a military that was institutionalized in the Western mode.

Ethiopia's encounter with Europeans and their alliance during the conquest and occupation of the nations in what is so commonly referred to euphemistically as "southern Ethiopia" demonstrated to the Abyssinians that success on that scale demanded a trained group of organized professional soldiers. Prior to the collaboration with Europe and the utilization of new forms of armaments and discipline, the military function in Abyssinia had not been centrally institutionalized. The old style of military organization was of a technological level, style of combat, system of recruitment, training, rewards, etc., suited to that decentralized form of social organization. This system had been forced to change in order to conquer and to occupy the colonies. There was a greater need to establish central administration. Having realized this at a fundamental level, Haile Selassie took a personal interest in the development of professional military institutions.

As Ras Tefari he had already begun to implement the institutionalization of the military, building on what had been initiated by Menelik. As early as the late 1920s, he planned to establish an institution for the training, equipping, and organizing of a standing force of bodyguards, to be followed by the creation of a military academy at Holeta in 1934.

The development of the institutionalized Ethiopian military was halted by the occupation of the empire by the Italians. But the Holeta Academy was brought to life immediately after what is gratu-

Ethiopia in the Era of Finance Capital

itously referred to as the "liberation" of the empire in 1941. The function and success of this academy was a high priority for the emperor. One of the first requests he made of Britain upon his return was to reactivate it. Its operation was in fact begun immediately under the direction of the British military mission. Patrick Gilkes describes the situation:

> Before 1941 there was no effective central army. The troops who fought the Italians were composed of levies called-up by, and under the control of, the individual governors of provinces plus the small imperial bodyguard that had modern training. Haile Selassie, having begun to train his own bodyguard before he became Emperor, sent a number of officers to study in France in the 1920s and engaged a Belgian Military Mission in 1929. This mission continued to train the Imperial Guard after his assumption of the throne in 1930. The Holeta Military Academy was also set up before the war, in 1934 ... (Gilkes 1975: 85).

John Markakis has offered an account of the emperor's interest in improving the capacity of his defense system:

> After the restoration and as a part of his centralization programme the emperor persuaded the British to finance and organize a military mission to train and equip ten infantry battalions as well as a regiment of artillery and one of armoured cars (Markakis 1974: 256).

By 1951, by which time the United States had taken over the function of leading Ethiopia, Britain had organized the military, assisted by Swedes. The Swedes in their own right took over the challenge of organizing the Air Force in 1947. As John Markakis has written,

> When the British military advisers were withdrawn from Ethiopia in 1951, they were replaced with Americans.

The Invention of Ethiopia

Ethiopia had already dispatched a battalion, equipped and transported by the U.S. to Korea in 1950. In 1953 the two countries concluded agreements governing the leasing of Kagnew Station in Asmara by the U.S. and the provision of military assistance to Ethiopia.... In return Ethiopia has received military and economic assistance continuously since 1951. Initially, the U.S. undertook to equip three Ethiopian divisions of 6,000 men each. American support now maintained four Ethiopian divisions for a total of 40,000 men—by far the largest military force in sub-Saharan Africa (Markakis 1974: 257).

Experimenting with Corporate Colonialism

The superstructure that existed in Ethiopia at the time of the United States arrival required little adjustment because it was itself a product of compromise between superpowers bent on single-country monopoly control, so it already contained the seeds of state built to accommodate collective access. And it was undeniably a product of the capitalist class of Europe seeking to satisfy its own interests in northeast Africa. The United States had become quite familiar with the principles and the instruments used by the absentee capitalists of Europe to construct the Ethiopian state.

The United States, like Britain before her, operated on the assumption that the implanted superstructure could in time generate indigenous classes to manage those institutions vital to protecting the interests of finance capital.

To achieve this objective, the United States set a plan in motion to strengthen those institutions by generating capital for the empire through gifts, loans and credit. The United States also agitated other countries to invest in the development of Ethiopia by initiating the investment programs beyond what already existed. The year 1950 is often noted as the year when Ethiopia's economy "took off" (see Marcus 1983: 90ff.).

250

Ethiopia in the Era of Finance Capital

Under the United States' umbrella land continued to serve as the main, if not the only, source of the "national" economy. Land was accessible and distributed only in the closely prescribed ways described above. The inherited state had been designed to sustain the production relations that were laid out in the land policy.

The soldier settlers and the Abyssinian aristocrats, collectively referred to as the neftegna, had become the chief local beneficiaries of this system and they developed a vital interest and role in maintaining and defending the arrangement. Due to the Italian policy of reorganizing the boundaries between the colonies, the emperor had been able to assume an even tighter control over the neftegnas when he resumed power than he had before the Italian invasion. Upon his return, the emperor redrew all the boundaries in such a way that there was no possibility for local fiefdoms to be formed. All landholding and associated power became completely dependent on the state. Only through it were the neftegna able to claim rights to and "ownership" of the property upon which they had been allowed to settle. The new refurbished Ethiopian state guaranteed them the right to participate in defending their position vis-à-vis the continued resistance of the indigenous inhabitants and to play a role in legislating laws that governed their interest.

Despite the fact that the substructure and superstructure of a dependent colonial state had been neatly designed, the social category of persons who could fill positions created by these new institutions and could run the empire had not yet been developed. The primary challenge left for the United States was to organize a petit-bourgeois group that could function as a class to manage the still-defective state. This situation was the converse of the classic model. In the classic model a class develops out of a specific historical condition and then builds a mechanism to protect its own interest. In this case, however, capitalist institutions were built up by a largely absentee class, the international capitalist class, to try to develop from a precapitalist society an indigenous class to administer the new type of overseer colonialist state.

By the 1950s, Ethiopia's empire already demonstrated that she would not be an economic burden to her patron, but, by virtue of

The Invention of Ethiopia

the neftegna administrative class consuming directly the produce of the tenants on the land, Ethiopia could in fact be considered "self-sufficient." A country was defined as self-sufficient in this new formula when it posed no undue economic burden on the sponsoring country. There was relatively little concern for how those conditions were created internally. The United States realized that if the potential of this area were properly developed the resources could satisfy the demands of not only this empire alone but of the entire Horn of Africa region and parts of the Middle East as well (Marcus 1983). Ethiopia's economic potential, though significant, was not of direct interest to the larger concerns of the United States at that time, however. Ethiopia was seen as an important asset in the process of achieving and proving other larger economic and political objectives worldwide. As a product of Western thought she appeared a secure and reliable staging ground for future United States activities in that area.

Soon after the advent of United States sponsorship, Ethiopia began to aspire to achieve the place of importance in the eyes of America that she had held in the eyes of European countries at a different time. This aspiration, however, was based on the kind of relationship and principles that had applied during the period of single-country monopoly colonialism. The changes that had taken place in the international order had done away with the more-or-less "exclusive" relationships that had dominated prior to World War II in favor of the corporate model. Since the United States had been the leader in designing the new order, she was not tempted to accede to Ethiopia's expectations. Ethiopia seemed convinced that she herself was responsible for successfully enticing the United States to assist her and believed that America could be enticed to pour millions of additional dollars into the country for general facelifting. Consequently, Ethiopia's leaders were very much disappointed when America was not willing to continue full-scale assistance.

It came as a rude awakening when Ethiopia began to realize the extent of America's several other third world interests and involvements. United States intentions to treat them all equally disappoint-

Ethiopia in the Era of Finance Capital

ed the emperor greatly. Ethiopia's experience had led her to believe that every gift she requested she would receive. Following the Anglo-Ethiopian Treaty of 1944, a treaty that formally declared the "independence" of Ethiopia, a technical and economic mission had in fact been sent by the United States, as Haile Selassie had requested. Furthermore, President Roosevelt had granted virtually every item on a long "shopping list" prepared by Haile Selassie in 1944.

To show her commitment to the U.S., Ethiopia had volunteered troops to be sent to Korea. Quid pro quo was United States support in the United States for Ethiopia's annexation of Eritrea. But as far as Haile Selassie's government was concerned the relationship was developing too slowly in the early years. Abyssinian culture recognized the principle of *belto mablat* (feed and be fed), and the Ethiopians soon began to feel that their commitments and loyalty were undervalued by the Americans.

Ethiopia began to complain in various ways about her treatment at the hands of her rich American patron. But the United States refused to be drawn into the kind of commitment in Ethiopia that Haile Selassie envisioned for the reason discussed above. Harold Marcus has pointed out that "... until 1956 Washington's development programs remained largely devoted to technical assistance administered under a Point Four agreement signed on 15 May 1952" (Marcus 1983:90). America's refusal to go beyond its own agenda prompted Haile Selassie, a very unhappy man at this point, to take his complaints to a joint session of the United States Congress. He explained that Ethiopia had done all in her power and that by comparison the United States had done very little. In this speech, he referred to Ethiopian mythology: "We read the same Bible. We speak a common spiritual tongue." Then he appealed for an American response saying, "So great are your power and wealth, that the budget of a simple American city often equals that of an entire nation" (Selected Speeches 1967: 109-118). He revealed his plans to refashion Ethiopia through "the closest possible association with the United States." Of course, the implication was that Ethiopia expected the United States to function like a traditional Abyssinian patron. When U.S. interests fell short of these expectations, Haile Selassie's

The Invention of Ethiopia

Foreign Minister Aklilu posed their dilemma very directly: "Ethiopia must ask itself again, just what place does Ethiopia actually hold in the eyes of the U.S." (Marcus 1983: 92).

One thing that needs to be understood is that the United States had no plans for disappointing Ethiopia. It was, after all, an empire that had taken the energy of three European colonial powers (Great Britain, France and Italy) almost one century to develop. The United States wanted to reformulate that dependence into their own model. They did not plan, however, to abandon others in Africa and the third world in the process, as Ethiopia expected them to do.

The United States responded to Ethiopian complaints made through John Spencer, Haile Selassie himself, and the foreign minister among others, by reexamining its involvement. James P. Richards of South Carolina, according to Spencer, served as "ambassador on a special mission to promote the Eisenhower doctrine for the Middle East designed to combat Communist inroads there" (Spencer 1984: 291). He revealed the general attitude in the United States about Ethiopian expectations when in 1957 he responded to a remark like that of Aklilu's above. Richards reminded Aklilu, "To listen to you, Mr. Minister, I ought to be ashamed to be an American. But let me tell you this, were it not for the United States, Ethiopia would not even be on the map today" (ibid). All told, however, the United States found development in the country to be far beyond its expectations. The United States was, in the end, forthcoming with additional aid though it was not the amount Ethiopia had requested. Eventually Ethiopia did go looking elsewhere for assistance and received it (see Marcus 1983: 94-7, Spencer 1984: 290ff.). Such efforts on the part of Ethiopia to expand her links with other supporters was perfectly in keeping with the United States formula for U. S.-led corporate control of the colonies.

Subsequent events confirm that though the United States did have a strong interest in Ethiopia, American policy continued to be guided by the effort to lead the way in implementing a new model for international order—distinct from the old British and French styles of colonial control that the colonies themselves had come to expect. Under the rule of finance capital, the United States was only

254

one of the controllers, not the sole controller of any one country. It is fair to assert, however, that she saw herself as the major shareholder among many. She saw her main task as preparing the way for the remaining partners by demonstrating that there was ample opportunity for profitable investment.

The United States did aid Ethiopia's empire by supporting substantial loans from the World Bank and the International Monetary Fund, in this way investing substantially in the success of the development of coffee exports.

A high priority for the U.S. was to create the conditions and the mechanisms through which investments could be made by others. This was the essential purpose for the United States to maintain a refined means of communication, from air and sea to ground transportation, and from radio to telephone to telegraph. Once the communication and transport networks were functional, the defense and legal systems could be raised to a standard that could govern modern business, and a bureaucracy could be established capable of accommodating investments in a way satisfactory to international capital. The U.S. made certain that these conditions existed by the middle of the 1950s and were subsequently maintained.

Transport and Communication Infrastructure Extended under the United States

When the United States arrived to provide major assistance to Ethiopia, one of her top priorities was to assure an improvement in the material infrastructure so that business interests would be attracted to the area. She took over the Italian-built transport and communication networks to maintain and refurbish them. A road team was brought in. Marcus reported that the United States Bureau of Roads worked under a contract with the Imperial Highway Authority (1983: 96). This agency, from the time of its creation to the end of the 1950s, had taken and maintained about 3100 miles of all-weather roads. The establishment and maintenance of these roads facilitated in some cases and initiated in others the movement of

The Invention of Ethiopia

many new products for external trade. The movement of produce generated small business establishments. The roads provided easy access for the settlers to the cities and enabled the cities to get what they needed from the colonies to survive and prosper.

Once the means of transport became cheaper and commodities could be transported more easily, business thrived. Easy access to the colonies was ensured through new transport links to previously existing roads. The United States projects greatly increased access to the existing railway line which remained the primary avenue for movement of commodities from the colonies to the international market and for the importation of consumer items for the settlers. These links encouraged external trade and ultimately agribusiness, all of which benefitted the settler class.

Both ground and air transport expanded tremendously under United States supervision. British moves in the early 1940s to monopolize the airport had particularly offended the United States, As Spencer tells it, "[t]he British demand for a monopoly over commercial air traffic was a restriction of particular concern to the Department of State, which feared that this provision would effectively exclude U. S. carriers" (1984: 99fn). When the United States moved in, it implemented a very different style of control, supplying a "national" airlines, the Ethiopian Airlines, with a great deal of visibility although the carrier amounted to little more than a subsidiary of the United States-controlled Trans World Airlines. The airport was open to all carriers in keeping with the style of finance capital. The airplane made accessible not only external regions but also opened up interior regions to the settlers who were running the government. By the end of the 1950s, planes could land in most of the coffee-producing regions of the colonies.

Under United States tutelage, telephone, telegraph and radio communication was expanded to reach most areas where settlers were located. Electronic media in general were activated during this period, functioning to their fullest possible extent. All offices and shops were equipped with telephones. The empire was connected to the center. By the end of the 1950s all towns in the empire could be reached in the time it took to dial a simple telephone. Ground

Ethiopia in the Era of Finance Capital

transport made it possible to travel from one end of the colonial area to the other in less than one week.

All these developments ushered in a new phase: the development of roads, telecommunication, railway linkage to the sea through the newly annexed province of Eritrea, the broader distribution of land, and, above all, the number of educated Ethiopians who began to agitate for more commercialization and urbanization.

The American program worked nicely with regard to Ethiopia's economic development. For example, coffee, the most important product in the country, yielded Eth. $17,004,350 in 1949 and had a yield of Eth. $30,000,000 in 1950—an increase of over 75 percent. Hides, skins, grains, peas, beans and oilseeds that had brought Eth. $40,000,000 in 1950 had been only Eth. $30,300,000 in 1949. Since shipments of coffee rose from 17,829 metric tons to 21,152 metric tons in 1950, revenues from duties went up from Eth. $24,000,000 to $31,650,000 (Marcus 1983: 95). By 1951 Ethiopia was made a virtually one-crop producing zone like so many of the dependencies in the new world economy.

> For 1951 the value of coffee soared to E$56,500,000, accounting for 50.5% of all Ethiopian exports; hides and skins were now 28% . . . [b]y 1952, coffee, now 54.9% of all exports was valued at E$83,000,000; the country's total trade was E$158,000,000, which yielded customs revenues amounting to E$42,989,981, against E$36,181,476 for the year before.
>
> 1953 was a big year for the Ethiopian economy: the coffee crop had grown to 37,000 tons, which sold at higher world prices for E$122,000,000, nearly 65% of the value of all exports (Marcus 1983: 95-96).

By 1954 when all of the above-cited complaints were aired by Ethiopia, the United States was the main recipient of Ethiopian coffee.

It should be remembered that all of these exportable commodities were brought to the market from the colonies of Abyssinia such as Oromia and Sidama. These developments were achieved by building upon the same economic base upon which the empire was founded, the production relation of neftegna-gabbar, protected by the state.

The United States had in essence held in place the system that kept the settlers in the colonial lands. The new formula merely improved the technological efficiency of the exploitation of that relationship. Through the process of intensifying colonial exploitation of Oromia, Sidama, etc., lands that had potential to produce a wide variety of crops were reduced to essentially a one-crop-producing colonial empire.

The settlers could well have been forced back to their kingdoms of origin had it not been for the armaments provided by the British and then by the United States in the same fashion for "internal security." The United States continued to arm the settler regime in a hidden colonial situation.

The Military Apparatus under the United States

The United States accepted the training and financing of all matters relating to the Ethiopian armed forces. Eritrea was of central concern. General Charles L. Bolte of the United States Army revealed this priority when he "... admitted that Asmara's Radio Marina was an area of mutual interest and testified that Washington would 'always take with great concern any danger to Ethiopia'" (Marcus 1983: 87). It is clear that the training and equipping of the Ethiopian army was in large part a tradeoff for access to and utilization of Radio Marina. The general clearly indicated, however, that the demands made by Ethiopia for defense were unjustified because Ethiopia had no need to fear external attack. He stated for the record that "... except for internal security, Ethiopia had 'little reason' to maintain national armed forces" (ibid). (As we will see below, however, the level of resistance from the conquered and subdued peoples in the empire made internal security a major concern.) He did suggest an American military mission or involve-

258

ment that lasted until 1975. Spencer, negotiating with the United States in New York on Ethiopia's behalf in 1952, ". . . voiced the emperor's concern that the commitments be long-term, particularly the provision of training" (ibid.: 89). As a result of both the United States and Ethiopian interest, on May 22, 1953, the two countries had agreed to the trade-off and signed a 25-year agreement which specified United States use of the Kagnew Station (as Radio Marina was renamed) and other facilities in Eritrea until 1978 and inaugurated "a standard military assistance treaty regulating the delivery of weapons and other equipment and providing for a Military Assistance Advisory Group (MAAG)" (Marcus 1983: 89).

Beginning from this point, the United States became intimately involved in training and equipping the Ethiopian military, as demanded by the emperor. Ethiopia represented an example of the way that the United States chose to implement its leadership in defending the world economic order—that is, would change to establishing a military base and taking responsibility for the direction of the development of the state apparatus of its client. Once this commitment had been made, Washington found it difficult to withdraw. In the case of Ethiopia, she did not withdraw until another superpower (the Soviet Union in 1977), aspiring to take the lead in the world order, stepped in to replace her militarily and otherwise.

United States experience in Ethiopia at the end of the 1940s and the beginning of the 1950s had shown, if not much else, the economic potential and strategic importance of this area. By this time, the United States had seen that the Ethiopian empire could be important not only strategically and politically for United States interest, in the Red Sea area in both the long and short term, but also that the area could be important for economic reasons. To secure the United States general global position, specifically in relation to the Persian Gulf, the Indian Ocean and the Mediterranean, which were threatened by the Soviet Union, the United States established Kagnew Station in Eritrea. This allowed the United States to secure an optimal site in this most strategic area. At this period in the twentieth century the United States together with NATO took over leadership in maintaining the global economy.

259

The Invention of Ethiopia

It became United States policy to try to keep all colonial territories as they were; the Ethiopian empire fell within this general model. The United States saw its role as supporting this longstanding empire. By underwriting and underpinning the central government that they inherited, the United States believed that she was implementing a new form of "self-determination."

During this period, the rest of the African continent was setting a timetable for "independence," or, in light of the above discussion, what could be better called a timetable for the transition from monopoly or single-country colonial rule (direct colonialism) to the American-backed rule of finance capital or corporate control. This move to corporate control has been alternately referred to as "independence of the colonies" and "neocolonialism." At the point of this transition conflict between the United States and the Soviet Union reached a new level (see Mahoney 1983, *JFK: Ordeal in Africa* for a discussion of this contest). The United States became intent on keeping the Soviet Union out of Africa, while the Soviet Union, which did not possess the financial clout to benefit from the corporate model of control, opposed the transition to this sort of "independence" and instead attempted to draw Africans into her own orbit, calling that "liberation."

In northeast Africa, the United States had Ethiopia in its bloc and had assisted in annexing the former Italian colony, Eritrea, to that dependent colonial empire. The Soviet Union gained no immediate footing in the area, despite its attempts to coax Eritrea to its side through demonstrating sympathy to her cause during the United Nations hearings on the Eritrean matter.

Among the areas that were given this kind of independence under the decolonization of Africa, Egypt was the first in the region to be so recognized. Others followed one by one. By the mid-1950s, Egypt had indicated that she inclined toward the Soviet bloc. This was confirmed when she eventually recognized the People's Republic of China. Soon she nationalized the Suez Canal companies and then began receiving economic and military aid from the Soviet bloc.

With these developments it became clear that the Soviet Union had entered into a campaign to acquire a share of the former

Ethiopia in the Era of Finance Capital

colonial market in Africa. The United States extended its program to keep the Soviet Union out of Africa by offering economic assistance to Egypt. At the United Nations the United States even opposed Ethiopia's annexation of Ogaden in order to prevent the Soviet Union from finding an entry into the Horn by way of disappointed Somalis. But by the middle of the 1950s the Soviet Union had begun to find a foothold from which to launch a successful challenge to the United States on the continent.

In the case of the Horn of Africa, the United States had already planned for the Soviet challenge and had instructed Ethiopia not to demand the Ogaden. Thus, America ended up supporting the Greater Somalia concept. This was done so as not to disappoint Somalia or push Somalia into the Soviet sphere of influence, not because the United States perceived Ogadenis as Somalians or supported their objectives. This temporary and opportunistic recognition of Greater Somalia by Washington made the Ethiopians very unhappy. Ethiopia began to express interest and make public overtures to the Soviet Union.

Upon achieving its independence the government of Somalia sought weaponry for the national security of Greater Somalia, just as Haile Selassie had before it. The Ogaden issue subsequently created a dilemma for the United States. The issue was where the United States should stand when Somalia became independent. Rather than abandoning Ethiopia, the United States held fast to its original strategy of supporting her. The consequences were far-reaching, as Spencer, a direct participant, reported:

> The Somali leaders wanted arms to back up the pursuit of their objectives. After independence, Somalia turned to the Soviet Union, and the United States, for all its diplomatic efforts from 1957 to 1960, was faced with a massive Soviet military presence to the south in the Horn (Spencer 1984: 359).

Up to this point, a major objective had been to keep Somalia within the Western bloc, but the presence of the Soviet Union had

261

The Invention of Ethiopia

made the United States react in a very friendly manner toward Ethiopia. The Soviet involvement in the Horn only intensified this relationship.

Augmentation of the Economic Base during the Period of United States Patronage

Although the minimal conditions for the building of a dependent state had been laid down by the 1950s, the state still lacked several features vital to its operation according to plan. It awaited a local social class fully equipped to operate it, although the conditions required to fashion this class were in place. Economically, the land grant system had been designed to expand the landholding group. Institutions had been formed to legitimize and safeguard settlers' ownership of land and to ensure their eventual control of the state.

The primary United States suggestion for improvement of the conditions of the sector of the society loyal to the state was the intensification of modernized agriculture. Haile Selassie's government was advised to intensify foreign investment in order to accomplish this.

Examples of foreign investment attracted to Ethiopia after the establishment of these policies are:

1. The Ethiopian American Coffee Company was financed by the U.S. (70 percent), with the remaining 30 percent carried by the Agriculture and Development Bank of Ethiopia which was also foreign-owned. AIDBE also financed individual Ethiopians in their coffee farming projects.

2. Livestock and hides production in the southern rangelands, the Hermatu Range Development and others (Gilkes 1975: 142).

3. A foreign-financed oil and gas project was located in Bale.

4. Gold in the Sidamo and Wallega region was jointly exploited by Abyssinians and Europeans.

Ethiopia in the Era of Finance Capital

5. The expansion of H.V.A., Wonji and Metahara lower down the Awash Valley was financed by an international corporation loan from HVA Holland, HVA Ethiopian government and private shareholders (Gilkes 1975: 151).

6. The British were the largest investors for the Tendaho cotton plantations.

7. Chilalo Agricultural Development Unit (CADU) and the Wallamo Agricultural Development Unit (WADU) were financed by the World Bank.

8. Most of the projects of the Awash Valley Authority (AVA) were financed or owned by foreign capital such as the United States, the World Bank and U.N.-financed loans.

It is important to point out that all of these projects are located in the conquered land, primarily in Oromia. Yet by law to get a job in any of the agricultural projects, CADU, WADU, AVA, etc., one must pass an Amharic literacy test (see Gilkes 1975: 124-150). During the 1950s the program of free land grants to loyal groups proceeded alongside the introduction of foreign investment and technology. By the mid-1960s agricultural modernization had begun apace under the direction of Ethiopia's new patron, the United States.

With a series of Five Year Plans, Ethiopia had embarked on a "modernization" program aimed at increasing production and moving the country toward capitalist development. The purpose of the first Five Year Plan (1956-1961) was to promote infrastructures to enhance the state's capacity to control the colonies. In fact only 13 percent of the total amount went to agriculture, the activity of 90 percent of the population, and most of that went to coffee cultivation. The Second Five Year Plan (1962-1967) was supposed to supply more food for domestic consumption, but the bulk went to production for export and agro-industry, which enhanced the benefits of the settler group. The Third Five Year Plan (1968-1973) adopted a "minimum package program" approach which promised to diffuse modern technology to a large proportion of the farming population. At the same time, however, the government encouraged

The Invention of Ethiopia

expansion of the modernizing agricultural sector by issuing an Investment Proclamation to offer incentives to foreigners, and the government itself, together with its landed aristocracy, participated directly in the expansion of commercial farms.

> The fastest development took place in the Awash Valley. By 1970-71, about 57 percent of the total estimated irrigable area in the upper valley had been developed. H. V. A. Wonji and H. V. A. Metahara cultivated 65 percent of these lands to produce sugar cane. In the lower plains, where a single feudal landlord owned 50 percent of the cultivated land in the region, 70 percent of the irrigable land was developed. In 1973 there was a total of 27 large and medium-sized agro-industrial enterprises functioning in the Awash Valley (Alula Abate and Tesfaye Teklu 1980: 8).

The advantages of mechanization and the profits to be gained through cooperation with foreign investment were not lost on either the government, hungry for revenues, nor the landed aristocracy. They began to look for development opportunities to be realized in huge regions in the colonies where fertile lands were tilled by resident tenants. Both government and private landlords began to clear the land to make it available for new economic opportunities. State-owned land, land that had not been settled by Abyssinians, was referred to as "unutilized government land," or "government unoccupied land." The designations "unutilized" and "unoccupied" should not be taken at face value. They referred to the colonies, the conquered lands filled with residents from the Oromo and other colonized nations who were utilizing it for their own subsistence. Since the land and people were of the crown by law, however, a number of bureaucratic devices were introduced, such as requiring people to produce receipts for tax payments for three consecutive years. Those without receipts were simply declared by the state to be illegally occupying the land and ordered off without alternative arrangements provided (see Stahl 1974 for a description of this process). The "cleared" lands were then turned over for modernized

Ethiopia in the Era of Finance Capital

agricultural units. Many agricultural projects financed by foreign capital were established on Oromo territories (for example, CADU, H. V. A., AVA, Wonji, and Matahara Sugar Plantation). The essence of a policy—the holding of large sections of colonial lands in reserve, allowing the colonized people to utilize them only until the state developed the capacity to penetrate and fully control them for the benefit of the settler class—became apparent during this period and was even more starkly revealed later during the Derg's era.

The 1960s brought expansion of these projects and the consequent evictions of tens of thousands of indigenous Oromo people who were officially considered to be "illegally" occupying the land simply because they were not capable of relating to the state that had introduced the laws and the means of enforcing them. The "modernization" process through which land was provided to a "developer," transformed the landed aristocracy of Haile Selassie's era into a class that directly served the interests of foreign or international capital. The objective of Michael Stahl's book *Ethiopia: Political Contradictions in Agricultural Development* (1974) is to address the issue of the contradictions in policies that were expressly designed to introduce technology to small cultivators when all political power in the country rested in the hands of a specific elite which the state was directly designed to serve.

Other writers such as Markakis (1974), Cohen and Weintraub (1975) and Ellis (1976) also discuss the process of eviction and the creation of a rural proletariat among the peoples of "the south." Their analyses stop short, however, of relating the position of these "southern" peoples to the specifically colonial nature of the state. Given the production relations, the people of the colonies were not "peasants," since they did not retain rights in even a small part of their lands. They had been transformed into tenants when the land was removed from them all at once and declared owned by the crown. Through the Menelik and Haile Selassie periods the land was unevenly distributed to people attached through various ways to the crown, i.e., to the colonial state. Haile Selassie and his foreign advisers introduced some changes that resulted in these privileged landowners relating to each other and to the world market through

The Invention of Ethiopia

capital and capitalist relations, but those innovations did not produce *structural* change in the relations between conqueror and conquered nations. Instead they sought to broaden the base of one group at the expense of the other.

As part of an orchestrated effort to broaden the neftegna class base, Haile Selassie's government established a Ministry of Land Reform and Administration in 1966. The task of this ministry was to study all the proposals, advice and criticism regarding the land grant system that had been presented to the government by foreign powers, to conduct its own studies, and then to produce a program for land reform. Several proposals were put forward by this institution. Eshetu Chole reported that

> among its priority considerations were the adoption and implementation of settlement and resettlement programs. The government appeared to attach great significance to the issue of settlements, both in terms of solving the problems of an excessive labor-land ratio in the North plateau regions, and in terms of the modernization of agriculture and improvements in agricultural productivity in the economy as a whole. What was envisaged included the removal and resettlement of surplus peasant households from Tigray, Gondar, Wello, and Shewa regions in the relatively densely populated lowland areas of the south and the plateau regions of the south-west (Eshetu Chole 1984: 6).

The government brought in a team of external consultants known as the Harvard Advisory Group. This group supported the proposal in essence. Again as Eshetu Chole put it,

> [a] 1971 report by a consultant for the Harvard Advisory Group advocated the idea of abrogation of the land-grant system and proposed a comprehensive planned utilization of government lands through an appropriate settlement policy. A key element in the policy was the support to be given to

individual initiatives and to low settlement cost programs (ibid).

Virtually the same suggestion was made in 1971 by USAID.

Haile Selassie's government faced the problem of internal rejection of these schemes. While the government was contemplating the policy and attempting trials on a small scale without implementing any proposal in full, the government was overthrown and replaced by the Derg (a word literally meaning "committee" in Amharic). The Derg government that replaced Haile Selassie moved to implement these schemes in a far more aggressive way than Haile Selassie dared to contemplate. The junta's advantage over him in this regard was that it was able to eliminate the opposition that came from the landed aristocratic fraction of the neftegna by eliminating that fraction altogether.

Education under United States Tutelage

All taken, these developments marked the beginning of the kind of business group that the United States had expected to develop. In addition, the Western-educated group was emerging from the schools and coming into political power, conversant with concepts and the skills created by the international capitalist class. These graduates constituted a new product, a new bureaucratic bourgeoisie which had been taught to understand the language of the state.

The primary function of the new type of educational institution was to produce an educated elite, who prefer to call themselves "intellectuals," prepared to serve in every department of the state apparatus and ultimately to safeguard the interests of capital first and of the Abyssinian settlers. The United States representatives believed that an educated class of experts, capable of taking over the state, could be developed by the end of the 1950s. In essence it was a program of trusteeship. The Americans felt confident in this belief because virtually all the children who attended school were in some way children of the land-owning group. If they did not yet own land

The Invention of Ethiopia

directly, people in this category were soon entitled to do so under the new land grant law.

The American advisers together with the Ethiopian functionaries were initially slow to accomplish much in this area, but it must be remembered that the major task during this period was laying groundwork for the future. By the time this major groundwork had been completed in 1950, though, the Ethiopian schools had shown the capacity to increase attendance by more than double the 1945-46 numbers. "By 1950 more than 500 schools offering primary education, not all of them complete—and four secondary schools had come into existence. About 56,000 students were enrolled. The budget for education rose from less than Eth. $1 million in 1943-4 to about Eth. $10 million in 1950" (Markakis 1974: 147). Once the organizational set-up was complete, it was a simple matter to funnel a large proportion of state resources into preparing this group to take over the operation of the state. Built into this system was a very tight and effective control over who was selected to participate in these educational opportunities. Amharic was kept as a requirement for participation. This is a critical point because it is the group shaped by these institutions that has displayed so much loyalty to the state in the 1970s and 1980s.

Most of the schools were to be found in towns and cities. Since towns in the colonies were built upon the foundations of old garrison posts that housed the soldier-settlers, the majority of those attending were children of the guncarriers (neftegna) living there. In the major cities the children of the absentee landlords, members of the northern aristocracy who were offered positions in the bureaucracy from the outset, and a handful of members of the conquered nations who had migrated to the towns seeking to attach themselves to the state for various reasons, were afforded higher education. Because of the existence of these groups, the United States believed that there was a critical mass from which a class could be developed to manage the already-fashioned state structure.

Just as Western institutions were basically organized by capitalist ideology, so were these Ethiopian institutions. The rapid development of a state structure that had been spawned by the Abyssinian-

268

Ethiopia in the Era of Finance Capital

European alliance had created a large demand for personnel trained to operate the state machinery. Consequently, all the training necessary could not be carried out in Ethiopia itself, at least not at first. Many students were sent abroad to Western schools for education. The products of both types of schools, whether trained in the United States, Europe, or in the Horn of Africa, were similarly equipped to function within the state administration at the completion of the training process.

Indeed the product of an Ethiopian school of this period was in most ways akin to his American counterpart—a person whose interests and tastes had been modified in similar directions in the process, but who could not identify a clear Ethiopian class to whom he felt responsible.

Upon graduation, the former Ethiopian classmates found that they shared no clear common social or economic denominator, other than their school experience, and their conception of their future as holding some kind of position in the state apparatus. There was no other common ground on which they could be brought together, certainly no economic ground. This is a very important point. Graduates of the European-inspired educational institution were as much products of a European system as they would have been had they trained in Europe. The ideas that had shaped the institutions were the ideas that shaped its intellectuals. Even the motivation to build the system itself was grounded in the ideology of a class largely resident in Europe. The products of these schools were in a real sense the product of the ideology of an absentee capitalist class. The Ethiopian petit-bourgeoisie was, and is still, the direct product of finance capital.

The first graduates of this essentially European institution were the product of an effort to produce a group that would serve and defend the imported state. They were tested in a 1960 coup attempt, and their behavior confirmed the thesis that they would remain loyal to the state. The Ethiopian petit-bourgeoisie demonstrated that they related to the state no differently than Western petit-bourgeoisie related to it. During the attempted coup d'etat, the petit-bourgeoisie of one sector attempted to take over the state, and the petit-bour-

The Invention of Ethiopia

geoisie of the other defended the crown with the same objective—to enhance their position within the existing state structure itself.

Eventually a class of local people was developed capable of managing this dependent state structure, as the United States chose to intensify the production of Western-educated Ethiopian bureaucrats. There was a reduction of the importation of personnel from abroad. In short, the Americans continued the policies that had been established for dealing with Ethiopia as a dependent colonial entity. For this purpose, their policies merely enhanced the kind of training and socialization received by the Ethiopian petit-bourgeoisie. The Americans began to diversify the kinds of training available in the empire.

> During 1952-54, a wide variety of schemes were planned and effected. In the area of agricultural education, a high school in Jimma, the college at Alemaya, and a crop improvement center in the Cobbo-Alamata area were established (Marcus 1983: 91).

Other experimental projects included ". . . locust control, a machinery pool in the Ministry of Agriculture, a coffee cooperative venture, animal disease control, a water resources survey, and well-drilling" (ibid). The other educational programs, such as an intensive survey of Ethiopia's academic needs, included,

> . . . the establishment of the public health college and paramedical training center at Gondar and a nurse and midwife training school in Asmara . . . a water supply and sewerage survey for Addis Ababa . . . [a] handicraft school in the capital, rural vocational and industrial arts . . . , a commerce and industry development center, health advisory services, an institute of public administration, and a program providing scholarships abroad (ibid).

Superimposed upon what had previously existed, the U.S. added much of its own style and personnel. Several colleges were founded

Ethiopia in the Era of Finance Capital

by the end of the 1950s. There were 170,460 students who had reached grades 1-8, and 8,919 secondary students. At the college level there were 827 students (Gilkes 1975: 91).

The Efflorescence of United States Patronage

Through the 1950s and 1960s the Ethiopian state flourished under the patronage of the United States. It was during this time that, playing on the strategic position of the empire (this time vis-à-vis the Middle East and Persian Gulf), the Ethiopian colonists set up the mutually beneficial arrangement in which Ethiopia agreed to allow the United States to build the Kagnew Station communications base in return for a supply of adequate arms to ensure "stability" in the empire, including in the former Italian colony of Eritrea, and to legitimize its rule in this annexed territory. Ensuring "stability" meant utilizing the weaponry to suppress constant uprising and resistance in the colonies and in the annexed territories against the imposed Amhara settler rule. The United States supplied more military assistance to Ethiopia than to the rest of Africa combined during this period.

The Ethiopian state became confident and assertive in its secure niche, again one created by the interests of a major imperial power. Haile Selassie perfected the art of presenting facades to the external world in every domain, from introducing television in major cities to sophisticated Five Year Plans. Keenly aware of the continued need for a wide circle of international friends, the emperor of one of the largest colonial empires in the continent invited the Organization of African Unity (OAU) to be housed in Addis Ababa, having hosted the founding conference in 1963. This move was symbolically significant as well as substantive, playing once again on the well-cultivated mythology about Ethiopia. What better candidate than Ethiopia, the empire that had the oldest tradition of "independence" on the continent, to champion the revised formula for corporate control of former colonies sponsored by the United States in the name of independence? Haile Selassie authored, proposed and orchestrated the passage of the OAU Resolution on Territorial Integrity (Greenfield 1982). This arrangement guaranteed that the economic basis for continued colonial exploitation would be preserved in the former colonies of Africa while a manager class was invited to step in to operate the largely unchanged state institutions built by the European capitalists. The managers of newly "independent" African states found themselves thrust into the position of championing and endorsing an Ethiopian colonial mythology about whose basis they were ignorant.

Haile Selassie encouraged the elaboration of the Ethiopian colonial mythology by providing extensive logistical support for those historians and scholars who would choose to focus on the glorious heritage of Abyssinia and the uniqueness of Ethiopian independence.

The 1950s and 1960s brought missionaries and U.S. Peace Corps volunteers who were willing to meet Haile Selassie's conditions for work in the colonies, such as speaking and advocating only the official state language, Amharic. Therefore, even foreign personnel became his unwitting colonial agents ensuring perpetuation of the fraud and the continuation of "Amharization" of the empire. By accepting these limitations on their own work, they were cut off from communication with the colonial peoples among whom they worked. These missionary and Peace Corps personnel swelled the staffs of schools. The foreigners in effect formed a cadre of a new generation of foreign advisers, providing skills and strategies that enabled the Ethiopian state to function and the settlers to remain in power.

Attempts of the Haile Selassie Regime to Cope with Discontent

By the end of the 1960s and the beginning of the 1970s the Ethiopian state under Haile Selassie was forced to face several severe crises simultaneously. Some of the programs designed for modernization had generated conditions which caused the regime to become

272

Ethiopia in the Era of Finance Capital

entangled with political-economic problems of resistance in the colonies and with opposition groups that began to form with the objective of reforming the state. On top of these problems troubling financial difficulties began to crop up which shook even the confidence and loyalty of workers and civil servants who were paid directly by the state.

When this latter group began to demand higher pay for the work done, Haile Selassie's regime embarked on several ambitious modernization programs which, in addition to certain political benefits that were to accrue, promised to raise revenues for the state to deal with economic demands. The modernization schemes were designed to disenfranchise the peoples of colonized lands on whose territories the programs were located. Feeling the pressure of discontent from several sectors of the empire, the Haile Selassie regime began to appeal for strategic "developmental" assistance from advisers and consultants from all over the Western world to design reforms that would quell the dissatisfactions and extend the life of the empire. Consultants responded enthusiastically to the challenge and by the early 1970s many of the requested reforms were complete and ready for implementation. These included major projects intended to install land reform, educational reform, refinements in the administrative machinery, in security, and in communication. Edmond Keller in his recent book has dealt in detail with the kinds of reforms that Haile Selassie's government had proposed by the mid-1970s (1988: 94-163).

To take the proposed reforms in education as an example, in 1972 the regime had authorized what was called the "Educational Sector Review," a study of Ethiopia's educational system that was called upon essentially to assess the condition of education in the empire and solve the twin problems of limited access to education among the rural poor and overproduction of higher level graduates (Keller 1988:171-172). Supported by UNESCO, the ILO, the World Bank, the United States Agency for International Development (USAID), and the Ford Foundation the study, not surprisingly, issued a series of proposals to restructure the educational system. The essence of the recommendations was the same as those that had

The Invention of Ethiopia

been made for other countries of the third world, i.e., that Ethiopia expand education in the lower grades among children in every part of the empire but limit the opportunities for higher education to be made available. At the same time it proposed reduction in teachers' salaries while increasing the work load. The review, formally introduced on February 8, 1974, met with vociferous protest from teachers and students. The students' loud protest against it was grounded in disagreement with its underlying plan. Students argued among other things that it was designed to hold back the opportunities of students in the remote (colonial) rural areas by making available to them only enough education to turn them into errand boys, while the elite would still be allowed to advance to higher levels of state power. Even the elite students who had better chances than others of obtaining access to upper levels protested because they were no longer guaranteed education to be funded by the state, as had been the case in the past. Instead, they were placed in the position of having to compete with each other for limited number of spaces. The protesting students were joined by the 17,500-strong teachers' organization (Ethiopian Teachers Union, ETU) which had unsuccessfully demanded salary increases and improvement in working conditions since 1968. The teachers went on strike. Haile Selassie's government was forced to reconsider both the program and the demand for a pay increment. The Educational Sector Review was officially withdrawn by February 22, 1974.

In keeping with the approach presented for this new kind of broad-based education, however, Work-Oriented Literacy Programs had been developed in cooperation with UNESCO in several of the major languages found in the empire. Materials had been fully prepared that presented the initial lessons in several indigenous languages written in Sabean (Amharic) script. This was done in order to provide stepping stones to the introduction of Amharic, the national language. Some of the printed materials representing the cumulative effort of several Ethiopian ministries and substantial foreign planning and financial support had been widely-circulated in the latter years of Haile Selassie's regime; other follow-up volumes

274

sat piled in warehouses ready for distribution by February 1974 (Alemitu 1970 and 1989, Debebe 1987).

The Haile Selassie regime had also begun to face repeated demands for larger agricultural projects, employment for urban migrants, resistance in remote areas and devastating famine in the rural regions of the empire. The World Bank and the Harvard Advisory Group stepped in to assist in addressing simultaneously these economic and social problems in the long-term. The proposal was to design schemes for resettling problematic populations from one region of the country into large mechanized farms established in another (Cohen 1987, Eshetu Chole 1984, Wood 1973). A few pilot projects were carried out in the early 1970s (Wood 1973), but conditions in the colonized areas were too precarious for the Haile Selassie regime to carry out large-scale resettlements at that time. When an extensive famine developed in Wollo, it was ignored and covered up (Shepard 1975), a response that exposed to the international sponsors as well as to the populations within Ethiopia the incapacity of the government to carry out the reforms designed as solutions to these problems.

Land reform, more than any other issue had long been a subject of great concern not only in Ethiopia but also among the foreign governments and businesses representing the interests of finance capital. These latter were interested in further penetration into the rural areas for developing large and small-scale projects in the empire. Extensive efforts had been made by Western consultants to find ways of tinkering with the land policies and suggesting "viable" proposals for implementing changes that would increase productivity. Each of these were effectively blocked by the Ethiopian Senate, the haven of that fraction of the landholding class that had accrued great personal profit as a result of their stranglehold on access to large tracts of land. Most of the changes put forward by foreign consultants could not be implemented directly because they undermined the particular formula for controlling the economic base that kept the neftegna in power during the Haile Selassie era. It had been the era in which the aristocratic fraction of the landholding group dominated due to the size of their holdings. The land issue was one

The Invention of Ethiopia

that had been widely discussed throughout the latter years of Haile Selassie's rule, and countless proposals were under active consideration by the government at the early 1970s (Cohen and Weintraub 1976, Hoben 1973, Cohen 1985, Halliday and Molyneux 1981, Markakis and Ayele 1978, Ottaway and Ottaway 1978, LeFort 1983, Gilkes 1975, Dessalegn 1985, Stahl 1974). Land, the basic means of production in the empire, became the central issue in the resistance to the state that was posed by the colonized peoples and, consequently, the student movements abroad had chosen to rally around the slogan "Land to the Tiller."

Plans for refining and extending the bureaucracy necessarily went hand in hand with proposals for land reform because the basic infrastructure was not yet refined enough to guarantee secure access to and control of the remoter regions where lands were fertile but where people were resistant to the government. Designs for improving central government penetration of the rural areas were also complete but not yet in place by the early 1970s. These plans systematically replaced the balabats with a new kebele organization capable of extending the reach and the control of the state deeper into the rural communities (for description of the proposed design see Cohen and Koehn 1980).

Through this period of the late 1960s and early 1970s while the Haile Selassie government and its foreign advisers attempted to save the empire by grappling with one major area of crisis, another more serious would rise up. Although several different groups were expressing discontent with the regime, in no way were the causes of their discontent similar. The issues raised by the people who challenged Haile Selassie's government in the 1970s easily fall into three categories. The first and most basic challenge came from the Oromo, Eritrean, Sidama, Afar and Somali nations, simply put, from the colonies. The issue they raised was one of political economy; they aspired to achieve self-determination through replacing the production relations that obtained under the Ethiopian state with new relations born of the values and imposed through the institutions grounded in their own very separate socioeconomic experiences.

276

Ethiopia in the Era of Finance Capital

The second category was the opposition groups who raised a political challenge to the sitting regime. They did not want to replace the system; they wanted to move into power in order to make the state function more smoothly and efficiently. They wanted reform. In this category fell the subordinated peoples, and intellectuals who had been trained to move into the state apparatus, both of whom aspired to take control in order to save the empire through improving it in different ways.

The third category raised economic issues. These were the taxi cab drivers, nurses, teachers, NCOs, labor unions, etc. These were people largely dependent on the state for livelihood. They had no aspirations for changing the state structure, nor did they want to move into power; they simply wanted an improvement in their allotment of what was available from the state as it currently functioned.

By the early 1970s, the demands of all of these groups began to be made simultaneously, rendering it extremely difficult for the regime to respond to each in turn. The ability of the Haile Selassie government to continue to safeguard the dependent colonial formula began to crumble. The chapters that follow a closer look at the nature of the resistance and opposition to the Haile Selassie government.

7 RESISTANCE TO THE FORMATION AND CONSOLIDATION OF THE ETHIOPIAN STATE

As the Ethiopian state has taken shape, fundamental challenges to the very existence of the state itself have developed apace. In earlier chapters mention has been made of some of the attempts that were made to suppress the expression of this kind of resistance. In the following two chapters we make a distinction between "resistance," the term we use to refer to efforts to dismantle the Ethiopian state by fundamentally altering the existing production relations, and "opposition," which is used to designate efforts to reform political relations within the existing state. The bulk of resistance originated among groups at whose expense the state was formed and developed for the most part outside the operation of the state structure.

It is true that at the same time that resistance was developing upon independent social bases, opposition began to emerge from within the state itself, among those who themselves were intimately connected with the state. There has been a great deal of confusion generated by those who fail to make the distinction between the kind of external opposition that we are calling resistance, and the internal opposition that is best characterized as movements for reform. In this book these movements are treated separately. This

The Invention of Ethiopia

chapter addresses the external opposition, i.e., the resistance. Within the frame of reference discussed in the introduction, the resistance comprises the forces for a revolutionary transformation of the mode of production imposed by that state. The opposition movements differ significantly from the resistance in that their fundamental objectives are to adjust the mechanism of the state rather than dismantle and replace it. The following chapter addresses the opposition.

During the creation of Ethiopia in the time of Menelik, the peoples of Oromia, Sidama, Ogaden, Afar, Gurage, and others were attached to Abyssinia by means of conquest. It has been our position that after a series of internal challenges to the state, Haile Selassie took this newly invented entity and firmly maintained its conquered peoples and territories in a colonial relationship. Settlers were joined by others who also called themselves "Ethiopians" in running the new state apparatus according to the advice and guidelines of Europeans. Haile Selassie also took several steps to expand the empire itself by extending the colonial relationship to other national entities. This is what occurred when Eritrea and the Somali Ogaden were annexed during his period of rule. The resistance of the peoples of these annexed constituted a force for transformation due to the position that they hold within the socioeconomic system and because of the nature of the changes that they advocate for the betterment of their nations.

The response to conquest from the victims at whose expense the expansion and consolidation took place is a dimension of the history of this empire that has been woefully and often intentionally neglected by scholars who have called themselves Ethiopianists. The evidence of massive resistance to the formation and consolidation of this state runs counter to the dogma that has been accepted as the definitive explanation for the creation and the independence of Ethiopia. The very fact that resistance has been ongoing exposes the mythology that the empire is a "naturally-existing African entity" that rallied its own forces to defeat European efforts to take it over, and after that was recognized in its pristine condition by the European powers. A complete, well-documented, and scholarly account

Resistance to Formation and Consolidation

of the nature and the scale of resistance put up by the peoples who were conquered and brought into the empire by force remains to be done, although a notable beginning has been made for the early period (see Mohammed Hassen 1990). Short of the type of full-blown study that a book-length work will bring, however, there is enough evidence available to make preliminary observations. Over the span of a century several neutral witnesses in the empire unwittingly recorded significant episodes of resistance of the colonized people while these witnesses were making records for other purposes. From their written records and from the oral history of colonized peoples we are able to document that colonized peoples have been intent upon transforming the production relations that exist in the empire. The efforts of these colonial subjects to liberate themselves from their subject position played a major role in bringing down the Haile Selassie government.

Oromia

The Oromo is the largest nation in the empire—60 percent of the population and a greater proportion of the land area. Historically, it was the first conquered. The conquest of part of Oromia provided the basis on which the Manz kingdom began to consolidate its power and gain an advantage in Abyssinia. That conquest provided the ground for Manz to conquer other nations and to gain recognition in the European world. Also the bulk of the economic resources claimed by Ethiopia and desired in the world market are located there.

The Oromo case is not unique, however. Many other independent nations of northeast Africa were conquered, occupied and colonized as part of the construction of the Ethiopian empire. The broad outlines of their experience in relation to the Ethiopian state have been similar to that of the Oromo in the essential features. Their histories and the accounts of their resistance have been subject to the same neglect and distortion as that of the Oromo. We have made the decision to elaborate upon the case of the Oromo as an

281

example of the experience of those nations brought into the Ethiopian empire by conquest and colonization.

Although Oromia and Abyssinia shared a long border for centuries, their cultural and linguistic roots are embedded in fundamentally different traditions. The Semitic Abyssinian background is linked to the Middle East, and the Cushitic Oromo heritage is tied to a language family that stretches across the central part of the African continent. The primary way that the Abyssinians related to the Oromo nation, up to and including the Sahle Selassie period, was to engage in raiding—entering Oromo territory on extensive looting and slave raiding expeditions. They were never successful in conquering or establishing themselves in Oromo territory for sustained occupation until the advent of European assistance, assistance which they received both in terms of weapons and schemes for extended occupation. When Sahle Selassie gathered substantial war material from Europeans, he became the first to introduce the phenomenon of guns as a major factor into the conflict between the Oromo and the Abyssinians, a conflict that up to that time had consisted of raiding by Abyssinians and resistance to the raiding by the Oromo. Besides the dramatic increase in number and style of armaments Sahle Selassie also brought a design that he had contrived with visiting Europeans. He planned in the long-term to use Oromo resources to obtain a secure supply of weaponry from Europe. It was this objective that required a fundamentally different way of relating to the Oromos than had been previously utilized; it required not just occasional entry but rather an occupation of their territory and a means of redirecting their economic resources away from the internal systems of distribution that operated under the indigenous Oromo production system.

With his new weapons, Sahle Selassie managed to establish several outposts among the resistant Oromo and maintain enough presence there that he declared himself King (negus) of Shoa. Once he had suppressed the indigenous Oromo systems of control over the resources that they themselves produced, Sahle Selassie entered into several agreements with Europeans desirous of the trade arrangements that he proposed. They were eager to supply arms that

Resistance to Formation and Consolidation

would be used to suppress the Oromo threat and guarantee the supply of what were regarded as Abyssinian products. What was happening here was the germination of the European-Abyssinian alliance that was specifically designed to change the economic base of the Oromo. Oromo resistance was aimed at reasserting Oromo control over their population, land and products.

This initial European-Shoan alliance lasted only until Sahle Selassie died and the alliance with the Europeans ended. Historians recount that at that point, there were "disturbances" among the Oromo who "rose in rebellion." What actually happened at that time was that the Oromo reclaimed their independence; the Abyssinian domination which had been imposed and held in place only by force of arms, proved to be temporary. The kingdom of Shoa "entered on a period of decline" (Darkwah 1975: 35-36). The issue at stake here was which form of production was going to prevail, the indigenous Oromo or the imposed Abyssinian form. In the absence of external assistance, the Abyssinian system could not prevail over the Oromo. Most of the occupied and annexed Oromo areas that had bordered on Manz were regained by the Oromo during the reign of Menelik's father, Haile Melekot, and Oromo production relations were reinstituted.

Menelik systematically attempted to implement the same kind of design to try to establish permanent control over the Oromo economy that his grandfather had used. The Oromo stood between Menelik's Shoa and the most direct route to the sea. If he could secure an avenue independent of the Tigray route through Eritrea, he could avoid Yohannes' more heavily armed forces; he could establish direct linkage with the Europeans to acquire virtually unlimited supplies of arms, and this would eventually lead to Shoan dominance over all of Abyssinia. He had to pass through Wollo Oromo territory to reach the British and French ports which would connect him to Europe and the outside world. Interestingly, information that sheds light on Menelik's design for establishing independent trade links is contained in the writings of Massaja, the man who served as Menelik's adviser and confidante until he was expelled by Yohannes (Marcus 1975: 37). It is quite likely that Massaja played

The Invention of Ethiopia

a key role in plotting with Menelik to fashion this design that required control of part of the Wollo Oromo.

Menelik met stiff resistance from the Wollo Oromo as he moved to implement his plans through their territory. Worqitu's armies and then Mastewet's forces resisted him strongly (Marcus 1975: 35-36) but were finally suppressed. Menelik was still able to strike deals with Oromo leaders at that early period in the relations between Oromo and Shoan leaders. Prior to the introduction of large-scale European weaponry into Shoa, Oromos would occasionally ally with Abyssinians in order to tip the balance in skirmishes between Oromo themselves. The Abyssinian component could play a contributing but not definitive role in the outcome of small encounters among Oromo. After the introduction of European armaments into the battles changed the nature and the outcome of the fighting, however, this practice stopped. Oromos themselves soon realized that they were no longer dealing with the Abyssinians alone, but that the European factor mandated a change in the way that they related to Shoans and other Abyssinians. This is a point that is often missed in the recounting of the early history of Abyssinian-Oromo relations. Whereas several writers have noted that at the early stages of European contact, Oromos would ally with one faction or another of Abyssinian force to fight another group of Oromos, they always refer to the phenomenon as evidence of endemic "divisions" among or "disunity" of Oromos. What they do not note is that prior to the advent of the large-scale use of guns, neither Abyssinian raiding nor participation in local Oromo disputes had a lasting effect upon the overall Oromo socioeconomic organization.

When the European factor entered in on the side of the Abyssinians, the Oromo met together in assembly and passed resolutions to go to war to defend the values of their fathers (lubba). They vowed in sacred oaths that the Oromo laws (sera) which had been publicly hammered out to formally embody these values would not be tampered with by the interference of the "Amara." Such assemblies have been recorded by Cerulli. The full text of the resolutions passed at such an assembly (which Cerulli calls a "parliament") is recorded for the Oromo of Gullallie. Cerulli (1922: 70-71) writes,

> The assembly of the Gullallie resolved to stand resolutely against the Amara led by Waldie. . . . Here is the text of the law passed by the Assembly. Like most Galla [Oromo] laws, it is drawn up in verse.

>> *luggama fardatti nbasin*
>> *addu Addarra nbufatin*
>> *miedhicha rkkarra nbufatin*
>> *tume sera*
>> *Mure sera*
>> *sera abba lubati*
>> *bokkudha*
>> *chaffiehda*
>> *chaffie abba Gallati*
>> *akka chaffiekienaballiesi*
>> *amara agabusa olcha*

This means, "Do not take the harness from the horse, the gear from your head or the weapon from your hand, because the law has been decided upon, the law of the lubba fathers. As proof, the specter is here, the parliament is sitting, the parliament of the fathers. According to our fathers, lay waste to the Amharas, force them to fast this and following nights."

When the law of the Oromo appeared to be threatened as it had not been earlier, the Oromo began to realize the extent of the threat and rose up together to defend it. This realization came in different ways in different parts of Oromia. There emerged several forms of response and resistance among the Oromo to what was a new Abyssinian threat. Some forms were successful and some were not. One of the most well-known cases of a response that was ineffective in the short run was that of Gobana Dacchie, a skilled Oromo fighter, son of an Oromo leader. Spotted by Menelik as an outstanding horseman, Gobana quickly rose to a position of leadership in

The Invention of Ethiopia

Menelik's army and was instrumental in bringing several Oromo regions under Menelik's domain. In some cases he was able to convince Oromo leaders to submit to him, in others, he defeated Oromos who could not be convinced that his schemes were in their best interests. Gobana's involvement enabled Menelik to extend the area of his control and was the determining factor in keeping the Gojjamis out of Oromia. Menelik promised Gobana the kingship of the conquered Oromo regions, but when the battles were over, Menelik and Taytu substituted loyal Abyssinians into the position that Gobana had expected to fill. Cerulli notes that Gobana made expeditions "without conquering the land" (1922: 72). It is true that the areas in the center and west of Oromia brought in under Gobana were spared the devastation that was wrought upon the east and south. Though these particular sectors were part of a nation that was brought into the colonial empire through conquest, the colonial relationship was extended into their territory by means of the control of local leaders. These leaders, often the heads of prominent families, such as the Jotee, Bakare or Jimma Abba Jifar families, accepted the colonial relationship for segments of the Oromo population for whom they were made responsible on the model of extended balabats.

There are two interpretations for Gobana's behavior. The first is that he was an outright traitor who turned against his own people for the hope of the personal glory of becoming king. In keeping with this interpretation, the pejorative term "neo-Gobana" is occasionally applied to an Oromo individual to indicate his betrayal of the Oromo cause. Another interpretation is that rather than betray an Oromo cause, Gobana miscalculated and made a tactical blunder that turned out to be devastating to the Oromo chances of retaining their independence.

This second interpretation assumes that as a man who had seen the firepower, the strategy, and the capacity of the Shoans to destroy and occupy Oromo country, he could have calculated that if an Oromo surrendered he could become a ruler of his own territory. An Oromo ruler who respects the tradition would be in a position to preserve many fundamental aspects of the society that someday

Resistance to Formation and Consolidation

the Oromo could build upon to regain their former strength. This could be seen as better than an Amhara who would try to completely destroy the societal system. The betrayal of Gobana himself by the Abyssinian ruler once his usefulness was over voided whatever plans Gobana may have had to form his own type of resistance. History has recorded only the fact that whether or not Menelik's general was an Amhara or an Oromo, the Oromo people fought against the occupationist army. On many occasions Gobana was defeated by Oromos resisting the invasion. Cerulli tells us that during one of the western expeditions,

> After the return of Gobana to falle, the Galla [Oromo] whom he had recently conquered took up arms against the Amhara. A league was formed . . . against this Galla confederation, Gobana sent [an expedition]. . . . The Amara were defeated in a battle at Gura Doba near the Wama river (1922: 75).

In an expedition Menelik charged Ras Darge to subdue Arsi. When he moved in, he faced the same kind of resolve and stiff resistance that Menelik's other efforts had faced. "The Arsi resisted desperately, led by Shiekh Nur Husseyn . . . an officer of Ras Darge, Fitawrari Dufera who was in the vanguard of the invaders, was defeated at Fugug and obliged to withdraw. After some other unfortunate combats, Darge himself was forced to retreat to Shoa" (ibid: 88).

When Menelik turned to try to conquer Harar (1887), he first asked Ras Darge to join, "but Darge, who had already been engaged in the war against the Arussi, refused." The Oromo of Harar repelled all subsequent attempts to take the land. Finally, Menelik himself carried out the invasion of Harar, and with a fully armed force he was able to claim a victory over the unarmed Oromo.

Once an Abyssinian victory over the Oromo in one area was considered complete, however, previously defeated groups would rise again. After the conquest of Harar, Oromos from the center "rebelled against the Emperor Menelik. He sent against them Ras

The Invention of Ethiopia

Darge, Makonnen, and other Chiefs. However, in spite of the boast of the Shoans, the Obborra together with the Abbiccu ... resisted valiantly for an entire year" (1922: 96). This kind of resistance was commonplace; the incidents that Cerulli offers were the norm throughout conquered Oromo territory. Oromo oral history provides a mine of detail concerning the incidents and issues at stake in uprisings against the conquering Abyssinians armed by Europeans. Further scholarly work into this area to address this issue is urgently required and will reveal the depth of the rejection of outright conquest and rule by European-aided Abyssinians. The phenomenon of continual uprisings among the Oromo earned them the label "warlike" and "rebellious" among Abyssinians and their European friends, both of whom were interested in eliminating all those dimensions of the Oromo social order that prevented their establishing control and secure trade in and out of Oromia. These constant uprisings among the Oromo were battles over control of the socioeconomic formation, specifically over what form of production relations would obtain in the domain of the Oromo. The resistance constituted attempts to throw off interference in their way of life and reinstate their own previously existing form of social and economic order.

The slow imposition of Abyssinian presence into the heart of Oromia was always accompanied by substantial armaments because of the violent resistance of the inhabitants to the changes that were being introduced at gunpoint. The settlers are called neftegnas (gunowners) to this day because the gun was the essential feature which made possible their very presence in the conquered areas. The name itself is testimony to the resistance that the conquered nations posed to settlement itself. Settlers could enter conquered areas only by means of building armed forts and garrisons. Through the administrators who lived in these garrisons new "laws" were declared and enforced which were tools for imposing the new production relations. These were primarily laws that had to do with the redistribution of the land. It was this change that constituted the transformation of the Oromo economic base. The Oromo land and its products were reallocated to play a central role in supporting the

Resistance to Formation and Consolidation

new Ethiopian state. Then the nationwide Oromo systems of communication, cooperation and assembly, which had sustained the superstructure of the Oromo society, were outlawed. When Oromo cultivators were parcelled out among the armed settlers, they were tied to the land. They were immobilized. Not only were they prevented from rallying troops, the Oromo were not able to travel or communicate with Oromo who had been arbitrarily placed into other "administrative" districts introduced by the state. There was a full-scale assault on Oromo culture—all aspects that enabled the Oromo to obstruct and prevent Ethiopian control of the people and resources.

Consequently, the arena of battle shifted from primarily the military field to the arena of day-to-day interactions where the Ethiopian state institutions were being introduced to suppress and replace all the ways that the previously existing Oromo mode of social organization had shaped social and economic life.

The forms of administration that were imposed on Oromia divided naturally occurring family and economic units and placed them into different sections of the administrative apparatus. Every "provincial" boundary drawn in the center, west, east and south of Ethiopia cuts through Oromo territory and divides internally-significant categories of Oromos from each other. This is true for Wollo, Tigray, Gojjam, Shoa, Wollega, Illubabor, Kaffa, Sidamo, Bale, Arussi, and Hararge. Every act that Oromos took to show defiance of these divisions was an act of resistance to the imposed state structure.

There was an immediate frontal attack on Oromo religion—all those who followed the traditional religion were termed "pagan" and were forced to convert to the Ethiopian Coptic Orthodox church. Massive numbers of Oromos throughout the country converted en masse to Islam in widespread acts of protest against the forced Christianization program of the Ethiopians. The enthusiasm that Oromos and other peoples showed for conversion to European and American missionary efforts must be seen in light of their political rejection of and their attempts to escape the continued use of coercion by the Ethiopian state to influence their religious affiliation. Of course the Ethiopian willingness to allow missionaries into the territories of Oromo and other conquered peoples was part of their attempt to eliminate the peoples' traditional beliefs, thus attempting to undermine the ideological basis for any resistance. Ideological resistance to these efforts was easily changed into political resistance and the consequent revolt.

There have been several acts of resistance large enough to have been heard in the outside world despite the tight control maintained by the Abyssinians over the communications system. These have taken place among the hundreds of smaller-scale acts that have gone unregistered in the official records of Ethiopian history. In 1928 there was massive participation by Oromos in the Azebo-Raya revolts. In 1936, there was an official petition for recognition by the League of Nations from Western Oromia where a provisional government of Oromos had been established. They also asked from Britain acknowledgement of their independence (Gilkes 1975: 210-14). In 1947 there was a similar petition from Oromos in Hararge. Oromos opposed the restoration of the rule of Haile Selassie after the Italian occupation in dramatic acts of resistance that have usually been ignored by historians intent upon praising the "restoration of independent Ethiopia." The Oromo rebellion in Illubabor is another case in point. There have been many. Oromo scholars are only now beginning to record and publicly expose aspects of Oromo history that have been ignored by those who have supervised and conducted research and writing of the history of this region.

To establish a system of colonialism, however, it had become necessary for the occupiers to begin an attack on the Oromo superstructure that had protected the economic base during the period of Oromo sovereignty. This process entailed enforcing new policies which prevent conditions from returning to the preconquest organization. This required replacing the Oromo norms, values, and customs that had been generating continual revolt with those of the class that had invented this new entity called Ethiopia. Much Oromo resistance to this attempt by the colonizers to replace the seedbed of their culture has been successful.

Resistance to Formation and Consolidation

Oromo oral history reveals that though Oromo throughout the country realized that their national defense system had failed to protect the people and the way of life from the onslaught of the Abyssinian-European alliance, they have continued to claim the inevitable liberation of their nation from the conditions that have been imposed upon them. The first claim of this nature was reported verbatim by a European observer who accompanied Menelik to battle against the Arsi Oromos. He noted that one of the defeated leaders of Oromo resistance named Roba Bultum stated a full five years after his defeat at Arsi, "The hour has not come, but it will come. Perhaps our children will see the departure of the oppressor." (Marcus 1969: 276) This statement is currently cited by the Oromo Liberation Front in its official literature aimed at mobilization of a broad spectrum of Oromo. This indicates that it continues to capture an attitude Oromo have maintained toward the occupying force from the time that the battles took place. This fundamental belief has become a shared dimension of Oromo national identity and can be found at the heart of continued resistance by Oromos to Ethiopian institutions.

In the face of Ethiopian domination several generations of Oromo have clearly shown an ability to preserve and find expression for norms, values and beliefs that remain characteristically Oromo. The capacity to maintain a separate identity and set of values plays a significant role in the effort to throw off or change colonial rule.

Oromos were successful in resisting the new norms that were imposed on them. They ran their own affairs on a day-to-day basis "akka gada ti," according to the Gada, the system by which Oromo society was governed before the advent of Ethiopian domination. Since Gada had once functioned as superstructure of the Oromo society, it permeated Oromo culture, and found expression in dimensions of life that could not be controlled by the Ethiopian state. It remained a cultural tool accessible to every Oromo for resisting assimilation to the new Ethiopian standard that was being imposed by the state.

Since a central function of Ethiopian state institutions is to outlaw and replace those dimensions of Oromo culture that obstruct

The Invention of Ethiopia

the smooth assimilation to an Ethiopian norm, imposition and enforcement of a new formal ideology on the residents has become one of the state's most powerful methods in the effort to cast the empire in an Ethiopian mold. In this regard, the state required that all courts, schools, offices, businesses, church services, even public addresses be carried out in Amharic throughout the empire. Complete assimilation to the Amhara standard became a requirement for participation in any affairs of government or business. Literacy tests in Amharic, official forms with Ethiopian court approval, evidence of receipts for payment of land tax, even having an Amhara name could be and often were used a requirements for participation in state-sponsored programs. Place names throughout the conquered regions of the empire were changed—traditional names were replaced with Amhara ones. Part of this effort has been the granting of clear preference to Christian converts in every arena of life. Such policies amounted to the systematic destruction of an Oromo ideological system embodied in custom, culture, identity and language. Oromo efforts to circumvent these measures and keep Oromo practices and values current constitute a profound and effective form of resistance.

Certain forms of Oromo resistance have sharpened over the years. Since the nature of the confrontation between those attempting to impose Ethiopian values and those defending Oromo values is that of a colonizer trying to replace elements of an indigenous culture, the weapon of traditional Oromo values has become more keenly honed in daily battles between the colonizer and the colonized in every type of arena.

When the Ethiopian government under Haile Selassie began to encourage foreign investment and big businesses to invest in the empire to create positions for their children, a simple literacy test in Amharic served as an effective device to assure the members of the neftegna class that the conquered peoples would provide little competition for settlers in the new posts.

These acts had the result of not only excluding the indigenous people from the new jobs that these ventures were creating, but they

Resistance to Formation and Consolidation

resulted in people being massively evicted from their lands which had been targeted for "development."

As regards the colonies, it was during Haile Selassie's era that the state acquired an increased capacity to alienate the colonized peoples (now tenants) from their ancestors' land. Such an eventuality had been built into the colonial formula at its inception, but the state's inability to implement it had shielded the people from the extent of their vulnerability. Their position in relation to the state became exceedingly clear through these moves. With mechanization, the land owned by primarily Amhara neftegna settlers became more profitable without the serfs' labor. Even Oromo who had been successful in renting their fathers' lands back from the state were prevented from doing so as rents were increased to realize higher profits for further mechanization. The lot of the conquered peoples who had become tenants became worse than ever. These conditions set in motion an open war of resistance in the regions where the policies were directly applied.

Armed uprisings of the Oromo peasants were smashed in Bale in the late 1960s by more heavily armed units of the government, specifically, airborne rifle squadrons. Just as in 1929-30 when British airplanes were used to put down the Oromo revolt in Azebo-Raya, assistance from a superpower was required in Bale to suppress the resistance. The Ethiopian empire was saved and Oromos were kept in their position not by the Ethiopian army acting alone, but with the help of the United States. Patrick Gilkes has written regarding the Bale rebellion in 1968,

> Air attacks were unsuccessful and the accuracy of the rebel bazookas caused some concern. It was at this time that American experts were brought in to improve the fire power on some of the jets (Gilkes 1975: 218).

This type of aggressive implementation of its policies by the Ethiopian regime set the pace for modern coordinated wars of resistance among the indigenous peoples fighting to defend their access to basic resources.

The Invention of Ethiopia

Sporadic acts of resistance took place on a regular basis. The government responded with force, however. By the 1960s the sporadic confrontations had caused many previously quiescent Oromo from every corner of Oromia to realize the possibility of responding systematically to the Ethiopian government's violence against them. The colonial government had provided no opportunity for Oromo nationals to express themselves as Oromo. The intellectuals resented that they stood in no better position than did their fathers with regard to the state.

Both the intellectuals, or as the Amharas designated them, civilized, "ye salatana Gallas," and the uncivilized, "yal seletana Galla," (as the Amharas called Oromo who had rejected the Amhara value system imposed by the state) began to utilize traditional forms of communication to send solidarity messages to the Oromo warriors in the Bale region. They were also agitating Oromo to join them. This was done in the best way available within the Oromo culture, that is, through song. Examples of some of the songs sung on the streets of Addis Ababa demonstrate this:

> *Bale dur esheda amma isani*
> *Mauzerin ya akka bishani*
> *Nolle negala kara issani*

which means in English:

> In the past Bale was called cowardly
> But guns (Mauser) started flowing like water
> Now we will join them.

and also this:

> *Jetti bitte*
> *Jarsa Bale fitta*
> *Jallen gabaru didde*
> *Sittu Beeka, Ya Jono*
> *Kan kana fidde*

Resistance to Formation and Consolidation

which translated means:

> You bought jets
> You killed the old men of Bale (because they would
> not stop their children)
> The youngsters refused to give in
> Oh, Jon Hoy (Haile Selassie), you are responsible
> You, who brought these problems.

These are examples of thousands of messages that were enthusiastically sung throughout the major towns during the period of the Bale rebellion. The transport system and general mobility allowed for Oromo who went to the urban areas as laborers had begun to provide avenues for Oromo who had once been isolated from one another to come into contact and to begin to experience their own strength. The messages generated enthusiasm and self-consciousness among the hearers.

As the oppression continued, so did the resistance. By the 1950s the resistance of the Oromo people had taken on another dimension; it began to become clear to Oromo intellectuals selected to receive formal "Ethiopian" education that once they had completed their training and were ready to step in to operate some part of the state structure, that they were being kept behind. They began to conclude that they would never be allowed to reach the critical positions of power, that these were being reserved for neftegnas by the neftegnas who controlled the state. Educated Oromo complained that they were always being watched for signs of loyalty and expected to prove themselves to the neftegna and even to the neftegna children. This realization caused them to see that if they were to achieve anything on the scale that they had hoped for their people, they would have to achieve it from a position that enabled them to relate directly to their people.

The phenomenon that has frequently been referred to as the "return to the source" following the writings of Amilcar Cabral (1973) occurred gradually in the 1950s and was galvanized by the birth of the Macha-Tulama movement in the mid-1960s. Accounts that have been publicized in Oromo student journals relate the unfolding of this awareness. They say that looking at what was going on in the empire, the students observed that the system intensified the oppression and exploitation of Oromo, Sidama, Ogaden and other nations. They observed that they were hemmed in from every side. Scholarships for study in foreign countries were awarded to the children of landlords, and arrangements were made through the Ministry of Education to assure these students positions in the state apparatus upon their return. They observed that although these policies were presented as an extension of Ethiopian modernization, they usually translated into increased misery for Oromo and others. They concluded that they were destined to serve the children of the settler class, who rather than transforming the situation, had merely learned a new technique for rule (Waldhaansso 1985, Sagale Oromo 1985).

The current armed resistance traces its roots to the period of the much-abused Macha-Tulama organization, a period when Oromos proudly spoke their own language on the city streets and began to feel their power as a force in the empire (Lubee 1980).

As had other Oromo before them, educated Oromo also began to realize that their condition would never change unless they took action independent of the state. Their resolve to take action led to the formation of types of organizations that reflected their familiarity with Western institutions. Their efforts were part of a general sentiment among Oromo to organize themselves as Oromo.

Up to the 1960s, the socialization of most Oromo children, whether urban or rural was quite similar. Those who had been selected for formal education by one means or another were still intimately familiar with the concerns of the Oromo peasantry. Many of these became involved in the formation of an Oromo organization that articulated matters of common concern to the Oromo populace at large. Having framed an Oromo self-help organization around issues such as building roads and opening schools, educated Oromo found a groundswell of response among the rural Oromo population as well as among the urban dwellers.

Resistance to Formation and Consolidation

After several attempts, Oromo finally managed to obtain approval from the neftegna government for the title "Macha-Tulama Self-Help Association" only because the names of two geneological categories that encompassed all Oromo without exception happened to correspond with place names found in Shoa province. The government could find no reason to prevent its formation, in light of the existence of several organizations of similar ostensible objectives. But the overwhelming response measured in the millions of members registered in both the rural and urban areas within months of its formation was perceived as a potential political threat to the government from the largest nation in the empire. The organization begun in 1963, after a remarkable showing in its initial period, was relatively short-lived. Its leaders were harassed and framed for an explosion in Addis Ababa's largest cinema in 1966, and it was finally forced underground in 1969. P. T. W. Baxter has documented the process of the development of what he terms "a pan-Oromo consciousness" in a groundbreaking article written in 1978 in which he recounts the growing self-awareness of Oromos in the army, the university, and even in the parliament. He was an eyewitness to developments in the country in 1967 and describes the Macha-Tulama movement as "flourishing" (Baxter 1978).

The government framed the leaders of the Macha-Tulama and attempted to dismantle the organization at the peak of its popularity. They only succeeded in forcing it underground. Norman Singer, writing up the trial as an evidence of human rights violations, describes the procedures used by the government to suppress what up to that time had been an expressly apolitical movement:

A bombing incident in an Addis Ababa cinema in November, 1966, led to the arrest of over 100 prominent Galla [Oromo], many of them officials of the Mecha and Tulema Association, a Galla self-help welfare organization. The nine who were charged with involvement in the incident and plotting to cause tribal hatred and overthrow the government pleaded not guilty. In the trial (from 1967-8), which was partly observed by a representative of the International

The Invention of Ethiopia

Commission of Jurists, the first judge attempted to dismiss the case, but he was himself dismissed from his post. Two defense lawyers were fined by the new judge (a military Colonel with no legal experience) and severely warned. Defendants were not allowed to choose their own lawyers and were kept in solitary confinement without access to lawyers until the trial, which was mainly in closed court. Several witnesses, claiming that they had been tortured, tried without success to withdraw their statements against the accused. They alleged they had been deprived of food for three days, then interrogated continuously for a week without being allowed to sleep or go to the toilet. They stated that they were put in separate lice-infested cells, bound hand and foot, beaten and forced to drink boiling hot drinks, swung from their arms until blood dripped, tortured by electric shock and other means. In the court's eventual verdict, General Tadesse Birru and Lt. Mammo Mezemir were sentenced to death; Col. (retired) Alemou Kitessa, Mekonnen Wessene, Haile Mariam Gemeda (a lawyer, who was unable to attend trial because of his tortures, which left him partially paralyzed), Lemessa Boru, Seifu Tessemma, and Dadi Feysa were sentenced to prison terms of between 3 and 10 years, while the witnesses all received 10 years imprisonment—Bekele Mekonnen, Tesfaye Degga, Tafesse Gemetchu, Corporal Fituma Hiksa, and Haile Mariam Dima (Singer 1978: 668-669).

Such acts of atrocity committed against Oromo leaders had the effect of intensifying rather than deterring Oromo demands and commitment to independent action.

In the rural areas, Oromo tenants had already succeeded in carrying out land liberation on the basis of Oromo cultural values by the late 1960s and early 1970s. The long-term efforts to chase landlords away from their farms and to organize the land and labor resources "according to the Gada" had become effective by that time (Clay and Holcomb 1986: 129). While the rural cultivators were

298

experiencing some dramatic success, intellectuals who had survived the banning of Macha-Tulama had gone underground to find a new approach. Those who had been able to leave the country were also searching together for alternative tactics and strategies to achieve the objective they had espoused and to find a new model for effective organization.

For a while these remnants from other groups used the name Ethiopian National Liberation Front, also known by its Amharic acronym EBNAG. But this name was short-lived since it introduced confusion as to their objective. A committee was formed called the Organization of the Oromo People's Liberation Struggle (OOPLS) which issued a political program from Finfinne (the Oromo name for the spot on which Addis Ababa was built). This group finally settled on the name Oromo Liberation Front (OLF).

These multifaceted attacks on the status quo, both passive and active, played a major and usually unacknowledged role in the demise of the *ancien regime* of Haile Selassie. A full accounting of the scope and depth of the history of the resistance of the colonized peoples in Ethiopia is a major piece of research waiting to be done.

Sidama

There are many small and larger communities of people occupying parts if the southwest and south central regions of the Ethiopian empire that are often lumped together by outside scholars and residents alike in a general reference to "the Sidama people." In the Oromo language, this term means literally "non-Oromo." George Peter Murdock in an anthropological survey of the Horn region used the term "Sidamo" to mean all the ethnic groups of south central Ethiopia, including the Bako, Gibe, Gimira, Janjero, Kafa, Maji,and the Ometo (Murdock 1959: 187-88). Anthropologist John Hamer uses the term Sadama "used to refer to the Gudela, Kambata [Hadiya], Tambaro, Alaba, and Walamo [Walayita]" who live in the general vicinity of Lakes Abaya and Awasa (Hamer 1987: 10). Getahun Dilebo names particular Sidama groups among the south-

The Invention of Ethiopia

ern Cushites (Getahun 1974: 93-96). In the early 1980s, a Sidama Liberation Front was formed and issued a political program which spoke for all those who use that term to refer to themselves (see 1982). Since the term Sidama is not specific, and does not apply to any one exclusive group, but has a history of being used as a non-pejorative generic term for the many small groups with separate identities that are indigenous to that part of the Horn, the term is used here to refer to the conquered and colonized non-Oromo. In this work the term Sidama refers to the many peoples of the center, south and west of the empire who were incorporated into Ethiopia through conquest, occupation, and colonization. Many people eagerly await the time when these peoples will speak in their own voice and make their own history and experience available in publicly accessible forms. Until the time that formal associations emerge from these peoples which reveal what names they call themselves, we choose to refer to them in this general way, knowing that their experience of colonization is a large unwritten chapter in the history of this empire.

The people referred to as Sidama have had an historical experience similar to that of the Oromo. They fought against the military conquest and colonization of their lands and population (Marcus 1969, Getahun 1975, McClellan 1978) and they relate to the Ethiopian state as colonial subjects. While there is little written about the resistance of the Sidama, oral histories indicate that the national experience of these peoples has been similar in type and direction to that of the other colonies. The primary difference between the Sidama experience and that of the Oromos in relation to the Ethiopian state is that the Oromo were the first to be conquered, and share borders with the Abyssinians. The conquest of the Oromo provided the basis for the creation and the expansion of the empire into the other areas; in some cases the Oromo language was used by the conquerors to communicate with these neighbors of the Oromo. Once that conquest had taken place, Ethiopian control over the Oromo and Sidama lands and people formed the core of the economic base of the empire.

Resistance to Formation and Consolidation

The objectives that the Sidama Liberation Front put forward in its 1982 political program clearly articulates that they were conquered and colonized as a nation and that as a nation they came to the 1974 February upsurge expecting that the neftegna settlers would leave and their means of production would be liberated to be administered on the basis of self-reliance. Liberation and national independence is their stated objective.

Ogaden Somali

The case of the Somali nation is a classic, if not *the* classic example, of a fully functioning national entity dismembered among colonial powers in the process of partition that occurred as a result of the Scramble for Africa. Members of the single Somali nation were divided among four colonial powers, Britain, France, Italy and Ethiopia, and have had five distinct experiences under colonial rule. France carved out a small section of the homelands of both Somali and Afar that surrounded the harbor they claimed as the port Djibouti. This was French Somaliland or as the French called it, the Overseas Territory of Afars and Issas (Somalis). The adjacent coastline territory to the south of the French bordering on the Gulf of Aden was taken as British Somaliland. Further south still the Italians staked out the remaining stretch of coastal area that ran along the Indian Ocean up to the British claims on British East Africa. The Somali territories that lay inland from both the British and Italian coastal colonies were conquered by the Abyssinians and were brought into the Ethiopian empire as Abyssinian Somaliland, the region more popularly known as the Ogaden. The Somalis whose territory fell into the British reach from their East African preserve ended up in the British East African colony. As a result of these partitions, various parts of the Somali nation experienced direct, single-country monopoly colonialism of the British, French and Italian type and the dependent colonialism of the Ethiopian empire.

The Invention of Ethiopia

The Somalis resisted each of these forms of occupation, defending their country and people against the intruders of all backgrounds (Perham 1969: 334-338, Laitin and Samatar 1987, Bereket 1980: 97-125). The leader who has become a symbol of Somali resistance during the period of the early 1900s is Mohammed Abdille Hassan (the Mad Mullah), who combined certain dimensions of Islam with Somali nationalism to fight all the colonizers at once. He was able to avoid capture and defeat by ignoring the artificial boundaries that had been drawn through Somali territory and to utilize indigenous forms of expression and communication to unite his vast numbers of supporters. This made it clear to both Somalis and outsiders that a living nation with its own forms of organization had been violated by the intrusion. His poetry bespoke Somali sentiment when he referred to the colonizers as "vultures hovering over my head, eager to dip their filthy beaks into my body" (cited in Bereket 1980: 99).

Margery Perham tells us that for many years

> [t]he majority of the Somalis in the Ethiopian section, especially in the low, more desert areas, never came under effective Ethiopian administration ... the Somalis were not easily subjugated by the Amharas ... Ethiopians detest the Somali country which contrasts sharply with their cool native mountains.... [I]t was a country, they said, for the Somalis, the infidel, and the hyenas, not for the Christian.... [I]t is therefore not surprising that reports from Ethiopia and from British frontier authorities were that administration was mainly conspicuous by its absence ... sovereignty was expressed chiefly by means of intermittent expeditions, not far removed from raids, in which stock was taken as tribute from more accessible groups (1969: 337).

Ethiopia had only built enough garrisons in the region of Western Somalia to prevent the British from establishing effective occupation, but not enough to be able to make an impact upon Somali society and cultural life. This latter observation is significant in that it supports the notion that the Somali of this region continued to

302

organize themselves according to their pre-existing modes of livelihood, thus preserving a basis from which to challenge colonial authority over them.

During the period of decolonization (demonopolization of colonial empires), the position of the Somalis under British, French and Italian control shifted in terms of how each related to the international order; each became directly or indirectly administered as part of a corporate colony. That of the Somalis under Ethiopian dependent colonialism remained legally unaffected. The only thing that changed is that the patronage of Ethiopia shifted from Britain to the United States. One effect of this change was that due to the increased financial and technical support offered to Ethiopia by her new patron in this era, the Ethiopian state finally acquired the capacity to penetrate and occupy the Ogaden region, an accomplishment that had evaded them during the earlier years. With United States assistance to Ethiopia, the part of the Somali Ogaden region that had fallen within Ethiopian Somaliland was occupied and colonized by Ethiopia. It was at this point that the administrative divisions introduced by the Ethiopian Ministry of the Interior began to be applied to the Somali of this region and they began to experience the systematic incursions of dependent colonialism. In addition to this, part of Somali territory that had been under British administration, the Haud region, was annexed to Ethiopia through diplomatic channels described in Chapter Six.

The systematic efforts of the Ethiopian administration to impose actual control over the annexed and newly occupied regions resulted in systematic efforts by the Somalis to repel the new forms of incursion. The Western Somali Liberation Front (WSLF) was formed in 1960. Throughout the 1960s fighting broke out when local governors of the Ethiopian state attempted to collect taxes, recruit forces for the army or carry out any activities that implied the control of Ethiopia over the Somali region. The Somali desire to push out the Ethiopian colonizers, defend their own rights and establish their own independence was similar to the aspirations of the other colonized peoples of the Ethiopian empire, those directly colonized by Ethiopia or later annexed. Somalis who fell into both categories shared the same objectives.

So the people of the "Ogaden" or "Western Somalia" carried out a struggle of resistance in an attempt to attain their freedom not only in the face of conquest and annexation by Ethiopia, but also against the Italians, the Abyssinians and the British before that. The question of whether they would seek independent status or choose to join the Republic of Somalia has remained an open one debated within the ranks of those who shared the objective of separation from Ethiopian empire.

After the Democratic Republic of Somalia was formed from the former British and Italian Somalilands, and began to operate within the United Nations model for corporate colonialism, the people living in the area called Ogaden had consistently fought dependent colonialism as the Ethiopian occupation of their land continued. They fought by means of an intensive war of liberation backed sporadically by the government of Somalia. This support has at times confused their direction. A major obstacle for them lay in the Somali government's tactics of support. In the current era, the role that the "decolonized" Somali Democratic Republic has played in relation to the Ogaden Somalis has been similar to the role of the dependent Ethiopian state—each acts indirectly as an instrument to pull the region more closely into the orbit of the international institutions dominated by finance capital.

The struggle of the people of Ogaden to be completely disengaged from the Ethiopian state and to follow a course of self-determination built upon their own separate institutional base made a contribution to the fall of Haile Selassie's government in 1974.

Afar

The Afar nation is made up of a Cushitic people whose pastoral homelands comprise the lowland region along the coast of the Red Sea. The area extends from the harbor that became the port of Djibouti in the south to the port of Assab in the north and stretches inland to border the lands of the Tigray and the Wollo Oromo to the west. During the Scramble for Africa the Afar were divided among the colonizing powers in the region, specifically among France, Italy and Abyssinia. The part occupied by Italy later became known as the Eritrean Danakil. The part occupied by France was incorporated into the French Territory of the Afars and the Issas, known since 1977 as Djibouti. The parts of Afar territory incorporated into the Abyssinian empire were forced into the administrative units of Wollo and Harar formed following the conquest of northern and eastern Oromia (known as Wollo and Harar). The colonial policies that were applied to the conquered regions were extended to the Afar in these units by means of the Afar sultanate, headed by the family of Ali Mirah.

Following the battles of conquest against all the peoples to the east of Abyssinia, the Afar were made subjects of Ethiopia by extension of the same colonial practices that were derived for the peoples whose lands were directly settled by Abyssinians. This control was made effective through the use of petty kings made to rule under the Ethiopian emperor who was called King of Kings. Just as the practice of rule through petty kings who functioned as extended balabats to implement colonial policy was followed in Wollega with the Bakare and Jotee families and in Jimma with the Abba Jifar family, so was it utilized in Afar with the Ali Mirah family.

The content of the Afar experience of Ethiopian colonialism remains to be documented. As little information as is available regarding the situation in Wollega or Jimma in Oromia, there is even less available about the Afar. This scarcity strongly suggests the need for Afar nationals to conduct in-depth studies of the Afar experience to make the information accessible to many who are ready to learn about the nature of Afar subjugation. From what data are in the public domain we know that especially after World War II, when several political units in Africa received international recognition as independent, Afar nationals thought that once the European colonizers departed, the Afar would reunite to form an independent Afar nation. Negotiations were underway with Haile

The Invention of Ethiopia

Selassie's government regarding this objective before that Ethiopian regime was overthrown. This diplomatic avenue was closed with the end of Haile Selassie's regime.

When the Derg came to power, the Afar experience changed. Afar officials were arrested and the leader of the Afar, Ali Mirah himself, was invited to join the new government. When Ali Mirah refused, the Afar land was nationalized directly. The Afar fiercely resisted this action and demonstrated their disapproval by taking up arms in the name of the Afar Liberation Front. The Derg's reactions were two. On the one hand, key Afar individuals were successfully enticed away from involvement in the armed struggle; on the other hand, the Derg moved mercilessly to crush the intensified armed resistance. While the Afar resistance has not been eliminated, it has been delayed, awaiting an opportunity pursue its objectives openly.

Eritrea

After defeat of the Axis powers in World War II and her unconditional surrender, Italy's colonies were taken. This turn of events brought Eritrea once again under yet another type of foreign rule, this time British. This arrangement was to hold until the fate of all the colonies, particularly that of the Italian colonies, was to be decided by the Allied powers sitting together. The Allied solution to this type of issue was the formation of the United Nations and the creation of international trusteeship.

Since the Italians had not destroyed Eritrean tradition, and Britain allowed, or at least did not discourage, political development of certain social sectors in Eritrean society, several social and economic associations were transformed into political and interest blocs. Some were formed into parties and leagues. The most visible among these were the Liberal Progressive Party led by Woldeab Walde Mariam and the Eritrean Moslem League, led by Abd el Kadir Kabira; the objective of both of these organizations was the independence of Eritrea. The Unionist Party led by Tedla Bairu put forth the objective of forming a united federal republic. There were also a number of smaller and less active organizations who supported the independence of Eritrea (Bereket 1989, also see Gilkes 1975, and Trevaskis 1960). In short, the Eritrean people had organized themselves into different sets based upon their own socio-economic interest and addressing their own future in a democratic fashion with only one party, the Unionist Party, an exception to the overall sympathy with independence as a political goal. The failure to demonstrate a popular base has been noted by Trevaskis (1960: 74), Gilkes (1975: 194), and Bereket (1989: 34), all of whom document the heavy support for the Unionist Party from the Ethiopian government and the Coptic Orthodox Church.

As previously noted, Eritrea's fate was not only of interest to and discussed by the Eritreans; the United Nations had been internationally recognized by the victors in the war to decide its fate along with that of the other colonies. Here is the forum where the United States brought arguments to defend her strategic interest and Ethiopia brought the matter of her desire for access to the sea. At the third United Nations session in which the Eritrean issue was discussed, the majority of the Eritrean people, those represented by their own socioeconomic and political groups, petitioned the United Nations to guarantee Eritrea her independence. "... the Eritrean bloc for independence, composed of eight political parties and associations, had asked the United Nations General Assembly, during its Third Session, for immediate independence" (Bereket 1989: 34). Besides the strong United States interest in the Radio Marina, which dovetailed nicely with the Ethiopian desire to obtain independent access to the sea, the Allies wanted to proceed cautiously regarding the mechanisms of trusteeship which was designed to determine the future of all the colonies. They were concerned that they proceed in an exemplary fashion.

Even John Foster Dulles, the head of the United States delegation to the United Nations, revealed that the United States was aware that the course his country was following was running roughshod over the expressed objectives of the Eritrean people when he said in a formal speech delivered to the United Nations National Security Council,

307

The Invention of Ethiopia

From the point of view of justice, the opinions of the Eritrean people must receive consideration. *Nevertheless* the strategic interest of the United States in the Red Sea basin and considerations of security and world peace make it necessary that the country has to be linked with our ally, Ethiopia (cited in Heiden 1978: 15 and Bereket 1989:37) [emphasis added].

It was clear to the participants in these decisions that the positions of the Eritrean people that had been expressed through organizations grounded in their own historical experience ran contrary to the United States' plan for designing the new world economic order. Having heard four major proposals regarding the Eritrean case (complete independence for Eritrea, complete annexation of Eritrea by Ethiopia, the partition of Eritrea between Sudan and Ethiopia, and Eritrea made a United Nations trust territory under Italy or Britain), the United Nations General Assembly endorsed the compromise position recommended by the godfather of the United Nations, the United States. The specific United States proposal was that an autonomous Eritrean government be formed and then this government be linked with that of the Ethiopian empire. Once the Eritrean constitutional rule had been established, then the federal Ethiopian government was to be responsible concerning foreign affairs, the defense budget, and commerce, which would give Ethiopians ultimate control of the sea ports of Massawa and Assab.

This arrangement formally placed full responsibility for the internal day-to-day activities into Eritrean hands. Patrick Gilkes described it as follows:

The Eritrean Government and assembly were to have full internal powers over all functions not vested in the federal government; and an Eritrean administration was to be set up and an assembly elected before the federation took effect (1975: 193).

Resistance to Formation and Consolidation

This assembly was to be elected on the basis of the political parties mentioned above that had begun during the period of British control.

Once this concept had been formally adopted by vote, it remained for the decision to be put into practice. Here at this point is where the first open conflict erupted between the political groups who represented these fundamentally opposed objectives for the future of Eritrea. In Gilkes' words,

> The political campaigning was fierce and sometimes bloody. One Moslem leader, Adb el-kadir Kebire, was assassinated in 1949, and other separatist leaders survived or failed to survive a number of attempts on their lives. The election for the assembly of 1952 was held under British control and resulted in a roughly equal Moslem/Christian division but with a Unionist party majority. This accepted the constitutional proposals of the U. N. as did Haile Selassie in Ethiopia, and the British departed in September 1952, leaving Tadla Bairu, the Unionist leader, as chief executive (1975: 194).

Immediately after the victory of the Unionist Party, even before the members of the party had an opportunity to prove their opponents in the independence camp wrong, the Ethiopian government began to pursue systematically the objective of undermining the federation arrangement (Bereket [1989] and Trevaskis [1960]). The dismantling of the Eritrean institutions happened very quickly. The Imperial Ethiopian government representative in Asmara began to interfere in the political process in Eritrea, using the same tactics as his counterparts in the rest of the empire. Eritrean newspapers were silenced, politicians were arrested, personal pressures, threats, and intrigues were utilized to undermine Eritrean institutions. Individuals were eliminated or forced to flee abroad for safety and more malleable individuals were appointed (not elected or nominated by party members) to top positions. Even Tedla Bairu left his position as Chief Executive in 1955 (Gilkes 1975: 195).

The Invention of Ethiopia

By the time of the 1956 elections, no political parties were allowed! In two years the assembly that was "elected" under these circumstances voted to discard the Eritrean flag. By 1959 Ethiopian law was extended over Eritrea to replace Eritrean law, so when the Eritrean government became the Eritrean "administration" in 1960, and then when the assembly "voted itself" out of existence it appeared as merely a formal exercise. In fact, Richard Greenfield, a close observer of events during that period, disputes the claim that a vote was ever taken; instead, a prepared statement was read by the chief executive (Bereket 1989: 52). In any case, the real coup d'etat had already occurred. Ironically, the proclamation which announced the "Termination of the Federal Status of Eritrea and the Application to Eritrea of the System of Unitary Administration of the Empire of Ethiopia," was issued under Order No. 27, an order that had been written by the American adviser, John Spencer, months ahead of time (ibid.).

What in fact had happened is that the arena of conflict had shifted. The Eritrean leaders who had been forced out of the country upon threat of losing their lives and the Eritrean people who had supported independence had simply opted to pursue their objective in a different arena, using different means, completely dismissing the assembly as a place where they could find justice.

The Eritrean people continued to demand independence, and were forced by circumstances to pursue it through different organizational forms. As early as 1958 the Eritrean Liberation Movement (ELM) was formed as a defense force by Eritreans who realized that the federation arrangement was a dead letter. This was the group that mobilized preexisting discontent among Eritreans who had aspired to independence into a broad-based movement and successfully communicated the real position in which Eritrea had been placed. The strikes and boycotts that this group organized came to a halt when the leaders were arrested by the Ethiopians. Then, in September 1961, the Eritrean Liberation Front (ELF) declared armed struggle. When Ethiopia officially violated the code that had been internationally agreed upon, destroyed the UN-imposed federation and openly annexed a nation whose expressed aspirations

Resistance to Formation and Consolidation

were independence, the Eritrean people began a war of self defense led by the ELF.

The Ethiopian government's actions starkly revealed, even to those Eritreans who had initially chosen to cooperate in the federal arrangement, that the only way to achieve independence was to support those who had taken up arms to defend the Eritrean social formation from further attack. The history of Eritrean armed resistance to Ethiopian colonial rule is a history of Eritrean attempts to safeguard the uniquely Eritrean social formation and to ensure its further development. When Eritrea refused to accept Ethiopian domination to the point of raising arms, the indignant Ethiopians exercised force from air and from land. The fighting escalated throughout the 1960s, with the Ethiopians enjoying the military support of the United States for this matter, which was regarded as another instance of difficulty with "internal security." The Eritreans, for their part, received the assistance of Middle Eastern countries, the Sudan and the Egyptian governments. By 1965 Eritrean forces were well armed. In that year the Sudanese government announced that it had discovered eighteen tons of Czechoslovakian arms at the Khartoum airport destined for the ELF (Gilkes 1975: 197). Syria and Iraq also supplied arms, training, and financial support.

Friends of Ethiopia, following the lead of the Ethiopian government line, have often called attention to the Middle Eastern source of much of Eritrea's support and reduced the Eritrean attempt to achieve independence from Ethiopia to an "Arab" or "Moslem" effort to weaken "Christian Ethiopia." Such positions do not take into account the social and economic institutions that the Eritreans have developed, incorporated and made their own through the course of struggle against first single-country monopoly colonialism and now against Ethiopian dependent colonialism. Any assessment of the Eritrean effort to be free of Ethiopian colonial administration must take a close look at the independent development of the social formation that they are fighting so hard to defend. The Eritrean capacity to transform the colonial production relation imposed upon them by the Ethiopians at annexation warrants examination.

311

The Invention of Ethiopia

The intensification of the conflict between Eritrea and Ethiopia through the 1960s led Ethiopia to carry out extensive destruction of the rural areas where the majority of Eritreans live, and highly visible massacres and reprisals, such as public hangings, carried out in the Eritrean major cities. Despite the military successes of the ELF, by the early 1970s a wing of the ELF had separated from the front with the expressed purpose of reorganizing in such a way that the social and economic dimensions of the struggle could be explicitly democratized. This was the origin of the EPLF, at first called the Eritrean People's Liberation Forces, but eventually renamed the Eritrean People's Liberation Front.

By the time Haile Selassie's government was overthrown, Eritrea had developed a highly organized liberation force, was in control of major parts of its territories, and was still demanding liberation, making Haile Selassie's U. S.- backed government pay very dearly for the refusal to accommodate them.

Had it not been for squabbles that developed between the ELF and the EPLF on issues of strategy, arguments which resulted in shared long-range objectives being sacrificed to short-range tactics, the liberation struggle of the Eritrean people would have been capable of taking over Eritrean affairs at the time of Haile Selassie's demise. At the juncture when the Derg took over the crown, the Eritreans presented the Derg with demands for independence and the dismantling of the Ethiopian colonial administrative apparatus. These demands embodying the quest for the free expression of basic democratic rights that Eritreans had demanded over three generations of colonial subjugation (Italian, British and Ethiopian) were formally recorded in the National Democratic Program of the EPLF issued in January 1977 (reproduced in Davidson, Cliffe and Bereket [eds.] 1980).

In offering an explanation for the downfall of the Haile Selassie government, it is important to assess closely and to separate the objectives held by the many groups who contributed to its ultimate demise and the methods the various groups used to pursue those objectives. Too little attention has been paid to the resistance put up against the regime by the conquered and annexed peoples whose very purpose was to prevent the government from operating effectively in their territorial or social domains. These peoples sought to dismantle the mechanisms by which the state functioned and to run their own affairs by instituting alternative forms of social and economic organization in their place; they sought self-determination. The objectives of these groups were fundamentally different from the aims of opposition groups who were seeking ways to make the existing state operate more efficiently or more democratically.

8 THE OPPOSITION MOVEMENTS: THE FORCES OF REFORM

Tigray: A Subordinated Nation

When the Ethiopian empire was constructed in the late 1800s, Tigray was forced into the state as a subordinated nation. The difference between her position and that of the colonized nations lies primarily in the economic relationship between her and the dominant Amhara nation and in the extent to which she shares elements of superstructure with the dominant nation. Though a subordinated nation is repressed and discriminated against, the ruling nation cannot and will not destroy or replace her institutions as it does those of the conquered or annexed nations because they share the same basic norms, values and beliefs. Since they do share common institutions, if the dominant nation tried to destroy the superstructure of the subordinated nation, it would amount to destroying its very own institutions, i.e, self-destruction. Because of the economic and social heritage they share, nations in this dominant-subordinate position could never develop a colonial relationship. In fact their shared superstructure provides a basis for reconciliation between them.

In this case, self-determination can be accomplished by the subordinated nation's attaining regional autonomy within the same

The Invention of Ethiopia

state structure. Such an arrangement would constitute reform within the state structure. The relation between Tigray and Amhara is a case in point.

Opposition of Tigray to Amhara domination dates back to period when the expansion of the Manz Amharas into Oromia created Shoa. By incorporating part of northern Oromia (see earlier sections of this book), Shoa's position in Abyssinia was so strengthened that the Shoans were able to dominate Tigray. This rise of Shoa contributed to all Abyssinian kingdoms being reduced to tributary status under the ruling kingdom of Manz, now Shoa.

Tigray, formerly an autonomous kingdom, lost not only its previous position of privilege to receive tribute, but also lost even its autonomy to Shoa. In an attempt to suppress Tigray and prevent Tigray from posing a direct threat to Shoan dominance in the empire, Tigrays were made second-class citizens within the Ethiopian empire. Since originally they had been contenders for the throne, the Tigray monarchy demonstrated its bitter disappointment over this shift of power. Tigray had held traditional symbolic and historic supremacy over the rest of Abyssinia. Beginning with Menelik's hastily and improperly taking the emperor's crown when the Tigray Emperor Yohannes died, it became a policy of successive Ethiopian regimes overtly to repress the Tigray people in order to secure a dominant position over them. The blatant abuse of Tigray was softened while Taytu was in the throne claiming part descent from Tigray royalty. When Menelik became ill, Taytu attempted to reestablish northern, including Tigray, dominance within Ethiopia. But as discussed in Chapter Four, the Shoan-European connection was already too strong by then. When the Haile Selassie government came into power, Tigray was forced to pay more taxes in relation to other Abyssinian kingdoms (not in relation to the colonies, however), a policy designed to weaken her. This continued until the Italians took over the empire in 1936 (Solomon Inquai 1981: 27-31).

After the return of the Emperor in 1941, the Tigray people demanded that their autonomy be restored. This demand was most clearly expressed through a 1943 mass uprising known as the

The Opposition Movements

Woyane Revolt (see Gebru 1977). "The failure of the Woyane revolt led to the disarming of the Tigrean population, the occupation of their land and the imposition of heavy taxation" (Bereket 1980: 89). The memory of Woyane has remained in the minds of Tigray people of every walk of life. It serves as a symbol of their repression and reduced status within the empire. Though the revolt was crushed militarily, none of the aspirations expressed through the revolt were satisfied. The resistance represented in that uprising went underground, but, as Bereket reports,

> ... members of the educated and commercial classes attempted to form professional and social welfare organizations as centers for the national resistance struggle. In the early 1970s, all these efforts were united under the Tigray National Organization (TNO), which began underground political activities. During the Ethiopian revolution, the TNO played an important role in publishing and distributing agitational material and in guiding popular demonstrations. It intensified its organization of underground cells, in view of the usurpation of the fruits of the revolution by the military in September 1974, and, after having analyzed the situation in Ethiopia and in Tigray, it began to prepare for armed struggle in the countryside (Bereket 1980: 89).

Tigray intellectuals for the most part did not remain in Ethiopian student organizations. Their grievance was not that they denied being Ethiopians at all (as did many members of colonized nations who left during the 1970s), but the issue they voiced as their reason for leaving was a lack of democracy within the associations themselves. These differences reflected the differences and demands expressed in the society at large. Tigrayans began to see that the most radical Ethiopian elements were represented by the children of the neftegna, and the direction of their policies became clear to Tigrays early on. Autonomy within a democratic structure, the condition that the Tigrayans were looking for, was not to be found.

The Invention of Ethiopia

Consequently, Tigray students chose to pursue these goals on their own.

While the students were trying to sort out these issues, the February mass upsurge broke out, and the military took over, arresting all the officials of the Haile Selassie government. Just as the military group asked all these officials to surrender, they also invited Mengesha Seyoum, the Governor of Tigray, to surrender to them. Mengesha's response was to refuse and to join an already-existing front calling itself the Tigray Liberation Front (TLF). This took place at a time when there was considerable conflict between the Shoan Amhara and the Tigray over what changes would be made in the organization of the empire. When other ousted bureaucrats, attempting to reinstate many of the features of the collapsing monarchy, formed an opposition organization called Ethiopian Democratic Union (EDU), Mengesha Seyoum joined that and left the TLF.

By this time the group of intellectuals who had left the Ethiopian student organization, moved to unite the Tigray National Organization (TNO) with elements of the Tigray Liberation Front (TLF) to form the Tigray People's Liberation Front (TPLF).

The formation of the TPLF, thus claiming descendency from the Tigray mass movements of the past, particularly the TNO and TLF, was declared on February 18, 1975, with the objective of looking after the affairs of the Tigray people. The TPLF came to represent all those who identified themselves first and foremost as Tigray nationals. Since it was on the basis of nationality that large segments of the Tigray population had been suppressed, the movement grew rapidly. The objective has not been to dismantle Ethiopia, but to reform and democratize it, guaranteeing the Tigray people autonomy and self-determination within a unified Ethiopia.

There are other subordinated nationalities within the empire who share several aspects of economic and social history with the nation that has achieved dominance within the Ethiopian state. Their position is similar to that of the Tigray.

The Opposition Movements

The Opposition of Intellectuals to Haile Selassie's Government

The Ethiopian empire state could not function without the input of foreign advisers or foreign-trained personnel who represented capitalist class interests directly or indirectly. European education was introduced into Ethiopia when the need for local personnel to be trained to fulfill this role was felt. In fact education in Ethiopia since the empire's formation has been conducted according to a European system. Abyssinian institutions could not provide the training needed to operate this empire for the simple reason that Ethiopia did not grow out of the Abyssinian social formation. Consequently, maintaining the state has meant cultivating Ethiopian functionaries (who prefer to be called "statesmen") to replace the many European functionaries who sat in every department of the government. Consequently formal Western education has been a top priority of the state from its creation.

But as soon as the graduates of these European-modelled schools began to emerge from the cocoon, conflicts erupted between them and the northern aristocrats who refused to give up their coveted and highly visible positions in the bureaucracy. These northern elites failed to acknowledge their dependence on the strategic input of their advisers and assistants. They saw these foreigners as their "employees." When the children of the new settler class arrived armed with European education, they were resented by the old guard. The conflicts broke out between the members of the "modern" school and this old guard who still held onto the positions of power in the state that the graduates wanted. The recent graduates felt that since they were now imbued with the European education that had been provided by the state itself, they could take over and operate without a European hovering over their shoulders. They wanted to become "independent."

This conflict was antagonistic in form but not in essence since those involved were all members of the same privileged Abyssinian classes, representing the same sector within the socioeconomic organization of the empire. It was a conflict between the traditional

The Invention of Ethiopia

(compradore) landlord and the modern (compradore) bureaucrat. Both were defenders of the dependent colonial state.

The first graduates of the "modern sector" conspired against the government of the "modernizer" himself, Haile Selassie. They opposed Haile Selassie's government because they opposed his group holding power. They called this group the "feudals." Since they could not get into the positions they wanted through democratic election because the state was not designed that way, they could not take power. Furthermore, these graduates did not have the social basis to wage a revolution, that is, to transform the society, so they attempted a coup d'etat in 1960, which ended in failure. The "modernizer" prevailed in putting down his own progeny, but then continued to produce more. He tried to keep them close to him and under his personal protection. He sponsored a students' organization calling its members his "Young Lions." But even that organization developed into an opposition student movement, because the members wanted their own share of power.

What could really be termed the Ethiopian student movement began sometime in the 1963-64 school year. It can be seen as the beginning of a second group of intellectual opposition. It started as the outcome of a field service program known as the National University Program which sent all college students to the country-side, usually in their third year, but occasionally after their senior year. Each student had to teach in a high school in one of the provinces. At base the program was not designed for the furtherance of their educational experience. It rather served the interest of providing manpower to the educational system and of delaying the graduation dates for students whose arrival into the workforce in such great numbers was becoming more and more problematic to the state.

Once the students were out in the rural areas, they saw that the empire was close to disintegration due to the widespread discontent among the conquered and subjugated peoples. The students were able to observe first-hand the movements of the tenants against the government on the issue of land. It became clear to them that if the government did not make some major change, the empire would fall

320

The Opposition Movements

apart. Their common slogan became, "Land to the Tiller!" They also began to see how they could apply the skills that they had been taught in school in a more effective way than those who were responsible for state management. In fact, most of them came out of the experience thinking that they could do a better job of keeping the state intact than the government in power. An alliance developed among these discontented students as they began to oppose the government that sent them out. The student movement provided an organizational network for them.

A very limited number of social forces impinged upon the student movement at the time of its formation, due to the students' relative isolation. One that did affect them was that several African countries who had become independent had sent students to Ethiopia, a country that they had looked up to as the symbol of black resistance to colonialism. A large proportion of these African students expressed their disappointment with what they found there and shared their own experiences with students in Ethiopia. This introduced a vision of the future full of possibilities for achievement far beyond what Ethiopia had attained.

Another factor that affected the dynamics within the student movement was that of differences that were inherent to the traditional Abyssinian social formation. When Ethiopia was formed, it was particularly the Amhara nation, especially the Shoan segment of it, that suddenly expanded to incorporate colonies and to subordinate former equals. Since this dramatic turn of events did not result from social or political dynamics internal to Abyssinia or the region, but rather it was due to changes that had taken place within the capitalist world, it skewed the balance of forces and relations that had previously developed within Abyssinia. The invention of Ethiopia, which resulted from the introduction of capitalist interests, capitalist advisers, and finally a capitalist social formation, established a form of conflict within Abyssinia itself over control of the state. This tension among Abyssinians found its way into the student group. As student debates and conflicts emerged, oftentimes they assumed a significance out of proportion to the specific issue under

The Invention of Ethiopia

consideration. Frequently the alignment of individuals who took particular stands reflected the conflicts internal to Abyssinia.

Another factor affecting the formation of the student movement was that the future prospects of individual students in Ethiopia were not turning out as they had been led to expect. The positions in the state structure that they had been groomed to fill were not materializing. As a category they began to realize that the creation of the field service itself had been a tactic used to postpone their disappointment over what awaited them. The students correctly felt that they were simply biding their time in waiting games.

The students who had been hand-picked by the government from the colonies to receive an education also played an important role in the movement and brought into it their dissatisfactions with conditions in the empire. These so-called minority groups took an interest in the struggles of other peoples in Africa and the rest of the world and helped to distribute literature regarding these struggles during the 1960s. Even at the beginning stages of the movement, though, some of the Eritreans refused to play a part in the Ethiopian student movement saying, "We are not Ethiopians, we are Eritreans!" The presence of some Eritreans played an important role in the history of the student movement by forcing it to confront several vital issues.

After the failure of the attempted coup d'etat made by the first group of students in the 1960s, a second group began to form, now in the 1970s, to take over the government, this time in the name of Marxism. It actually turned out to be Abyssinian beneficiaries of the state employing Bonapartist-type tactics, advancing a popular slogan that was borrowed from Russian Marxists of the twentieth century, "Land to the Tiller."

In this case there was a fascinating double meaning buried in the slogan. Part of the Ethiopian mythology was that Abyssinians were the original and only true "farmers" or tillers of the soil in this part of the world. The argument was that all other groups, Oromos, Sidamas, Somalis, and others were essentially "nomads" and "herders" or "ensete tenders" prior to Abyssinian introduction of the concept of tilling to these people. Buried within this component of

322

The Opposition Movements

Ethiopian mythology lay the notion that the Abyssinians had introduced a "civilizing influence" on surrounding peoples and the idea was brought in as a means to justify Abyssinian supremacy over the conquered peoples. (This argument was made in spite of substantial evidence that agriculture was practiced among the conquered groups from time immemorial.) However, when the student movement put forth the slogan, "Land to the Tiller," Abyssinians supported it because it carried the implication that the land rightfully should be in the hands of the neftegna who had become the legal owners and for whom the land was now tillered. This was the message received by many. These saw the slogan applying to absentee landlords.

On the other hand, members of different conquered nations and nationalities, whose people claimed traditional rights to the land that they were made to till for settlers, called for "Land to the Tiller" for a different reason. It was a demand for return of the lands to their rightful owners, those nations such as the Oromos, the Walayitas, the Somalis, etc, from whom it had been forcefully taken during conquest. Because the same slogan carried different ideological meaning to different groups, its double meaning enabled groups with fundamentally opposed objectives to voice the same phrase. These basic differences among the students did not emerge until the time came to implement the policy referred to in the slogan. At that time the social divisions surfaced. This occurred later when the Derg tried to implement that very same slogan.

Whether the slogan itself is viewed as Bonapartist or as Marxist-Leninist, whether the students are seen to represent a new sector or not, there is no question about the fact that the second generation intellectuals opposed Haile Selassie's government from within. The Young Lions group was transformed into an opposition force that contributed to the subjective condition of discontent within the empire. They and their European friends have been largely responsible for writing the history of this period, and have consequently attributed to themselves most of the force of opposition to the Haile Selassie government. This approach has obscured the wide range of forces that brought down the Haile Selassie regime. Major sectors

The Invention of Ethiopia

of the society with grievances far deeper than those expressed or even understood by the students had posed basic challenges to the government. The dependent colonial empire was coming apart at the seams. The students, though vocal and by their own account, radical, were not at the forefront of any of these sectors.

At this point it is important to address the issue of Marxism within the student movement, which has often been cited as evidence of student "radicalism." The practice of studying Marxism had been part and parcel of the very establishment of the student movement. By 1965 most of the Ethiopian student generation, both inside the country and abroad, had been exposed to Marxism-Leninism. Many students had begun to subscribe to socialism as a matter of personal principle. Part of that seemed to be unquestioning adherence to the notion of a one-party system as the slogan "Proletariat dictatorship, yes! Feudalism, no!" indicates. It was the most popular slogan of the day. Assigning themselves as the vanguard of a posited proletariat dictatorship, and labelling the old aristocrats who held the government positions that they wanted to hold, the slogan served the purpose for the students of voicing their aspirations. The wide use of this particular slogan was symptomatic of much of the movement—there was a widespread and highly opportunistic use of borrowed phrases taken from dissimilar situations. The absence of a proletariat and of classic feudalism in Ethiopia testifies that the leaders of the student movement either had not assessed independently the conditions within Ethiopia itself in determining the use of the slogan, or were using a conscious effort to obscure from the dissidents the distinctions among themselves. It was successful in deterring the members of the colonies from clearly assessing the condition of their own people within the empire.

Marxism was regarded as a widely recognized oppositional doctrine and was taken up by the disgruntled students without much inspection. The concept of "class struggle" within the empire was also embraced virtually without examination of the specific conditions obtaining. Espousal of these ideas, once accepted by a leadership, was largely enforced among the students by the students

The Opposition Movements

themselves through the cultural instruments of intimidation and deference to authority and leadership. Neither critical assessment nor critical discussion was allowed. Use of these types of slogans, regardless of content and applicability, had become merely an indicator of opposition to "the feudal government." At face value there was nothing wrong with the issues that the students raised, the problem lay in the fact that many were not applicable to the situation in the empire and the students' own evaluation of their position.

In short, the student organization did not, even from the outset, address basic conditions within the empire. Instead, they were guided by issues arising from their own day-to day confrontations.

In its early days, several cliques were formed among the members of the Ethiopian student movement. Part of this was a result of the close social and personal contact among members due to the isolation and elite status they had experienced as students in the empire. The cliques had formed around such criteria as which high schools and colleges members attended, who was personally related to whom, what personalities they chose to be associated with, who had been in the organization longer, what national group the members were born into, the internal differences among the Abyssinians mentioned above, etc. Once the cliques were formed, the members tended to align in the same groups on any issue that was brought before the organization, regardless of whether it was substantive or trivial. These alignment of the factions had been expressed long before matters of importance in the empire were brought before the organization. When such matters did come, the position of the cliques aligned in the same old way. The eventual battles carried out in the streets of Addis Ababa between the All-Ethiopia Socialist Movement (MEISON) and the Ethiopian People's Revolutionary Party (EPRP) were largely a manifestation of cliques formed in the student movement.

Even such a matter as the issue of "the national question," clearly a matter relevant to Ethiopia, and a timely issue of the day, fell victim to the politics of the cliques within the Ethiopian student movement. Two positions were articulated but not on differences in principle, but on criteria that would allow members of predetermined groups to stay together on the issue. In retrospect, it is quite clear that even the national question itself became a vehicle or focal point for the expression of other differences.

The matter of the national question was first raised within the student movement, over the Eritrean question in 1971, and then over the formation of the Ethiopian National Liberation Front (ENLF or EBNAG) in 1972. As soon as the ENLF was announced and its program distributed (ENLF Program), the burning issue of the day became what position would the student movement take on this new front, which was primarily a question of Oromo nationalism. Although it was ostensibly appropriate to raise the issue of the ENLF, the manner in which it was raised within the student movement revealed that there was no conception among the members of what real issues were at stake or what was the distinction between a student movement and a liberation front. The Ethiopian student movement splintered over the matter according to preexisting cliques, cliques that had been formed along lines unrelated to the issue of national question. These cliques became known as the Federationist (after Worldwide Federation of Ethiopian Students) and the Unionist (after Worldwide Union of Ethiopian Students) groups.

The Unionist group in Europe had earlier introduced several conditions before its members could support the Eritrean cause. The Unionist leadership uncritically and oftentimes by intimidation supported the ENLF. The Federationists, who had supported the Eritrean question without conditions, basically rejected ENLF by postponing a decision until further study, which was never carried out. They were not prepared to support any cause that had been taken up by the Unionists.

This division had already been created among the students when the mass upsurge occurred in February 1974. By that time the discontent within the empire was felt in the capital and it was clear that the majority of the people refused to be ruled in the same way. At that time the matter of how to bring the divided intellectuals (the Federationist and Unionist groups) together dominated the student

The Opposition Movements

movement both abroad and in Addis Ababa. Scholars and analysts who tried at the time and have tried since then to address the students' split over the national question as if it were based on some substantive issue have understandably been frustrated and disappointed. Without taking account of the cliques within the movement, it is not possible to assess properly the debate over this or any substantive issue. To outsiders the materials put out by the different cliques appear so similar that they could have been written by the same person on different days of the week. Old members themselves, however, can distinguish in the writing of a rival group specific wording and phrases which have acquired significance over the history of specific clique confrontations. New members were forced to defend certain positions on the basis of loyalty rather than understanding.

When the February upsurge broke out, members of the student groups abroad rushed home to Ethiopia, quickly took positions on what was going on, and began to communicate with the general public by means of underground newspapers. Negotiations to bring these splintered "intellectuals" together continued even after they were back in the country to take part in what they called a "revolutionary situation." Reconciliation failed and the two factions began to produce two physically independent publications. The Federationist group began releasing a publication called "Democracy" (Democracia), and the Unionists released "Voice of the Masses" (Ye Safewo Hiszba Demits) Each of these was soon followed by the issuance of new names and party programs which contained very minor differences. The Federationists called themselves the Ethiopian People's Revolutionary Party (EPRP) and the Unionists became known as the All-Ethiopia Socialist Movement (MEISON). Most of the members of the opposition student movement had expected to lead their adult lives as party members of some kind trying to find ways to defend and lead the empire that created them as a group. They immediately seized upon the opportunity. By 1975, these same two cliques had put out quite similar political programs and had given themselves new identities: Unionists as MEISON and Federationists as the EPRP.

The Invention of Ethiopia

The squabbles that had been born in the student movement abroad were taken back to be continued in Ethiopia. A struggle for dominance continued between the two groups. Although they called themselves "revolutionaries" and their politics "revolutionary," the opposition of the bulk of the student generation to Haile Selassie's government had originated in a desire to see the old bureaucrats out of office in order to make way for themselves to institute reforms in the state apparatus. They were not trying to dismantle Ethiopia. As events in the empire began to unfold, they found allies in the military who were capable of clearing the way for them to step into the positions to which they aspired.

9 CONTINUITIES OF EMPIRE UNDER SOVIET PATRONAGE, 1974-THE PRESENT

The February Upsurge

The cracks in Haile Selassie's government began to be revealed for all to see and then to widen during 1974. The discontent of the colonized peoples, who were taking concrete steps to break out of the neftegna-gabbar relationship, was the deepest fault line running through the society. Rumblings along this line which threatened the very foundations of the empire had been felt at increasing intervals. There were also definite cracks due to aging and rigidity within the particular political coalition that had been constructed by Haile Selassie in order to rule during his era. Policies like his retaining honorary senior aristocrats in charge of ministries and major departments frustrated the young trainees fresh from schools at home and abroad, who had no idea of how they might bring about change in the empire unless they held government offices. This educated group longed to fill the spots held by Haile Selassie's hand-picked appointees. There were also crevices in the facade of the state that represented the economic complaints voiced among groups who had no other dissatisfactions except that

329

they wanted minor adjustments in the state's support of their interests. Each of these social forces had a different set of grievances.

A widespread and highly visible public protest occurred in February 1974, a period generally known as the February Upsurge, when all the grievances of these many groups erupted into a cacophony of voices. Each social force that participated in the tumult was acting on its own behalf, each expressing its discontent with a different dimension of the state's condition. The colonies wanted liberation from the authority of the state altogether. The oppressed nations wanted to change the state through democratizing it, while intellectuals wanted to change it by removing Haile Selassie and his traditional statesmen from office in order to replace them.

In addition, a third very outspoken category of dissidents who had no deep-seated problems with the nature or the organization of the state emerged; they just wanted it to run more smoothly. This group constituted those protected by the state who were simply expressing their unhappiness with the particular economic conditions that prevailed. This included employees of state institutions, workers who wanted fair pay for fair work, small businessmen protesting the failure of the state to take enough measures to counter the effects of inflation, a specific segment of the military, and others. The most well-known example of this latter category of economic complainants is the taxicab drivers who objected to a rise in gasoline prices.

The February Upsurge, triggered by this protest of the taxicab drivers in Addis Ababa, opened a brief but significant chapter of mass discontent in the empire that was closed by the military on September 12 of the same year. This period marked the transition of power from the Haile Selassie government to a military committee known as the Derg. Understanding how the military came to take power is essential for tracing what has happened to the dependent colonial state. Was there a revolution led by low-ranking members of the military, representing the proletariat, in which the fundamental relations of production in the empire were changed, as many have claimed? No, there was no revolution. The Derg itself, despite its claims to lowly origins and its eventual public embrace of radical Marxism-Leninism, constituted upon its formation a specific fraction of the privileged landholding group in the empire. Each move that was made in the course of its rise to power was designed to eliminate rivals for its position in the state and to weaken the capacity of resistance movements to challenge neftegna rule. By moving into power in the manner that it did, the Derg was able to preserve and strengthen the dependent colonial state and the formula that keeps it alive.

It has taken years for both analysts and participants in the concentrated series of events that began in February 1974 to separate the various issues and to reconstruct what was going on in the empire at that time. There are several detailed accounts of what occurred in Ethiopia in February 1974 and of the emergence of the ruling group that ultimately replaced Haile Selassie's government. Many scholars have offered complete and easily accessible accounts of the events of this period. Among them are Marina and David Ottaway in *Ethiopia: Empire in Revolution* (1978), Edmond J. Keller in *Revolutionary Ethiopia: From Empire to People's Republic (1988)*, Rene Lefort in *Ethiopia: an Heretical Revolution?* (1983) and Fred Halliday and Maxine Molyneux in *The Ethiopian Revolution* (1981).

It was an international oil crisis, which had caused inflation worldwide, that hit Ethiopia in early 1974 and resulted in a rise in the import price of oil in Ethiopia. The public transportation system in Ethiopia had from its inception manifested a high degree of external dependency. When the gasoline prices went up, the widespread reaction in the society only demonstrated the continued extent of the dependency. The urban protests also came at a time when the colonies were engaged in the kind of widespread resistance against the position that they held within the empire as described in Chapter Six. Their resistance had been effective enough that when the state was confronted by the need to generate more revenue, it had not been able to establish enough local control to force the colonies to bear the additional costs brought on by inflation. To so force the colonies would only further inflame the revolt going on there. The empire could not withstand that. Consequently, the government could no longer shield from the direct consumers in the urban areas the enormous costs of complete dependency and moved

The Invention of Ethiopia

to raise the price charged for oil to the consumers in the cities. Through this government move, other sectors of the society began to feel the impact of the problems in the colonies, although few of them saw the full implications. Ironically, it was the loud protest from the taxi drivers and other small businessmen in the cities that opened the way for the simultaneous expression of dissatisfaction from other sectors of the society—including those who had been demanding revolutionary change in the mode of production and those who demanded reform—who took their demands into the streets of Addis Ababa and were heard along with those who were simply demanding better state services. Their joint protest, the "upsurge," indicated that the dependent colonial state had been weakened significantly.

The period of joint protest in the empire that lasted from the first days of February 1974 until September 12, when the old regime was officially deposed and a new regime was begun, has been characterized in many different ways. Many participants remember it as pure anarchy, the most chaotic period in the life of the empire. Others call it the only period in which every social category that existed within the empire could and did exercise the opportunity to express itself freely. It was clearly a period in which the true nature of the empire was exposed and the myriad groups that had been made to live together by force of arms and by an imported and imposed formula for law and order publicly registered their views about their condition. This tumultuous situation created a politically open environment in which the revolt could take any direction. The direction that was ultimately taken was a natural outcome of the history and structure of the empire and a direct result of recent events.

By the beginning of the 1970s the Haile Selassie regime had become entangled with not only political problems but also economic difficulties. The government had attempted to cope with these problems through modernization programs which designed a series of reforms—land reform, political reform, and reforms of the educational, bureaucratic, communication and security systems. It was during the time many of these projects had met resistance of was during the time many of these projects had met resistance of one kind or another or still lay on the drawing board that the changes in the world economic order caused the rise in gasoline prices. It appeared that the gas hit an already-smoldering fire. When the cabdrivers went on strike, they were supported by students who had been protesting the handling of the Wollo famine and other issues.

At this time in early February 1974 the students were already protesting the policies embodied in the Educational Sector Review which called for limited opportunities for higher education in the empire and increased burdens on teachers. The teachers joined in the protest and went out on strike against the review, causing the government to withdraw it.

Within days of these uprisings, noncommissioned officers (NCOs) and enlisted men of the Fourth Division stationed in Neggelle, Sidamo, rose up in protest over their abysmal working conditions and low pay. When a water pump that broke was not repaired for weeks, they took hostage their superior officers until demands for improved conditions and more pay (to cope with inflation) were met. Haile Selassie's government responded positively to their demands, in hopes of hushing up the event. Word leaked out, however, and similar incidents took place among technicians and NCOs elsewhere. By February 10 at the Debre Zeit Air Force Base near Addis Ababa and by February 25 in the Second Division in Asmara enlisted men and NCOs had risen up in similar protests. In the Asmara case, those in revolt virtually took over the city and commandeered the radio station.

Enlisted men and NCOs were recruited from the less privileged portions of the society to serve primarily as the bulk of the military's labor force. They held positions that offered little chance of advancement, recognition or power. This is the group that contributed to the howls of protest that went up from those who had solely economic complaints. In voicing their economic grievances, these low-ranking members of the armed forces were simply demanding more comfortable working conditions and higher pay to cope with inflation. They had no further objectives, political or otherwise. In

care how the state was organized as long as it provided the services they had come to expect. And, as if to prove this point, when the government made concessions on the issues that concerned them, they went back to their barracks.

The rest of the society was already in an uproar over the myriad of grievances mentioned earlier. They were watching closely the government's response to the demands from within the military. In the Asmara incident not only was the radio seized and senior officers arrested, but the international airport was closed. These were highly visible acts. The Ottaways report that "[a]fter the ritual pledge of allegiance to the Emperor," the mutineers put forth twenty-two demands which concerned a limited range of economic grievances (listed in their entirety in Ottaway and Ottaway 1978: 46-47). They go on to say that

> The rebels' statement was read over Asmara radio, and the messages of support for which the mutineers appealed started pouring in immediately from units all over the country, most notably the Third and Fourth Divisions, the Royal Navy, and the Air Force Base at Debra Zeit. Some units sent not only messages of support, but also mutinied in turn and arrested their own senior officers (ibid.).

The open support of all units in the empire for this Asmara revolt forced the hand of Haile Selassie's government. Within forty-eight hours another salary raise was approved for the soldiers, but immediately afterward the government crumbled. The emperor remained seated but accepted the resignation of the man who had been his prime minister since 1958, Aklilu Habte Wold, together with his entire cabinet. Having received most of what they had demanded, the military released their hostages and returned to duty. The immediate effect of the soldiers' actions, however, was lost on neither the other aggrieved segments of the population nor on the new government that came in to replace that of Aklilu.

When the emperor nominated Endelkatchew Mokonnen to become the new prime minister, he announced at the same time that a new constitution would be issued providing a framework for new reforms. The new government was faced with a torrent of demands from the civilian population, specifically from the Confederation of Ethiopian Labor Unions and the Ethiopian University Teachers Association. It was immediately clear to the new prime minister that he must have the support of the military to be able to deal with unrest throughout the society. He began to move to guarantee their loyalty. As it happened the civilian population moved simultaneously to rally the support of segments of the military which they could influence through family and social class lines.

This is the period—immediately after Endelkatchew moved into power—that a portion of the struggle taking place in the society at large began to be acted out in the military. Members of the military began to protect their own material interests.

Endelkatchew began from the assumption that he would have a virtual blank check for any action he ordered from the military, due to the double increase in salary that they had just received. He also enlisted the help a relative of his, Colonel Alem Zewde Tassemma, the commander of the Fourth Division's Airborne Brigade. This commander thought that with the help of Colonel Atnafu Abate, he could successfully step forward at this time and assert that he had been a member of the first military group that claimed to represent the armed forces. This claim was to have given him some legitimacy to speak on behalf of at least one of the committees that had successfully rallied the armed forces and obtained such concessions from the government. In fact there was no record of Alem Zewde's participation. The Ottaways write that "[h]e had not been a leader in any of the early uprisings by junior officers and NCOs" (1978:50). Keller, drawing on many observers, points out that,

> between January and July 1974, at least six separate military groups claimed to represent the armed forces. The most important ones proved to be two that developed in the Fourth Division headquarters at Addis Ababa and another group of radical airmen at Debra Zeit. The first Addis group to demonstrate its political disposition was a group

of thirty NCOs who claimed to represent every military unit except the navy. The group appeared sometime between January and February 1974 and *quickly came under the influence of a second group of officers of intermediate rank.* The officers' group was a collection of politically oriented and well-connected moderates and radicals (1988: 181) [emphasis added].

Throughout published accounts of the development of the Derg from the earliest days, there are similar references to shifts in membership of the committee that eventually took power and held it. These shifts are of central importance to the analysis offered here because they signify a change in composition of the organizing group from NCOs and enlisted men to commissioned officers who represented fundamentally different segments of the society. The latter had landholding interests.

When the enlisted men and NCOs went back to their barracks in late February after the spectacular successes they had achieved, several groups of young officers began to step forward to claim credit for and to pick up the reins of the abandoned committees that had been formed to negotiate for government concessions. These young commissioned officers had not initiated or played much of a role in the early stages of the rebellion; they had not been subjected to the same working conditions during their military experience, had not been driven by circumstances to take the same risks to express the same outrage or grievance. These people were of different social origins from the NCOs. They had been raised in landholding families. They had been accepted to officers' training institutions where they had mingled with others of their higher status. Their families and friends were connected to civilians of the landed middle ranks within Ethiopian society. Most importantly, they themselves were landholders or potential landholders who became intent upon preserving the state in which they had vested landholding interests.

As February turned into March and April 1974, there was a mounting tension felt within and outside the military over what was becoming of the empire's land. The colonized peoples were expelling landlords, claiming land on historical and cultural grounds, taking possession of it, and threatening to dismantle the empire! Their success would mean to the military and to those of their social and economic category the end of their position of privilege and rights to land. The unfolding events of those months convinced the young neftegnas, including those in the military, that neither the old regime nor its new aristocratic replacement was capable of protecting the empire against these forces of resistance.

There had been considerable mention made in the literature of the pressures that were placed on the military during this February to June period in 1974 from other segments of the urban population who were not content to let them rest on that minimal accomplishment while so many in the society remained aggrieved. When the civilian population began to experience frustration in achieving their own goals, they turned to their brothers, sons, friends, schoolmates, neighbors, and relatives who were in the armed forces to take some action on their behalf. These appeals came primarily from beneficiary groups whose objectives were those of reform. This kind of agitation forced those in the military to consider seriously where their own interest lay. Though others tried to push them, the military officers of the Derg moved to take advantage of the military's access to tools of force to protect the interests of their own class. Theirs were the interests of the landholding class. In the view of the bulk of the urban population they were performing the originally intended purpose of the armed forces.

The transition of control of the armed services coordinating committee away from NCOs and enlisted men to young middle-level officers was the single most significant event in determining the direction of events. It occurred over several weeks and months and became the focus of intense struggle. It represented a shift to the dominance of a new fraction of the neftegna landholding class itself away from the old aristocratic fraction.

The old emperor had attracted the military into the landholding group when he broadened the base of this class through a land grant system of land reform described in earlier chapters. This mechanism had succeeded in bringing many members of the military into the

337

The Invention of Ethiopia

neftegna class by directly allotting land to some of them and making the rest with their families eligible for land grants. This move reinforced connections between land, military service and class. Even those members of the armed forces who were not yet actual land-holders were aware of their incipient rights of access.

As the situation developed further, the members of the military began to discover more precisely that their interest lay with the landholding group.

When the military responded to pressures from the other neftegnas to take power, it was an act which achieved a modicum of peace within the neftegna class itself. No other armed group was able to challenge them initially. The armed men performed the role of safeguarding the interests of their friends and relatives, the young neftegna, by demanding, as a compromise, the removal of the old statesmen from office in order that they be replaced by young and responsible educated elements. This group was also a product of the Ethiopian state, having been produced by one of Haile Selassie's own institutions, the revamped educational apparatus. The emperor himself responded positively to this turn of events. He was familiar with the moves required to allow for a shift of power. It was a scenario very similar to the one that prevailed when Taytu and Lij Iyasu had been systematically taken from office when Haile Selassie himself had moved into power. At that time he had acted to elimi-nate the old statesmen from office so that he could focus sharply on preserving the essential elements of the dependent colonial formula and protect the interests of the neftegna.

It was young middle-ranking officers who finally prevailed within the military itself and then moved into the wider arena of public government. They acted as Ras Tefari had done before them, to use their power ultimately to eliminate several sectors of the society who had assisted them to achieve power.

It was this particular landholding segment within the military that laid claim to the heritage of the Coordinating Committee of the Armed Forces (which is translated Derg) and claim to its history as well.

Continuities of Empire Under Soviet Patronage

The takeover occurred during the period between the first dropping of leaflets "To All Ethiopian People" on March 4, 1974, and the disposition of the emperor. Several incidents in March and April indicated that there was a move afoot to coordinate the armed forces. When one group would act, another would be rallied by the government to quell it.

Every sector of the society was trying to apply pressure to influence members of its group within the military. This competition included the old aristocratic sector as well. When Endelkatchew came into power, he tried to bring the military to his side through his relative Colonel Alem Zewde. And when Alem Zewde claimed that he had been part of an earlier committee of the armed forces, he was making a bid for legitimacy to take preemptive action against other segments within the military that might attempt to use the organization as a base for power. This was all part of the struggle over Alem Zewde, who did indeed try to close off the avenue of the military committee to all other segments of the society by announcing the formation of a committee on April 24 and then immediately declaring it to be disbanded on April 29. In doing this he demonstrated his loyalty to the aristocratic segment of the landholding group, the group that was desperately trying to hold onto the reins of power. He was almost successful in creating confusion and division by this move.

There was, however, a section of the middle-ranking officers who took the position that the aristocrats had failed at maintaining the empire and moved to organize themselves apart from Alem Zewde's high-ranking officers. They demonstrated through their actions that they were afraid the empire might be lost to the resistance forces of the liberation fronts if the old guard were allowed to stay in power. By July, this group moved to arrest aristocrats, high officials and generals in the military itself, before the old guard had a chance to arrest them. The motto they put forth to the rest of the population was loud and clear: Ethiopia Tikdem—Ethiopia First. In other words, they were declaring to the rest of the society that they were going to step in to save the empire from the forces of disintegration. It is clear from this slogan and their subsequent acts that

339

they were acting on their own behalf first, and on the behalf of the interests of neftegna.

Before long, these elements within the military who had acted to save themselves, discovered where the power lay and realized that they were capable of physically taking over the key positions in the state apparatus. What they also realized was that they were lacking ideologues with the strategic skills to organize them to get what they wanted. Consequently, they sought what every Ethiopian regime has sought since the creation of the empire—advisers capable of organizing and managing this state. Foreign advisers seemed not to be needed since there was an abundance of foreign-trained neftegna and assimilated candidates who were willing to give the service that they were trained for. An open invitation was extended, and personal as well as general calls went out for the educated to return from abroad to save the motherland. A search went on for some months, and positions were offered to young Ethiopians found in every corner of the world. In response to the call, intellectuals from every corner began returning home, some of them rushing back to have some power for themselves, some coming slowly but positively to play a role in shoring up the empire. With this call both the military and the educated "intellectuals" got what they wanted.

Advice also came pouring in from all over the globe. By midsummer the demands of the military committee had changed from their original ones for higher wages to a political takeover that enabled them not only to raise their own wages but their status as well. These military men who had served the crown were now quite capable of seeing that the crown without the army and the intellectuals was powerless and empty. Part of this realization was that the army could not take over the crown without the intellectuals. The only workable solution put forth by the Derg and agreed upon by all in power was that the young officers of their class take over power and that the young intellectuals of their class provide the strategy for maintaining order. The military, in alliance with those intellectuals who had come forward to assist the move, took over power from the crown on September 12, 1974. Once this accord was reached, a sigh of relief went up from the neftegna that the empire had been saved, and the excitement that filled the air at the prospect of implementing the plan was palpable. There were celebrations, and "Long Live Ethiopia!" was chanted in the streets.

At this juncture the military declared that they no longer held their position of power in order to defend the emperor but rather to defend the empire. This is the act that has been considered so widely as a revolutionary act and the basis for a social/political transformation. This is the point at which the Derg announced the establishment of the Provisional Military Administrative Council (PMAC) and put forth the Ethiopia Tikdem slogan. In the first proclamation the PMAC dismissed the constitution and proclaimed that strikes, demonstrations and public gatherings were prohibited.

Once the tacit agreement had been reached between the military and a sector of the intellectuals to take power in September 1974, the old and once-powerful statesmen and generals peacefully submitted themselves to the officers of their own class. Haile Selassie instructed them all to submit to the coordinating committee and give in to the Derg's demands one after the other.

Haile Selassie and his noblemen may have held out a hope that to give in to their children would prompt the leaders of the liberation movement to put down their arms thinking that their worst enemies had been arrested. This old guard could not or would not realize that the objectives of the liberation fronts were not to remove them personally as individuals from state power—that was actually the objective of their own children. The liberation fronts had been widely regarded by the old guard of the Haile Selassie regime to be made up of discontented individuals. They saw the battles with the liberation fronts to be struggles between individuals rather than between defenders of a system of rule on the one hand and those who aimed to alter fundamentally that system on the other. The liberation fronts were resisting the system itself. Consequently, many of the early overtures made to the liberation fronts were aimed at individuals and as such were ineffective.

As soon as the military had declared the formation of a government, there were wails of protest from many sectors who had wanted the top job themselves, the elements of the students and

The Invention of Ethiopia

those intellectuals who had not allied with the military, the labor unions and others who called immediately for the formation of a "civilian" government. Just as immediately it became clear to the Derg that its first task was to consolidate its power. Its members knew that it could not fight all its rivals for power at once. They took the issues and the groups and dealt with them swiftly one by one. Many issues had been raised but most had been postponed. The Derg began to act more quickly.

What changed the nature and the pace of the slow scenario of change, which many participants, including the old guard, had hoped to be reversible, was that within the military committee a leadership began to come forward, led by Mengistu Haile Mariam, a man who was at first looked down on by all and appeared to have nothing to lose by making bold moves. He and his peer group had not only grown up around the palace but they had the best adviser on palace intrigues at their ear—the man reputed to be Mengistu's biological father, Daj. Kebede Tesemma. These men were not at all intimidated by palace affairs nor enamored of palace mystique. Of Mengistu himself it is widely believed that he took on decisions for summary action and even killings as his personal responsibility (Dawit 1989: 18-9, 22, 29). Such a perception conveniently matches a notion prevalent in Abyssinian culture that in order to be successful, a leader must be feared and must rule by terror. This characteristic symbolically represents strength in the Abyssinian value system.

From the vantage point of the military committee Mengistu's group had tested and assessed the power of the crown and found that it was fallible. They had shaken the intellectuals and found them to be helplessly unorganized as a group and extremely servile as individuals. When it became clear to the military men that the same Ethiopian intellectuals that they had greatly respected were divided over relatively trivial matters and without a clear agenda or leadership, they concluded that the decisive leadership was meant for them. They saw only one force standing in their way, the liberation fronts. The military, who had become familiar with the liberation fronts on the battlefield, next tested these fronts with regard to their program of dismantling the empire and found that they were unshakable by comparison with the other forces.

The quick conclusion was that if someone did not make a rapid move to seize power and give the state a direction, the colonies, especially the Eritreans, would be successful in their attempts to liberate their country. Such an outcome would mark the success of Oromos and others and the end of both the dominance of the landlord class (which included themselves) and its ability to protect its interests. That would mark the end of the empire. This realization by the military was shared by the members of the landholding class. Once the military had taken power, they moved to establish themselves in relation to other forces in the empire.

By November 1974 the military group betrayed the trust of those of the old guard who had placed their hope in them by deciding to kill all the statesmen who had surrendered to them. A mass execution of the key leaders under Haile Selassie's government was carried out in November 1974 without due process of law. This fundamentally altered the pattern for change.

The Derg, which had come forth as the protector of the empire, was immediately faced with the matter of addressing the demands of those who had risen up against the Haile Selassie regime and participated in bringing about the change. Among these were the two groups who had renamed themselves as EPRP and MEISON. Their chief demands were that they move in to take state power for themselves. The two groups had not yet settled squabbles that had been born in the student movement; they now returned to Ethiopia and continued their disputes over the issues then current. The competition between the two old rival groups continued even after the MEISON group had made an alliance with the Derg and actually stepped into state power. They argued that it was indeed possible to engineer a revolution from within the state apparatus itself. The alliance had been formed quickly since the Derg needed strategic intellectual support and MEISON needed assistance in reaching the top. EPRP, MEISON's rival group, immediately declared itself against the Derg or any form of military government.

Their rivalry was eventually played out through massacres in the streets.

After the Derg had taken power, other groups also were formed in opposition, challenging its claim to state power. The Ethiopian Democratic Union (EDU) was one of these. Its objective also was to claim state power and save the empire. It was then possible to see that on one side two generations of the landlord class had lined up to save the empire in one way or another—the Derg, MEISON, EPRP, EDU, and several smaller and insignificant groups who joined them. The Tigray People's Liberation Front (TPLF) had a different position; it also sought reform in the form of the democratization of the empire. The condition of the people of Tigray, as mentioned in the previous chapter, was that they were subordinated and made to hold a place in the empire second to the Amharas. Thus the Tigray people also came to stand against the Derg. At the initial stage they did so by making their alliance with the colonies. Subsequent efforts to align their position with that of the colonies has caused them to disassociate themselves from the colonies' positions.

Opposed to all of these Ethiopian groups stood the conquered and annexed nations who had taken the initiative in trying to uproot the Haile Selassie government. They still aspired to break the power of the settlers and to dismantle the empire. These were the Oromo, the Eritrean, the Ogadeni, the Sidama, the Afar and all other colonies that revolted against the Ethiopian landlords. These forces were led by their respective vanguards, the Oromo Liberation Front (OLF), Eritrean People's Liberation Front (EPLF), Eritrean Liberation Front (ELF), Western Somali Liberation Front (WSLF), Sidama Liberation Front (SLF), and Afar Liberation Front (ALF).

The contending forces were divided into two major camps. One was composed of those who defended the empire and its legacy, and the other was made up of those who sought to dismantle it. The issues raised on the two sides differed fundamentally. The colonies were raising the issue of liberation and eliminating their colonial status by dismantling the state itself. This would open the way for the establishment of separate and independent existence as nations.

Continuities of Empire Under Soviet Patronage

The neftegna defended the continued existence of the Ethiopian empire.

There is no question that the convergence of events leading to the February Upsurge provided the occasion for the transfer of power from Haile Selassie's government to another set of neftegnas represented by a military committee. When the tumult began to subside it became clear that the same old state structure had merely acquired a new set of bureaucrats. This assessment is confirmed by a series of events that took place once the Derg was able to consolidate power.

Plans for projects that had been designed by the Haile Selassie regime and assisted by the advice of Western consultants who represented the institutions of international finance capital were not destroyed by the Derg. Throughout the period of upheaval the plans for reform that had been drawn up by the Haile Selassie government remained on the drawing boards in the appropriate government ministries. Already-prepared materials and equipment sat unmolested in the warehouses. Trained personnel inside and outside of Ethiopia stood by during the tumult, holding their breath, waiting to learn the fate of plans in which they had invested a great deal of expertise and money.

Eventually the Derg eliminated, crippled, or coopted those fractions of the landholding class who had once posed obstacles to the implementation of reforms by blocking access to land and privilege. Then the Derg found ways to pull the reform projects of Haile Selassie's government out of mothballs and implement them as they had originally been intended. The very programs designed during the Haile Selassie era for altering the educational system, for tightening and streamlining administrative control, for redistributing Abyssinian populations into the colonized regions through resettlement, and even for reforming access to land were carried out under the banner of "Revolutionary Ethiopia."

Although the land reform has been touted as the single most revolutionary act performed by the Derg, a close look reveals that through its implementation it deflected resistance and then consolidated control and benefits from the land into the hands of those

The Invention of Ethiopia

segments of the landholding class who were willing to follow the lead of the military fraction. The PMAC's reformist character and its true class nature are revealed starkly in its implementation of the programs which were the progeny of the regime that the Derg formally rejected as "feudal" and "reactionary." To kill the "feudal" aristocrats and reject their patrons as "imperialists" and then to implement by force of arms the same programs that these so-called "reactionaries" and "imperialists" designed demonstrates the true nature of both the Derg and its patrons. They are themselves defenders of the same system of dependent colonialism and international imperialism.

The difference was that before the defenders of Ethiopian dependent colonialism were able to carry out the reform programs that were designed to save the system of relationships embodied in that state, some force had to silence or eliminate all those groups that had been obstacles to the objectives of the state. That was the function performed by the military committee. Nothing demonstrates the extent to which the Derg saved the dependent colonial formula in Ethiopia more clearly than to look at how closely it was made to follow the path of its predecessor regime.

The issues among the neftegna were two: (1) whether or not to reform the empire, and if so, how, and (2) the question of who should assume state power. There had been some elements of the neftegna who saw that the people of the colonies were striking at the root of the system—trying to change the economic base. They had been attacking the landlords and the agents of the crown trying to replace the governing principle with another set of values. This was widely described by the neftegnas and Ethiopianists as "anarchy" in the rural areas.

It was primarily the young neftegnas sent to the rural areas in service to the state who had seen this situation developing. After having assessed the circumstances, their prescription for saving the empire collided with that of the old landed aristocracy. They saw that they had to mollify the masses, inject themselves into the thick of the battles, and find a way to reverse the direction that the colonized people were taking. This group truly believed that if they

346

fully utilized their mental powers to analyze the situation, they could find a way to tinker with the state creatively enough to resolve all problems that the empire faced. Their background led them to believe two things—that since they were the ones who were educated, they were the only ones who could arrange a satisfactory outcome, and that the few members of the conquered and oppressed nationalities who had been processed with them in the educational institutions would go along with and assist them.

The neftegna class led by the Derg decided that they had to put Haile Selassie's government that represented the old landed aristocracy aside in order to strengthen the hand of those who would save the state. The economic base had to be made secure. Hence the Derg was forced to deal with the pressing issue of land reform.

While within the camp of reformists, elements of the settler class had been battling it out in the urban areas over whether the Derg with MEISON would stay in power or the EPRP would move in to take their place, the forces of revolution had been engaged in chasing the landlord settlers out of the countryside away from their colonial holdings. These forces of revolution were the colonial subjects who demanded liberation of their traditional lands. These tenants had taken concrete steps to destroy the relationship that lay at the heart of the economic base of the empire—the neftegna-gabbar relationship. Absentee landlords were denied the opportunity to claim produce when they arrived to collect it. The tenants in the colonies were successfully liberating their land and their own labor as well, administering both according to principles which eliminated the Ethiopian dependent colonial formula. Research done by Clay, Holcomb and Niggli among Oromo farmers who participated in this process sheds some light on what went on during that period,

> ... Oromo had formed their own associations "in order to isolate the landlord." The tenants agreed to contribute money for oxen in order to plow for themselves and to keep the produce or redistribute it according to their own agreement (Clay and Holcomb 1986: 129).

The Invention of Ethiopia

The basis for peasant land allocation was clear.

> They had redistributed land, according to traditional
> Oromo principles of allocation [the principle known as
> Gada], in many of the Oromo regions discussed (ibid.).

When the process of peasants chasing the landlords out of their
settlements by force began to intensify, the elements of the neftegna
class who had seen this coming, preempted the movement by
arranging to nationalize the land itself. This occurred through the
land reform proclamation made on March 4, 1975. There were three
conditions that forced this proclamation. (1) The tenants' refusal to
obey the Derg's initial orders which were to stop liberating the land;
their efforts continued and even intensified. (2) During that time
there were several conscious Oromo and other nationals from
colonized regions who, working through the Ministry of Land
Reform, had agitated for changes in land policies. (3) Fear of the
revival of Oromo resistance groups, such as the remaining elements
of Macha-Tulama, and fear of intellectuals from the colonized
nations who had begun to join the peasant movement, prompted the
preemptive action in this matter.

Now the Derg faced a problem. Unlike the old group of
neftegnas whom it had now pushed out, it had no physical presence,
no representatives, in the rural areas. This fact alone provides clear
evidence that the Derg had no political or economic connections in
the conquered areas which would provide a basis for successfully
controlling the revolt, implementing a "revolutionary land reform,"
or consolidating power in the colonies. The land reform that was
announced was presented as if it were a response to the demands of
the conquered peoples. When the land was nationalized, it was
declared to be the "collective holding of the Ethiopian people." This
measure was inherently ambiguous since there was no agreed
definition of "the Ethiopian people" and the basis for collective
holding had not been politically nor economically established.

The confusion that resulted from this ambiguity made it
possible for the cultivators in the colonized areas to be told that

Continuities of Empire Under Soviet Patronage

their demands had been met. Their resistance was thus diffused. It bought time for the regime to continue on its course of consolidating its position in relation to the reformists who desired to unseat the military. The colonies, interpreting nationalization to mean liberation, settled down to implement their own plans. They saw the proclamation as a recognition of their efforts and turned from active resistance to the Derg. This predictable response from the colonies gave the Derg an aura of legitimacy and provided an opportunity to be rid of problems that were mounting against them in the cities. They chose to send the troublesome students out of Addis Ababa and into the rural areas "to administer the land reform." The students and members of the Ethiopian Teachers' Association were to go to the countryside and teach the objectives of Ethiopia First. This act represented a kind of adventurism—very public and very dramatic. It made it possible for the Derg to take over Addis Ababa, which had not been possible with the students there. This also removed the students and their criticisms away from the watchful eyes of international media. The proclamation itself silenced the civilian intellectuals and caused a setback in the momentum of the Oromo national resistance movement among the rural cultivators, both of which benefitted the Derg. All in all the Derg benefitted ideologically, politically and economically from the land reform proclamation.

The launching of the student exodus to the countryside, called a Zemecha program, actually amounted to sending agents into the countryside. When the Derg ordered students to the rural areas for the ostensible purpose of "helping the peasants to organize peasant associations," and teaching the philosophy of Ethiopia First, they were orchestrating an enormous stage play. The implication here was that some kind of connection had been built between the Derg and the rural populations and the overriding message sent to all onlookers was that the Zemecha would strengthen the Derg's existing base. Less important to the Derg was what the students might say when they arrived to address the farmers. Since the student body of 60,000 was not all comprised of members of the neftegna or beneficiary class, however, and since some of the teachers and university students were sympathizers of opposition groups, and since the philosophy of Ethiopia First had no ideological underpinning, the teaching of the peasants was not uniform. In fact, there were cases when members of the student group fought each other as EPRP, MEISON, or liberation front sympathizers. These acts demonstrated the ideological bankruptcy of the Derg and further exposed that the Derg had failed to rally successfully even its own class. Those who were directed to teach the Derg's philosophy ultimately were absorbed into various resistance and opposition groups.

Back in the urban areas, the Derg confronted the labor unions (CELU) and the remaining urban intellectuals. Members of CELU had been to a considerable degree affected by the squabbles among the intellectuals over power. Their leadership consisted of persons who belonged to the traditional beneficiary groups who had their own political ambitions that clashed with the Derg and with each other. When clashes broke out among themselves and escalated from verbal conflict to physical attack, the Derg took the opportunity to step in and close the CELU headquarters by May 19, 1975. In the midst of a media campaign against the CELU, the Derg ordered new elections in which its own hand-picked people were appointed. By July 4, 1975, the union was under new leadership and the Derg's problem with labor was over. New directives were issued and by December of that year, the CELU had become a part of the Derg's state apparatus as the All-Ethiopia-Trade-Union.

The Familiar Game

Having quite literally cleared out its student problem and its problems with the only organized sectors of manpower, i.e., the teacher's association and labor, the Derg turned to dealing with the urban-based intellectuals. Soon after assuming power, the Derg created an advisory board made up of civilians (Civilian Advisory Board or CAB) and also organized a political bureau. Individual citizens were invited to participate in the CAB, political organizations, specifically MEISON and EPRP were asked to join the political bureau. The civilian board was ignored as soon as it was formed, however, and never became a factor in the Derg's government. The tactic was similar to that used by Haile Selassie with regard to the Council of Ministers—the body was condemned to oblivion by neglect. The formation of the political bureau, on the other hand, became part of the contention between MEISON and EPRP. When MEISON accepted the Derg's invitation, the EPRP immediately rejected the entire notion of cooperating with the Derg. It was from behind the barricade of the political bureau that MEISON members plotted the destruction and then attacked their rivals, the EPRP. The physical attack led by MEISON, who now drew on the military resources of the Derg, had the effect of transforming the EPRP into an urban guerilla movement intent upon recruiting as many young people as possible to retaliate in kind. The ensuing bloodbath, which led to the massacre of thousands of urban young people hastily recruited by both sides, has been called the Red Terror. The scope and brutality of the battles fought in the streets of Addis Ababa were documented daily by journalists of the international media and stand out as one of the features of the "revolution" in most accounts of the Derg's rise to power.

These battles between EPRP and MEISON continued and a condition of terror prevailed in the urban areas until the Derg settled its own affairs internally using much the same violent means. Once a specific faction within the Derg had prevailed, the Derg itself shifted its policy away from an indirect one of allowing these urban groups to eliminate each other to one of direct action against all urban opposition groups. This shift in policy evolved over several months.

A tactic preferred by one faction within the Derg was to appeal to all forces to unite. Teferi Banti formally presented to all Ethiopians a call for united front action:

The Invention of Ethiopia

The appeal I make to all progressive Ethiopians at this particular moment from this square is that you unite, establish a party and form a common front. As long as this is not done, our revolution will continue to be on the verge of disaster. (cited in Ottaway 1978: 143)

Soon after the call was issued, a shootout ensued within the Derg's own ranks. Teferi Banti was killed; his faction lost and the faction led by Mengistu Haile Mariam triumphed. Mengistu is reported to have said, "We ate them for breakfast while they were preparing us for lunch."

Subsequent interpretations of these events have designated Teferi's faction as "moderate" and Mengistu's faction as "radical." In fact the disagreements among the Derg's members did not originate with this call of Teferi's. Both were intent upon eliminating the troublesome opposition. The issue was one of tactics. The public call for unity triggered a violent reaction by a faction that was impatient to step into power in order to take over and physically liquidate all opposition when necessary. This faction preferred to call itself "radical." Mengistu began his ascent by first liquidating those close to him, members of the Derg who stood in the way of his rise to power.

At a victory party, or what could be better dubbed his "inauguration speech," on February 4, 1977, Mengistu explained that the "revolution" had reached a new and offensive stage. He then proceeded to step up the war against external opposition, beginning with the EPRP and the EDU. In this speech Mengistu declared:

As a result of the determined and decisive step taken Thursday by the provisional military administrative council against the internal collaborators and supporters of the EPRP, EDU and ELF, our revolution has, in keeping with the demands of the broad masses, advanced from the defensive to the offensive position. Henceforth, we will tackle enemies that come face to face with us and we will not be stabbed from behind by internal foes. . . [cited by Ottaways 1978: 145]

Beginning the following March, the Derg took control of the urban war by organizing a search-and-destroy squad which specifically targeted the EPRP. By mid-July of the same year the Derg turned its guns against MEISON, now known as the Politburo. Until this time, the Derg had equipped MEISON to eliminate EPRP, who was a threat and competitor to both of them. This final move against MEISON came after MEISON had begun to try to upstage the Derg. (This was done by, for example, agitating for student demonstrations in which people carried placards praising MEISON by name.) The Red Terror thus turned against the Derg's own allies. From that time onward the faction of the Derg led by Mengistu moved in to rule over the empire of Menelik and Haile Selassie.

The process was remarkably similar to the way that Haile Selassie moved into power from among a wide field of candidates, eliminating opposition, orchestrating a massive slaughter among groups whose only differences were over who would assume state power. Such narrowing of the field had the effect in both the cases of Haile Selassie and Mengistu of making it possible for the victor to take any and all means necessary to reinstitute those segments of the dependent colonial formula that were being challenged from within the circle and without.

One consequence of the programs of elimination that the Derg carried out, killing or driving away all the intellectuals, was that the Derg severely reduced the sources of its supply of strategic ideas necessary to keep a dependent colonial state running. These ideas were needed for deciding how to contain the demands among the disaffected within the empire, how to manage the state apparatus itself, and how to conduct foreign affairs. The shortage of strategists led to a desperate search for what we have called mental labor or strategic planning assistance. It was at this point that the Derg was forced to turn to a superpower to provide the appropriate conceptual skills to enable the military committee to continue in power. The

The Invention of Ethiopia

United States' and Western Europe's sympathies, however, remained with the students who had been trained by them in the Western universities. They preferred to see their graduates stay in power since they had been imbued with the ideas of their intellectual motherland to implement back in their home country. The United States and Western Europe condemned the killing off of the products of their educational institutions, and refused assistance to Ethiopia on human rights grounds. Consequently, the Derg turned to the Soviet Union and the Eastern bloc for strategic assistance; they had no where else to go. They simply could not manage the dependent colonial state without the two most critical ingredients, guns and strategic or ideological guidance.

Use of Foreign Expertise

Haile Selassie had willingly placed his empire under the wing of one of the major imperial powers of the day. Mengistu also willingly placed his empire under the Soviet Union, and employed advisers from eastern European countries. He imported, without understanding or knowledge, the model of eastern European Marxism-Leninism. Just as designated members of the settler group had been packed off to Europe or the United States in years past to learn and try to apply the new "ideology" of the adoptive guardian power, scores of young people were sent off to the Soviet Union and Eastern Europe, where they became overnight Marxist-Leninists, without the background to carry out a deep investigation into its application in the empire. The Eastern European Marxist-Leninists also came to the aid of the dependent colonial state using a very imperialist approach, that is, without understanding or trying to understand the conditions prevailing within the empire, simply assuming that they could force the situation.

Mengistu talked about socialism and used the slogan "Ethiopian Socialism," just as Haile Selassie had talked of modernization when the United States advisers had his ear. The Soviet Union took on the role of foreign adviser, supplying the conceptual expertise to

Continuities of Empire Under Soviet Patronage

Mengistu talked about socialism and used the slogan "Ethiopian Socialism," just as Haile Selassie had talked of modernization when the United States advisers had his ear. The Soviet Union took on the role of foreign adviser, supplying the conceptual expertise to guide the dependent empire through the vagaries of internal and external crises. Mengistu introduced a Soviet-style party structure on paper as the model of government, complete with a central committee and a politburo. All the trappings were brought in, including, for the central committee, a first, second and third secretary. The country was renamed the People's Democratic Republic of Ethiopia, and Mengistu placed himself in the presidency. But the imperial style remained, down to the last details that sent clear cultural messages to the populace about the extent of continuity with the past. Where the picture of the monarch had been placed in the upper left corner of the daily newspaper, on the frontispiece of all government issue publications, prominently placed in all courtrooms, etc., the photograph of Mengistu was placed instead. The only differences were the name and the face in the frame. The monarchy was intact.

The willingness of the Soviet Union and the Eastern bloc countries to step in to play the role of supporter, strategic adviser, and supplier of weapons to the dependent colonial state indicates the degree to which the Soviet Union herself was committed to upholding the principles of finance capital and the global order that were embedded in that state.

What changes have been made after August 1977, when MEISON was eliminated by the Derg and the Soviet Union entered to provide the strategic assistance to maintain the state? The Derg had originally declared itself to be on the side of the peasant masses because MEISON had cultivated the peasantry from the outset, trying to establish a base there. What happened is that Mengistu began to make the initial moves necessary to meet the USSR's requirement that a party be formed to provide some legitimacy to the new turn they were about to take. Mengistu proceeded to declare that "the revolution belongs to the oppressed masses. Therefore, there can be no conflict among us over who was the first quently, assorted former members of MEISON, the EPRP and EDU accepted Mengistu's invitation and submitted to the Derg's authority in order to take some position in the state. This victory of Mengistu's group put a stop to the majority of the bickering among the members of the class fraction, and opened the way for Mengistu's faction to take the lead in constructing what so many have enjoyed calling a political "party." Hereafter, Mengistu was able to take into his own hands the task of perfecting the state without the obstacle of demands and compromises with any other sectors of the society or even of his own class. This is just as Haile Selassie had done before him.

Securing the Economic Base

The first major challenge the Derg faced was to establish a firm control over the economic base of the empire. This required taking a series of actions to reverse the momentum of events that were taking place among the colonial subjects who were trying to do away with the essence of the neftegna-gabbar relationship. The primary contact that the peoples of the colonies had had with this government had been when the Zemecha students arrived and approved the actions that the peasants had taken. The students had told the tenants that the local organizations that they had formed to do away with the landlords and to redistribute land among themselves were officially recognized by the new government. The only provisos were that the lands be divided into 3000-acre units, and that they be called "peasant associations." The farmers had raised no objections to these alterations. Officers who had served in the original organizations were elected as officers of the new associations.

It was on the basis of the government's recognition of the already-functioning associations that the farmers in these areas accepted the new regime. As long as this was the case, the farmers saw no reason to oppose the new government, and they did not. They believed that the Derg had endorsed their claim to their lands on the basis of their national rights to the land. This is what taking possession of the land meant to these farmers. Consequently they accepted the Derg's emissaries. "Collective ownership by the Ethiopian people" carried one specific meaning for the peoples of the colonized regions, that is, the immediate possession and disposition of the lands according to the nationally derived value system already represented in their established associations. These associations constituted the parameters of the unit of "collective ownership."

This understanding formed the basis on which the peasant farmers initially accepted the Derg's land reform, peasant association structure, and, by implication, the Derg's authority.

For the period of two years, farmers in the colonized areas operated according to their original principles of organization. During the 1975-1976 and 1976-1977 agricultural years, farmers reported dramatic increases in production and consumption.

Commentators have often remarked that the land reform measure taken by the Derg was far more radical in nature than any observers had anticipated. Halliday and Molyneux observed:

> Against the advice of Chinese, Yugoslav and Russian embassy officials, the PMAC enacted extremely far-reaching measures. No legal ownership of rural land was henceforth permitted: only a "possessory" or "usufructuary" form of tenancy was allowed (1981: 105).

These authors comment in a footnote, "The question of why the land reform measure was so radical has not been clarified" (1981:fn 105). The answer to this question is that a less far-reaching measure would very likely have been rapidly rejected by the once-conquered populations. Had the peasant farmers been given an early indication that their own associations were unacceptable to a new regime moving into power, they probably would have risen up to oppose it. The ambiguity and confusion over the issue bought time for a neftegna regime to secure control of the state apparatus before turning around to confront the colonial peoples with a fortified version of the dependent colonial formula.

The Invention of Ethiopia

By 1977-78 the Mengistu-led faction had taken control in the urban areas by eliminating much of the opposition they faced from class competitors and by turning to the Soviet Union for strategic and military assistance. The new Derg then moved to reestablish the old relation that lay as the centerpiece of the dependent colonial formula—landholder-laborer or neftegna-gabbar. An Oromo peasant interviewed by one of us in 1985 commented about the period by saying, "The Derg and we were both fighting the old landlord. But we wanted to have no landlord. The Derg wanted to become our landlord" (from a 1985 interview by Holcomb with a farmer from Wollega).

Another simply stated, "You see, the government's plan and our plan were not the same" (1985 interview by Holcomb).

A restructuring of the peasant association organization took place in 1978-79. The colonized peoples refer to this as the period of "the Derg's betrayal." This is given proof in extensive purges of elected leaders that took place throughout the country in those years. In many areas, the imposition of central government authority on the local peasant association occurred through demands from newly appointed woreda officials for sharply increased taxes, land redistribution, forcible recruitment from the peasant associations for military service, etc. These requirements embodied the norms and values that were going to be reimposed by the state superstructure by the Derg from then on. These values directly opposed, in fact were designed to destroy the pattern of reorganization that the colonized people had begun to implement. This change of policy set the stage for a series of sharp confrontations which have eventually given strength to the national liberation fronts.

Reorganizing the peasant associations in 1977-78 introduced the means for returning control over the basic means of production in this agricultural society to the state. Control had been slipping away. At that period the food supply to the urban areas and to the massive armies that had been called up by the Derg was threatened. The Land Reform Proclamation had provided the rationale for seizing the means of production, but the state had initially lacked the tools to do it. Once they reestablished a firm grip on the economic base

358

in the colonies, the Derg attained the ability to control the rest of the empire.

Above all, however, the reorganization of the peasant associations constituted a return of the landlord-laborer relationship between the government and the peoples of the colonies. The Derg faced the same dilemma that all governments of Ethiopia have faced, the need to secure control over the workers and to find solutions to the labor problem in a still technologically undeveloped society. The peasant association structure as it was implemented provided a device for extending administrative control over the entire work force. The farmers in the colonies were quickly reduced to the role of laborers on state land.

It is not surprising that the Derg reestablished the basic economic relations that had always obtained between the colonized peoples and the colonial state when the Derg utilized the old superstructure to do its work. Once the Derg was able to establish itself in a position to orchestrate events it introduced into every branch of government the programs that the Haile Selassie government had already designed, and in some cases, had already begun implementing during its latter days.

Peasant associations have always been highly touted as evidence of "socialist" administration of the revolutionary new land reform system, but in fact their introduction constituted a refinement to the old Ministry of the Interior that Haile Selassie's government had tried and thus far failed to achieve. This fact has enormous implications for widely accepted claims by the Derg and by the vast majority of onlookers that a "revolution" took place led by the Derg. Those who had been responsible for managing the state under Haile Selassie's government, both the Western-trained Ethiopians and those who formed the continual parade of foreign experts and advisers to the regime, had several experimental programs under consideration when the government fell. Each of these programs was intended to extend the life of the state in the face of the increasing number of challenges discussed above. On some of them, action had not yet been taken; they were still on the drawing board, while others had already been tried out.

The Invention of Ethiopia

This even applies to the program that has always been considered the Derg's most radical achievement—the advent of the peasant association. When the Derg came into power, Ethiopia had already begun experimenting with different styles of administration. It had been considering a removal of the miktal woreda system in order to expand the number of woredas. This project was to be tested on eighteen awarajas.

> ... at least one from each province was selected for the 1974 local administration development program. The project was under the general supervision of a vice-minister in the Ministry of Interior. A list of awraja administrators was selected carefully and approved by the emperor. A review of the backgrounds of these men and the characteristics of the selected awrajas suggests that the two criteria for choice of a model awaraja were security and development potential (Cohen and Koehn 1980: 58).

By January 1974, when the new plan was put to the test, the awaraja administrators did not know yet how many woredas would be found in any given awaraja, "... since the Miktal woredas appeared to have become de facto woredas when order No. 86 replaced decree No. 1 without mentioning Miktal woredas" (ibid.: 59). This was a project case study for awaraja self-government. Such a program would facilitate greater penetration of the rural areas by the government administration. It was this same project that the Derg took and put into practice with the eventual institutional addition of the All-Ethiopia Peasant Association (AEPA).

The Derg recognized that the organization of the peasantry was relatively independent up to 1977. By 1977, however, the peasantry had already been penetrated by the Derg's cadre to the extent that they were able bring a "reorganization" of the peasant associations. The peasants were disarmed with promises of higher caliber weaponry, then only Derg-selected militia were rearmed. The All-Ethiopia Peasant Association subsequently replaced the self-organized peasant associations. Schwab tells us that "AEPA was founded to coordinate the activities of the many peasant associations. . . . " (Schwab 1985: 26) This is merely another way of saying that the peasant associations were drawn into the old state apparatus.

The Derg's changes to the structure and organization of administrative and economic units of the Haile Selassie state apparatus were minimal throughout. Regarding provincial organization, during Haile Selassie's period (around 1964) there were fourteen provinces and ninety-eight awarajas. In 1975 under the Derg the fourteen provinces were retained with the revolutionary change that they were now to be "administrative regions." The name was changed from Teklay Ghizat to Kifle Hager. There were 102 awarajas. With regard to the smaller units, the number changed from 444 woreda in 1964 to 583 woredas in 1975. Miktal woredas numbered 1328 in 1964. The Derg replaced the Miktal Woreda administration at the lower reaches of government with administration through peasant associations.

From Balabat to Peasant Association Officials: the Building of a New Cadre

During the Haile Selassie period, governors appointed by the emperor administered the provinces (Teklay Ghizat). The awaraja governors were also appointed by Haile Selassie. After the Derg took power, the title governor was changed to administrator. But these provinces continued to be governed in the same top-down fashion by an administrator appointed directly by Mengistu, and the awaraja administrators were chosen in the same fashion. The difference lies in the precise number of awarajas, woredas, miktil woredas and kebele (which had been called atbia). The balabats had been the state's local representatives. But the system was not functioning smoothly; the colonized had been able to exert themselves too much. By co-opting the locally organized peasant associations and transforming them into lower branches of the dependent colonial state, the Derg was able to do what Haile Selassie had been unable to do—penetrate further into the colonial regions in order to exert tighter control over the people and the resources of the colonies.

Writing of the Haile Selassie period, Cohen and Koehn have noted that:

> In all provinces of Ethiopia, a number of informal grass-roots officials provided a link between the lower levels of the Ministry of Interior and the residents of their particular areas. The titles, functions and duties of such local leaders were highly localized and varied significantly throughout the country. In the absence of many case studies, the types and roles of informal local officials cannot be placed within a specific classification system (Cohen and Koehn 1980: 30).

The Derg's contribution to streamlining the dependent colonial state was to provide a classification for this category of official that operated in the state's behalf at the local level—the peasant association official.

By expanding and tightening this All-Ethiopia Peasant Association organization, the Derg was also able to provide the kinds and numbers of jobs for the petit-bourgeoisie that had been lacking under Haile Selassie. Shortages of jobs for this group had been one of the sources of dissatisfaction with the former regime. The smaller units in the rural areas also enabled the state to increase control over the discontented countryside people. The remaining structure of the administration was left as it was organized under Haile Selassie's Ministry of the Interior.

The similarities in structure between the Derg's and Haile Selassie's administration of this dependent state can be shown as follows:

Haile Selassie	*Mengistu*
The crown council	Derg
Ministry of the Interior	Central Planning of Interior Ministries

Continuities of Empire Under Soviet Patronage

Provincial governor	Provincial administrators
Awaraja governor	Awaraja administrators
Woreda	Woreda administrators
Atbia	Peasant association (kebele)
Balabat	Peasant association officers

The AEPA operated as an instrument of control. The coordination of the peasant associations not only led to the replacement of democratically elected leaders with persons selected or hand-picked by the state, but the new leaders, the peasant association chairmen, had wide powers. They sat as the judges, dispensing the new directives and proclamations that issued from the center, and they directed the newly armed police force (the militia) to begin the imposition of the Derg's economic policies. Raising and collection of taxes and land use fees was the first order of business.

The Superstructure Remains Intact

Regarding bureaucratic expansion, the bureaucracy of Mengistu's government mirrored the Haile Selassie model. Actually, Haile Selassie tinkered with the bureaucracy a lot more than the Derg did when they came to power and he was not immediately claiming to have effected a "revolution." Where Haile Selassie took over five ministries and developed them through time into twenty distinct ministries, the Derg took over those twenty ministries and expanded the number to twenty-five.

The usual process of expansion was that when a specific department in the bureaucracy was overwhelmed, it became transformed into a ministry. The function of the ministries and the responsibilities of the chief administrators are exactly what they were during the Haile Selassie period. The most obvious change was that of the title given the officials, a change from governor of the unit to administrator. Even this change was arranged under Haile Selassie and only implemented by the Derg.

From ministry to ministry, the Derg's pattern of adopting Haile Selassie's programs was repeated. The Ministry of Education provides an important example. The Derg became well known for and received a UNESCO award for its literacy campaign. This program was designed, approved, and carried out under Haile Selassie with the name Meserata Temeheret—or basic education. When it took power the Derg retained the same staff and merely distributed the books already printed and stored in warehouses (A. Ibssa 1989). Even the set-up of the educational system was the same, with the exception of cadre training through political education on the Soviet model. The non-Amharas, especially those in the colonies (with a special emphasis on the Oromos) continued to be the targets of an assimilation campaign. The Derg's literacy campaign is set up to begin the teaching of Amharic script in a wide range of languages and then revert to teaching only in the Amharic language for the advanced lessons.

Even those sympathetic with the Derg politically and those who have praised the "revolution" of the Derg have admitted that there was no transformation of the state apparatus under the Derg. The superstructure remained intact.

Regarding the substructure, many writers have concluded that since the Derg has been able to implement the so-called nationalization of the land, industry, urban houses, etc, the society indeed has been transformed into a socialist economy (Schwab 1985, Ottaways 1981, Clapham 1988, Harbeson 1988, Mulatu and Yohannis 1988). Their writings assume that this type of reorganization was necessary to bring benefits to all.

The so-called state socialism of the Derg is little more than a return to the old maderia land model of Menelik. The land has a use value but no exchange value. The land belongs to the new crown, albeit one with a red star on it. A previous holder of the crown, Menelik, used to settle northerners in the colonies. Haile Selassie continued and expanded the policy and the class base, bringing more settlers, hoping that they would remain in that position permanently. Mengistu did nothing more than eliminate the complications introduced by Haile Selassie by reverting to the original form of the edict "all lands belong to the crown, all peoples are subjects of the crown." The role of the superstructure is to hold this relationship in place.

Resettlement: The Process of Extending the Dependent Colonial Relationship

One of the key accusations made against Haile Selassie's government by the Derg was that it had handled the Wollo famine badly. In August 1974, a new commission known as the Relief and Rehabilitation Commission (RRC) was established by the Derg with the blessing of Haile Selassie. The major task of this new group was to organize distribution of food aid that had been sent during the Haile Selassie period for famine victims in Wollo and Tigray and to continue the resettlement of famine victims to new lands.

The Derg's contribution in fact was merely to implement old schemes. All of the studies of settlement as an aspect of land reform were carried out under the auspices of the Haile Selassie government and were at the disposal of the Derg when that committee took over. The new government, in need of an institution to implement some of the proposals, temporarily assigned the Awash Valley Authority to conduct further studies of its implementation. By 1978 an autonomous unit was established within the Ministry of Agriculture to deal with settlement issues; it was called quite descriptively the Settlement Authority. In 1979, by means of proclamation No. 173, the Relief and Rehabilitation Commission was reorganized to bring all the settlement projects of the Awash Valley Authority and the work of the Settlement Authority together under the newly-organized commission.

The Invention of Ethiopia

The Derg's government was able to carry out its land policies with the same kind of free hand that Menelik enjoyed in the days when he declared all land in the empire to be a possession of the crown. In the initial stages the Derg feared none of the internal opposition groups that had dogged the steps of Haile Selassie's government. They had been eliminated. Since the "nationalization" of land carried a different interpretation among the colonized peoples, the Derg was given virtually a free hand regarding land policy.

The Derg chose to implement several of the land projects started by Haile Selassie's government. This move also effectively silenced criticism from a significant group of western intellectuals, who had been directly involved in formulating the plans and/or closely advising former Ethiopian officials regarding the proposals. Once Western advisers saw that their strategies might be implemented by the Derg, they fell silent. Taking the settlement project proposed by the Harvard Advisory Group as an example, the Derg adopted many of the basic features involving the movement of peoples but eliminated the element of voluntary participation. The West, happy to see its programs implemented in some form, refrained from harsh criticism of the manner in which the programs were carried out. Early in its tenure the Derg showed a great deal of public contempt for any opposition from the West to any of the programs, despite the fact that these ironically originated as Western programs designed to extend the life of dependent colonialism. When inquiry and investigation were attempted by the West, the Derg spokesmen simply asserted that the settlers who participated in these schemes were volunteers, without granting opportunity for investigation. Subsequent research revealed otherwise, but there was still little outcry.

The Derg's disregard for the voluntariness of its land programs placed it in the role of colonizer of the settled lands. The objectives of the settlement program were not to seek ways to improve the well-being of the people as a whole but rather to find ways and means to retain and control the colonies so that the needs of the ruling groups would be met.

366

Continuities of Empire Under Soviet Patronage

The settlement design that had been drawn up called for a planned and systematic relocation of people beginning on a small scale and continuing slowly over time. The Derg, however, beginning at the point of greatest vulnerability of the target groups, rushed the program through, conducting a massive relocation in a short period of time. There have been many public complaints from the West about the *manner* in which the Derg carried out the program but virtually no criticism of the concept behind it. A close examination reveals that there was little difference in essence or in form between the actual programs of the governments of Haile Selassie and the Derg.

Due to its lack of a political base in the rural regions of the colonies, the Derg has been unable to conduct agrarian reform in the empire.* The Derg has only been able to accomplish land reform, meaning that it arranged to distribute the conquered (colonial) land to a growing new cadre of neftegnas.

The land reform enabled the ruling committee to deceive the Oromo and other colonial peoples who had raised the question of land into thinking that they had made great progress. It also blunted criticism that the previous Ethiopian regime had faced from foreign critics whose complaints were based on the inability of international finance capital to penetrate the colonial lands. The neftegna hold on the land had proved to be too strong. The policy of land reform also created sufficient confusion to enable the Derg to bring a greater number of settlers to the colonies to supplement the number of old settlers thus furthering the objective of retention of those territories by the neftegna-run state.

---

* Agrarian reform, however, requires a fundamental change of production relations i.e. the reorganization of the production, consumption and distribution patterns. Only when land reform is followed by the repatterning of other forces, the means and tools of production, has agrarian reform taken place. In the case at hand such a transformation would lead to a shift in the position of the laborer, for example, the state's legitimizing and protecting the farmers' say in organizing their own production. This type of change has not occurred in the empire.

The Invention of Ethiopia

The Derg realized that implementing new settlements would not be an easy task in terms of human and financial resources, so the government was forced to organize a bureaucratic device to take care of this task. It was given to the newly organized and autonomous Relief and Rehabilitation Commission (RRC). The RRC was only to report directly to a council of ministers.

Since the technical groundwork had already been laid by studies and pilot projects conducted in Haile Selassie's day, and since the bureaucratic apparatus of All-Ethiopia Peasant Association was in place to implement the program on both the sending and receiving ends, all that remained was for the financial needs to be met. The 1984 drought provided an ideal opportunity to arrange for all settlement to be funded by the infusion of cash, foodstuffs and other resources into the government and into the economy in general through the generosity of international humanitarian agencies. The job left for the RRC was to collect the funds and to organize part of the means of transport. The Soviet bloc provided most of the transport. The program was pushed through in the midst of international lament for the victims of famine. Local officials were ordered to fill quotas, so they forced people into the program by means that varied from place to place. This amounted to dumping people into areas already designated by planners in other departments as settlement sites. The Derg succeeded in placing into the colonial regions more Abyssinians whose function is to help retain the colonies. (The details and consequences of this program are available in Clay and Holcomb, *Politics and the Ethiopian Famine* 1986; also in Niggli 1985; in Clay, et.al. 1989 and Harris 1987). Through the resettlement program, the ranks of the settler class were swollen with populations who had been unwilling to move, but had been forced to do so. The long-term strategy is one of reinforcing the dependent colonial state by expanding the category of settlers dependent directly on the state for their very livelihood.

The Derg believes that through these programs, it has created the political basis for control of both land and labor in the country. Mengistu has asserted that those loyal to his government constitute the "New Ethiopians;" in fact, he claims that the new settlers are more Ethiopian than the old settlers. They are certainly more dependent on the state for their existence. He also acknowledges that some further changes must come from him in order to secure the land in the hands of these "New Ethiopians." It is clear that the settlers on whom the regime depends will not live all their lives from beginning to end without the additional satisfaction of acquiring some rights to the land that they till and all the benefits that come with it.

Consequently, the Derg has had to plan that the land reform will probably change. There is no doubt that it will have to confront the issue of agrarian reform, the only question is one of time. The Derg believes that this issue can be postponed until after the settlement and villagization programs are completed and all the settlers are in positions to defend their gains. The Derg or its the successors will be forced to guarantee the settlers not only the use value of the land they till but also the exchange value. This means an inevitable return to some form of ownership as in the Haile Selassie period. The Derg has introduced the model of collective ownership of the means and tools of production, but it does not have the socioeconomic base to sustain true collectivization through producer cooperatives. If Mengistu stays in power, the Derg will certainly be forced to return to individual ownership of land before he reaches his 60th birthday. Now that it has reorganized the population and secured the settlers' function, it is going to have to allow the settlers access to the benefits. This is the essence of "Ethiopia First."

One thing is clear: Anyone who follows Mengistu will be faced with the land issue. Mengistu will have succeeded in his retention program if the settlers that he has installed in the colonies acquire state-supported rights in the land they till.

If Mengistu's formula holds, the model of New Ethiopia will be sustained. If the national liberation fronts are successful in their programs, however, there will be an end to this formulation of "Ethiopia" and an end to settlerism. Mengistu's contribution in this regard remains to be seen. His successors will determine whether his

The Invention of Ethiopia

efforts to implant and secure new state-supported settlers in the colonial areas will affect or determine future production relations.

It is the Derg's hope that initial resistance from the settlers themselves will evaporate when the Derg judges that it is safe enough to liberalize the land policy. By offering private rights in land the defenders of New Ethiopia will be doing what Haile Selassie did for the children of Menelik's settlers. Such a move would be designed to cause the resistant settlers to acquiesce. Perhaps the degree of liberalization will be decided by the Derg's successor neftegna regime, if the neftegna colonial system survives.

Ironically, the resettlement program designed to re-establish dependent colonialism has been touted in many corners as one of the "revolutionary gains" of the regime. Up to the end of the 1980s, the Derg's accomplishments amount to the refining and implementing of institutions designed by the preceding colonial regimes. This process is called "protecting the revolutionary gains."

Background of the Workers Party of Ethiopia

It was in 1984 that the Derg announced the formation of a political apparatus that could serve the ruling group, the Workers' Party of Ethiopia. After having searched for several years for an ideology, this group that called itself a party officially declared itself to be guided by Marxist and Leninist ideologies. It organized a legislative body called The Shengo to go with the party formation and ideology and issued a new constitution. It has declared that Ethiopia is no longer an empire, but has been transformed into a people's republic.

There is widespread interest in and sympathy for Ethiopian efforts to form a party and to establish a socialist government in that empire. The Derg has found many defenders who take the announcements and declarations at face value, ignoring that these changes form part of the Derg's attempt to legitimize its hold on power in the eyes of the Eastern bloc nations. Recent literature is full of commentary concerning the credentials of the Derg's party and the uniqueness of the socialist experiment.

It has been argued that although the Derg and its revolution may have been off to a rather shaky start, since a party was formed in 1984 and the state is now capable of giving an ideological direction, a true revolution is finally underway. The argument also goes that since a party is the vanguard of a class, its formation should be seen as an indication that there is or has developed a force with an empire-wide capacity to accomplish a revolution. This view of the party tends to explain away or overlook all of the Derg's past difficulties.

It is therefore necessary to examine the social and political origins and the process of party formation in the empire. The idea of the party was introduced into Ethiopia's political life by way of the Ethiopian student movement. As part of the legacy of Marxism in the student movement, the notion of a "one-party state" had achieved great popularity. During the years 1974-76, members of both left organizations, EPRP and MEISON, set out to implement this notion in Ethiopia and held extensive debate and discussions on the issue of party formation, how different social issues should be handled, who should take the state power, and how they themselves could or should participate. For example, MEISON argued that all forces in the country had already participated in the mass upsurge in their own right without any leadership. Consequently, MEISON accepted the Derg as a provisional government for this already accomplished fact. MEISON's position was that an all-encompassing party should be organized and all should be invited to come to take part in the formation. The EPRP's position, on the other hand, was to insist on a popular government elected from each sector of what they designated as revolutionary elements—teachers, students, military, trade unions, etc. In contrast to MEISON, EPRP argued that a party had to be formed first and then all revolutionary classes could join if they were qualified. Both took the position that all forces should be part of their party. They disagreed on the terms.

The two groups expressed differences on almost every issue, but a close examination of the differences reveals that all were tactical

The Invention of Ethiopia

matters and points of strategy, hence, reconcilable if the real problems lay in the issues. But since these groups were at base divided on matters other than these issues, they continued to oppose each other to the extinction of both of them. These debates took place in meetings, in the pages of *Democracia* and *Voice of the Masses*, and in places where old school friends (who now began to call themselves "comrades") could meet.

While the intellectuals were debating these matters, the Derg was taking over the decisionmaking process by force. The EPRP became very popular among several sectors of the urban society, particularly among the labor unions, the university students, high school students, even among the old members of the Ethiopian Democratic Union (EDU) and others, primarily by extending its network of contacts through family and school connections. *Democracia* became much more popular than *Voice of the Masses* because of its opposition to the Derg.

MEISON was losing ground to EPRP until the Derg invited all the intellectuals to join them and to help the Derg accomplish its objectives. EPRP rejected the invitation, choosing to rely on its own base of support, while MEISON accepted it and took over the task of organizing the Derg's Politburo. MEISON's most visible leader, Haile Fida, automatically became the chairman of the Politburo, and the Politburo itself was filled primarily with MEISON members, MEISON supporters from earlier days, and other anti-EPRP individuals. MEISON had, in effect, joined the Derg's government. After the alliance of MEISON with the Derg in the Politburo, the MEISON was put into key positions. The Politburo soon organiz ed institutions such as an ideological school to produce cadre and the Provisional Office of Mass Organizational Affairs (POMOA) to organize local-level kebeles. The Politburo also initiated political education programs (PEP) at the kebele level. These Political Education Programs provided an opportunity to determine in small local meetings who was advocating what political philosophy; in other words, the PEP planners implemented political surveillance, hoping that they could discover EPRP members or sympathizers. Ultimately this plan was not successful.

Continuities of Empire Under Soviet Patronage

After the PEP ploy, the Politburo suggested (and the Derg accepted) that they publicly invite all underground organizations to come forward to make their organizations legal and form at least a united front with the possibility of forming a party. At this point the old animosities emerged, and verbal battles between the EPRP and MEISON broke out in public and expanded to include the Derg. While MEISON's tactics were to leave EPRP exposed and unprotected, the Derg's method of dealing with a problem was to eliminate the opposition directly. When MEISON had suggested study groups and then invited all clandestine organizations to come and join the struggle by becoming legal, EPRP predictably rejected both "invitations."

Other groups that had been organized by or approved by MEISON and the Derg accepted. These others were MALERED, Seded, Waz League (Ader), and ECHAT. Together they formed the Union of Ethiopian Marxist-Leninist Organizations (Amharic acronym: EMALEDEH). The group known as Seded or Abyotawit Seded (literally revolutionary wildfire), was composed of military officers calling themselves a party; they had been organized by Mengistu Haile Mariam personally and were chaired by Legesse Asfaw. A labor league was formed that became known as Waz League (for an Amharic word symbolizing labor) whose members were civilians who had chosen to support the Derg but were not part of MEISON or EPRP. Actually it turned out that they were civilians who were organized by the Derg specifically to strategize against MEISON and to fill in for MEISON in case MEISON left the Derg for any reason. The Waz League was led by a man who had been a long-time political activist, a mechanical engineer and karate instructor in the Air Force, Dr. Senay Lique. MALERED (the shortened form of EMALERED, the Amharic acronym for Ethiopian Marxist-Leninist Revolutionary Organization) was a MEISON product, organized by the MEISON and pro-MEISON, led by Gulilat. ECHAT (Amharic acronym for Ethiopian Oppressed Masses Revolutionary Struggle) was an organization reportedly chaired by Baro Tumsa. It was made up of member groups of oppressed peoples who were trying to protect themselves from

373

attacks by EPRP, Derg and MEISON by joining forces determined to push out the EPRP. By responding to the Derg/MEISON call to be a part of this Union of Ethiopian Marxist-Leninist Organizations, they sought cover from MEISON, the Derg and Seded against a common threat. None of these groups that accepted the Derg's invitation trusted the others. They sought protection under the umbrella of Marxist-Leninist organizations. ECHAT was a bit of an exception here in that it was made up of member groups of oppressed nations whose purpose was reportedly to protect the interests of the colonies from their adversaries.

Among these who responded, the most powerful groups were those supported by the military, that is, Seded and MEISON. MEISON was powerful because it had become the intellectual base of the Derg and, as such, was budgeted by the Derg to organize several institutions. MEISON was responsible for setting up almost all the extended institutions of the Derg. Plans to implement the POMOA, the kebele system, the All-Ethiopia Peasant Association, the militia, youth, and women's organizations were all the work of MEISON. In fact, MEISON became so confident that it had begun asking the Derg for the control of militia. In the southern provinces, which were the colonial provinces, MEISON had worked to build up a rural base of support to counter EPRP's urban base and ultimately to counter the Derg. No one was in a better position than MEISON to have seen the ideological bankruptcy of the Derg. But, when MEISON so seriously misjudged the situation that it was decimated by those whom it tried to outsmart, MEISON's own ideological shortcomings were exposed for all the world to see. MEISON had specifically assigned its own people from the region as provincial governors, awaraja and woreda leaders, etc. This was done, however, to abort the growing Oromo resistance. The Derg did not like this arrangement at all and organized the military officers under Seded specifically to watch MEISON. Seded and MEISON, who had worked for the Derg as two peas in a pod, eventually came head to head over who would control the ideological school and what would be the role of the POMOA.

Continuities of Empire Under Soviet Patronage

MEISON's strategy of exposing the EPRP led to the Red Terror campaign in which the EPRP was crippled, if not destroyed. Right on the heels of that extermination, MEISON and the others who were legally organized under the Derg's umbrella became the victims of intimidation and elimination. MEISON eventually lost at its own game. The other two groups, MLRO (MALERED) and Waz League, plus a few remains of MEISON, were swallowed up by Seded. ECHAT dispersed. Since ECHAT member organizations had only responded to the Derg's invitation in order to protect themselves temporarily from the physical attack of EPRP while paving a different way for themselves, its members joined the armed struggles in the colonies. It was the only group among them whose members had a base in the rural areas. Therefore it was the only one of these groups whose members were not destroyed or absorbed in urban battles. The only groups remaining in contention for the Derg's sanction were MEISON and Seded. As the Derg members began to be suspicious of MEISON's moves, the Derg organized all intellectuals who remained in support of the Derg faction into a group offering tactical support of Seded. It became inevitable in such an atmosphere that only one of these two groups would prevail. As it turned out, only Seded, with the Derg's explicit backing, survived. MEISON, when it lost the Derg's sponsorship, met its demise. Once MEISON was eliminated, the Derg simply renamed the remaining group Commission to Organize the Workers' Party of Ethiopia (COPWE). COPWE was formed on December 18, 1979, again to be renamed in 1984 the Workers' Party of Ethiopia (WPE).

Thus, Seded became COPWE. As WPE recounts these events:

> Confronted with such a problem, the remaining members of the Union of Ethiopian Marxist-Leninist Organizations had mapped out an altogether new strategy for the establishment of the vanguard party of Ethiopia (Committee for the Founding of the People's Democratic Republic of Ethiopia 1987: 56).

The Invention of Ethiopia

So the WPE version of these events is that all of these groups tried and failed to implement the Ethiopian Revolution. According to the WPE account, Mengistu Haile Mariam became the savior of the Ethiopian Revolution since he was able to do what none of these other organizations could do. WPE goes on to say:

> All those genuine revolutionaries who had practically demonstrated their dedication and loyalty to the triumph of the Ethiopian revolution . . . all those genuine revolutionaries [are] to be led by Comrade Mengistu Haile Mariam, who through his ceaseless efforts and decisive leadership had symbolized the determination of the Ethiopian people to build a new society free from exploitation and oppression.

So after the process of elimination resulted in only one surviving fraction of the petit bourgeois class, that fraction was called a party. What this event really indicated was that a one-group military party was formed. This is the segment of society that began to refer to itself, continues to refer to itself, and is referred to by others as a vanguard party. Such a party could never be regarded as or become a vanguard party, however. The day that five different groups lost to Seded by force and disappeared was the day that even the neftegna lost the opportunity to claim that they had established any kind of vanguard. This group that remains cannot by any standard claim credentials to call itself the vanguard party even of the neftegna, let alone of the empire. Others, who might claim the position of vanguard party of the neftegna, whether MEISON or EPRP, even EDU, have not yet lost the bid for leadership of the neftegna class. While the Workers' Party of Ethiopia (WPE) claims to represent workers, despite its ambitious name, it represents only the military fraction of the petit-bourgeoisie within the Ethiopian empire. The Derg's party does not embody either neftegna interest or workers' interest. There are some small additional sectors of the petit bourgeoisie represented, but these are so limited in relation to the society at large as to be insignificant to the total picture.

376

Continuities of Empire Under Soviet Patronage

The social base for this party formation was so narrow as to represent only a clique within a fraction of a class. Yet there is support for the notion that this self-declared party should be regarded as the vanguard force of the workers in the empire.

Once Seded was victorious in the power game, it was given a new name (COPWE) and a new set of tasks. Created for the narrow purpose of serving as a counterweight to MEISON, COPWE immediately had to step into the role as the organizer of a workers' party. Its very purpose and function within the state became to be determining how to justify calling itself a party at all. Building a party was a requirement for Soviet patronage, so the effort could not be abandoned, regardless how fruitless it was. After five years of feeble and failed attempts, it was merely announced that COPWE was to be inaugurated as the vanguard party. This audacious move generated surprisingly little international criticism.

The Derg's declaration of the formation of what it called the Workers' Party of Ethiopia occurred amid great fanfare and expense in 1984, the year of the great famine. It was touted as the vanguard party of Socialist Ethiopia which continued to be governed by the PMAC (Provisional Military Administrative Council). By 1987, on the thirteenth anniversary of its rule, the Derg declared in the same fashion that the People's Democratic Republic of Ethiopia (PDRE) had been formed.

Haile Selassie's government was shattered by several social forces, each representing a different dimension of the socioeconomic formation of the empire. The people of the colonies became involved by fighting for the liberation of their nations; the workers became involved by demanding fair wages from the state (this group included the NCOs of the Derg who had originally rebelled against the government for higher pay); the small businesses struck for improvement in the conditions that affected their income, and the students and intellectuals demanded changes that would give them the access to good positions in the state that they had been led to expect. When Haile Selassie's government fell under the weight of opposition from all these forces, only the committee of armed military men called the Derg was in the position to prevent any other group from taking over state power. This group quickly moved to eliminate the real vanguards of all the social forces and sectors of the social formation that were genuinely represented at the initial stage. Having done this, they recognized their handpicked elite group as the vanguard party of the entire colonial empire.

How could a group that could not even assume the leadership of its own class, the petit bourgeoisie, claim to serve in that role for the entire society? The group did not merely fail to accomplish a difficult task, the group that claims to be a party, could neither theoretically nor practically assume a true vanguard position in relation to the varied social forces in the empire. The production relations that were fashioned upon the creation of this empire were intrinsically antagonistic and have never been transformed. Hence, no common ground has been nor could be created for these forces to ally for any common objective. Furthermore, the class base of the group claiming representation of the whole is itself is petit bourgeois, i. e., heterogeneous; it has been patched together from classes that have far deeper and enduring interests. It is therefore subject to be splintered apart over a number of issues. The very existence of this class has been determined by the needs of other classes. Its members merely vie for recognition in how best to serve the other classes. As a group its members do not have the common economic foundation necessary to establish a shared ideological or political position.

In Ethiopia there was no indigenous class equipped to lead he country in such a way that this petit bourgeois group could choose to serve it. As a result, its only choice was to move to defend the state itself, as indicated in the slogan "Ethiopia First." The petit bourgeoisie was in practice allying with the international capitalist class that created the state in the first place to accomplish its own ends. Since the petit bourgeoisie did not move into state power in order to resolve a defined social or economic question for a mature class to which it was answerable, it had no set of shared values on which to base a reorganization of economic and political matters. The petit bourgeoisie has no other options available except to rule with brute force. The only alliance it finds is with the gun that the imperial patron supplies. Using a gun to enforce a system that it did not design is the way it serves the class that created it in the first place, the international capitalist class. Since the petit bourgeoisie is not anchored anywhere as a group, its reason for being becomes nothing more than consolidating control over the administrative apparatus which it finds in its possession. It tries to use administrative control as a tool for political domination and even tries to create from that control a source of economic power.

This kind of behavior from the petit bourgeoisie is not an unheard-of phenomenon by any means. Early on, Antonio Gramsci characterized in no uncertain terms the performance of the petit and middle bourgeoisie who move into state power when the classes that had originally built the state move into the background. According to him, once these elements have taken power, a struggle follows between them and the working people.

> This struggle took place in the only way it could take place: it was disordered and tumultuous .... But this struggle was connected, albeit indirectly, to the other higher class struggle between capitalists and workers. The petit and middle bourgeoisie is in fact the barrier of corrupt, dissolute and rotten humanity that capitalism uses to defend its economic power: a servile abject hoard of hirelings and lackeys, that has now become a *serva padronna* and wants to extort a booty from production that is larger than even the booty grabbed by the capitalists themselves (Gramsci 1977: 135).

The Ethiopian stateholders represent a classic case of petit bourgeoisie in open war against the productive sectors of the society. They do so from within the barricade of the state structure itself, which embodies the ideology of its framers, who built it as a tool of colonial domination.

In the Ethiopian case, the concept of Greater Ethiopia, created as the ideological support for the dependent colonial empire, proved to be powerful enough that the new stateholders did not offer a replacement ideology. Instead they clung to it even more tightly

The Invention of Ethiopia

than did the previous regime. They started from there to plan their course, a course which put them in direct confrontation with the victims of that state.

By eliminating those who represented the challenging social forces in the empire, the Derg did not succeed in eliminating the issues they represented. Consequently, the concerns and demands of these groups that had required a revolution within the society continued to find expression, this time taking the form of opposition to the Derg's government. The nature of their efforts changed rather than the nature of their interests and demands.

Opposition to the Derg from People Desiring Autonomy

The issue of nationalities constituted a significant portion of the basis for the overthrow of Haile Selassie's government. Were the issues raised by the nationalities addressed or answered?

Having taken over the state structure and having taken the steps to safeguard the economic base of a colonial empire, the Derg turned to deal with the demands of the people. The Derg did not grant the Tigray demands for national autonomy within a democratic structure. Tigrayans had begun to see that the Derg represented the children of neftegna and had seen the direction its policy was taking. The TPLF was formed with the specific objective of protecting the interests of the Tigray people in the face of threats to their goals by the Derg. The TPLF represented all those who identified themselves first and foremost as Tigray nationals. Since it was on the basis of Tigray nationalism that large segments of the Tigray population had been suppressed, the movement grew rapidly. After the downfall of Haile Selassie's government, the democratic demands that the TPLF made were not honored by the Derg. The Derg's response to Tigray demands was a series of military attacks.

Continuities of Empire Under Soviet Patronage

The Colonial Question: Colonized Subjects Confront the Derg

The strategy for land reform created a critical and important ambiguity between the *liberation* of land and the *collectivization* of land. The former would have met the demands of the national liberation movements and created the basis for autonomy up to independence (or later, voluntary federation) of regions where traditional landholding systems varied considerably. The Land Reform Proclamation was widely interpreted in the colonies to mean liberation of land, that is, endorsement of the former tenants' rights of possession to the plots they had been farming and also endorsement of the collective actions they had taken through the local associations.

Peasants had the opportunity to implement their own values, and when they did, production rose and peasant consumption rose. Taxation during the early period was nominal and primarily symbolic but adequate to maintain a line of communication and authority in keeping with that of the emperor's government.

After the city massacres known as Red Terror were over, the battle for direction and control of events moved to the countryside, and the Derg's design for the collectivization of land was exposed. It was found to be in direct contradiction to the liberation of land that had been implemented in large parts of the once-conquered Oromo, Sidama and Somali territories to the south, east, and west of Addis Ababa, in the once-subdued lands of the Tigray to the north and in the annexed territory of Eritrea also to the north. This is when the values of the opposing sides came into direct and open conflict.

By this time, 1977-78, the Derg had secured its position in relation to other contending parties, had secured a route of access to substantial quantities of military hardware from the Soviet Union, had begun a large-scale confrontation with the colonized Somalis who were backed by the Somali Democratic Republic and the annexed Eritreans led by the Eritrean People's Liberation Front (EPLF) and the Eritrean Liberation Front (ELF). The Derg had also extended assurances to new and loyal sectors of the petit bourgeoisie that the state would sustain them in return for their services. The arrangement on which Ethiopia was founded was that colonized nations were to provide labor power and agricultural products to the neftegna state. By this time the arrangement was condemned by the colonial peoples. The urban areas and the armies were hungry, the weaponry had to be paid for, and the Derg had arrived to revive the arrangement. These factors set the stage for the Derg to confront the rural populations for access to their labor and resources. Several steps came in rapid succession. Taxes were raised and then raised again. Large quotas were set for the recruitment of able-bodied rural farmers into the military for the wars with Eritrea and Somalia. The product of communal plots was trucked to the cities to sustain the army and the growing populations of urban-based bureaucrats. Enormous sacrificial "contributions" were required from all rural sectors, particularly from the conquered southern regions.

All of these measures were designed to be implemented through the Derg's improved state apparatus—improved through the addition of peasant associations. One farmer, speaking in 1985, remarked, "The peasant association is the face of the Derg." Demands, quotas and instructions were passed through the All Ethiopia Peasant Association to the local branches. Resistance was widespread. When a wave of condemnation of locally elected leaders—leading to executions, imprisonment and formal accusations against the peasant association leadership—was registered across the rural countryside, the resistance of the colonized people was forced into a new stage. Imposition of the old order was felt with every new edict. New "elections" were held at gunpoint in many regions. Any opposition to the state measures was harshly punished, and those who voiced the opposition were labelled "anti-Ethiopia" or "counterrevolutionary." Peasant associations were restructured in such a way that officials hand-picked and responsive to central directives were placed in a position to reimpose a landlord-laborer relation. They were empowered to extract all the previous obligations the state had demanded of its subjects, i.e., to determine how the peasants' labor time would be utilized, to decide how land would be redistributed and to enforce higher and higher taxes, fees and quotas for grain sales for individual farmers (see Clay and Holcomb 1986: 123-153 for detail).

In short, implementation of military control over the means of production crystallized the disparity between the needs and demands of two fundamental political categories in the empire. One was the class that had been formed by the state itself and which was intent upon defending, strengthening and continuing to benefit from the state; the other was made up of those groups who had been victimized in the very process of state formation and alienated from the state apparatus. Groups in this latter category were intent upon transforming or replacing the mechanisms that had held them in a subject position for several generations.

The conflict between these two political groups became sharply defined during the period after 1978. Confrontations began to occur which revealed that Derg strategy merely streamlined and reinforced the relations of production that had been put into place by its predecessors. The activity of the national liberation fronts and rural support for them grew in direct relation to the realization among the tenants that their position vis-a-vis the Derg government was identical to their position vis-a-vis Haile Selassie's government and that of Menelik before him.

This crystallization of the battle lines after 1978 was reflected, for example, when several traditional Oromo songs and stories which served as repositories for strong sentiments of protest against those who conquered and subjugated the Oromo were sung about the Derg. The label neftegna, guncarrying settler, began to be actively applied to the Derg's personnel as armed alien functionaries arriving to demand taxes, contributions, manpower and to impose onerous obligations on the populace. Protest songs that had been recorded as early as the 1890s when Menelik was attacking and occupying the independent Oromo country and sung widely throughout the Oromo countryside during unrest in 1912 in the west, 1922-27 in the central regions, and in the 1960s in the central and eastern regions were sung in the 1980s in the eastern, southern, central and

The Invention of Ethiopia

western parts of the Oromo country. Translations of some of these songs have appeared in print (Cerulli 1922, Triulzi 1980, Nagaso 1982 and Tamane 1983). Triulzi had written regarding earlier Oromo revolts in Wollega

> ... these songs appear interesting to me because they fully express the deep feelings of hatred, anger and frustration of the Qellem Oromo gabbar under the neftanna [neftegna] rule of their Amhara overlords and tell us directly—apart from the severe sets of rules and obligations of the gabbar-neftanna relationship—how people felt towards and reacted to, an administrative structure of oppression which had so deep a part of Qellem history, or for this matter in the history of many southwestern provinces. These songs are also important because they give us the psychological background to one of the few recorded peasant revolts in Wallega history, that of 1909-1912, which for a short spell freed Qellem of the occupying Amhara forces, was the cause for the subsequent military occupation of the country, and eventually led to several thousand gabbar families leaving Qellem... (1980: 2).

The very songs that Triulzi refers to were adapted in the 1980s to include the new neftegnas who called themselves socialists. The designation neftegna was applied by the peasantry with vehemence to Mengistu's representatives as early as 1978, when the implementation of land policy revealed to them the Derg's rejection of Oromo aspirations.

The national liberation fronts, whose roots lay in the systematic resistance to the earlier incarnations of alien settlers, functionaries and landlords who alighted upon the conquered people and claimed their labor and land, flourished. Continuity with forms of resistance utilized in the past had been maintained in different ways in different national territories. Organizational resistance was followed by armed resistance when the Derg itself arrived fully armed to impose

Continuities of Empire Under Soviet Patronage

a streamlined model of dependent colonialism on populations who had been brought into the empire by force.

The colonial relations among the parts of the Ethiopian empire lie at the heart of the conflict that has ravaged the region throughout the 1980s and looks to persist into the 1990s, continuing the devastating legacies of famine, heavily armed military confrontations, and exhaustion of enormous international resources. The invention and official international recognition of an artificial unit in the Horn for the purpose of accommodating superpower interests generated problems for the peoples of the empire that they are struggling to overcome. But a lack of global perspective on events in this region has concealed Ethiopia's position in the world order, prevented people from easily identifying the forces in conflict there and led to errors of policy of tremendous proportions up to and including the period of the Derg's rule. Ethiopian mythology which claims uniqueness of the empire prevails even on the verge of the 1990s when a military regime defends colonial rule in the name of a "unique" kind of Ethiopian socialism and the "first and only" fully functioning communist party in Africa.

Ethiopian colonial mythology is exposed for what it is when the politics of empire become clear. Once the powerful illusions about Ethiopia—illusions of a unique, ancient, sovereign, internally united, Christian nation whose problems have been caused by nature and hostile imperial forces—are set aside and a cool discerning judgment is made about the nature of the crisis in the region, then the objectives and activities of national liberation fronts in Oromia and Sidama and Afar as well as in Eritrea and the Somali Ogaden may be properly evaluated. Their challenge to the system of Ethiopian colonialism is fundamental. National liberation movements have already begun to construct new sets of institutions which embody the values and the social and economic relations denied legitimate expression throughout a long period of subjugation. The task which faces anyone interested in the prospect of peace in region is to assess thoroughly the alternative social formations that are being generated by these movements that are in the process of eliminating the colonial relation upon which the empire was built.

10 SUMMARY

The key to understanding the creation, expansion, and continuity of the Ethiopian empire lies in the position that it has held within the global political and economic order. When Ethiopia was first invented at the turn of the twentieth century it was born out of a need for contending superpowers to find some way of avoiding war with each other over which one of them would move in to monopolize the strategic region of northeast Africa. They became involved in fashioning the Ethiopian state as a solution for managing a potentially devastating conflict among themselves. Then they recognized "Ethiopia" to be "independent," though it was for all intents and purposes a collaborative effort of all of them to keep the region free from the monopoly control of any individual superpower.

The participation of these European capitalists in Ethiopia was far-reaching. Advisers who represented various capitalist countries were initially involved at every stage in forming the empire, and then at every level of the new government. These advisers were the conduits through which the capitalist ideology, embodied in strategy, was implemented in shaping Ethiopia. The advisers were involved in bringing surrounding peoples under the control of Abyssinian settlers (neftegna), in arming and equipping the favored Abyssinian ruling group, in assisting to enforce new neftegna-gabbar relations of production upon the conquered peoples, and in cooperating to fashion a new state apparatus designed to maintain those relations of production.

The Invention of Ethiopia

The ideological basis of Ethiopian colonialism, the basic paradigm that gives shape to the state by creating the categories around which the features of the state are organized, is predominantly that of the European capitalists. The representatives of capitalism were not only influential in fashioning the state but also took an active role in advising during its development and refinement. The ideological underpinning is embodied in the hierarchical model in which control is assured by a centralized bureaucracy that extracts value and ensures compliance from all populations within its domain. The Ethiopian colonial mythology strives to obscure the fact that the state is a European-Abyssinian hybrid and that an imported design lies at the center of the empire's formula for control.

The neftegna-gabbar relation is as central to the ideology as it is to the economic base. It guarantees dominance of settlers in the conquered and annexed regions. From their position in the colonies, the neftegna are empowered to control the rest of the country as well. The political dimension of the empire is the set of policies which assure that their dominance is preserved. Without it there is no empire.

The story of the development of Ethiopia is the story of the formation, expansion, consolidation, and entrenchment of the neftegna as the only class to become established empire-wide. It is the story of the role that the neftegna as a tiny minority have played in receiving the blessing of the superpowers to manage and defend a state apparatus that met basic needs of the Europeans interested in preventing each other from gaining control of the region.

As a result of position that the neftegna acquired, many people from the conquered regions were evicted from their homelands during conquest and remained refugees with no relation to the land. Many others who fought became martyrs to the cause of resistance. Those who remained behind became subjects of the settlers. Following the conquest and occupation of these neighboring regions that until then Abyssinians had only aspired to possess, Menelik's government decreed that all conquered lands henceforth belonged to the Ethiopian crown and that all the indigenous people who had failed to cooperate were to be subjects of the crown. The signifi-

Summary

cance of the initial decrees of Menelik regarding the possession of the land and the people by the crown is that they laid the groundwork for the introduction of new production relations in the conquered regions and within the newly formed empire. By these decrees the conquered regions became colonies under the control of the institutions that were fashioned to accommodate an Abyssinian-European alliance. These institutions comprise the Ethiopian state.

Neither Abyssinians nor any combination of indigenous Africans created Ethiopia. It was cooperation between Abyssinia and Europe that fashioned the Ethiopian state; the state embodied the needs and interests of both parties and could not have been instituted without either party. Without this cooperation, the occupation of the conquered regions and the construction of the new institutions that transformed the regions surrounding Abyssinia into colonies would not have taken place. Neither the conquest nor the subsequent colonial control of the Oromo, Sidama, Somali and other nations that surrounded Abyssinia would have been possible without European input in the form of weapons and technical and strategic assistance. Without the Abyssinian settlers willing to carry the imported guns in return for a piece of the spoils, the participation of several groups of Europeans would not have been possible. The combined forces of Abyssinian armies with European officers assisting, however, were able to move into the territory of neighboring nations and physically seize their material means of existence, i.e., their means and tools of production.

This settler-system has not been wholly ignored in writing on Ethiopia, but its significance and formative character have not been placed at the center of analysis. Thus, analyses often go astray on assumptions such as the one that all residents function as citizens or that settlers blend with the members of the region to which they have moved to claim land. The neftegna-gabbar relation has been at the heart of Ethiopian colonialism. It constitutes the crux of the economic base of the system. Despite claims that it has been eliminated, it remains the basic feature that the entire Ethiopian superstructure is organized to maintain. Once this fact is clear several aspects of the state take on particular significance.

The Invention of Ethiopia

Haile Selassie did his part to maintain this relation, as shown in Chapter Four, by taking over what had been built under Menelik and extending it. He did not replace the basic neftegna-gabbar relation; indeed, he took steps to strengthen it by broadening the base of the landholding neftegna class itself. In order to assure his generation and the next the continuation of this neftegna-gabbar system, he issued assurances to those who had held maderia and siso lands under Menelik that their possessions were secure and then extended their rights across generations to their children. Consequently, all settlers' rights to their possession of land would be lasting as long as his state structure remained intact. Henceforth they fought to defend and protect that state because they had acquired a permanent interest in land that was attached to it.

Then he introduced a "free land grant" system that parcelled out government lands to specific categories of eligible recipients. Through this kind of move, he recruited individuals from preselected sectors of the society to join the already-established group of settlers and thus broadened even further the base of neftegna whose interest lay in defending the state. In retrospect we can see that it was military men who had been made eligible for land rights through this land grant system who rose to defend the state most vigorously during the 1974 change of power. At the time it was carried out, the land grant system was promoted as land reform and modernization, though it constituted merely an extension of the original settler-tenant laborer relation.

One key feature of the neftegna-gabbar system is that the gabbar are not allowed access to land ownership. Consequently their physical labor and its product were guaranteed to be available to both the settlers who became landlords, determining the disposition of the product, and to the state. The settler state was sustained on the value produced by this arrangement. The European interests were served by this arrangement, too, because the Abyssinian system alone could not have sustained the costs of maintaining a state structure suitable to European needs and interests. The neftegna-gabbar relationship forced the colonies to supply the material support which kept the neftegnas in place and footed the bill for the

Summary

type of state that met the minimal European standards without requiring the treasuries of Europe to do so. It was cost effective for the Europeans. The colonies' supplying the revenues directly to the settler state represented a great savings to European powers, who had become greatly concerned over the high costs of maintaining colonies in the many regions where they had already established direct monopoly control. In light of this massive indirect benefit, they were less preoccupied with the direct export of raw materials from Ethiopia to Europe.

Once the continued supply of labor and produce to the neftegna state was guaranteed by denying huge populations of conquered people access to landholding through state-supported devices, Haile Selassie's objective shifted. His government began to intensify the training of Ethiopians in the technical and intellectual skills that would enable them to take over the state directly and run it without continued dependence on the mental labor or strategy that Europeans advisers still provided. It was a plan for a kind of intellectual import substitution. Hence, as part of Haile Selassie's modernization program, more schools were opened in the European tradition and more students were imbued with the ideological orientation of the superpowers. The majority of students selected for this training were children of the settlers. In reality, through their education they were equipped to be able to defend their fathers' possessions and, by extension, their own future holdings through managing the state.

Imperial powers were very much interested in the Ethiopian experiment and were fascinated by how capitalist forms of control would penetrate the agricultural sector and whether educated Ethiopians could become effective agents of a capitalist social formation. The development of commercial agriculture occurred alongside the increased emphasis on higher education, beginning with such projects as the Wonji sugar plantation, Awash Valley Authority, CADU, WADU, etc. Once these schemes were established, the cadre newly recruited to the neftegna class began to show their loyalty to the state in promoting and faithfully managing the projects. The developments not only began to increase the size of the settler communities but also played an important role in effectively clearing from the lands those peasant farmers who were opposed to the expansion of the state.

The Emergence of the Petit Bourgeoisie

While efforts to further secure the economic base of the empire were underway through agricultural modernization during Haile Selassie's rule, difficulties began to be registered at the political level among those being trained to take over the state. The executive roles in the state that had been promised to the trained children of the settlers were not being created rapidly enough to accommodate all of the aspirants. Having been refashioned to see themselves destined for salaried administrative posts, positions far above anything their fathers held, these educated young people began to compete for the small number of those positions that were available. The competition that developed among these educated individuals spawned groups and alliances based on incidental criteria such as acquaintance, personality, or alma mater. The emergence of this kind of competition caused the government to seek ways to slow down the production of graduates from these modern schools. One such step taken during the last days of Haile Selassie's regime was to institute the Educational Sector Review limiting the number of students accepted for higher education and limiting access to high school level training. Initially the college entrance examination was made to be one of the narrowest bottlenecks in the empire. A very small number were "passed" on to college. Also, unless a student maintained a given grade point average and excelled in reading and writing the Amharic language, he/she could not continue in school.

For those who passed through all these obstacles, a new hurdle was introduced. They were required to serve one year of national service, the obligation to be completed usually after the third year of college. It turned out that this exposure to the real conditions in the rural areas, a great proportion of which were colonial areas, had a politically significant effect upon this group. When the students were sent to teach in the provinces, the differences in background

Summary

among them began to emerge and take on new meaning. A significant split began to occur that was not based on personality or school attended. The students constituted a mixed group of persons from the colonized and dominant nations, some of whom served in the colonies and some in the motherland.

Upon return from service, their alliances began to change. It became clear that their observations in the country had led them to assess the condition in the empire as it affected their futures. Both groups saw the inevitability of armed conflict in the countryside. Those from the dominant nations saw the seeds of united national resistance movements in the making among the colonized peoples and concluded that this situation endangered their future plans. Those from the colonized and oppressed nations saw to what extent their parents were disenfranchised and concluded that they had an obligation to side quickly with the peasant movements (that happened to be comprised of their parents).

Students who had been in the provinces observed that the national movements had the potential to develop into a powerful convulsion. This situation became their major concern. As a result, an ambiguous slogan was raised that received the endorsement of both groups and became popular among the entire student community. It was imported from the Russian revolution—"Land to the Tiller." Events subsequently showed that the students held fundamentally different interpretations of this slogan, however, just as colonized and colonizer groups throughout the empire had sustained deep divisions over this matter. In fact the differences and divisions within the student movement on the land issue reflected very closely the divisions in the rest of the society regarding land. The position of the colonized peoples was that land must be returned to the colonized nations from whom control had been wrested at conquest but who continued to till the land for the new owners. To the colonized peoples land to the tiller was a demand for change in the production relations. Those from the colonizer group, however, were not interested in a change in production relations that would return land to the colonized. They were interested only in wresting control from the aristocratic fraction of the settler neftegna class in order to expand access to land through enlarging the settler category. There was no way that the two interpretations could both be implemented because they were inherently contradictory. The differences between the two positions within the student movement came to the surface through debates that took place on the Eritrean question in 1971 and the Oromo question in 1972, as detailed in Chapter Seven. Although the student intellectuals were raising the land issue quite vocally, it received attention only because this was the question being raised by the colonized people who were developing more and more successful ways of resisting the power of the state to enforce neftegna control over the colonized nations.

The Rise of the New Neftegna

Of many different demands made during the 1974 February Upsurge, the issue of land raised by the conquered and colonized peoples was the most fundamental. But the response of these peoples to the crisis has often been misrepresented by persons who themselves were student intellectuals. The most common interpretations offered for how the Derg moved into power are that a) the proletariat, led by the noncommissioned officers in the military, affected a genuine revolution within the empire and introduced a new state apparatus to defend it, or b) members of the military, who were heavily pressured and influenced by progressive intellectuals, took over state power from a feudal class, bringing about a revolution in the empire. This latter version, which asserts that the student and intellectual roles were of primary importance, condemns the military committee for leading the revolution astray, mainly by its refusal to return the state to civilian rule as soon as the feudal regime was successfully ousted. By civilian rule writers are usually referring to their group; that is, the rule of the specially educated intellectuals who originally were trained to manage the dependent colonial state.

The interpretation offered here accepts neither of these explanations for the rise of the Derg. The military committee that eventually outmaneuvered the aristocratic faction within the military was no

Summary

longer the group led by noncommissioned officers who had originally protested their working conditions. These NCOs had gone back
to the barracks. Instead, a group of junior commissioned officers
moved forward to protect themselves from elimination by the
aristocrats and to protect their own interest within the empire as
landholders or potential landholders according to the state provisions. Although this military group initially allied with intellectuals
from its own neftegna class against the intellectuals and cultivators
of the colonized regions, its members were never acting as anyone's
puppets. They were defending their own position and the position
of other neftegnas within the empire by protecting the state from
dissolution at the hands of the aggrieved colonized peoples. The
slogan that they immediately put forward upon seizing power,
"Ethiopia First," sent this message loud and clear to all those with
an interest in defending the settler state. At that point all in the
neftegna category were relieved and excited that the empire had
been saved. Subsequent battles that erupted between the intellectuals
and the military were conflicts between different fractions of the
same neftegna class over which of them should hold state power, not
over the overall objective or purpose of the state. The military
committee refused to transfer power to the intellectuals or "civilians"
for the same reasons that they seized the power from the aristocrats
of their own class—they did not think that either group was capable
of protecting the empire and guaranteeing their rights better than
they could. All sectors of the neftegna knew that their rights were
secure as long as the empire remained intact.

Chapter Nine describes the moves made by the military sector
of the neftegna class to silence both the colonized peoples and the
student intellectuals by presenting a Land Reform Proclamation
which had the ostensible purpose of satisfying all those who had
demanded "Land to the Tiller." The fundamental contradiction
embedded in this slogan finally emerged into open conflict during
the delayed implementation of the land reform program. By 1977
the ambiguity was eliminated. The interpretation of the colonizers
was upheld by the state. The land was not liberated, nor were the
production relations changed. The neftegna-gabbar relation was

The Invention of Ethiopia

systematically reinstituted through regulations imposed through the All-Ethiopia Peasant Association (AEPA). This was an effective ploy because this instrument was able to forcibly reorganize the peasant associations that had been established at local initiative. As these peasant associations became branches of AEPA throughout the colonized regions, the means of production was placed firmly back into the hands of the neftegna class. This occurred through a series of devices such as enforcing universal land redistribution, flushing out the former leadership and calling for repeated new elections in each association, dictating new use of labor time, multiplying taxes and introducing quotas for scores of government needs. Each of these reversed the steps that colonized peoples had taken to alter production relations. Consequently, each was vigorously resisted at the local level. In the two years since the local peasant associations had been formed, however, the military had turned to a new superpower patron and armed itself sufficiently to force the required changes upon the people. Henceforth, the land question and the national question came to be openly recognized as inseparable parts of one another, and "narrow nationalism" was denounced as treason. It was clear that nationalism threatened the economic base of the empire.

Initially intellectuals had encouraged the Derg to nationalize all the land and to declare that the land belongs to all "Ethiopians." This was done in the name of all the people. It was soon made clear that to oppose this scheme was to be "anti-Ethiopia." In advising this step, the new generation of intellectuals confirmed their prescribed role as protectors of their class interest. Their predecessors had advised other rulers in the same way.

Technically speaking, until the end of Haile Selassie's era, the lands occupied by Oromos and other conquered peoples belonged directly to the crown, and the inhabitants were officially subjects of the crown. Those in the colonies had never considered themselves to be and had never been treated as Ethiopians. It becomes significant to ask who then was the Derg referring to in the declaration on behalf of the Ethiopian people? Certainly not the people of the colonies. Of the Ethiopians Mengistu had said, "Where today *we* roll

Summary

tanks, tomorrow *we* will roll tractors!" This statement, of course, referred to the offensive war that real Ethiopians were waging against the resistant people of the colonies and to the long-range plan to uproot the people of the colonies for state-sponsored agricultural schemes. These schemes were organized to feed the real Ethiopians, i.e., the new neftegna who rallied behind the Derg.

A close look at the failure of Haile Selassie's government to implement properly the "free land grant" program sheds some light on the nature of the Derg's reform. According to the land grant proclamation issued under Haile Selassie, all people who had rendered services of some kind to the Ethiopian state were entitled to a reward of some government land. This program ran aground, however, because nearly 80 percent of the grants made went to high-ranking government personnel. The middle-ranking military was only one group which was entitled to land but in reality was barred from receiving it. What this category of potential beneficiaries really wanted was for the land to be equally divided among themselves. The Derg land reform was little more than a means by which the land grant program of Haile Selassie's regime could be implemented as it was originally intended.

Continued Expansion of the Neftegna Class Base

We have noted that the first oath that the Derg made to the neftegna ruling class in adopting the slogan "Ethiopia First" after stepping into power was to protect the empire from the "rebels" and "bandits" who threatened it. The Derg was committed to fight to keep neftegna property from being taken and to implement neftegna policies. Once the Derg had accomplished its first order of business, which was to exert control over the economic base of the empire, the way was clear to expand the political base by broadening the neftegna class itself. This proved not to be a complicated step because when the Derg took power, there was already a proposal on the books designed by Haile Selassie's government for a program of massive resettlement of northerners into colonial lands. The Derg

397

adopted it and implemented it, evicting many more indigenous people who resisted the plan, and forcing the remainder to serve the incoming settlers. By implementing this proposal, the Derg repeated a pattern that had been reinforced by Haile Selassie and, in so doing, further entrenched the production relations. Beginning from the late 1970s, almost all of those settlers who did arrive in the colonies (now called "nationalized lands") as part of this program, were forced to leave their homelands against their will, particularly those from Tigray and Wollo. These settlers were moved to lands falsely called virgin and unoccupied, terms which have come to mean in the Derg's vocabulary areas of the colonies that had not yet been tightly settled by the neftegna. The settlers have often been trained and armed by the government after they arrive in the new settlement site. Though these settlers did not choose their position initially, they have been offered one way out of the rigors of agricultural work in the settlements—that is to take up arms to use against the indigenous people. In the same fashion as neftegna settlers before them they are granted rights at the expense of the colonized peoples. It is quite likely that the Derg or a neftegna regime which follows the Derg, if the empire remains intact, will extend to these newly settled peoples rights of some kind in the lands where they have been settled. Such a move would give even these reluctant settlers a stake in the government and in the empire, providing for them a reason to defend it.

What the Derg really did with regard to resettlement was to execute what Ethiopian intellectuals as well as the usual foreign advisers had counseled Haile Selassie's government before them to do as part of the neftegna state's effort to defuse the national movements. They did the same thing with regard to other major branches of the state, be it in administrative policy, educational reform, or judiciary reform. No part of these programs that were initially introduced by the Derg in fact originated with or were designed by the Derg. Rather, all major "renovations" of the state were projects that had been in progress during the Haile Selassie regime. What differed from Haile Selassie's regime was the Derg's

Summary

"harsh" methods of implementation of the programs; they cleared away the obstacles that had stood in the way of Haile Selassie.

The Derg provided for a great expansion of the bureaucratic class—that group that is sustained by the state itself. Since the military committee had had no independent political/social base different from that which sustained Haile Selassie's administration, the inherited state itself quickly became the source of livelihood for those who showed great loyalty to the Derg. Ironically, such an expansion of the state machinery had been one of the demands made by the intellectuals who originally advised and supported the Derg before the Derg blocked their access to state power. Many of these intellectuals had aspired to move into executive positions as soon as the administrative buildings were cleared of the old guard whose presence had prevented them from achieving their career objectives earlier. The revolution was successful in clearing the offices. With the first group of intellectuals gone, the Derg nevertheless retained their model and trained their own loyal cadre as bureaucrats.

Many people observing the change of government from a distance supported the Derg believing that the change had transformed the life of all the people in the empire. Such people cite the land reform proclamation, the peasant associations, the National Democratic Revolution program, the constitution and the party as proof of revolution, social transformation, and democratization. Many have argued that the existence of a party organization provides the ideological basis for fundamental changes. Yet these same people do not focus on the ideological basis of the Derg's so-called party. It is true that the party of the Derg has an ideological basis, but it is not revolutionary, as onlookers assume it must be; it is the ideological basis of the neftegna or the colonialist.

The Question of Transformation

The Derg's government did not alter the relations of production that existed between the parts of the empire when it took power, rather it tightened the neftegna-gabbar relation and reinforced the

399

state institutions designed to protect it. Consequently, under Derg control there have been no changes that constitute transformation. What has happened is that the basic productive resources of the society that were once owned in monopoly form by their fathers are now collectively held by both established and newly added settler groups. Land reform must not be confused with transformation, as it often is. Whenever readjustment is made within a social formation to safeguard the interests of the dominant group, it is reform that has taken place, not transformation. The Derg's changes are classic examples of reform. Transformation occurs when the dominant social formation and its institutions give way to a new production relation enforced by new ideas and a new set of institutions.

It is important to note here that without a change in production relations in a way that systematically reverses what was put in place, transformation will never be realized. It is equally significant that transformation cannot come from a class that is a beneficiary of the dying order. Those who come forward from this group come not to change the production relation at work, but to maintain it. This is the group that arrives to help when the old order is about to die.

The inability of this category of people to bring fundamental change to a situation they may deplore has nothing to do with their will or desire to effect change. They cannot bring the change they want because they themselves are products of the old system; they do not possess a material or organizational basis separate enough from the dying order to provide the leverage necessary to dismantle it. In the case at hand, the neftegna are part and parcel of the Ethiopian system; they cannot transform it. Their position is dependent on the continued existence of the empire. Intellectuals, by contrast, are products of the state as a group, and for the most part come forward to breathe life into it. As individuals, however, they have the choice of allying with any of the contending classes.

Let us take a closer look at the character of these contending classes that are found in the empire. When writing about the February Upsurge of 1974 in Chapter Nine, we pointed out three categories of individuals who rallied around issues that were raised from within the society at the time when Haile Selassie's govern-

Summary

ment was brought down. The first was the issue of political economy that was raised by the Oromo, Eritrean, Sidama, Afar and Somali peoples, or, more simply put, raised by the colonies. The political issue was one of self-determination. The economic aspect was the liberation of the land—specifically the release of the land from the grip of the state—and the release of human resources, the labor, from the same grip.

The second group included those who raised a purely economic issue—the taxi cab drivers, the noncommissioned officers, the nurses, teachers, members of the labor union, etc. These had been affected by the inflation that had seized the world. They were wage earners who had not been paid on time, or those who demanded wage increases. Their issue was to gain some purchasing power within the existing state system.

The third group was comprised of those who raised a purely political issue. It was made up of the subdued nationalities, intellectuals who were products of the state moving forward to claim their positions in the bureaucracy, and students. They brought forward a number of political issues that were being poorly handled by the dying regime, the issue of land, of modernization, of freedom of assembly, the press, the national question, of feudalism, of bureaucratic capitalism, etc. They would raise any issue as long as it exposed the shortcomings of the old regime.

The second category, those demanding increased purchasing power, were easily and quickly satisfied. Even before it left office, the Aklilu government was able to appease the economic demands of this group. The solutions offered by the Derg could not satisfy the two remaining categories, those who raised political-economic issues and those who raised political issues. These two groups are once again standing in opposition to a government which has failed to silence or eliminate either category. One still demands a dismantling of the state. The Derg has expended more resources on fighting to keep them in the empire than it has expended on the populations who remained inside. They have only become stronger in resistance. The other group consists of variety of political factions, each identifying itself as Ethiopian, each laying a claim on

401

state power, each once again bringing forth any issue that is being poorly handled by the dying regime.

The Derg can accommodate neither of these politically. Each of the Ethiopian factions has sprung back to life, some even multiplying after the Derg systematically rejected them during the process of party formation. The procedure for forming the party increasingly narrowed the base for eligibility and did it so completely that it succeeded in eliminating or alienating all neftegna groups except Seded, which was the Derg's own creation. This process is coming back to haunt the Derg. The lack of credentials of the so-called Workers Party of Ethiopia has been exposed. It has become patently clear that the party does not hold either a social or economic base across the empire as a whole. It is also revealed that the Derg has not even managed to provide a vanguard role for the neftegna, the only existing empire-wide class that it could have represented.

The political groups who call themselves Ethiopian and who oppose the Derg each aspire to remove the Derg from power and take over control of the state apparatus. The reemergence of the EPRP (Ethiopian People's Revolutionary Party) and MEISON (All-Ethiopian Socialist Movement), EDU (Ethiopian Democratic Union) and several other groups, such as EPDM (Ethiopian Peoples Democratic Movement), EPDA (Ethiopian Peoples Democratic Alliance), and the alliance of EPDM and TPLF, is a direct consequence of the way that the party was formed. Their very existence serves as proof that the development of Seded, which became COPWE (Committee to Organize the Workers Party) and then WPE (Workers Party of Ethiopia) did not even achieve leadership within its own class. If it could not lead its own class, it cannot be surprising that it has been unable to lead the empire. Those who were alienated have come forward to take over the reins of the state. They criticize Mengistu and the Derg, but never the formula on which Ethiopia is founded.

The programs and tactics of the Ethiopian opposition groups for achieving a united Ethiopia, as well as their political philosophy, are based on changes that would take place after they have seized state power. These are most of the same groups who encouraged the military at the initial stages in 1974 to take over power at any cost.

402

Summary

Their position then was based on the same assumptions of wresting control from an evil regime in power in any way possible. Now portions of the same groups have revived in order to express the same desperate need to replace the Derg. They now publicly encourage even the liberation fronts to participate in an open season on trying to rally the population to support some kind of coalition government or "united front" that would be thus empowered to step into the same offices once held by the predecessor regimes. All of the Ethiopian factions still believe that change can (and should) come from the top. All claim historical responsibility to seize the state power of Ethiopia.

The colonized peoples have pursued their objective of liberation of their lands and people from the grip of colonial control along very different lines. From their vantage point in the colonies, the liberation fronts are leading the people to dismiss the state institutions of Ethiopia, not to seek to take them over. Consequently the national liberation movements of the colonies propose to implement alternative institutional forms that follow a new design, the design of the peoples' own independently developed values and ideas. They want nothing to do with the legacy of the colonial state. They have chosen to invest in a new infrastructure and to fashion a substitute.

As these two categories rise to express their demands, they find themselves facing each other from opposite poles, looking beyond the dying Derg regime. The liberation fronts and the Ethiopian (neftegna) organizations represent the colonized peoples and the colonizing system who confront each other still. Their conflict concerns the meaning of democracy and freedom and their respective visions of the future for the region and its peoples. The Ethiopian groups from their public statements do not seem to understand that the power behind the liberation wars is the power of subjected peoples unleashed through organizations that are wholly their own. Ethiopians are deeply divided over the national question. This needs to be assessed, not as a political threat, but as a practical reality.

For its part, the Derg has revealed through its political and military choices that it is deeply concerned with the threat posed to neftegna rule by the national liberation movements. What have been

The Invention of Ethiopia

referred to in the media as "coup attempts" have been in truth preemptive attacks by Mengistu made against any and all individuals remaining in his government or in his military organization who could possibly rally around themselves disaffected peoples from the conquered and annexed nations. These moves demonstrate his awareness of the relative power of the national groups who challenge the system he defends.

The Issue of Self-Determination

The national question cannot be ignored or absorbed by a neftegna state. At the heart of the national question lies the nature of the relations of production. The national question is raised both by cries of protest by subject nations against exploitation and by actions taken together by a people against whatever prevents them from realizing or practicing their nationhood. It is a matter raised by a people who act together as a unit, usually a people who share a common language, territory, economic life, and psychological make-up expressed through a common culture. Just as there are different forms of oppression, there are different strategies required for a nation to liberate itself from a subject position. In the case at hand, the place of particular nations within the unit of Ethiopia has been determined by how those nations were brought into the empire in the first place. In this difference lies the distinction between the conquered, annexed and subdued nations and nationalities in the empire. The differences in the form of solutions that each seek also lie here.

Nations that were first brought into the orbit of the empire through conquest were forced in because there was no other way to incorporate them. Their socioeconomic formation was so alien to the conqueror that there was no common ground upon which to base an attempt to assimilate or subdue them. Military conquest alone, however, would not ensure that the people and the resources of these nations would remain available to the conqueror. The conquered countries were occupied by agents of the conquering

Summary

system in order to impose new production relations by force of arms. Force was continued because the moral and political power of the conquered people's previous way of life continued to assert itself and overwhelm the conqueror's edicts. Ultimately, in order for a conquered region to be incorporated into a colonial system, the previously existing superstructure of the colonized region must be dismantled and replaced by the superstructure of the occupying force. It is this act added to the act of occupation that introduces colonial relations of production between the conquered and conquering systems. The national question among conquered peoples is a question of reasserting sovereignty over themselves and the means of production that were once wholly within their domain by reinstituting production relations free of external control.

Nations that were brought into the Ethiopian empire through annexation shared with the other colonized peoples the process of having their independently formed social formation placed in a subject relationship with the colonial system. Annexed nations such as those of Eritrea and Ogaden Somali have been politically rather than militarily defeated at the hands of the colonial system in league with superpower allies. In such cases, just as in the cases of conquered nations, the superstructure of the colonial system is imposed on them by military force with the colonizer's attempt to destroy their independent basis for asserting sovereignty. Henceforth the exercise of control over the colonized nations, whether brought into the empire by conquest or by annexation, is the same. The solution for the national question raised by annexed nations in Ethiopia is also the assertion and defense of their own social formation—one fashioned outside the control of the Ethiopian state—with the objective of putting it forward to replace the colonial superstructure and the colonial relations of production that had been imposed on their nation by force.

In the case of subdued nations such as Tigray, the oppressor and the oppressed groups share several key institutional forms. Although the subdued nation has been discriminated against, repressed and thwarted in achieving its ambitions as a people, the institutional matrix within which they function as a people is not destroyed. The

The Invention of Ethiopia

ruling nation cannot and will not destroy and replace the institutions of these subdued nations as it did in the conquered and annexed nations because in the case of the subdued, the oppressor and oppressed share the same basic norms, values and beliefs. Since they have common institutions, if the dominant nation tried to destroy the superstructure of the subdued nations, it would amount to destroying its own social structure and inflicting damage upon its own ruling system. The dominant system did not have something wholly alien to impose upon the subdued in order to completely disenfranchise and totally control them. The position of a subdued nation in many ways resembles the position of a subordinate class within Abyssinia. The reason that the Shoan became capable of oppressing the Tigray within Abyssinia was that the Europeans ultimately favored the Shoans in assisting them to conquer the Oromo and other neighboring nations.

The current resistance against the government of the Ethiopian state from among colonized peoples who were first conquered emanates from the event of the conquest itself and the forcible rearrangement of the relations of production. At the time of the conquest, previously flourishing cultures attached to specific systems of production were forced underground. Despite several sustained efforts to assimilate these peoples into an Ethiopian nationality, the deposed cultures continued to flourish in hibernation, generating, informing, invigorating, and nourishing alternative forms of socioeconomic organization. It is from the strength of these militarily defeated but not destroyed cultures that the indigenous peoples put forward institutions to replace those of the Ethiopian state. These suppressed cultures have functioned as seedbeds for generating institutional designs shaped by values and an ideology fundamentally distinct from that embodied in the structure of the Ethiopian state. Self-determination for these nations would constitute a move to organize and govern their society according to these values. Such a move would represent a revolutionary transformation of the relations of production in the empire.

The key to resistance among nations that were colonized by annexation is that prior to annexation they established the social

Summary

basis upon which they are constructing an institutional matrix wholly distinct from that of the Ethiopian. Nourishing this gives them an alternative structure through which to achieve a transformation in their relations of production.

Since the relations of production in the subdued nations do not change upon their loss of rights, their systems retain many important aspects of the superstructure that they share with the ruling system. This position leaves open the opportunity for the subdued nations to seek an internal solution to their oppression. Indeed, the Tigray want to solve their problem by achieving full democratic rights within Ethiopia. They have some basis for reconciliation and a ground upon which to reform the system that they share with other Abyssinians.

Whoever seeks to contribute to peace in this empire, whether through political, humanitarian, or business involvement, must do so taking these fundamental issues into account and addressing them directly. Rather than postponing the key issues through ambiguous slogans and exploiting the confusion of various participants in order to step into power, what is needed is a clear, hard look at and recognition of the real demands of colonized peoples. The challenge of the colonized peoples to the Haile Selassie regime was the major cause of that regime's downfall; likewise their challenge to the Derg's government has rendered that regime bankrupt and paranoid. This same challenge will undermine any regime that follows the Derg in an attempt to patch up and defend the settler colonial state. The issue of the colonized peoples has plagued and will continue to plague all supporters of Ethiopia who choose to dismiss or disregard it.

The colonial relations that exist among the parts of the empire lie at the heart of the conflict and crisis in the Ethiopian empire. Until these relations that hold the empire together are dismantled and replaced with those of the peoples' choosing, there will be no peace in this region.

BIBLIOGRAPHY

These listings have been prepared to reflect the fact that for most people of Northeast Africa the primary name for identification is the first name. Therefore, for example, Alemitu Ibsa is identified according to Alemitu under A rather than Ibsa under I.

Abir, Mordechai
1968   Ethiopia: the Era of the Princes. The Challenge of Islam and the Re-unification of the Christian Empire, 1769-1855. New York: Frederick A Preager

1980   Ethiopia and the Red Sea. London: Frank Cass

Alemitu Ibsa, et. al.
1970   Work-Oriented Adult Literacy Project, Ethiopia Family Living Survey: Wonji, Shoa. Addis Ababa: IEG/UNDP-SF/UNESCO

1989   Interview regarding the scope and continuity of Work-Oriented Adult Literacy project. October, Washington, D.C.

Alula Abate and Tesfaye Teklu
1980   "Land Reform and Peasant Associations in Ethiopia: a Case Study of Two Widely-Differing Regions," Northeast African Studies, II(2): 1-51

Anderson, Perry
1962   "Portugal and the End of Ultra-Colonialism," New Left Review III (6): 83-102, (16): 88-123, (17): 85-114

Bibliography

Aren, Gustav
1978   Evangelical Outreach in Ethiopia: Origins of the
                     Evangelical Church Mekane Yesus. Uppsala: Studia
                     Missionalia Upsaliensia XXXII

Arrighi, Emmanuel
1972   Unequal Exchange. New York: Monthly Review Press

Asiwaju, A. I. (editor)
1985   Partitioned Africans: Ethnic Relations Across Africa's
                     International Boundaries, 1884-1984. New York: St.
                     Martin's Press

Ayoob, Mohammed
1978   The Horn of Africa: Regional Conflict and Superpow-
                     er Involvement. Canberra: Australian National Uni-
                     versity

Babu, Abdul Rahman Mohamed
1981   African Socialism or Socialist Africa? London: Zed
                     Press

Bailey, Sydney D.
1963   The United Nations: A Short Political Guide. New
                     York: Frederick A. Praeger, Publisher

1964   The General Assembly of the United Nations: A
                     Study of Procedure and Practice, Revised Edition.
                     New York: Frederick A. Praeger, Publisher

Bairoch, Paul (translation by Cynthia Postan)
1977   The Economic Development of the Third World
                     Since 1900. Berkeley and Los Angeles: University of
                     California Press

Baran, Paul A. and Paul M. Sweezey
1966   Monopoly Capital: An Essay on the American Eco-
                     nomic and Social Order. New York and London:
                     Monthy Review Press

Baxter, P. T. W.
1978   "Ethiopia's Unacknowledged Problem: the Oromo,"
                     African Affairs 77 (308): 283-296

Bender, Gerald J., James Coleman and Richard Sklar (editors)
1985   African Crisis Areas and U. S. Foreign Policy. Berke-
                     ley: University of California Press

410

Bibliography

Benns, F. Lee
1954   Europe Since 1914: In its World Setting: New York:
                        Appleton-Century Crofts, Inc.

Bereket Habte Selassie
1980   Conflict and Intervention in the Horn of Africa. New
                        York and London: Monthly Review Press

1988   "Empire and Constitutional Engineering: The PDRE
                        in Historical Perspective," In Proceedings of the
                        Third International Conference on the Horn of
                        Africa, pp. 88-103. New York: Center for the Study of
                        the Horn of Africa

1989   Eritrea and the United Nations and Other Essays.
                        Trenton, NJ: The Red Sea Press

Berry, Sara S.
1985   Fathers Work for Their Sons: Accumulation, Mobility
                        and Class Formation in an Extended Yoruba Com-
                        munity. Berkeley: University of California Press

Betts, Raymond F. (editor)
1966   The Scramble for Africa: Causes and Dimensions of
                        Empire. Lexington, Massachusetts: D. C. Heath and
                        Company

Bukharin, Nikoklai
1973   Imperialism and World Economy. New York and
                        London: Monthly Review Press

Cabral, Amilcar
1973   Return to the Source. New York: Monthly Review
                        Press

Carr, E. H.
1971   Foundations of a Planned Economy, 1926-29. Volume
                        II. New York: The Macmillan Company

Cerulli, Enrico
1922   The Folk-Literature of the Galla of Southern Abyssin-
                        ia. Harvard African Studies III. Cambridge, Mass.

Clapham, Chistopher
1988   Transformation and Continuity in Revolutionary
                        Ethiopia. Cambridge, England: Cambridge Unversity
                        Press

Bibliography

Clay, Jason W. and Bonnie K. Holcomb
1986   Politics and the Ethiopian Famine 1984-1985. Cambridge, Massachusetts: Cultural Survival and Trenton, NJ: The Red Sea Press

Clay, Jason W., Sandra Steingraber and Peter Niggli
1988   The Spoils of Famine: Ethiopian Famine Policy and Peasant Agriculture. Cambridge, Massachusetts: Cultural Survival

Cohen, John M.
1985   "Foreign Involvement in the Formulation of Ethiopia's Land Tenure Policies: Part I and II," Northeast African Studies VII (2) & VII (3): 1-20

Cohen, John M. and Nils-Ivar Isaksson
1987   Villagization in the Arsi Region of Ethiopia. Rural Development Studies No. 19. Uppsala: International Rural Development Center

Cohen, John M. and Peter Koehn
1980   Ethiopian Provincial and Municipal Government: Imperial patterns and Postrevolutionary Changes. East Lansing, Michigan: African Studies Center, Michigan State University

Cohen, John M. and Dov Weintraub
1975   Land and Peasants in Imperial Ethiopia: the Social Background to a Revolution. Assen: Van Gorcum

Committee of the Founding of the People's Democratic Republic of Ethiopia
1987   Ethiopia From Feudal Autocracy to People's Democracy. Addis Ababa: PDRE

Crummey, Donald
1972   Priests and Politicians: Protestant and Catholic Missions in Orthodox Ethiopia 1830-1868. Oxford: Oxford University Press

Crummey, Donald (editor)
1986   Banditry, Rebellion and Social Protest in Africa. London: James Currey and Portsmouth, NH: Heinemann

1986   "Banditry and Resistance: Noble and Peasant in Nineteenth-Century Ethiopia," In Crummey (editor), pp. 133-149

Bibliography

Darkwah, R. H. Kofi
1975   Shewa, Menilik, and the Ethiopian Empire, 1813-1889. London: Heinemann

Davidson, Basil, Lionel Cliffe and Bereket Habte Selassie (eds.)
1980   Behind the War in Eritrea. Nottingham: Spokesman Press

Dawit Wolde Giorgis
1989   Red Tears: War, Famine and Revolution in Ethiopia. Trenton, NJ: The Red Sea Press, Inc.

Debebe Hurissie
1987   Transition from Haile Selassie's to Derg's Rule. Interview. Washington, D. C.

Dessalegn Rahmato
1985   "The Ethiopian Experience in Agrarian Reform," In Fassil G. Kiros (editor), pp. 197-224

Ellis, Gene
1976   "The Feudal Paradigm as a Hindrance to Understanding Ethiopia," Journal of Modern African Studies XIV (2): 275-295

Engels, Frederick (edited by Eleanor Burke Leacock)
1978   The Origin of the Family, Private Property and the State. New York: International Publishers

Eshetu Chole and Teshome Mulat
1984   Land Settlement in Ethiopia: a Review of Developments. December, Unpublished MS

Fassil G. Kiros (editor)
1985   Challenging Rural Poverty: Experiences in Institution-Building and Popular Participation for Rural Development in Eastern Africa. Trenton, NJ: Africa World Press

Fernyhough, Timothy
1986   "Social Mobility and Dissident Elites in Northern Ethiopia: The Role of Bandits, 1900-69," In Crummey (editor), pp. 151-177

Gadaa Melbaa
1980   Oromia: a Brief Introduction. Finfinne, Oromia

413

Bibliography

Garretson, Peter
1980   "Ethiopia's Telephone and Telegraph System, 1897-1935," Northeast African Studies II (1): 59-71

Gartley, John
1984   "The Utilization of Communications Technology During the Reign of Menelik II," In Rubenson (editor): 297-300

Gebru Tereke
1977   Rural Protest in Ethiopia 1941-1970: A Study of Three Rebellions. Unpublished Ph.D. Dsstn, Syracuse University. (see especially, "The Rebellion in Bale," pp. 227-351)

Getahun Dilebo
1974   Emperor Menelik's Ethiopia, 1865-1916: National Unification or Amhara Communal Domination? Unpublished Ph.D. Disstn. Howard Unversity, Washington, D.C.

Gilkes, Patrick
1975   The Dying Lion: Feudalism and Modernization in Ethiopia.New York: St. Martin's Press

Gilmour, T. Lennox
1906   Abyssinia: The Ethiopian Railway and the Powers. London: Alston Rivers, Ltd.

Gramsci, Antonio (translated by John Mathews)
1977   Antonio Gramsci Selections from Political Writings 1910-1920. New York: International Publishers

Greenfield, Richard
1965   Ethiopia: A New Political History. London: Pall Mall Press

1982   Paper presented to the Conference on Oromo in the Horn of Africa. Minneapolis, MN, November

Haile Selassie (translated and annotated by Edward Ullendorf)
1976   My Life and Ethiopia's Progress 1892-1937. Oxford, England: Oxford University Press

1967   Selected Speeches. Addis Ababa: Haile Selassie University Press

Bibliography

Halliday, Fred and Maxine Molyneux
1981   The Ethiopian Revolution. London: New Left Re-
                        view, Verso Edition

Hamer, John H.
1987   Humane Development: Participation and Change
                        among the Sidama of Ethiopia. Tuscaloosa: The
                        University of Alabama Press

Harbeson, John
1988   The Ethiopian Transformation: the Quest for the
                        Post-Imperial State. Boulder and London: Westview
                        Press

Harris, W. Cornwallis
1844   Adventures in Africa. Philadelphia: T. B. Peterson

Harris, Myles F.
1987   Breakfast in Hell: a Doctor's Eyewitness Account of
                        the Politics of Hunger in Ethiopia. New York: Posei-
                        don Press

Heiden, Linda
1978   "The Eritrean Struggle for Independence," Monthly
                        Review 30 (2)

Hess, Robert (editor)
1978   Proceedings of the Fifth International Conference on
                        Ethiopian Studies, Session B. Chicago: Office of
                        Publications Services University of Illinois at Chicago
                        Circle

Hoben, Allan
1973   Land Tenure among the Amhara of Ethiopia: the
                        Dynamics of Cognitive Descent. Chicago and Lon-
                        don: University of Chicago Press

Hobsbawm, E. J.
1975   The Age of Capital 1848-1875. London: Weidenfeld
                        and Nicolson Ltd.

Hobson, J. A.
1938 (orig. 1902)   Imperialism: a Study. Ann Arbor: University of Michi-
                        gan Press

Holcomb, Bonnie K. and Sisai Ibssa
n.d.   Examining the Bases of Self-Determination. Work in
                        progress

Bibliography

Huntingford, G. W. B.
1962   "The Constitutional History of Ethiopia," Journal of
                          African History III (2): 311-315

K. Teferi
1987   Events in the Ethiopian Royal Court during Tefari's
                          Rise to Power. Interview given in Washington, D.C.

Keller, Edmond J.
1988   Revolutionary Ethiopia. Bloomington: Indiana Uni-
                          versity Press

Keller, Edmond J. and Donald Rothchild (editors)
1987   Afro-Marxist Regimes: Ideology and Public Policy.
                          Boulder, CO: Lynne Rienner Publishers

Kennedy, Paul
1987   The Rise and Fall of the Great Powers: Economic
                          Change and Military Conflict from 1500 to 2000.
                          New York: Random House

Laitin, David D. and Said S. Samatar
1987   Somalia: Nation in Search of a State. Boulder, CO:
                          Westview Press

Lefort, Rene
1983   Ethiopia: An Heretical Revolution? London: Zed
                          Press

Lenin, V. I.
1972   What is to Be Done? Burning Questions of Our
                          Movement. New York: International Publishers

1968   National Liberation, Socialism and Imperialism:
                          Selected Writings. New York: International Publishers

1939 (orig. 1917)   Imperialism, the Highest Stage of Capitalism. New
                          York: International Publishers

1971   Selected Works. Moscow: Progress Publishers

Levine, Donald
1965   Wax and Gold: Tradition and Innovation in Ethiopian
                          Culture. Chicago and London: University of Chicago
                          Press

1974   Greater Ethiopia: the Evolution of a Multiethnic
                          Society.Chicago and London: University of Chicago
                          Press

Bibliography

Louis, Wm. Roger
1978   Imperialism at Bay: the United States and the Decolonization of the British Empire, 1941-1945. New York: Oxford University Press

Lubee Birru
1980   Background to the Development of the Macha-Tulama: an Eyewitness Account. Interview given March 14-5

Mahoney, Richard D.
1983   JFK: Ordeal in Africa. New York: Oxford University Press

Marcus, Harold
1969   "Motives, Methods and Some Results of the Unification of Ethiopia during the Reign of Menelik II," Proceedings of the Third International Conference of Ethiopian Studies, Addis Ababa, 1966, pp. 269-280. Addis Ababa: Institute of Ethiopian Studies, Haile Sellassie University

1975   The Life and Times of Menelik II: Ethiopian 1844-1913. Oxford: Clarendon Press

1983   Ethiopia, Great Britain, and the United States, 1941-1974. Berkeley, Los Angeles, and London: University of California Press

1987   Haile Sellassie I: the Formative Years, 1892-1936. Berkeley, Los Angeles, London: University of California Press

Markakis, John
1974   Ethiopia: Anatomy of a Traditional Polity. Oxford: Clarendon Press

Markakis, John and Nega Ayele
1978   Class and Revolution in Ethiopia. Nottingham: Spokesman Press

Marx, Karl
1964   The Class Struggle in France (1848-1850). New York: International Publishers

1964   The 18th Brumaire of Louis Bonaparte. New York: International Publishers

Bibliography

1970   A Contribution to the Critique of Political Economy. New York: International Publishers

1974   Capital, Vols. I-III: a Critical Analysis of Capitalist Production. Moscow: Progress Publishers

Marx, Karl (edited and with an introduction by Eric J. Hobsbawm)
1972   Pre-Capitalist Economic Formations. New York: International Publishers

McClellan, Charles
1978   "Perspectives on the Neftenya-Gabbar System: the Example of Darasa," Africa 33.

1979   Reactions to Ethiopian Expansionism: the Case of Darasa, 1895-1935. Unpublished Ph.D. Dissertation: Michigan State University

1980   "Land, Labor and Coffee: the South's Role in Ethiopian Self-Reliance 1889-1935," African Economic History 9: 69-83

1983   State Expansionism and Social Reconstruction in Ethiopia: the Lure of the South. Paper delivered to the African Studies Association, Boston, MA. November

Mekuria Bulcha
1984   The Social and Economic Foundations of the Oromo States of the Nineteenth Century: Social Differentiation and State Formation among the Macha Oromo, circ. 170-1900. Hanledare: Goran Ahrme

1988   Flight and Integration: Causes of Mass Exodus from Ethiopia and Problems of Integration in the Sudan. Uppsala: Scandinavian Institute of African Studies

Mohammed Hassen
1990   The Oromo of Ethiopia: a History 1570-1850. Cambridge: Cambridge University Press

Morris-Jones, W. H. and Georges Fischer
1980   Decolonization and After: the British and French Experience. London and Totowa, NJ: Frank Cass

M'Quera, James
1968   The Journals of C. W. Isenberg and J. L. Krapf in the Years 1839, 1840, 1841, and 1842. London: Frank Cass

Bibliography

Mulatu Wubneh and Yohannis Abate
1988   Ethiopia: Transition and Development in the Horn of Africa. Boulder, Colorado, Avebury and London: Westview Press

Murdock, George Peter
1959   Africa: Its Peoples and Thier Culture History. New York: McGraw-Hill

Nagaso Gidada
1982   "Oromo Historical Poems and Songs: Conquest and Exploitation in Western Wallaga, 1886-1927," Horn of Africa V (3): 32-40

New African
1982   "The Military in Africa," October issue, 48-51

Niggli, Peter
1985   Ethiopia: Deportation and Enforced-Labor Camps, Doubtful Methods in the Struggle Against Famine. Berlin: Berliner Missionswerk

Norberg, Viveca Halldin
1977   Swedes in Haile Selassie's Ethiopia, 1924-1952: a Study in Early Development Co-operation. Uppsala: Scandinavian Institute of African Studies

Ottaway, David and Marina
1981   Afrocommunism. New York: Africana Publishing Company

Ottaway, Marina
1987   "State Power Consolidation in Ethiopia," In Keller, Edmond J. and Donald Rothchild (editors), pp. 25-42

Ottaway, Marina and David
1978   Ethiopia: Empire in Revolution. New York: Africana Publishing Company

Oromo Liberation Front
1979-present   Oromia Speaks. OLF, Box 1830, Khartoum, Sudan

Payer, Cheryl
1974   The Debt Trap: the International Monetary Fund and the Third World. New York and London: Monthly Review Press

1982   The World Bank: a Critical Analysis. New York: Monthly Review Press

Bibliography

Pankhurst, Richard
1961   Introduction to the Economic History of Ethiopia: From Early Time to 1800. Lalibela, Ethiopia: Lalibela House

1967   "Menelik and the Utilization of Foreign Skills in Ethiopia," Journal of Ehiopian Studies V (1) 29-86

1968   Economic History of Ethiopia, 1800-1935. Addis Ababa, Ethiopia: Haile Sellassie University Press

Pearce, R. D.
1982   The Turning Point in Africa: British Colonial Policy 1938-48. London and Totowa, NJ: Frank Cass

Peoples' Democratic Republic of Ethiopia (PDRE)
1987   Report of the Provisional Military Administrative Council. Addis Ababa, Ethiopia

Perham, Margery
1948   The Government of Ethiopia. London: Faber and Faber

1969   The Government of Ethiopia, Second Edition. Evanston: Northwestern University Press

Prouty, Chris
1986   Empress Taytu and Menilik II: Ethiopia 1883-1910. London: Ravens Educational and Development Services and Trenton: The Red Sea Press

Robinson, James Harvey and Charles H. Beard
1908   The Development of Modern Europe: an Introduction to the Study of Current History; Volume II, Europe Since the Congress of Vienna. Boston, New York, Chicago, London: Ginn and Company

Robinson, Ronald and John Gallagher with Alice Denny
1961   Africa and the Victorians: the Official Mind of Imperialism. London: The Macmillan Press, Ltd

Rosenfeld, Chris Prouty
1978   The Medical History of Menelik II, Emperor of Ethiopia (1844-1913): a Case of Medical Diplomacy. Munger Africana Library Notes Issue 45/46. Pasadena: California Institute of Technology

Bibliography

Rubenson, Sven
1966   King of Kings: Tewodros of Ethiopia. Addis Ababa:
               Haile Sellassie University Press
1976   The Survival of Ethiopian Independence. London:
               Heinemann

Rubenson, Sven (editor)
1984   Proceedings of the Seventh International Conference
               of Ethiopian Studies, University of Lund, 26-29 April
               1982. Addis Ababa: Institute of Ethiopian Studies

Salmon, E. T.
1970   Roman Colonization Under the Republic. Ithaca,
               New York: Cornell University Press

Sbacchi, Alberto
1985   Ethiopia under Mussolini: Fascisim and the Colonial
               Experience. London: Zed Books Ltd.

Schwab, Peter
1985   Ethiopia: Politics, Economics and Society. Boulder,
               CO.: Lynne Rienner Publishers

Scott, George
1973   The Rise and Fall of the League of Nations. New
               York: Macmillan and Company, Inc.

Shepard, Jack
1975   The Politics of Starvation. Washington, D.C.: Carne-
               gie Endowment for International Peace

Sidama Liberation Front
1982   Political Program. Mimeographed Typescript

Singer, Norma J.
1978   "Ethiopia: Human Rights, 1948-1978," In Robert
               Hess (editor), pp. 663-678

Skinner, Robert P.
1906   Abyssinia of Today: an Account of the First Mission
               Sent by the American Government to the Court of
               the King of Kings (1903-1904). New York: Long-
               mans, Green and Company

Smith, Tony (editor)
1975   The End of the European Empire: Decolonization
               after World War II. Lexington, Massachusetts, To-
               ronto, London: D.C. Heath and Company

421

Bibliography

Solomon Inquai
1981   "The Hidden Revolution in Tigray," Horn of Africa Journal IV (3): 27-31

Spencer, John H.
1984   Ethiopia at Bay: a Personal Account of the Haile Sellassie Years. Algonac, Michigan: Reference Publications, Inc.

Stahl, Michal
1974   Ethiopia: Political Contradictions in Agricultural Development. New York: Africana Publishing Company

1978   New Seeds in Old Soil: a Study of the Land Reform Process in Western Wollega, Ethiopia, 1975-76. Uppsala: The Scandinavian Institute of Arican Studies

Tamane Bitama
1983   "On Some Oromo Historical Poems," Paideuma 29: 317-325

Thesiger, Wilfred
1912   Report submitted from Addis Ababa to Sir Edward Grey, British Foreign Office. London: British Archives FO 371/1571

1913   Report submitted from Addis Ababa to Sir Edward Grey, British Foreign Office. London: British Archives

Thomson, David
1957   Europe Since Napoleon. New York: Alfred A. Knopf

Trevaskis, G. K. N.
1960   Eritrea: A Colony in Transition 1941-1952. London: Oxford University Press

Triulzi, Alessandro
1980   "Social Protest and Rebellion in Some Gabbar Songs from Qellam, Wallagga," In Tubiana, J. (editor)

Trimingham, J. Spencer
1952   Islam in Ethiopia. Oxford: Oxford University Press

Tubiana, J. (editor)
1980   Proceedings of the Fifth International Conference of Ethiopian Studies, Session A. Rotterdam: Balkema

Bibliography

Ullendorf, Edward
1973   The Ethiopians: An Introduction to Country and People, Third Edition. London, Oxford, New York: Oxford University Press

Union of Oromo in North America
1976-present   Waldhaansso. UONA, Box 21044, Washington, D.C.

Vanderheym, J. G.
1896   Une Expédition avec Negous Menelik. Paris: Librarie Hachette et Cie

Waugh, Evelyn
1936   Waugh in Abyssinia. London: Longmans
1931   Remote People: a Report from Ethiopia and British Africa, 1930-31. London: Penguin Books (reissued 1985)

Winks, Robin W. (editor)
1969   The Age of Imperialism. Englewood Cliffs, NJ: Prentice-Hall, Inc.

Wood, Adrian
1973   Resettlement in Illubabor. Liverpool, England: University of Liverpool
1983   "Rural Development and National Integration in Ethiopia," African Affairs 82 (329): 509-539

Woolf, Leonard S.
1919   Empire and Commerce in Africa. London: Allen and Unwin

Work, Ernest
1935   Ethiopia, a Pawn in European Diplomacy. New York: The Macmillan Company

Workers' Party of Ethiopia
1988   The Sole Truth and Only Solution. Addis Ababa: PDRE

Wylde, Augustus B.
1901   Modern Abyssinia. London: Methuen and Co.

INDEX

Abbay River 96, 122; see also Blue Nile
Abbiccu Oromo 288
Abd el Kadir Kabira, Abd el-Kadir Kebire 306, 309
absentee landlords 268, 323, 347
Abu Bakr 165
Abuna 80, 137 Abuna Mattewos 150, 153, 164
Abyotawit Seded 373; see also Seded
Abyssinia 1-11, 23, 32, 34, 36-38, 59, 74-76, 78-80, 82-85, 87-90, 92, 94, 99-102, 106, 107, 112, 117-119, 122, 126, 128-131, 133, 135-137, 139, 155, 161, 164, 171, 173, 178, 192, 201, 209, 233, 234, 236, 240, 242, 248, 257, 272, 280-283, 304, 305, 316, 321, 322, 388, 405 Abyssinian confederation 74, 92 Abyssinian heartland 10, 145, 189, 207, 209
Abyssinian kingdoms 1, 3, 6, 79, 84, 87, 88, 91, 99, 101, 135, 316 see also Gondar (Bege-meder), Gojjam, Manz, and Tigray
Abyssinian Somaliland see Ogaden 301
Adal, Adalites 95, 162, 165; see also Afar
Adal, Adel Ras 95
Addis Ababa, Addis Abeba 94, 98, 102, 104-107, 127, 140, 146, 156-158, 160, 162, 165, 169, 176, 178, 180-182, 196, 201, 224, 230, 246, 270, 271, 294, 297, 299, 325, 326, 330, 332, 333, 335, 349, 351, 381
Aden 93, 301
Ader see Waz League
administrator, adminstrators 55, 66, 113, 115, 117, 128, 160, 203, 207, 288, 360-364
adviser, advisers 9, 15, 25, 65, 77, 90, 94-96, 98, 102, 125, 128, 136, 141, 156, 163, 176-77, 185-187, 204, 215, 219, 222-225, 227, 229, 231, 234, 236, 243, 246, 247, 249, 265, 268, 272, 276, 283, 310, 319, 321,

Index

340, 342, 353-355, 359, 366, 386, 390, 397
Adwa, Battle of 7, 8, 106, 112, 126, 131, 136, 137, 192
Afa Negus 241
Afar, Afar people 3, 159, 276, 280, 301, 304-306, 344, 400
Afar Liberation Front 306, 344
Afar sultanate 305
Afghans 137, 138
African Orientale Italiana (AOI) 195
agencies 60-64, 228, 368
agrarian reform 367, 369,
agribusiness 256
agriculture 60, 130, 140, 197, 236, 262, 263, 266, 270, 323, 365, 390
Agriculture and Development Bank of Ethiopia 262
agropastoral 121
Air Force 249, 333, 334, 373
air transport 256
Aklilu Habte Wold, Prime Minister 254, 334, 400
Alaba 299
Albania 50
Alem Zewde Tassemma, Colonel 335
Alemaya 270
Alemou Kitessa 298
Alexandria 93
ALF see Afar Liberation Front
Algeria, Algiers 33, 41
Ali I 74, 83
Ali II, Ras 74, 75, 80-82, 89
Ali Mirah 305, 306
Ali the Great 74, 83

All-Ethiopia Peasant Association (AEPA) 360, 362, 363, 368, 374, 395
All-Ethiopia-Trade-Union 350
All-Ethiopian Socialist Movement see MEISON
Allah 165
Allied powers, Allies 15, 45, 50, 52, 54, 68, 157, 161, 162, 167, 211, 217, 220, 233, 306, 307, 328, 353, 404
America 28, 31, 32, 52, 57, 202, 217, 218, 222, 224, 225, 229, 247, 252, 253, 261, 326
American 28, 35, 56-59, 138, 176, 182, 215, 216, 218, 219, 222-227, 233, 236, 247, 250, 253, 254, 257, 258, 260, 262, 268, 269, 289, 293, 310
American advisers 215
American colony 28
American cotton 58
Amhara, Amhara people 8, 10, 81, 85, 90, 103, 109, 110, 113, 117, 118, 128, 143, 145, 148, 150, 152, 195, 196, 207, 210, 247, 271, 285, 287, 292, 293, 294, 302, 315, 316, 318, 321, 344, 364, 384
Amhara hegemony 10, 247
Amharic, Amharic language 106, 108, 113, 119, 128, 129, 165, 187, 196, 245, 263, 267, 268, 272, 274, 292, 299, 364, 373, 391
Amharization 247, 272
Andreone 123

Index

Anglo-Ethiopian agreements 204, 206, 210, 215, 220-222, 224, 231, 241, 253

Angola 33, 37, 39

annexation, annexed nations and territories 3, 234, 235, 237, 257, 271, 280, 283, 303, 310, 312, 315, 344, 381, 387 403-405

anti-Ethiopia, as a political label 382, 395

anti-imperialist behavior of Iyasu 160

anti-Oromo stance of Kassa (Tewodoros) 82

Arabic 158, 165, 197

Arabs 136, 138

Arero 110

aristocracy 113, 135, 139, 146-148, 172, 209, 264, 265, 268, 346, 347,

Armenians 136, 138

Arnoux 93, 94

Arsi Oromo, Arussi 105, 152, 287, 289, 291; see also Oromo people

Asia, Asian 28, 32, 50, 199

Asmara 250, 258, 270, 309, 333, 334

Assab 93, 122, 182, 304, 308

assimilation 10, 19, 291, 292, 364

atbia 363

Atlantic Charter 52, 202

Atnafu Abate 335

Australia 32, 33

Austria 30, 40, 42, 43, 161

Austria-Hungary 40, 42, 161

Austro-Prussian War 30

autonomy, national 121, 131, 155, 195, 315-318, 380, 381

AVA see Awash Valley Authority

awaraja, awraja, awarajas 121, 174, 175, 181, 207, 237, 239, 360, 361, 363, 374   function as fiefdoms 174

Awasa 299

Awash River 96, 98, 110, 123, 124, 263, 264, 365, 390

Awash Valley Authority (AVA) 263, 265, 365, 390

Axis powers 194, 202, 203, 216, 226, 231, 306

Axum, Axumites 75, 80, 82, 101

Ayshal, Battle of 82

Azebo-Raya 290, 293

Azores 33

Ba'uchis 138

Baffana 95, 96

Bakare, Bakere 286, 305

Bako 299

balabat, balabatship 120, 174, 175, 208, 237, 238, 361, 363

balance of power 5, 29-31, 34, 36, 39, 40, 43, 44, 46, 50, 51, 56, 58, 73, 149, 191, 193, 194, 203, 216, 217

Bale 262, 289, 293-295

Balkan, Balkans 38, 41, 47, 50

bandits see shifta

Bank of Abyssinia 128, 137

Baro Tumsa 373

Bartleet 182

Bashillo River 96

Begemeder 82, 168

Bekele Mekonnen 298

Index

Belgian Military Mission 249

Belgium 23, 34-37, 44-46, 49, 59, 78

Beni Shangul 182

Berlin 34, 36, 41, 103, 191, 194, 219

Berlin Congress 34, 36

Beshah Wired 87

Beyene, Dejazmatch 167

Bezzabbeh, Bezzabboh, Bezzabeh 83, 88, 89

Bianchi 123

Bible 76, 253

Big Five, big powers 22, 35, 42, 48, 49, 54, 217, 220, 229, 232, 234

Birru Aligaz 81

Birru Goshu 81

Bismarck 34

Blowers, George, American governor of the State Bank of Ethiopia 223, 224

Blue Nile 1, 73, 122, 125 see also Abbay river, Nile

Boer War 39

Bonaparte, Bonapartism 30, 39

Book of Laws 239, 240

booty, taken at conquest 63, 101, 104, 105, 379

Borana, Borena 110, 152

bourgeois, bourgeoisie 29-32, 43, 67, 251, 267, 269, 270, 362, 376-379, , 381, 391

bridge, bridges 40, 98, 122-124, 134, 180, 182

Britain 242, 249, 250, 254, 290, 301, 303, 306, 308

Britain, British, Britons 6, 7, 8, 11, 12, 28, 30, 32-42, 44, 46, 49, 50, 52-59, 68, 72, 73, 78, 79, 84-87, 90, 91, 98, 102, 105, 124-127, 129, 131, 137-139, 145, 146, 155, 159, 161, 175, 181, 182, 189, 192-194, 197-211, 215-219, 221-225, 229, 232, 234-237, 239, 241, 243, 244, 246, 247, 249, 254, 256, 258, 263, 283, 293, 301-304, 306, 308, 309, 312

British empire 56, 202

British Commonwealth 46, 198, 199, 203

British reinstatement of Haile Selassie, "liberation" of Ethiopia 215

British Somaliland 235, 301

Bulgarians 138

Bure 181

bureaucracy, bureaucratic 15, 60, 135, 173-175, 183, 195, 207, 210, 213, 225, 236-239, 255, 264, 267, 268, 276, 319, 332, 363, 367, 368, 387, 398, 400

bureaucratic bourgeoisie 267

Burma 33

Butler, R. A., British foreign minister 219

CADU see Chilao Agriculture Development Unit

Cairo 6, 39, 225, 240

Cambodia 33

Cameroons 35

Canaries 33

Cape Colony 33

Index

Cape Verde 33

capitalism 12-14, 18, 20-25, 27-29, 31, 44, 51, 55, 71, 72, 136, 379, 387 400

capitalist 3-5, 13, 14, 21-26, 28, 30, 31, 41, 42, 45-47, 54, 55, 57, 60-64, 72, 77, 107, 111, 114, 122, 123, 125, 130-135, 182, 187, 188, 191, 192, 200, 201, 223, 224, 228, 229, 246, 250, 251, 263, 266-269, 319, 321, capitalist 378, 386, 390

capitalist class 21-26, 28, 30, 31, 45, 54, 55, 72, 107, 111, 132, 133, 188, 191, 224, 246, 250, 251, 267, 269, 319, 378

Caribbean 33

cars, motor cars 180, 181, 249

CELU see Confederation of Ethiopian Labor Unions

Central Africa 93

Central powers 45, 159

Ceylon 33

Charles L. Bolte 258

Chefneux, Leon, foreign affairs adviser to Menelik 94, 125, 129

Chilalo Agriculture Development Unit (CADU) 263, 265, 390

China 33, 38, 48, 52, 54, 57, 192, 217, 260

Chinese 138, 357

Christian, Christianity, Christianized 4, 5, 10, 76, 81, 84, 96, 100, 109, 113, 140, 141, 143, 158, 159, 161, 164, 165, 292, 302, 309, 311, 385; see also missionary, Orthodox, proselytization

church 75, 80, 97, 109, 113, 121, 137, 142, 165, 211, 240, 246, 289, 292, 307; see also Orthodox

Churchill, Winston 52

city, cities 50, 106, 107, 125, 135, 163, 169, 182, 253, 256, 268, 271, 296, 312, 332, 333, 349, 381, 382; see also urban

civet 122

civil servants 64, 211, 213, 273

Civilian Advisory Board, of the Derg (CAB) 350

class 18-20
    see bureaucratic bourgeoisie, capitalist class, finance capitalist class, management class, merchant class, middle class, monopoly capitalist class, petit-bourgeois class, proletariat, regional finance class, ruling class, settler class, wage-earning class, working class

coalition government 402

Cobbo-Alamata 270

Cochin-China 33

code of conduct 12, 17-18, 20, 114, 142

code of law, Ethiopian 239

Codification Commission, for Ethiopian legal system 244

coffee 7, 83, 122, 255-257, 262, 263, 270

collective security 46, 49, 55, 192, 218

Index

collectivization, of land 369, 380, 381

colonial ideology 226

colonial mythology 8, 10, 141, 192, 199, 230, 272, 385

Colonial Office (War Office) British 200-203, 205, 236, 244

colonialism 2, 3, 9, defined 11-26, 32, 33, 37, 45, 65-67, 106, 109, 116, 133, 135, 142, 149, 162, 196, 197, 201, 208, 223, 226, 236, 247, 250, 252, 260, 290, 301, 303-305, 311, 321, 346, 366, 370, 384, 385,387 388; see also dependent colonialism

colonization 3, 18, 19, 72, 100, 112, 116, 132, 282, 300

COMECON 68

commissioned officers, in the Ethiopian military 336, 394

communal courts 210, 242

communication 13, 20, 83, 88, 111, 122, 127, 129, 134, 135, 177, 179, 182, 207, 235, 236, 255, 256, 272, 273, 289, 294, 302, 332, 381

communist party 232, 385

comprador, compradore 189, 320

Concert of Europe 31, 43, 45

Confederation of Ethiopian Labor Unions (CELU) 335, 350

conflict 1, 2, 6, 8, 10, 23, 24, 26, 30, 31, 38, 44, 45, 51-54, 60, 64, 66, 67, 73, 116, 135, 146-148, 157, 187, 190, 191, 200, 209, 219, 238, 260, 282, 309-311, 318, 319, 321, 350, 355, 381, 383-386, 392, 394, 402, 406

Congo, Congo river 34, 35, 39, 59

Congress at Berlin see Berlin, Congress

conquered land 107, 160, 263

conquest 1-3, 9, 17, 19, 20, 23, 33, 84, 85, 88, 92, 94, 99-103, 106, 109, 110, 114-117, 120, 131, 132, 143, 198, 199, 237, 242, 248, 280-282, 286-288, 300, 304, 305, 323,387 388, 392, 403-405

Constitution of 1931 184-189, 206, 209, 210, 240

Constitution of 1955 187-188fn, 233, 335, 341

Constitution of 1987 188fn, 370, 395

Coordinating Committee of the Armed Forces 338

Coptic Christianity 240, 289, 307

COPWE 375-377, 401

Coronation 97, 154, 170, 179, 183, 184

corporate colonialism defined 24-26, 54, 250, 304 corporate control 216, 254, 260, 271 corporate model 55, 56, 252, 260

Council of Ministers 155, 235, 351, 368

counterrevolutionary, as a political label 382

countryside 110, 134, 317, 320, 347, 349, 362, 381-383, 392

Index

coup 95, 149, 152, 162, 163, 166, 169-172, 178, 269, 310, 320, 322, 403; see also rural

coup d'etat 95, 169, 171, 269, 310, 320, 322

Crimean War of 1854-56 30, 32

criminal code 240

Crispi, Italian official 140, 141

Crown Council 148, 362

Crown Prince 168, 171, 175, 180, 181, 183, 186, 208

Cuba 33

culture 17, 150, 253, 289-292, 294, 342, 403

Cushitic 5, 282, 304

Czechoslovakian 311

Czechs 138

Dadi Feysa 298

Dahomey 33

Damot 75

Danakil 305
    see also Afar

danya 175

Darge, Ras 287

David, Rene, Swiss jurist 245

Dawit Wolde Giorgis 233

Debra Berhan 97

Debra Tabor, Battle of 81

Debra Zeit 334, 335

decolonization 14, 20, 24, 25, 56, 224, 260, 303

defense 1, 45, 50, 68, 111, 114, 135, 142, 183, 198, 200, 248, 249, 255, 258, 291, 298, 308, 310, 404

deGaulle, President of France 57

dejazmatches 74-76, 132, 139, 143, 175

Democracy (Democracia) publication of EPRP 327, 371, 372

Democracia see Democracy

Denmark, Danes 30, 49, 138

dependent colonialism defined 22-26, 37, 109, 116, 133, 149, 162, 196, 197, 208, 226, 236, 301, 303, 304, 311, 346, 366, 370, 384; see also colonialism

dependent colonial empire 1, 2, 192, 206, 209, 260, 324, 379

dependent colonial state 3, 4, 71, 98, 112, 132, 139, 140, 142, 145, 206, 248, 251, 320, 330-332, 353-355, 361, 362, 368, 393

Derg 3, 265, 267, 306, 312, 323, 330, 331, 336-338, 340-377, 379-388, 396, 398-405, 409

Dessie 155, 182

Djibouti 7, 99, 127, 180, 225, 301, 304, 305

Djote see Jotee

drought 100, 101, 117, 368

Dufera, Fitawrari 287

Dulles, John Foster 307

Dumbarton Oaks 52-54

Duparchy and Vigoroux 126

Dutch 32, 33, 138 see Netherlands, the

Dutch East Indies 33

East African empire 19

Eastern Europe, Eastern bloc 41, 354, 355, 370

Index

ECHAT see Ethiopian Oppressed Masses Revolutionary Struggle

Economic and Social Council (ECOSOC), of the United Nations 60

Economic and Technical Mission, U.S. to Ethiopia 228

economic base 15-18, 106, 112, 116, 117, 123, 145, 160, 208, 212, 224, 236, 258, 262, 275, 283, 288, 290, 300, 346, 347, 356, 358, 380, 387 388, 391, 395, 396, 401

economic crisis, crises 23, 29, 31, 79

economic substructure 12

economics 18, 19, 73

Eden, Sir Anthony 199, 204, 205, 219

EDU see Ethiopian Democratic Union

EEC see European Economic Community

education 25, 60, 64, 98, 114, 142, 188, 196, 197, 210, 235, 246, 247, 267-270, 273, 274, 295, 296, 319, 322, 333, 364, 372, 390, 391

effective occupation 36, 103, 111, 302

Egypt, Egyptians 7, 38, 59, 72, 73, 75, 79, 87, 90, 137, 138, 199, 225, 232, 240, 260, 261

Eisenhower Doctrine 254

elections 233, 309, 350, 382, 395

ELF 310-312, 344, 352, 381

Elifingi Askalkaye 167

EMALERED see MALERED

Embabo 99

Endelkatchew Mokonnen 334, 335, 339

ENLF see Ethiopian National Liberation Front, EBNAQ

enlisted men, in Ethiopian military 333, 336, 337

Entente Cordiale 146

Entente powers, Triple Entente 42, 45, 49, 127, 146, 157, 159, 164, 190, 198; see also Central Powers

Entotoo 85

entrepreneurs, European 6, 32, 36, 71, 72, 74, 76-80, 86, 122, 123, 129, 132, 133, 137

EPDA see Ethiopian People's Democratic Alliance

EPDM see Ethiopian People's Democratic Movement

EPLF 312, 344, 381

Eritrea, Eritrean people 3, 187, 195, 225, 229-235, 237, 244, 253, 257-260, 271, 276, 280, 283, 305-312, 322, 326, 343, 344, 352, 380-382, 385, 390, 397, 401   Eritrean Assembly 234

Eritrean Liberation Front (ELF) 310-312, 344, 352, 381

Eritrean Liberation Movement (ELM) 310

Eritrean Moslem League 306

Eritrean People's Liberation Forces 312

Eritrean People's Liberation Front (EPLF) 312, 344, 381

Estonians 138

Index

"Ethiopia First" 339, 341, 349, 350, 369, 378, 394, 396

"Ethiopia Tikdem" see "Ethiopia First"

Ethiopian Airlines 256

Ethiopian army 204, 210, 258, 293

Ethiopian colonialism 3, 9, 135, 305, 385,387 388 see also colonialism, dependent colonialism

Ethiopian Democratic Union (EDU) 318, 344, 352, 372, 376, 401

Ethiopian judicial system 241, 242

Ethiopian Minister of War 225

Ethiopian National Liberation Front (ENLF or Amharic: EBNAQ) 299, 326

Ethiopian Oppressed Masses Revolutionary Struggle 373-375

Ethiopian patriots 199

Ethiopian People's Democratic Alliance (EPDA) 401

Ethiopian People's Revolutionary Party (EPRP) 325, 323, 343, 344, 347, 350-353, 355, 371-376, 398

Ethiopian Railway Company 126

Ethiopian Railway Trust and Construction Company Ltd. 126

Ethiopian Socialism 354, 385

Ethiopian student movement 320, 322, 325, 326, 371

Ethiopian Studies 2, 239

Ethiopian Teachers Union (ETU) 274

Ethiopian Teachers' Association 349

Ethiopian University Teachers Association 335

ETU see Ethiopian Teachers' Union

Euro-Abyssinian 103, 135, 160, 206

European adviser 90, 96, 128, 236 see also advisers

European Economic Community (EEC) 68

European Powers 1, 4, 32, 33, 40, 41, 44, 58, 59, 102, 106, 111, 140, 141, 143, 147, 171, 189-191, 205, 280, 390

European-style cabinet 147

export 20, 59, 137, 182, 263, 390

extended balabat 237

Famine, in Europe 31 in Abyssinia 101, 108, 117 in Ethiopian empire 275, 333, 365, 368, 377, 384

Far East 6, 53, 72

Faris Aligaz 75

Fashoda 39

February Upsurge 301, 327, 329, 330, 345, , 393, 399

federation of Abyssinian kingdoms 87 of Ethiopia and Eritrea 188, 233, 234, 308-310 381

Federationist, in the Ethiopian student movement 326, 327

Fetha Nagast 113

feudal, feudalism 3, 12, 19-21, 28, 131, 142, 210, 264, 324, 325, 346, 393, 400

feudal-bureaucratic 210

feudalism 19, 20, 28, 324, 400

Index

fiefdoms 174, 250
finance capital 13, 21, 22, 24–26, 43, 47, 51, 52, 54, 55, 64, 66–68, 140, 189, 191, 192, 200–202, 215, 217, 218, 223, 227, 229, 250, 255, 256, 260, 269, 275, 304, 345, 355, 367
finance capitalism 20, 24, 27, 51, 55
finance capitalist class 22, 26, 45, 55, 224
finance capitalists 46, 53, 54, 57
finfinne 106, 107, 299
Finland 50
firearms 1, 9, 80, 81, 86, 88, 91, 100, 102, 112, 245 arms treaty of August 21, 1930 183
First World War see World War I
Fituma Hiksa 298
Five Year Plan, Five Year Plans 263, 271
Food and Agriculture Organization, of the United Nations (FAO) 63
Ford Foundation 273
foreign advisers, strategists 9, 15, 25, 98, 136, 141, 185, 186, 219, 231, 265, 272, 276, 319, 340, 354, 397; see also advisers
foreign affairs 94, 98, 156, 190, 219, 224–225, 229, 231, 234, 308, 353
foreign investment 213, 262–264, 292
Foreign Office, British 126, 155, 200–203, 205, 221, 223
Formosa 40

fourteenth province 234
Fourth Division, of Ethiopian army 333, 335
France, French 6–8, 11, 28, 30, 32–35, 37–42, 44, 46, 49, 50, 54–59, 72, 73, 78–80, 85–87, 90–94, 98, 102, 103, 123–127, 129, 131, 137–139, 145, 146, 159, 161, 162, 166, 167, 175, 189, 192–194, 196, 198–200, 217, 218, 232, 245, 249, 254, 283, 301, 303–305
Franco-German War 32
Franco-Prussian 30
Franklin D. Roosevelt 52
free land grants 211, 263
freehold grant 211
Fugug 287

Gabbar, gabbars, gabars 108, 115, 118, 135, 145, 160, 211, 258, 329, 347, 356, 358, 387, 389–392, 397, 401
gada 114, 115, 291, 298
"Galla," "Gallas" 81, 87, 96, 103, 104, 109, 110, 122, 158, 197, 285, 287, 294, 297; see also Oromo
Gambela 181
garrison, garrisons 110, 112, 118, 121, 134, 181, 268, 288, 302
gashas, unit of land 174, 212
Ge'ez 158, 240, 245
Gebre Selassie 151
General Assembly 60, 61, 232, 307, 308
Georgians 138

Index

German, Germans 32, 37, 38, 39, 41, 49, 50, 53, 137, 138, 146, 159, 164, 181, 193, 194, 198

German East Africa 37

German Southwest Africa 37

Germany 32, 34, 35, 37-42, 44, 46, 47, 49-54, 78, 161, 190, 193, 194, 198, 202, 221

Gibe 299

Gimira 299

Giyorgis Iotis 122

global dominance 26, 51, 53

Goa 33

Gobana 285-287

Gobaze of Lasta 92

Gojjam, Gajjami, Gajjamis 75, 78, 81-83, 90, 95, 99, 122, 152, 286, 289

gold 7, 31, 73, 83, 122, 182, 262

Gondar, Gonder, Gondari 74, 75, 78, 80-83, 90, 101, 152, 168, 266, 270 see also Begemeder

Gore 181

government land 119, 212, 264, 396

governor-general 195, 238, 239, 242

governors 118, 174, 175, 195, 207-209, 249, 303, 361, 374

governorship, governorships 149-151, 153, 154, 195

Grand Alliance 52

Great Bitter Lake 225

Great Demonstration Against Corruption 173

Greater Somalia 261

Greece 50

Greek 122, 181

Greeks 136, 138

Grey, Wilfred, British Foreign Office 155, 156

Gudela 299

Gugsa, Ras, ruler in Gondar 74, 75

Gugsa, Ras of Begemdir 168, 177

Guinea 33

Gulf of Aden 93, 301

Gulilat 373

Gullallie 285

gult, tenure 119, 120; see also land tenure

guncarrier see neftegna

Gura Doba, Battle of 287

Gurage 280

Habte Giorgis 147

Hadiya 299

Haile, Mardazmatch 95

Haile Fida 372

Haile Mariam Dima 298

Haile Mariam Gemeda 298

Haile Selassie, emperor 3, 48, 49, 94, 112, 151, 154, 162, 166, 168-171, 178, 183-185, 187-189, 194-196, 198-201, 205-215, 219-221, 223-228, 231, 233-237, 240, 241, 245, 247-249, 253, 254, 261, 262, 265-267, 271-277, 280, 281, 290, 292, 293, 295, 299, 304, 305, 309, 312, 316, 318-320, 323, 328, 329-334, 338, 341, 343-345, 347, 351, 353, 354, 356, 359, 361-370, 377, 380, 383, 389, 390, 391, 395-399, 406

Index

Haile Selassie's empire   49, 194-196, 198, 200
Haiti 48
Hajj Abdullahi 164
Hakim Zahn 137
Hanafi 165
Harar   102, 149-154, 160, 164, 165, 169, 174, 182, 195, 246, 287, 305
Hararge 289, 290
Harrington, John 127
Harvard Advisory Group 266, 275, 366
Haud, Somali region   234, 235, 303
Hawaii 51
Hayla Giorgis 162
Hermatu Range Development 262
High Court, Ethiopian 204, 210, 242-244
Hitler 50, 57
Holeta Military Academy 248, 249
hostages 90, 334
House of Braganza 59
House of Deputies, Chamber of Deputies, in Ethiopian parliament 188, 189, 209
Hull, Cordell 56, 57
Hungarians 138

Ichege 80
ideological guidance 354
Ideological School 372, 374
ideologues 109, 340
ideology 18, 19, 30, 54, 72, 76, 78, 123, 135, 140-143, 186, 187, 226, 246, 268, 269, 292, 354, 370, 379, 386,387 405

Ilg, Alfred   98, 123-125, 127, 129, 141, 219
Illubabor 289, 290
IMF   see International Monetary Fund
Imperial Guard 249
Imperial Highway Authority 255
Imperial Railway Company 126
imperialist 1, 7-9, 11, 62, 160, 354
import, imports 13, 58, 133, 137, 182, 241, 331, 390
independence, independent status 1, 4, 8, 10, 14, 15, 28, 39, 46, 54, 56, 61-64, 66, 68, 78, 83, 88, 89, 90, 92, 94, 96, 97, 114, 120, 130, 132, 136, 141, 142, 158, 174, 184, 187, 192, 195, 196, 199, 201, 203, 207, 209, 215-217, 220, 227, 234, 242, 253, 260, 261, 271, 272, 279-281, 283, 286, 290, 296, 298, 301, 303, 304, 305-312, 319, 321, 327, 344, 360, 381, 383, 386, 398, 404
India, Indians 33, 57, 65, 87, 136, 138, 247
Indian Ocean 6, 259, 301
indigenous   19, 25, 26, 99, 106-108, 110-113, 120, 124, 135, 139, 142, 158, 159, 164, 185, 241, 245, 246, 250, 251, 265, 274, 282, 283, 292, 293, 300, 302, 378,387 388, 397, 405
Indochina 33
industrial   5, 6, 24, 27, 30-32, 38, 50, 76, 124, 130, 218, 228, 264, 270

Index

industrial capitalism see monopoly capitalism

industry 5, 28, 32, 60, 93, 125, 182, 236, 263, 270, 364

infrastructure 34, 53, 72, 98, 110, 116, 120-122, 124, 129, 131, 134, 136, 177, 179, 180, 182, 183, 197, 205, 210, 229, 255, 276, 402

institutions, as components of social formation 16-27, intellectual, intellectuals 13, 63, 64, 67, 142, 247, 267, 269, 277, 294, 295, 299, 317-320, 323, 326, 327, 330, 340-343, 348, 349, 350, 353, 366, 372, 374, 375, 377, 393-395, 397-400

Interior 130, 140, 174, 177, 207, 208, 236-239, 256, 303, 359, 360, 362

internal public order 183

internal security 258, 311

International Bank for the Reconstruction of Europe 62

International Labor Organization, of the United Nations (ILO) 63

International Monetary Fund 62, 68, 69, 255

International Postal Union 129

internationalization, of Ethiopia 8, 127, 180, 191, 215

invention, of Ethiopia 9, 11, 215, 321, 382

Iraq 311

Ireland 50

Islam, Islamic 80, 159, 164, 165, 196, 289, 302; see also Moslems, Muslims

Issas 301, 305; see also Somali, Somalis

Italy 7, 8, 34, 37, 38, 40, 42, 46-49, 53, 54, 59, 78, 98, 102, 127-129, 141, 145, 146, 159, 161, 189, 190-195, 197-200, 210, 211, 232, 254, 301, 304, 306, 308

Italian, Italians 7, 49, 50, 58, 93, 103, 112, 122, 123, 126, 128, 131, 137-141, 149, 158, 160, 162, 178, 179, 182, 190, 193-201, 204-208, 211, 215, 220, 225, 228, 231, 232, 241, 247-250, 255, 260, 271, 290, 301, 303, 304, 306, 312, 316

Italian Communist Party 232

Italian Somaliland 231

ivory 7, 33, 73, 83, 122

Ivory Coast 33

Iyasu, Yasu, Eyyasu 145, 147-149, 152-171, 174, 175, 179, 338

James P. Richards 254

Janjero 299

Japan, Japanese 38, 40, 46-54, 138, 192-194, 202, 217

Jijjiga 165

Jimma 152, 164, 182, 270, 286, 305

Jimma Abba Jifar, Jimma Abba Jiffar 164, 286

Jon Hoy 295
    see also Haile Selassie

Jotee, Djote 165, 286, 305

Index

Judges 169, 204, 242, 243, 245, 363, 369
Jules Ferry 34

Kafa, Kaffa 152, 156, 259, 299
Kagnew Station (Radio Marina) 250, 259, 271
Kaiser Wilhelm II 38
Kambata 299 see Hadiya
Kassa, Dejazmatch 75, 81, 82; see also Tewodoros, emperor
Kassa of Tigray 90-92, 94; see also Yohannes, emperor
Kebede Tesemma 342
kebele, kebeles 237, 276, 361, 363, 372, 374
Kebrat Amba 89
kela, customs posts 128
ketema, ketemas 110, 111; see also garrisons
Keynes, Lord John Maynard 60, 62
Kinfu 75
King Leopold 34, 35
King of Italy 195
Kolmodin 185
Korea 40, 51, 250, 253
Krapf 86
Kruger 38

Labor unions 277, 335, 342, 350, 372
Lakamti 182
Lake Tana 182
Lakes Abaya 299
land grant system 212, 213, 262, 266, 337, 389

land reform 211, 212, 266, 273, 275, 276, 332, 337, 345, 347-349, 357-359, 365, 367, 369, , 380, 381, 389, 394, 396, 398, 399
Land Reform Proclamation, of the Derg 348, 349, 358, 381, 394, 398
land tenure
    see collectivization, freehold grants, gult, maderia, rist, rist-gult landholding system, siso,
land use fees 363
landholding 188, 209, 211, 237, 251, 262, 275, 331, 336-339, 343, 345, 346, , 381, 390
landlord 115, 143, 147, 209, 213, 264, 320, 343, 344, 347, 358, , 382
law 5, 17, 74, 86, 91, 109, 110, 113, 121, 167, 185, 186, 189, 239-243, 245, 263, 264, 268, 285, 310, 332, 343
League of Nations, world organization 46-49, 53, 54, 176, 191-193, 198, 221, 226, 290 "Ethiopian case" 48
Lebanese 137, 138
Legesse Asfaw 373
Lemessa Boru 298
Lenin 12, 13, 32, 35, 37
Liberal Progressive Party, in Eritrea 306
liberation movements 2, 381, 385, 402
"liberation," of Ethiopia by Britain see reinstatement of Haile Selassie

Index

Line of Solomon 80

literacy, literacy tests 263, 274, 292, 364

Lithuanians 138

London 41, 50, 190, 197, 198, 205, 219, 220, 222, 224, 230

Lord Chesterfield 127

lubba 284, 285

Lusitanian see Portuguese empire

Lush, Brigadier Maurice 201

Macha Oromo 92; see also Oromo

Macha-Tulama, Oromo organization 295-297, 299, 348

"Mad Mullah" see Mohammed Abdille Hassan

Madagascar 59

maderia, landholding system 119, 120, 209, 211, 364, 389

Mahazar Bey 165

Maji 299

Makonnen, Ras 128, 149, 165, 167, 168, 288

Makonnen Desta 247

Malaysia 65, 66

MALERED see Ethiopian Marxist-Leninist Revolutionary Organization

Mammo Mezemir 298

management class 62

Manchuria 40, 47, 51, 193

Manz, Manzians 75, 78, 80, 82-84, 86, 88, 90-92, 132, 281, 283, 316

Maqdala 89, 90

market 21, 27, 42, 55, 56, 62, 63, 66-68, 84, 87, 99, 122, 181, 192, 194, 203, 216, 224, 229, 256, 257, 261, 265, 281

market trusteeship 229

Marseilles 93

Marx, Karl 18, 30

Marxism, Marxist 322, 324, 330, 354, 371

Marxism-Leninism, Marxist-Leninist 323, 324, 330, 373-375

Masqal 164

Massaja 90, 91, 96, 97, 283

Massawa 93, 308

Mastewet, Oromo leader 284

Mathew, Charles, British judge 243

means of production 10, 115, 116, 211, 276, 301, 358, 382, 395, 404

media 127, 128, 176-179, 256, 349-351, 403

Mediterranean 221, 259

MEISON (All-Ethiopia Socialist Movement) 325, 327, 343, 344, 347, 350, 351, 353, 355, 371-376, 401

Mekonnen Wessene 298

mekwannint 152, 168

Menelik, Menilik, emperor 3, 7, 8, 80, 88-103, 105-109, 112, 113, 116-119, 122, 123, 125-129, 131, 135, 137, 140, 141, 143, 145, 146, 147-149, 152-154, 157, 165-168, 172, 174, 175, 177-180, 183, 188, 195, 199, 211, 212, 219, 236, 240, 246, 248, 265, 280, 283-287, 291, 316, 353, 364, 365, 370, 386, 384-386

Index

Mengesha Seyoum 318

Mengistu Haile Mariam, president 342, 352-357, 361-363, 365, 368, 369, 373, 375, 376, , 384, 395, 401, 403

mental labor, ideologues see advisers

mercantile capitalism 20

merchant capitalist class 28

Merson, Dejazmatch 81

Meserata Temeheret (basic education) 364

Metu 181

"middle" class, in Europe 29

Mikail, Ras then Negus 104, 109, 155, 169

miktal woredas, miktel woredas 121, 360, 361

militarization 10

Military Assistance Advisory Group (MAAG) 259

military blocs 67, 69

militia 360, 363, 374

"minimum package program" 263

Minister of Justice 242, 243

Minister of the Interior, Ethiopia's Colonial Office 130, 174, 177, 207, 208, 236-239, 303, 359, 362

ministries, creation and function 60, 130, 140, modelled on European style cabinet 147, 173, 177, 186, 195, 208, 210, 235, 236, 238, 241, 274, 329, 345, 362, 363

Ministry of Agriculture 140, 270, 365

Ministry of Commerce and Industry and Agriculture 130, 140, 236

Ministry of Finance 130, 140, 238

Ministry of Foreign Affairs 130, 140, 220, 223

Ministry of Interior 360, 362

Ministry of Justice 130, 238, 239, 242-244

Ministry of Land Reform and Administration 266

Ministry of Land Reform 266, 348

Ministry of the Pen 235

Ministry of Post, Telephones and Telegraphs 128, 130, 140, 230

Ministry of Public Works and Communication 130, 140, 235

Ministry of War 236

missions, missionary, missionaries 58, 76, 77, 93, 137, 224, 230, 272, 289, 290 role in reconnaissance 76,

mode of production 16-18, 20, 114, 142, 280, 332

modern education 25, 64, 246, 247; see also education

modes of production 13, 114, 131

Mohammed Abdille Hassan, the Mad Mullah 302

Momina 165

monopoly, monopolists 7, 13, 14, 20-27, 32, 34, 35, 39, 42, 47, 49, 51-57, 59-62, 64, 66, 67, 71, 72, 74, 76, 98, 124, 132, 133, 143, 146, 190, 191-193, 200, 202, 216, 217, 221, 250, 252, 254, 256, 260, 301, 311, 386, 390, 399

Index

monopoly capitalism, monopoly capitalists 13, 14, 20-23, 25, 27, 32, 71, 72, 76, 124, 133

monopoly capitalist class 21, 24, 54, 132, 191

monopoly powers 21, 22, 24, 25, 52, 55, 57, 60, 146

Morocco 38, 41

Moscow 230

Moslem, Moslems 158, 159, 306, 309, 311; see also Islam, Muslims

Mozambique 33

Muhammad, Prophet 165

multinational institutions 22

Muslim, Muslims 158-161, 164, 165, 232, 243

Mussolini 49, 198

mythology 1, 8, 10, 11, 141-143, 159, 176, 178, 192, 199, 230, 253, 271, 272, 280, 322, 323, 385, 9

Napier Expedition 7, 90, 98, 125

Napoleonic rule 28, 29

narrow nationalism, as a political label 395

"National Democratic Revolution" 2

national question 325-327, 395, 400, 402-404

National University Program 320

nationalism, nationalistic in Europe 21, 22, 25, 29, 50, 67 in the Horn of Africa 302, 326, 380, 395

nationality 3, 19, 138, 158, 178, 208, 405

nationalization, of land and property by the Derg 349, 364, 366

nation, nations 1-5, 9-12, 17-23, 26, 30, 37, 40, 42-49, 51, 53-55, 60-67, 80, 88, 94, 102, 103, 107, 109, 112, 114, 115, 117, 120, 133, 142, 176, 190-192, 197, 198, 200-203, 216-218, 221, 226, 231, 232, 233, 236, 244, 248, 253, 260, 261, 264, 266, 268, 276, 280-282, 286, 288, 290, 291, 296, 297, 301-308, 310, 315, 317, 318, 321, 323, 330, 344, 348, 370, 374, 377, 381, 387, 392, 393, 403, 404-406

NATO see North Atlantic Treaty Organization

Nazi 53

NCOs see noncommissioned officers

neftegna 76, 108, 111, 113-117, 131, 135, 143, 145, 154, 156, 160, 161-164, 172, 174, 175, 187-189, 197, 206, 207, 209, 211, 212, 237, 245, 247, 250-252, 258, 266-268, 275, 292, 293, 295, 297, 301, 317, 323, 329, 331, 337, 338, 340, 345-349, 356-358, 367, 370, 376, 381-384, 386-390, 392-399, 401-403; see also gunowner, guncarrier, settler, settler class

guncarrier 76, 108, 135

neftegna-gabbar 108, 135, 145, 160, 258, 329, 347, 356, 358, 386-389, 394, 398

Neggelle, Sidamo 333

Index

neocolonialism 24, 25, 140, 260
Netherlands, The 33, 49
New Caledonia 33
New Zealand 32
Nile 1, 6, 7, 38, 73, 122, 125; see also Abbay
noncommissioned officers, in the Ethiopian military (NCOs) 277, 333, 335-337, 377 393, 394, 400
Noppe 181
North Atlantic Treaty Organization (NATO) 68
northern principalities 99, 100; see also Abyssinia
Norway 49

OAU see Organization of African Unity
Obborra Oromo 288
Obok 6, 93
occupation, of territory 1, 9, defined 17, 19, 22, 34, 36, 85, 99, 101, 103, 109, 111, 112, 118, 132, 134, 197, 200, 203, 205-207, 211, 215, 216, 220, 241, 248, 282, 290, 300, 302, 304, 317, 384, 387 388, 404
Odonga 155
Ogaden, Ogadeni 3, 39, 219, 225, 229, 230, 234, 235, 237, 261, 280, 296, 301, 303, 304, 344, 385, 404
OLF see Oromo Liberation Front
Ometo 299
OOPLS see Organization for the Oromo People's Liberation Struggle

Operation Sea Lion 50
opposition, movements 18, 19, 273, 277-280, 313, defined 315-316, 317-328, 344, 350-353, 355, 357, 366, 372, 373, 377, , 382, 397, 398
Organization for the Oromo People's Liberation Struggle (OOPLS) 299
Organization of African Unity (OAU) 227, 271, 272
Oromia, Oromians 2, 38, 39, 84, 85, 91, 99-101, 103, 106, 107, 109, 122, 143, 156, 258, 263, 280-282, 285, 286, 288-290, 294, 305, 316, 385
Oromo, Oromo people 2, 3, 5, 9, 74, 75, 79-82, 84-87, 92, 93, 99, 100, 103, 105, 106, 108, 113-116, 122, 124, 154, 156, 159, 160, 172, 178, 195-197, 264, 265, 276, 281-300, 304, 322, 323, 326, 343, 344, 347-349, 358, 364, 367, 374, 381, 383, 384, 388, 393, 395, 400, 405
Oromo Liberation Front (OLF) 291, 299, 344
Oromoffa, Oromo language 196
Orthodox, Christianity 10, 113, 128, 143, 177, 240, 289, 307; see also Christian, Christianity
Ottoman Empire 12

Paris 46, 47, 49, 126, 129, 190, 197, 230
Paris Peace Conference, of 1919 46

Index

parliament 186, 209, 234, 244, 285, 297,

partition of Africa 35, 41, 58, 59; see also Berlin Congress, Scramble for Africa

party 31, 79, 142, 163, 185, 210, 232, 306, 307, 309, 324, 325, 327, 352, 354-356, 370-373, 375-378, 385, 388, 398, 401

Party formation 370, 371, 376, 401

Peace Corps, United States' 272

Pearl Harbor 51, 52, 202

peasant associations 349, 356, 358-361, 363, 382, 395, 398; see also AEPA

Peking 33

People's Democratic Republic of Ethiopia 355, 377

PEP see political education programs

Persia 38

Persian Gulf 6, 259, 271

petit-bourgeois, petit-bourgeoisie 67, 251, 269, 270, 362, 376-379, 381-384, 394

petty king 237 see extended balabat

Philippines 40, 219

PMAC see Provisional Military Administrative Council

Poland, Polish people, Poles 138, 402

police 117, 175, 204, 236, 239, 242, 363

Politburo, political bureau 350-354, 372

political education programs (PEP) 372

politics 18-19, 30, 59, 73, 159, 161, 225, 325, 328, 368, 385

Polynesia 32

POMOA 372, 374

Portugal, Portuguese 14, 23, 32-37, 39, 50, 78

Portuguese colonies, Lusitanian empire 14 "overseas provinces" 56 "ultracolonialism" in 14

postal system, in Ethiopia 129

Prague 230

producer cooperatives 369

proletariat 30, 265, 324, 330, 393

proselytization 93, 109

protectorate 141, 203, 205

provinces, administrative regions 56, 119, 179, 196, 207, 210, 236-238, 242, 245, 249, 320, 361, 362, 374, 384, 391, 392

Provincial Court 210, 242

Provisional Military Administrative Council (PMAC) 341, 352, 377

Provisional Office of Mass Organizational Affairs (POMOA) 372

Prussia 30

Public Health College, at Gondar 270

Puerto Rico 33

Qarra Haymanot 96

Qellem 384

Qur'an 164, 165

Index

Radio Marina 258, 259, 307; see also Kagnew Station

railway, railroad 6-8, 59, 98, 124-127, 129, 146, 180, 181, 204, 225, 230, 256, 257

Ramadan 165

rases 74-80, 94, 122, 123, 129, 132, 139, 143, 177, 184, 242

Raynton-Robinson project 218

reconnaissance 76

Red Sea 6, 8, 59, 93, 259, 304, 308

Red Terror 351, 353, 374, 381

reform 16, 156-158, 207, 211, 212, 266, 273, 275-277, 279, 315, 316, 318, 332, 337, 344-349, 357-359, 365, 367, 369, , 380, 381, 389, 394, 396-399, 406

regent 95, 148, 152-154, 167, 168, 181

regional finance class 56

regional organization of the colonies 210

relations of production 16, 17, 160, 330, 383, 386, 398, 403-406

Relief and Rehabilitation Commission (RRC) 365, 368

Rennell Rodd 129

resettlement 266, 345, 365, 368, 370, 396, 397

resistance, national 12-14, 19, 84, 99, 101, 103, 105, 110, 201, 203, 208, 211, 248, 251, 258, 271, 273, 275-277, 279-313, 316, 317, 321, 331, 332, 337, 339, 345, 348-350, 369, 374, 382, 384, 387 392, 400, 405

revolution 2, defined 16, 30, 44, 66, 121, 317, 320, 330, 331, 343, 347, 351, 352, 355, 359, 363, 364, 370, 371, 375, 376, , 392, 393, 398

Revolution of 1848 30

rist, rist-gult landholding system 119, 120, 209
  see land tenure

Rhodes, Cecil 71

roads 104, 134, 179, 181, 182, 255-257, 296

Roba Bultum 291

Rochet 85-87

Rome 12, 194, 230

Roosevelt, Franklin D., U. S. President 52, 53, 62, 216, 225, 227, 228, 253   Roosevelt's "plan for world peace" 203

Roosevelt, Theodore, U. S. President 58

route to the sea 92, 96, 283

Royal Navy 334

RRC see Relief and Rehabilitation Commission

ruling class 18, 19, 43, 127, 162, 178, 185, 187, 233, 396

Rumania 40, 42

rumor, rumor-mongering, as a political strategy 163, 167, 172

rural 85, 110, 112, 134, 135, 159, 181, 265, 270, 273-276, 296-298, 311, 320, 346, 348, 349, 357, 360, 362, 367, 374, 375, 382, 383, 391

Russia, Russian, Russians 30, 31, 38, 40, 42, 44, 47, 49-53, 78,

Index

102, 137, 138, 183, 187, 193, 232, 322, 357, 392

Russian empire 49

Russo-Japanese War 40

Russo-Turkish War of 1877 30

Sagale 169, 296

Sahle Selassie, King of Shoa 75, 80, 83-89, 91, 92, 282, 283

Salimbeni, Samlimbeni, Count Augusto 123, 140

San Francisco conference, regarding United Nations 53

Sayo 181

schools 63, 113, 195-197, 246, 247, 267-269, 272, 292, 296, 319, 325, 329, 390, 391 see education

Scramble for Africa, Scramble 4, 5, 32, 33, 36, 37, 81, 191, 219, 301, 304

Second Division, of the Ethiopian army 333

Second World War see World War II

Secretariat, of the United Nations 61, 238

security 46, 48, 49, 52, 55, 60, 68, 73, 93, 99, 111, 131, 135, 183, 192, 193, 210, 218, 236, 242, 258, 261, 273, 307, 308, 311, 332, 360, ,

security apparatus 210

Security Council, of the United Nations 60, 307

Seded 373-376, , 401

Seifu Tessemma 298

self-determination 46, 66, 202, 203, 260, 276, 304, 313, 315, 318, 400, 403, 405

semon, church landholding 121

Senate 47, 188, 189, 209, 275

Senay Lique 373

Senegal 87

Senigov, Russian artist in Ethiopia 137

Serbia 43, 45, 46, 48, 50

serfs 108, 115, 293

Settlement Authority 365

settler, settlers 3, 8-10, 17-19, 24, 26, 28, 100, 107-118, 121, 128, 130, 131, 134, 143, 145, 146, 148, 150, 152, 157, 161, 162, 172, 174-177, 180-182, 189, 195-197, 202, 203, 206-210, 244, 247, 250, 256, 258, 262, 263, 265, 267, 268, 271, 272, 280, 288, 289, 292, 293, 296, 301, 319, 323, 344, 347, 354, 365-370, 383, 384, 386-391, 392-394, 397, 399; see also neftegna

settler class 9, 10, development of Ethiopian 106-114, 176, 180, 207, 256, 265, 296, 319, 347, 368, 389-406; see also neftegna

settlerism 369

shareholder land tenure 55

Shawa Ragga, daughter of Menelik 147

Sheikh Nur Husseyn 287

Shengo, National 370

shifta, bandits 75, 396

Shoa, Shewa, Shoan, Shoans 7, 8, 75, 83, 86-106, 111, 117, 123,

Index

124, 128, 143, 145, 148-152, 154-158, 160, 162, 163, 167-169, 182, 195, 201, 266, 282-284, 286, 287, 289, 316, 318, 321, 405

shum, shums 173, 188

Sidama, Sidama people 3, 38, 39, 99, 101, 156, 258, 276, 280, 296, 299-301, 322, 344, 381, 385, 388, 400

Sidama Liberation Front (SLF) 300, 301, 344

Sidamo 110, 152, 195, 197, 262, 289, 299, 333

Sinclair Oil Corporation 225

Singapore 65, 66

Sino-Japanese War 40

siso, land tenure system 119, 120, 209, 389

Skinner, R. J., American envoy to Ethiopia 58, 59

slave-raiding, slavery 12, 108, 134

SLF see Sidama Liberation Front

slogan, slogans 276, 321-325, 339, 341, 354, 378, 392, 394, 396, 406

small, smaller nations 42, 45, 190, 233 powers 48, 228 states 35, 42, 46

social formation defined 16-18, 134, 135, 229, 311, 319, 321, 377, 390, 399, 404

social organization 13, 15, 16, 114, 131, 133, 136, 141, 143, 145, 248, 289

social transformation defined 15-19, 398

socioeconomic formation, organization 13, 17, 131, 133, 284, 288, 319, 377, 403

soldiers 81, 100, 104, 107-109, 111, 117, 118, 120, 121, 169, 176, 211, 248, 334

Somali, Somalis 159, 162, 165, 234, 235, 261, 276, 280, 301-304, 322, 323, 344, 384, 388, 391, 403, 407

Somali Democratic Republic 304, 381

"Somaliland" 39, 126, 230, 231, 235, 301, 303

songs, protest songs 104, 294, 383, 384

South Africa 6, 23

South America 32

South Pacific 33

Soviet bloc 68, 260, 368

Soviet Union, Soviet 31, 54, 56, 57, 62, 63, 65-68, 187, 232, 259-262, 329, 354, 355, 357, 364, 368, 377, 381

Spain 28, 33, 34, 50

Spencer, John 199, 201, 204, 205, 219-226, 229, 234, 254, 256, 259, 261, 310

spheres of influence 36, 38, 59, 126

St. Michael 84

Stalin, Joseph, Soviet leader 53

state, the 8, 10, 11, defined 18-26, 61, 65, 111, 113, 116, 117, 130, 131, 135, 137, 142, 143, 150, 152, 156, 160, 172, 173, 177, 178, 196, 197, 205, 207, 209-213, 221, 223, 224, 228,

Index

229, 235, 244-246, 248, 251, 258, 259, 262-265, 267-269, 273, 274, 276, 277, 279, 280, 289, 291-296, 312, 315, 316, 319, 320, 321, 322, 328-331, 334, 336, 340, 343, 344, 346, 347, 353, 355-359, 361-364, 367, 368, 370, 371, 377-379, 383, 386-391, 393, 394, 397-402

State Bank of Ethiopia 223, 224, 229

State Department, Department of State, U. S. government 220, 221, 256

state religion of Ethiopia see Christianity, Orothodox

Stockholm 230

student, students 196, 239, 246, 268, 269, 271, 274, 276, 296, 317, 318, 320-328, 333, 341, 343, 349, 350, 353, 356, 371, 372, 377,387 388, 389, 391-394, 397

student movement, Ethiopian 320-328, 343, 371, 392, 393 cliques within 325, 327

subdued nations 90, 258, 384, 403, 406-409
  see also subordinated nations

subordinated nations 16, 21, 131, 277, 315, 318, 344; see also subdued nations

substructure 12, 15, 251, 364

Sudan 38, 155, 182, 199, 308, 311

Suez Canal 1, 6, 34, 72, 73, 79, 125, 225, 260

superpower, superpowers, role in creation and maitenance of Ethiopia 4, 9, 11, 23, 33, 35, 65-67, 102, 126, 190-194, 201, 215, 222, 226, 237, 231, 235, 250, 259, 293, 353, 385-387, 390, 395, 404

superstructure, superstructural 12, 15-18, 20, 23, 26, 44, 46, 51, 60, 67, 114-116, 124, 235, 250, 251, 289-291, 315, 358, 359, 363-365, 388, 404, 405, 406

Suppe 181

Supreme Imperial Court, of Ethiopia 210, 241

Sweden, Swedes 50, 138, 249

Swiss 98, 125, 137, 138, 182, 245

Swiss Polytechnic Institute 98

Switzerland, Swiss 50, 59, 78, 98, 215, 137, 138, 182, 245

Syria 33, 311

Syrians 137

TAB see Technical Assistance Board

Tadesse Birru 298

Tadla Gwalu 83

Tafesse Gemetchu 298

Tahiti 33

Tajura 93

Tasamma, Ras, Regent for Iyasu 149-155

Tambaro 299

tax, taxes 10, 113, 115, 119, 156, 160, 174, 208, 213, 264, 292 303, 316, 358, 363, 382, 383, 395

Index

Taytu, Taitu, empress 98, 106, 107, 145, 148-153, 155, 170, 175, 178, 286, 316, 338

Technical Assistance Board, of the United Nations (TAB) 63

Technical mission 228-230

Tedla Bairu 306, 309

Tefari 149-151, 153, 161-164, 166-169, 171-184, 192, 195, 208, 247, 248, 338

Teferi Banti 351, 352

Tekle Giorgis 80

Tekle Haymanot 99, 122

telegraph 127, 128, 134, 140, 177-179, 230, 255, 256

telephone 127, 128, 134, 177-179, 204, 230, 255, 256

tenancy, tenants 109, 115, 116, 118, 139, 212, 213, 252, 264, 265, 293, 298, 320, 347, 348, 356, 381

Tendaho cotton 263

Tesfaye Degga 298

Tewodoros, Teodros, emperor 75, 81, 87-91

Thavenot, A., British judge on Ethiopian High Court 243

theological disputes in Abyssinia 91-92

Thesiger, Wilfred, British consulate officer in Ethiopia 155, 156

third world 13, 60, 64, 66, 252, 254, 274

Tigray, Tigrayan, Tigrays, Tigrayans, Tigreans 3, 7, 75, 78, 80, 81, 83, 89-92, 94, 102, 132, 148, 151, 152, 266, 283, 289, 304, 315-318, 344, 365, 380, 381, 397, 404-406

Tigray Liberation Front (TLF) 318

Tigray National Organization (TNO) 317, 318

Tigray People's Liberation Front (TPLF) 318, 344, 380, 401

tiller, "Land to the Tiller" 276, 321-323, 392, 394

Tiso Gobaze 83

TLF see Tigray Liberation Front

TNO see Tigray National Organization

towns 110, 112, 134, 181, 256, 268, 295; see also cities, urban

TPLF see Tigray People's Liberation Front

Trans World Airlines 256

transformation defined 15-20, 120, 280, 288, 341, 364, 367, 398, 399, 405, 406

transport, transportation 6, 13, 20, 39, 72, 134, 179-182, 226, 230, 255-257, 295, 331, 368

Tripartite Treaty 8, 38, 39, 59, 116, 127, 146, 161, 180, 190, 191, 194

trusteeship 46, 54-57, 60-62, 217-220, 227, 229, 232, 267, 306, 307

Tunisia 34

Turkey 30, 50, 161

Turks 138

UNESCO 63, 64, 273, 274, 364

Unionist Party, in Eritrea 306, 307, 309

Index

Unionists, in Ethiopian Student Movement 326, 327
united front 4, 50, 82, 351, 372, 402
United Kingdom 83
United Nations 54, 55, 60-67, 226, 231-233, 260, 261, 304, 306-308
United Nations Charter 55, 226
United Nations Model for World Order 60
United States 28, 33, 40, 44-49, 51-58, 60-63, 65-68, 191, 202, 203, 215-229, 231-233, 235-239, 244, 245, 248, 249, 250-263, 267-271, 273, 293, 303, 307, 308, 311, 353, 354
United States Agency for International Development (USAID) 267, 273
United States Bureau of Roads 255
United States Navy 221
United States patronage 225, 262, 271
urban 131, 140, 181, 275, 295-297, 331, 337, 347, 350, 351, 353, 355, 357, 358, 364, 372, 374, 375, , 381, 382; see also cities, towns
USAID see United States Agency for International Development
USSR see Soviet Union
usufruct rights, in land 119, 120 see land tenures

Vanguard 287, 324, 371, 375-378, 401

vanguard party 375-377
Verona, Congress of 31 Treaty of 36, 41
Versailles, Treaty of 46, 49
Victoria, Queen of England Queen 90, 92
Vienna, Treaty of 29-31, 36, 41 Congress of 29
villages 107, 110
villagization 369
Vitalien 146
Voice of the Masses (Ye Safewo Hiszba Demits) 327, 371, 372

Wadera, Treaty of 96
WADU see Wallamo Agricultural Development Unit
wage-earning class 30
Wal-Wal incident 193
Walayita, Walayitas 103-105, 299, 323
Waldie 285
"Walamo," "Wallamo," "Wollamo" 104, 105, 263, 299; see also Walayita
Waldmeier, Theophilus 93
Wallamo Agricultrual Development Unit (WADU) 263, 265, 390
Wallega 262, 384
War Office, British see Colonial Office, British
Warsaw Pact 68
Waz League (Ader) 373, 375
Welles, Sumner 56
Wello see Wollo Oromo
West Africa 6, 33
Western Europe 52, 60, 353, 354

Index

Western Somali Liberation Front
(WSLF) 303, 344
Western Somalia 302, 303
White, J. G., Engineering Corpo-
ration of New York 182
White Nile 7
Willan, Brigadier, of British Colo-
nial Legal service, president of
the Ethiopian High Court
243
Wilson, Woodrow, U. S. President
46
Wolde Giorgis, Ras 104
Woldeab Walde Mariam 306
Wollamos see Walayita
Wollega 289, 305, 358, 383
Wollo, Wello Oromo 74, 92, 96,
147, 152, 169, 275, 283, 284,
289, 304, 305, 333, 365, 397;
see also Oromo people
Women's organizations, under the
Derg 374
woreda, woredas 121, 174, 207,
208, 237, 239, 358, 360, 361,
363, 374
Work-Oriented Literacy Programs
274
Workers' Party of Ethiopia (WPE)
370, 375-377, 401
WPE see Worker's Party of Ethiopia
working class 29, 31
World Bank 60, 62, 68, 69, 255,
263, 273, 275
world economic order 9, 20, 21,
24, 27, 54, 67, 201, 223, 259,
308, 333

World War I, First World War,
1914-18 war, "European"
conflict 7, 38, 42, 44, 47, 52,
54, 137, 161, 191, 203, 217
World War II, Second World War
49-51, 53, 54, 190, 192, 193,
202, 216-218, 252, 305, 306
Worqitu, Oromo leader 284
Woyane, rebellion in Tigray 317
WSLF see Western Somali Liberation Front
Wube, Dejazmatch, of Tigray 75,
80-82, 89,

Yalta, conference 53, 218, 219,
225
Yejju Oromo 74; see also Oromo
people
Ye Safewo Hiszba Demits see
Voice of the Masses,
MEISON publication
Yilma, Dejazmatch 167
Yohannes IV, emperor 7, 83, 91,
93-99, 101, 102, 125, 283, 316;
see also Kassa of TIgray
Yugoslav 357

Zewditu, Zawditu, Queen of
Queens 167-170, 175, 185
zemecha, zemetia 108, 349, 356